THE ESSENTIAL HISTORY OF
ENGLAND

FOREWORD BY SIR GEOFF HURST

ANDREW MOURANT AND JACK ROLLIN

headline

First published in 2002
by HEADLINE BOOK PUBLISHING
for WHSmith, Greenbridge Road, Swindon SN3 3LD

First published in paperback in 2004
by HEADLINE BOOK PUBLISHING

10 9 8 7 6 5 4 3 2 1

ISBN 0 7553 1364 X

Numerous interviewees have, over the years, illuminated various periods of England's history. In particular, the authors would like to thank Sir Tom Finney and Maurice Norman for vivid recollections of the 1940s, 50s and early 60s. Thanks also to FA librarian David Barber and receptionist Sian Thomas for their help and goodwill at a crucial time; and Julian Flanders, Lisa Hughes, Carole McDonald and Kathie Wilson at designsection.

Text design by designsection, Frome, Somerset
Cover pictures: front cover (clockwise from top left) John Terry, Sol Campbell, Sven-Goran Eriksson, Michael Owen, Wayne Rooney, David Beckham; spine Steven Gerrard; back cover (top) England's World Cup winners celebrate with the trophy, (below, left to right) Stanley Matthews, Tom Finney and Johnny Haynes. Pictures on the following pages are from Getty Images, Hulton Archive: 4, 12, 17, 21, 27, 29, 34 (all), 37, 38, 44, 45, 48 (both), 51, 56, 58, 60, 67, 69, 71, 72, 74, 76, 77, 78, 93, 243, 246, 247, 248, 249, 255, 264, 266, 267, 275, 276, 279 and 282; picture on page 10 from Mary Evans Picture Library.

Printed and bound in Great Britain by Clays Ltd, St Ives PLC, Bungay, Suffolk

Headline's policy is to use papers that are natural, renewable and recyclable products and made from wood grown in sustainable forests. The logging and manufacturing processes are expected to conform to the environmental regulations of the country of origin.

HEADLINE BOOK PUBLISHING
A division of Hodder Headline
338 Euston Road
London NW1 3BH

www.headline.co.uk
www.hodderheadline.com

Contents

Foreword
by Sir Geoff Hurst

Mine has been a full and satisfying life, both in football and business, but nothing has surpassed those moments between 1966 and 1972 when I played for England. I was lucky enough to play for my country 49 times and, even today, still feel a little flutter of emotion when I watch the modern England players competing in the World Cup or the European championships.

What an honour it is to represent your country in any field of endeavour. I can still remember the pride I felt when we stood in line to sing the national anthem before a game. In my case, playing football for England provided a sense of achievement and contentment that the club game simply couldn't match. I had a wonderful club career at West Ham along with my World Cup colleagues Bobby Moore and Martin Peters. All three of us had chances to move to more glamorous clubs in the aftermath of the World Cup triumph in 1966 but we stayed together for another four years because we felt no need to satisfy any desire for recognition beyond Upton Park. Wearing an England shirt satisfied and fulfilled all our wider ambitions.

In those days playing for England elevated you to a new status within the game. The honour of playing for your country raised your public profile, enhanced your value in the transfer market and significantly increased your earning potential. You were made to feel that you were one of the sport's elite. Is it the same in the modern game? I hope so, but I'm not sure. Playing international football today should be just as much an honour, but I suspect that the call to represent England isn't valued quite as highly as it was years

Left: *Geoff Hurst celebrates the goal that beat Argentina in the 1966 World Cup quarter-final.*

5

ago. For a professional 30 years ago, winning an England cap was not just an enormous privilege, it also opened the door to richer pastures.

Many of today's players are rich long before they play at international level and some are rich without ever playing for their country. Fame, along with fortune, is no longer dependent on achievement.

The nuts and bolts of my own playing career suggest that achievement was the platform for all that followed. In my case fame and fortune followed England's historic win in 1966.

That team, put together by Sir Alf Ramsey, remains the most famous in England's history – and it's famous because of what it achieved. Alf was a great patriot who inspired loyalty and commitment in his players. Until he came along, team selection had been the responsibility of a committee. Alf accepted the job on condition that he alone would pick the team. He wanted the England team to be his creation and not a patchwork gathering of players determined by favouritism, parochialism and a show of hands by the blazered committee men of the Football Association. He got his way and, as a result, England won the World Cup for the first, and only, time.

That 4-2 extra-time win over West Germany at Wembley in 1966 was obviously the single most memorable moment of my own career and not a week passes without someone reminding me of my three goals, a record that I thought Ronaldo might equal when Brazil met the Germans in the 2002 final in Yokohama. He scored both Brazilian goals in the first 79 minutes and I thought he might add a third. I smiled to myself when he was substituted just before the end. Later that evening I received a text message on my mobile phone from my grandson Jack. 'Grandpa,' it read, 'you've still got the record!'

Sir Geoff Hurst

Chapter One: 1872-1914
The First Home Internationals

In 1872, Britain was an indomitable imperial power. Its people were colonising disparate corners of the world, usually taking their culture and traditions with them. It was also a milestone in sporting history: the year of the first international football match. Eleven men from England faced eleven from Scotland, brought together by idealistic pioneers. To 21st century eyes the game they played at the Partick cricket ground in Glasgow, on a late autumn day, was a strange one. But for all its quirks, it was the genesis of international competition destined, in time, to flourish across the continents on an unimaginable scale, with the games played for astronomically high stakes.

The roots of football are to be found in public schools such as Eton College, Harrow, Winchester and Rugby, where vigorous young men were experimenting with a new sport. Each institution's version had its quirks and variants and it was far from the great game as we know it, but as the same young gentleman footballers converged on Oxford and Cambridge Universities, intent on continuing their sport, a consensus on the rules became necessary. Writing in 1905, Alfred Gibson and William Pickford, editors of *Association Football and The Men Who Made It*, said, 'The old boys at the Varsities were verging upon the adult stage of life and felt that the absurdities of school rules were not fitting for the pastimes of men.'

By 1862, when football clubs had sprang up around the country from Sheffield to Blackheath, ten simple rules had been drawn up. These were based on those that had evolved at Cambridge 14 years earlier where, at Trinity College, 'the Eton men howled at the Rugby men for handling the ball.' For all their eccentricities – Rule 4 stated that 'A player may not kick the ball whilst in the air' – these were the basis of the modern association game, and a committee of representatives from Eton, Harrow, Shrewsbury, Marlborough and Westminster agreed them.

This initiative came from J.C. Thring, by then a schoolmaster at Uppingham. In 1863 his rules were further refined by university players at Cambridge and within months of this 'Cambridge Convention' representatives of several old boys' clubs met in the Freemasons' Tavern, Great Queen Street, London, to try to organise an association; to band together under one set of rules.

This wasn't easy. Clubs outside London were few and isolated, communications across the country were rudimentary and some schools remained reluctant to give up their cherished rules. One month later, in November 1863, an irreconcilable divide manifested itself at the Association's fourth meeting, for while the Association's own laws, Rules 9 and 10, permitted running with the ball, hacking and tripping, the Cambridge Rules said nothing about handling the ball. Moreover, holding, pushing, shinning and tripping were banned. It was a debate based on manliness or, depending on one's point of view, licensed unarmed combat. Mr F.W. Campbell, the representative from Blackheath, believed that hacking was sacrosanct – 'the true football game' – and soon afterwards Blackheath resigned from the Association. The game was set on two divergent paths: rugby and football were about to be born.

The Game Gets a Guiding Star

In its fragile, fledgling state, football needed a firm hand to guide it, and it was the game's great fortune that three years later C.W. Alcock, a member of the Wanderers, was elected to the Association. A man of 'fine and commanding presence who had the happy knack of... being free from narrow views and yet of being able to persuade others,' Alcock's passion for expanding and unifying the game was demonstrated in the establishment of the FA Challenge Cup. However, it also went beyond club level and, soon after becoming Football Association honorary secretary, Alcock wrote to a Glasgow newspaper inviting applications from Scottish players who might like to take part in a contest against England. The initiative resulted in five matches between the English and the Scots at the Kennington Oval, London between 5 March 1870 and 24 February 1871, but none of them were officially recognised since the Scottish teams were selected only from exiles living in England.

The first rugby international between Scotland and England was played at Edinburgh in 1871 and this further spurred Alcock. The idea of an official fixture affronted the Scottish rugby establishment, which regarded the Association game as an upstart. Football was in its infancy north of the border, with Queen's Park the only club of note, and rugby grandees wrote indignantly to The Scotsman, expostulating that no team drawn from a minority had the right to represent Scotland.

Alcock had a stout ally, though, in the shape of Archibald Rae, the Queen's Park secretary. Earlier that year his club had travelled to London to play the Wanderers in an Association Challenge Cup tie. A correspondent for the sporting paper *Bell's Life* observed: 'Unquestionably the pluck evinced by members of that club in being the first to travel so long a distance... had the greatest effect in producing the first visit of an Association eleven to Scottish soil.' The meeting of minds and determination of Rae and Alcock was crucial in bringing about the first football international, but it is worth bearing in mind the obstacles that existed 130 years ago. *Bell's Life* reports: 'On both sides there were difficulties in the way of any practice games, as the Englishmen were, in many cases, so separated that all chances of meeting were impossible and the weather in Scotland proved fatal to the success of the attempts at practice made by the Scotsmen. C.J. Chenery, C.J. Morice, R.C. Welch and J. Brockbank were unable to leave

C.W. Allcock, first secretary of the FA and instigator of the first ever international football match.

London until Friday evening and thus had the enjoyment of travelling all night.' Alcock himself was one of several first choice men injured – he had played in four of the five unofficial games – and was restricted to acting as an umpire.

The match kicked off at Glasgow's Partick cricket ground on 30 November 1872 at 2.20pm – 20 minutes late. After pre-match drizzle the weather was fine and the crowd was estimated at 4,000, the biggest assembly at a football match in Scotland, and included a 'large number of ladies'. While Scotland played a formation of goalkeeper, two full backs, three half backs and five forwards, England took to the field with a goalkeeper, one back, one half back – and eight forwards. The Englishmen were: W.J. Maynard (First Surrey Rifles), goal; R.C. Barker (Herts Rangers), back; E.H. Greenhalgh (Notts), half back; F.C. Maddison (Oxford University), J. Brockbank (Cambridge University), C.J. Ottaway, captain (Oxford University), A.S. Kirke-Smith (Oxford University), J.C. Morice (Barnes), C.J. Chenery (Crystal Palace), J.C. Clegg (Sheffield) and R.C. Welch (Harrow Chequers), forwards.

A selection of sketches from Scotland v England, 30 November 1872.

The outcome was a 0-0 draw. While a goalless match is usually synonymous with tedium, one Scottish journalist was enthused by 'the skilful and always pleasing dribble'. According to *Bell's Life*, it was 'one of the jolliest, one of the most spirited and pleasant matches that has ever been played according to Association rules. The enthusiasm at the finish was displayed in marked manner by the spectators, and each member of the two sides was greeted by a volley of applause as he entered the pavilion.'

England wore white jerseys with the arms of England as a badge on the left breast, white knickerbockers and dark blue caps, while the Scots were in dark blue jerseys with the Scottish lion as a badge, white knickers, blue and white stockings and, on their heads, pixie-like red cowls. No photographic record exists of this encounter, but there is a fine reminiscence from Scotsman Walter Arnott, who attended the match as a 10-year-old boy and later became a fine full back for his country. Having walked five miles only to find he could not afford the price of admission, Arnott watched sporting history unfold perched on top of a cab. He was, for one so young, an astute observer.

'The English team was by far the heavier one,' he said. 'Their forwards played an individual game and were much faster than those on the Scottish side, whose forward work was done in pairs. What a treat it was to see Clegg or Ottaway getting the ball near their own goal and making off at a great pace down the field, and only being robbed of it by someone in the last line of the Scotch defence. Then again to watch Jamie Weir, the prince of dribblers... the gallant attempts of Billy McKinnon, also a wonderfully fine dribbler and splendid shot, to score; the grand manly charging that was indulged in by both sets of players; the resolute kicking of the half backs; the cool, and at times daring, saves by the goalkeepers... I make bold claim to say that some of the play I witnessed in that first international would put to shame what I have seen in recent years in first-class club games.'

50 Greatest Players

G.O. SMITH Centre forward

Club: Oxford University, Old Carthusians, Corinthians

Debut: v Ireland, 25 February 1893

Appearances: 20   **Goals:** 11

G.O. Smith was a classic product of his time. Educated at Charterhouse and Oxford University, he then became a talisman for Corinthians, the amateur side of public school sportsmen formed in 1882 to resist the encroaching scourge of professionalism. However, if Smith's background were typical, his gifts were extraordinary and commentators of his era considered him the finest centre forward of all time.

He packed a deadly shot and his brilliant passes constantly outmanoeuvred defenders. 'On the wettest muddiest day, when the ball was heavy with clay or greasy as a Christmas pudding, his passes never went astray,' wrote commentators Gibson and Pickford. He may have lacked the physique and height to play a bruising, hard-running game, but he endured the buffeting of brawny defenders without flinching.

If not the greatest sprinter, few, if any, could run faster with the ball at their feet. But it was as a thinker as much as a practitioner that Smith stood out: 'He opposed subtlety to force, intellect to mere strength... in full cry... you saw a king among athletes.'

The encounter, rounded off by three cheers from each team and a dinner at the Carrick's Royal Hotel, was a resounding success. From it came the momentum for international contests that would, in time, be played around the globe.

Four months later, on 8 March 1873, England and Scotland locked horns in a rematch at London's Kennington Oval. For England, only C.J. Chenery and E.H. Greenhalgh survived from the original team and England also modified their formation to mirror Scotland's 2-3-5. This time the outcome was decisive and England won this second international fixture 4-2, with eye-catching contributions from R.W. Sealy-Vidal, 'one of the finest dribblers that has ever played'. For Scotland, Captain R.W. Renny-Tailyour, also a Kent cricketer, 'was a centre forward of almost unexampled ability, strength and robustness,' but despite his prowess England walked away the victors.

In 1878, the Scots won their third successive match against England, 7-2 victors at Queen's Park (usually known as the First Hampden).

Money taken at the gate amounted to £106 1s, with tickets sold in advance yielding a further 6s 9d. A balance sheet discovered by Sir Frederick Wall, secretary of the FA from 1895-1934, showed where the money went: hire of ground £10; ground expenses £2; loan of tent £1; printing bills £1 5s; bill-sticking 12s 6d; printing cards 10s 6d; cost of football 12s 6d; police 17s 6d; luncheon to Scottish team £2 12s 6d; and dinner to Scottish team £13 2s. The balance of £73 8s 6d went to the Association. Missing were any expenses for the England team who, Wall noted, 'evidently entertained themselves'.

The fixture had become a firmly established annual event, usually played in March, either in Glasgow or at the Kennington Oval. Scotland won for the first time at Partick in 1874, 2-1, having looked a more solid unit than England and having had, on the day, a better understanding among the forwards. The following year, C.W. Alcock, so instrumental in establishing the fixture, captained the England team in a 2-2 draw. The years 1876, 1877 and 1878 saw England suffer three successive defeats, the latter a rout, beaten 7-2. Among England's defenders on that inauspicious day was the headmaster of Eton, the Hon. Edward Lyttelton. The Scots had evolved tactically and their understanding of playing to a formation was more highly developed, while England still had a fondness for the dribbling virtuoso rather than passing players who used the pitch to good effect. In England, being dubbed 'the prince of dribblers' was the ultimate accolade and the chosen player would often be followed around by a 'backer-up', in case the ball ran loose or rebounded.

In January 1879, Wales, who already had played three matches against Scotland, took on England for the first time at the Oval. This encounter, watched by a crowd estimated at just 200, had the flavour of an impromptu kickabout on a local park. Because the weather was bad, both captains agreed to cut the playing time to 30 minutes each half; and one of the English players, William Clegg, despite arriving late, was allowed to join in after 20 minutes. The Welsh, who put up stout resistance, were able to draw confidence from a narrow 2-1 defeat.

This low-key curiosity of football history was soon eclipsed in the memory by a scintillating see-saw encounter with Scotland, wherein England emerged 5-4 victors and, according to Gibson and Pickford, debutant E.C. Bambridge scored 'possibly the finest goal ever seen in football'. In a triumph of individualism, 'he ran practically the full length of the field and then put the goal past the lengthy Parlane... a man of giant stature and consistently clever between the posts.'

Soon the balance of power shifted towards Scotland. England was producing many fine players yet persisted in drawing from a small pool, often ignoring the regions in favour of London. 'For years, the Association was accused of slighting provincial players. Sometimes the accusation was justified, sometimes it was not,' say Gibson and Pickford. However, as the 1880s unfurled, the game began slipping from the grasp of the talented gentlemen amateur. To widespread consternation, the battle for professionalism had begun, its crucible a small Lancashire mill town 200 miles from the capital.

The Great Amateurism v Professionalism Debate

Football had taken root in many pockets of northern England. By the mid-1850s, two clubs had been established in Sheffield, influenced by local men who had been to public school. By the 1860s there were numerous clubs in the city and they had formed an Association of their own. In the early 1860s football was played by pupils of Leeds Grammar School, though with a jumble of rules more akin to rugby. The FA Challenge Cup, Alcock's brainchild, had propagated wider interest, and in 1883 was won for the first time by a northern side, Blackburn Olympic, 2-1 victors over the Old Etonians. However, according to Gibson and Pickford, some Lancashire clubs had been paying players – strictly against FA rules – since 1877.

In east Lancashire the release of mill workers from their labours on Saturday afternoons had helped establish team sports. The popular game was a mixture of Association and rugby rules. There were few Association clubs until, in 1878, under the leadership of the Darwen club, the Lancashire FA was formed. In the following year Darwen took on two Scottish players, Fergie Suter and Jimmy Love, to reinforce their assault on the FA Cup: a campaign that ended with defeat by the Old Etonians in the quarter-finals after two replays, and caused a big stir.

Darwen denied paying Love and Suter, yet there seemed to be clear evidence of payment in kind. Both had better jobs than when in Glasgow, and Darwen also arranged a benefit for them. Other Scotsmen soon followed in their wake to join ambitious northern clubs. Traditionalists in London talked of banning teams with professionals from the FA Cup but C.W. Alcock, although reared as an amateur, recognised the tide was unstoppable. 'I cannot be called a supporter of professionalism for when I played football it was played only by amateurs,' he said. 'But I consider veiled professionalism the evil to be repressed. Professionals are a necessity to the growth of the game.'

The passage of time had not impaired Alcock's far-sightedness. The man who had fostered international football was remembered by a contemporary as 'a good a judge of a player's form and abilities now as when he himself took part in the rough and tumble of earlier days; just as he is as keen to note a weak point in an argument or loophole in a rule... but with a blend of good nature that declines to press too hard on a luckless defender. He is the Grand Old Man of the Football Association, loved and respected by everybody.'

Others found reality harder to come to terms with. As rows and rumours festered, Major William Sudell, the chairman of Preston North End, became the first figurehead to admit publicly that his players were indeed being paid. His reason was quite simple: he intended to build the best team in the country and he saw no other way of doing it. His admission cost the club a one-season ban from the FA Cup.

By 1884, the FA was bitterly divided, but then a series of repressive measures, seemingly designed to throttle professionalism, forced the issue. When 31 clubs met in Manchester and resolved to break away from the Football Association, causing a schism that threatened to plunge the game into chaos, diplomacy prevailed. Following a meeting in London 20 July 1885 at the Anderton's Hotel Fleet Street, professionalism – albeit with strings attached – was made legal. A year later, James Forrest of Blackburn Rovers became the first paid player to pull on an England shirt.

Against this backdrop, Corinthians, a club self-consciously raising the standard of amateurism while meeting professional sides on equal terms, was formed. Founded in 1882, the driving force it was N. Lane Jackson, the FA's assistant secretary, to whom professionalism was a scourge. Jackson's belief – and that of like-minded colleagues – was that if the public school old boys and Oxbridge men who were mainstays of the England team practised together enough, they could achieve the coherence of professional teams.

Corinthians also embraced the ethos of sportsmanship and fair play. Their achievements confounded the cynical modern adage that nice guys finish last. For more than 20 years, before professionalism took root in London, they flourished, even though one Corinthian rule stated that they should not compete for cups and prizes. They gave the professional northerners much to think about. Shortly after Bury beat Derby 6-0 in the FA Cup Final of 1903, the Shakers headed south to play Corinthians and received a gentlemanly hammering, losing 10-3. The England side of 1894 that beat Wales 5-1 in Wrexham, and the one that drew 1-1 with the Welsh in 1895 at the Oval, comprised all Corinthian players.

Amid such upheavals, international football continued to broaden its base. In 1882, England and Wales both played Ireland for the first time. The 1883-84 season saw the inaugural British international championship, contested by England, Scotland, Wales and Ireland; a tournament that survived two world wars, only to be brought down a century later by the withdrawal of England and Scotland, on the grounds that it had outlived its usefulness.

In 1888, the Football League was established, professionalism was in full swing, and Preston North End seemed invincible. The trouble for England was that most Preston players were Scotsmen, but the superior methods of training and teamwork that came with professionalism soon brought benefits to the England camp. In March 1888, England thrashed the Scots 5-0 in Glasgow, ending a run of nine games without victory. Englishmen from Preston, backs Percy Walters and Bob Howarth, and forwards John Goodall and Fred Dewhurst made a crucial difference.

The days of patrician English rule by gentlemen from Eton, Oxford, Cambridge and the Royal Engineers were over. The victors of 1888 also included Tinsley Lindley of Nottingham Forest, Dennis Hodgetts of Aston Villa and Harry Allen of Wolverhampton Wanderers. Suddenly the team sheet had a contemporary ring. The Scots – 'defeated, disgraced and annihilated' – were not helped by a cumbersome selection process in which a committee of 38 picked their side.

50 Greatest Players

STEPHEN BLOOMER Inside forward

Clubs: Derby County, Middlesbrough
Debut: v Ireland, 9 March 1895
Appearances: 23   **Goals:** 28

Eye-witness reports of the phenomenal Steve Bloomer, a magnificent inside forward for Derby County, Middlesbrough and England, read like a portrait of a modern striker; the classic goal-poacher.

His aim was to get goals and 'not be a party to mere finesse'. Slight, pale-faced, an unlikely looking athlete, 'full of wire and whipcord, usually as hard as nails', Bloomer was a predator who did his effective work in a trice. One moment he appeared idle; the next he was pouncing on the ball, leaving opponents for dead, mesmerising goalkeepers. Bloomer won the first of 23 caps against Ireland in 1895. He was the tormentor of all opponents, shrugging off the attentions of defenders whether fair or foul, 'slippery as an eel... much given to dealing out electric-like shocks to goalkeepers at the end of a run'. He was no less deadly from 25 yards than with an open goal; his precise passes could inflict as much damage as his lethal shot.

After 14 years at Derby, Bloomer, to the consternation of all at the Baseball Ground, joined Middlesbrough in 1906; though he returned four years later and inspired Derby's return to the top flight as Second Division champions in 1912. In 1914, with hapless timing, he went to coach in Germany where he was interned after war broke out. Afterwards, he continued his association with Derby as coach and general assistant. He died in 1938 and is still revered by some as Derby's greatest ever player.

By 1892, when England beat Scotland 4-1 in Glasgow, the only remaining amateur was Old Etonian A.T.B. (Arthur) Dunn. New professional stars, such as winger Billy Bassett from West Bromwich Albion, were emerging. This was a man with swift feet, who was capable of crossing with wicked accuracy, and after the match he declared England's 19-minute, four-goal blitz the finest display he had ever witnessed. Such was England's strength that they could put out two different sides on the same day – to play Ireland in Belfast and Wales at Wrexham – with both English sides winning 2-0.

The England team that won the Home International Championship in 1895 included Billy Bassett (seated front row, extreme left) and Stephen Bloomer (seated next to him).

The Scots, on the other hand, were still locked into amateurism. They had protested vigorously when Forrest was first included in an England team in 1885 and held out against the professional game until 1893. During the decade 1886-96, paid English players regained the upper hand in Britain's great domestic rivalry, winning five, drawing three and losing three of the encounters. It was thanks largely to Scots schooled in the English professional game that, in 1896, Scotland won for the first time in seven years, 2-1 victors in Glasgow.

The First Forays Abroad

In 1899, the FA sent a touring party to Germany, a first tentative step in extending football relations to mainland Europe. There was a reciprocal visit two years later, when the Germans came to England and played a couple of representative matches, one against the amateurs, the other against professionals. Whether their opposition was paid or unpaid, it made little difference: the Germans were routed 12-0 by the amateurs at Tottenham and, four days later, 10-0 by the professionals at Manchester City. For the Germans, only one star emerged from these maulings: goalkeeper Luedecker, but for whom the indignity would have been even greater. In 1891, new opponents had also appeared on the fixture list when Canada arrived for a friendly at the Oval. England duly dispatched them 6-1.

Action from the 1905 encounter between England and Scotland at Crystal Palace. England won the match 1-0 with a goal from J.W. Bache of Aston Villa.

The extent to which the Association game had spread from its birthplace became obvious when, on 21 May 1904, representatives from Belgium, Denmark, France, the Netherlands, Spain, Sweden and Switzerland met in Paris to found FIFA, the international federation of football associations. It said much about British insularity that at first all the home countries stood aloof from this pioneering body. England joined in 1905, Ireland, Scotland and Wales duly followed, but the relationship was ever bumpy. The British withdrew after World War I, wanting nothing to do with former enemies; and again in 1928 over the issue of payments to amateur players in lieu of time taken off work. England was to remain an outsider until 1946.

The national team's next foray abroad was a summer tour to central Europe in 1908, but they encountered little in the way of serious opposition. England won the first of two games against Austria in Vienna 6-1; the second, two days later, 11-1. On 10 June they decamped to Budapest and beat Hungary 7-0, and still had plenty in reserve to beat Bohemia in Prague 4-0 on 13 June. England's new talisman, Tottenham centre forward Vivian Woodward, for whom amateurism remained an article of faith throughout his career, feasted on the easy pickings, sharing 14 goals with George Hilsdon of Chelsea.

The final match achieved curiosity status as the 'official international that never was', for Bohemia was merely a province of the Austro-Hungarian Empire, with players from the Slavia club of Prague. However, if at kick-off playing England was regarded as an honour, niceties were jettisoned by the final

50 Greatest Players

VIVIAN WOODWARD Centre forward

Clubs: Tottenham Hotspur, Chelsea
Debut: v Ireland, 14 February 1903
Appearances: 23   **Goals:** 29

Vivian Woodward, the Tottenham centre forward, was the last great amateur. As an attacker, he had the complete armoury of skills: the great pass; excellent close control; the sniffer's ability to convert a half chance; a turn of speed; and a body swerve that left opponents for dead. If he had a deficiency, it was a lack of physical strength. Bruising defenders were wont to bounce him off the ball, so much so that he had to restrain professional colleagues from retaliating on his behalf.

Woodward played many amateur internationals and twice captained his country to victory in the Olympic Games. He was a prolific scorer, though many of his goals were bagged against flimsy opposition.

Although not of the officer class, Woodward was a true gentleman, so faithful to the amateur ethos that he used to decline Spurs' offer of the bus fare to White Hart Lane. In later life, as he pursued his hobbies of photography and fishing, Woodward never lost his aversion to the money-driven game. 'Shocking,' he murmured when, while in hospital in 1950, he learned that transfer fees had burst through the £20,000 ceiling.

whistle. *The Times* reported that the Czech spectators 'were greatly excited, made a demonstration against the referee and attacked and beat him severely.'

Little is recorded of how Woodward plundered seven goals playing an amateur international against France in 1906 – England won 15-0 – or his six three years later when England beat their counterparts from Holland 9-1. The incidentals conveyed in newspaper reports suggest that standards of concentration, at what was then the highest level, were comically short of modern expectations. It is hard, for example, to imagine a modern day goalkeeper committing the error perpetrated by Woolwich Arsenal's Jimmy Ashcroft against Scotland at New Hampden Park on 7 April 1906. Watched by 100,000, a record attendance, Ashcroft conceded an own goal in absent-minded circumstances, safely gathering a shot but then, ball in hand, drifting behind the goal line while shaping to throw it out.

50 Greatest Players

ERNEST NEEDHAM Half back

Club: Sheffield United
Debut: v Scotland, 7 April 1894
Appearances: 16   **Goals:** 3

Few would contradict claims that 'Nudger' Needham was the finest left half England had before World War I. Yet for someone with such accomplishments – Needham was also a gifted cricketer – he was, according to one contemporary, the 'most modest and unassuming man whoever grew into first rank'.

Needham's undistinguished debut against Scotland in Glasgow in 1894 was a poor advertisement of what beckoned during an international career that spanned eight years. His terse summary of the half back's role – 'keep an eye on your wing man, and lend what help you can to the centre half now and then' – belied a wealth of talent.

His pivotal role on the left in England's 3-1 triumph against the Scots four years later, playing ingenious clever triangles with forwards Fred Wheldon and Fred Spiksley, displayed great confidence and positional awareness. In defence, he would hover between the winger and inside forward, rarely committing himself early, astutely picking off a pass or, with a great surge of speed, harrying his wide man into a corner.

Needham was a pioneer midfielder. He was destructive and constructive; blessed with great control and an awkward curling shot; would pop up out of nowhere at critical moments; and was inexhaustible. He was, in short, the most precious commodity a team could wish for.

Scotland were 2-1 winners and Ashcroft, as *The Times* noted dryly, 'rather damaged his reputation'. For their part, the Scots actually credited the goal to their own player, James Howie, of Newcastle United.

Ashcroft's was not the only reputation damaged that day. A crunching tackle by Menzies on England wing half Makepeace became notable, or rather notorious, for the culprit's unapologetic departure from the scene – in the eyes of the man from the *Daily Mail*, 'the one objectionable feature of the match'. There was a broader field of controversy as England, playing for safety, shamelessly exploited the offside law as it stood at the time, with almost the entire team advancing upfield and camping deep in Scottish territory. 'It is questionable,' another reporter noted tartly, 'if it is sportsmanlike for an international team to resort to this desperate move to keep down the scoring.'

Within ten years football had made its imprint upon northern and central Europe. The first international meeting between two non-British sides took place in October 1902, with Austria beating Hungary 5-0 in Vienna. By 1912, the football tournament at the Olympics in Stockholm had attracted teams from Sweden, Norway, Denmark, Finland, Russia, Austria, the Netherlands, Germany and Italy. England, who included players with professional experience, were fully stretched beating Denmark 4-2 in the Final.

Up until World War I, matches between the home countries remained sufficiently even for the tournament not to become too lop-sided, although England was the dominant force. From 1896 to 1914, England won the home championship eight times; Scotland five; Wales and Ireland once each. But inevitably England's clash against Scotland was the centrepiece and sometimes it took a braveheart – or a madman – to join the thronging crowds.

During the 2-2 draw at Glasgow in April 1894, some of the 45,000 crowd crammed into Parkhead behaved, according to one journalist struggling to hold his ground, 'so badly as to sweep away the tables on which the press men were supposed to be sitting, and cause an exodus to the opposite side of the ground. Few of all those press men saw much of the game save myself, for, hoisted on a table top which was in turn held in place by my colleagues against the surging crowd's encroachments, I saw sufficient to be able to dictate something of its progress to those beneath, and who wrote for dear life under supreme difficulties.'

But far worse was to come. Glasgow Rangers, having built a new west stand, had wrested from Celtic and Queen's Park a monopoly of international matches. On 5 April 1902, a fervent mob poured into Ibrox, probably many thousands more than its official capacity of 80,000. A stand at one end, iron-framed but otherwise made of wooden planks, became dangerously overcrowded, the crowd swaying for some time before kick-off.

After a railing dividing some of the tiers snapped, and with the game just a few minutes old, a 20-yard portion of planking at the back gave way, plunging people on to the ground below. Twenty-five died; hundreds were injured; there was a scene of terror and consternation; and yet, with players and most of the enormous crowd oblivious, the match ran its course, ending in a 1-1 draw. It is difficult to exaggerate the horror. There was, in the words of the *Daily Mail*, 'a scene too terrible to contemplate, as a great groan arose from this mass of humanity. Nothing could better illustrate the vastness of this stadium than that 400 should drop through a hole and the rest remain in ignorance.' The match was subsequently declared an unofficial international.

Such fervour became an awful characteristic of Scotland's home matches with England. For the last international before young men all over Europe and beyond would be forced to take up arms, Hampden Park became a seething mass. This is how a reporter from *The Times* described it: 'Getting to the ground was a matter of the utmost difficulty... Hundreds arriving after the gates were shut climbed the hill that faces the grandstand and watched from there. Watched was a polite fiction... they could only see the ball when it was kicked very high. Yet there they stood and apparently enjoyed themselves. "What fools these mortals must be," said Puck. But some forms of

Ibrox Park, April 1902: 'a scene too terrible to contemplate' as 25 died and hundreds were injured after falling through a hole in the stand.

madness are good for a nation. The huge bank opposite the grandstand was a misty sea of faces: mostly a coloured blur, like baby balloons.'

The match itself was brisk, lively and showed the Scots in a more sophisticated light. England's half backs seemed uncomfortable with the ball and the forwards, often isolated, squandered what chances they had. But Scotland were eager to play and only brilliant goalkeeping by Aston Villa's Sam Hardy saved England, who lost 3-1, from a trouncing.

Yet that season, with the prospect of war looming, the championship went to Ireland, who were 3-0 victors over England and came back from a goal down with only nine fit men to draw against Scotland in Belfast. This asked intriguing questions about the balance of power in British international football, which were destined to remain unanswered as eager young footballers were soon reporting not to their clubs but to recruiting depots, some never to return.

Chapter Two: 1920-39
The International Game Comes of Age

Across the world, football was being played to the same rules but with a different character. For instance, within a few years of being transplanted to South America, the game there forged its own style, one which, according to Terence Delaney, author of *A Century of Soccer*, made it 'florid and passionate, an emotional game of swiftness and delicacy, where skills with the ball flourished, and the robust shocks of bodily contact so necessary and "manly" to the English Victorians, seemed crude and irrelevant'.

Post-war Olympic tournaments emphasised the game's speedy evolution beyond British shores. The 1920 Olympiad at Antwerp showed English amateurs were no longer good enough to cope with the best sides of the emerging nations. After England were knocked out of the first round 3-0 by Norway, they steered clear of the 1924 Olympics in Paris and those of 1928 in Amsterdam. The potential that lay in South America came to the attention of the wider world when Uruguay came to Paris and bowled over all-comers, beating Switzerland 3-0 in the final. The other vanquished teams included Yugoslavia, 7-0, the United States, 3-0, France, 5-1, and Holland, 2-1.

When home internationals resumed, the old order, dominated by England and Scotland, was still out of kilter. Indeed, England re-entered the tournament looking alarmingly brittle. The intoxication of a goal within 30 seconds in the first game against Ireland in Belfast soon wore off: Ireland were much the better side, subjecting England to constant pressure and equalising through Belfast Celtic forward Ferris.

Wales won the title with four points from three games, their prize scalp being that of England whom they beat 2-1 at Highbury. The English had surrendered a seventh-minute lead, their attack generally ponderous and inclined to fritter away chances. On a tricky, hard-rolled pitch covered in surface water, it seemed an indictment of home defenders that Billy Meredith should give them the runaround. 'For a man of 44 years of age, he showed a wonderful turn of pace at outside right,' *The Times* reported. Yet however admirable the Welsh triumph, it was the clash between England and Scotland that became etched in the memory, as pulsating an international as the old adversaries have ever served up.

Great Matches

HOME INTERNATIONAL CHAMPIONSHIP Hillsborough, 10 April 1920

England 5	Scotland 4	Attendance 40,000
Cock	Miller 2	
Quantrill	Wilson	
Kelly 2	Donaldson	
Morris		

For the crowd craving some escape from the vile weather that enveloped them, the English and the Scots concocted supreme entertainment, with a match that teetered towards one side, then the other, before England finally grasped it by the throat.

The ground was slippery and everything, according to one commentator, conspired against good football, yet early goals, when such was their scarcity that there was talk of modifying the offside law, caused the game to erupt. After 22 minutes the score was 2-2, Scotland having twice pulled back England's advantage. The quality embellished the enthralling action: Quantrill's goal was a 'theatrical achievement'; Wilson's 'a moment of brilliance' when he pulled down the ball with his right foot then rifled it into the net with his left.

Scotland then seized control and at half time went in 4-2 up. England players had tended to over-elaborate, conceding possession. But with rain starting to fall, they switched to a passing game in the second half and the tables were turned. After a wonderful swift exchange of passes Morris equalised; and then, with just minutes to go, Quantrill embarked on a long dribble and, closing in on goal, passed for Kelly to score his second of the match. For Scotland, this was the *coup de grâce*. Greater drama was hard to imagine.

England: Hardy (Aston Villa), Longworth (Liverpool), Pennington (West Bromwich Albion), Ducat (Aston Villa), McCall (Preston North End), Grimsdell (Tottenham Hotspur), Wallace (Aston Villa), Kelly (Burnley), Cock (Chelsea), Morris (West Bromwich Albion), Quantrill (Derby County)

Scotland: Campbell (Liverpool), McNair (Celtic), Blair (Sheffield Wednesday), Bowie (Rangers), Low (Newcastle United), Gordon (Rangers), Donaldson (Bolton Wanderers), Miller (Liverpool), Wilson (Dunfermline), Patterson (Leicester City), Troup (Dundee)

Victory against the Scots was to be savoured because, as the 1920s progressed, England's form against the old enemy – and that of the other home nations – became indifferent. Indeed, England had to wait until 1927 to beat the Scots again, and during those intervening seven years, they lost twice to Wales (1-2 in 1924; 1-3 in 1926) and also to Northern Ireland (1-2 in 1923). Four defeats and two draws against Scotland appeared stark evidence that better footballers were being produced north of the border.

The 2-0 defeat of England by the Scots in Glasgow in 1925 drew scorching criticism from the football correspondent of *The Times*, who wrote, 'Everywhere, except in goal, England were outmanoeuvred and outplayed. The Scots retained the outstanding joy of association football – the dribbling runs which make passing movements sometimes better than a mere rapid dispersal of the ball over the field. Englishmen no longer seem to have the capacity to do anything other than to swing the ball about mechanically or wildly. The English forwards were broken up with ridiculous ease.'

England selectors responded to this impasse by opting for youth. Among the side picked to play Scotland at Hampden in 1927 was Joe Hulme of Arsenal and Louis Page of Burnley, both of whom wrought havoc on the flanks with their pace and uninhibited style. At centre forward, another young player destined to unnerve defences at home and abroad was emerging. Two months earlier, Dixie Dean of Everton announced his arrival with two goals in a 3-3 draw with the Welsh at Wrexham. Now his touches were to finish off Scotland. During an electric 15 minutes before half time, the English swept the Scots aside, more or less silenced the 110,000 crowd, and Dean, 'a splendid opportunist', was on hand to score two decisive goals.

Form is Hard to Find

A summer tour of Belgium, Luxembourg and France, games won 9-1, 5-2 and 6-0 respectively, were grounds for assuming that England, even allowing for the shortcomings of the opposition, had recovered some supremacy. But the home international championship of 1927-28 rudely brought them to earth. In turn, Ireland (0-2), Wales (1-2) and Scotland (1-5) sent the English packing, leaving them with the wooden spoon. Defeat by the Scots at Wembley was every bit as crushing as the scoreline suggests: England were bamboozled by the slick passing and sharp shooting of a team of wizards, the supreme maestro among them Alex James.

The reviews were as scathing as anything England had ever endured. After a deluge of rain at the start, only Scotland, their players generally smaller and much nimbler, seemed able to keep their feet. There was, *The Times*, reported, 'a period in the second half when the football bordered on the ludicrous... Scotland players giving and taking their passes at walking pace... moments when they seemed to indulge in the artistic pleasure of playing with the mouse rather than killing it outright. The England half backs from beginning to end looked bewildered and lost. The forwards never

50 Greatest Players

DIXIE DEAN Centre forward

Club: Everton
Debut: v Wales, 12 February 1927
Appearances: 16   **Goals:** 18

Dixie Dean is best known for the nickname that he hated – he much preferred to be called Bill – and for scoring 60 goals in one superabundant season as Everton stormed to the First Division championship in 1927-28. Dean's record, achieved in 39 outings, is almost certainly unassailable and says as much for his powers of recovery as for his technique. A motorcycle accident in 1926 left him unconscious and with severe head injuries, yet through sheer guts and physical fitness, he was back in an Everton shirt within three months, playing for the reserves.

Imperious in the air – though at 5 feet 10 he was no colossus – perhaps no one in the history of the game has surpassed Dean's ability to connect with crosses from the wing. In 16 matches for England, he kept up his fabulous average, scoring 18 times. But his value also lay in the openings he fashioned for teammates through precise deflections, his ability to shoot with both feet and his acute positional sense. Tommy Lawton, his successor at Everton, regarded Dean 'as the most complete centre forward you could possibly wish to meet'.

Dean liked a practical joke. He would send a bottle of aspirins to Liverpool goalkeeper Elisha Scott before derby games saying, 'Sleep well – I'll keep you awake tomorrow.' Yet although he scored 379 goals in 473 league games for his three clubs, Dean's international career suffered arrested development, thwarted not only by 'stopper' centre halves but also by the whims of England's selection committee.

got together as a line.' Under the circumstances, it may have been fanciful to suggest that, 'The dribbling and passing of James must have delighted even the most fervent England supporter.'

It was clear that England had deep-rooted problems. The 14-strong selection committee was forever tinkering and there was an absence of strategic thought. Four of the team routed by Scotland – right back and captain Roy Goodall, centre half Tom Wilson, inside right Bob Kelly and left wing Billy Smith – were Huddersfield Town men, key to the club's pursuit of

Dixie Dean, always deadly in the air, climbs above Ireland's McCluggage to head England's winner at Goodison Park in 1928.

a League and Cup double and facing an FA Cup semi-final replay 48 hours later. It is hard to imagine that under such circumstances their commitment was not compromised.

Says Brian James, author of *England v Scotland*, the era was one 'in which the slenderest evidence could promote a man to a cap; the simplest error hustle him to oblivion. Nearly every team played in the period (1921-1930) provided its example of optimistic team selection, of experiment almost instantly regretted.' It was true that World War I had taken a terrible toll on young life; that without serious competitive matches the fitness and technique of surviving players had suffered; but that was equally the case for the Scots. Moreover, in England obvious talent was being ignored. There was widespread and lasting consensus that Sunderland inside forward Charlie Buchan was a top drawer player, yet he was only ever awarded six caps. In all probability, Buchan's independence of mind and willingness to speak it provided the explanation.

But as the 1920s advanced, there were some signs of England becoming less insular. Games against continental opposition assumed more importance; the net was spread further. In May 1929, England's tour of

Europe included a fixture against Spain in Madrid. The match, played in suffocating heat, was a trial in every sense. The Spanish public were so eager for the game that they had formed a mile-long queue four hours before kick-off; and they were so anxious to play their part that when play stopped, supporters ran on to the field with sponges to cool off the home players.

Had centre forward George Camsell, scorer of six goals in the opening games of the tour, not been injured playing Belgium, the outcome might have been different. Nevertheless, England were rocked by the sophisticated way in which the Spaniards mixed up their game, splicing orchestrated link-up play with virtuoso bursts of dribbling. Two up at half time, having shown neat footwork in attack although with hints of fragility in the half back line, England wilted in the heat. The Spaniards, fast and fit, gained the upper hand, each goal in their 4-3 victory greeted by a pitch invasion from exultant fans, chased by a company of civic guards, their swords drawn.

Further notice that the football world had become a bigger, more exacting place, was served in May 1931, when Scotland, hitherto considered by England their only peers, embarked on a close season tour, losing 5-0 to Austria in Vienna, then 3-0 to Italy in Rome. The calibre of the Austrians was underlined in 1932 when, coached by Jimmy Hogan, they arrived in London to play England at Stamford Bridge. Hogan, who had played with Bolton, Burnley and Fulham, had been schooled by the Scotsmen he had played with in London in the short passing style with an emphasis on ball control.

At home and abroad the clash was eagerly awaited as a trial of strength and quality. Austria were backed by a large and vocal support and circumspect English commentators who predicted a severe examination of the home team were proved right. England won, yet constantly struggled to deal with clever opponents. Although scoring after three minutes and maintaining a lead throughout, by full time the older legs in the team were hanging on grimly. Austria had pulled back to 4-3 with five minutes left, England often chasing shadows, as the visitors showed technical superiority.

World Cup Kicks off Without England

The warning was clear: England risked being left behind by the game it had created. Two years earlier the first World Cup tournament had been held in Uruguay with Europe represented by four teams – France, Belgium, Yugoslavia and Romania – but none of the home countries. While simply staging the tournament, in which the rest of the teams save the USA all came from South America, was an exercise bedevilled by politics and rows, it became the foundation stone for all global competition.

A form of football is said to have been played by British sailors on Brazilian shores in the 1870s, but the acknowledged catalyst of the game on the continent was Charles Miller, the son of British immigrants living in São Paulo. Miller went to study in England and returned to São Paulo in 1884 with kit, footballs and a mission to foster the game among local industrial workers. British emigres also brought the game to Argentina, forming a club in Buenos Aires in the 1860s, though for some years only ex-patriots played for it. It took a wave of Italian immigrants, settling in the early 20th century, to spread the game across the country. By then the Argentina Football Association had been formed with a Briton, Alexander Watson Hutton, as president.

Britain had also exported the game to neighbouring Uruguay. British workers building the Uruguayan railway founded Peñarol, the country's most famous club. The game flourished in a country where there was no racial discrimination and, at national level, an enlightened approach to training and pre-match preparation. South America's first, unofficial, championship was held in 1910, a triangular affair promoted and hosted by Argentina with Uruguay and Chile, and won by the home team. Brazil joined the contenders in 1916, Paraguay in 1921, Bolivia in 1926 and Peru in 1927. Football had taken a firm and impressive grip.

Jules Rimet (left) presents the World Cup to Dr Paul Jude, president of the Uruguayan FA. Uruguay beat Argentina 4-2 in Montevideo in July 1930 to win the first ever tournament in which England did not compete – they had withdrawn from FIFA in 1928 for politicial reasons.

The founding father of the World Cup was FIFA's third president, Frenchman Jules Rimet, who took office after the First World War and retained it until 1954, yet there were moves towards establishing a global competition even earlier. The Dutch FIFA representative, C.A.W. Hirschmann, first mooted the idea of an international championship in 1905, and plans were drawn up for European groupings the following year, but no one entered formally. For more than 20 years, international football on a knockout basis was catered for principally by Olympic competition until the inevitable collision between amateurism and the professional game.

Rimet's compatriot Henri Delaunay, secretary of the French Football Federation, saw this coming in 1924. 'Today's international football can no longer be held within the confines of the Olympics; and many countries, where professionalism is now recognised and organised, cannot any longer be represented there by their best players,' he said.

The success of the Paris Olympic football tournament in 1924 acted as a spur to Rimet to achieve a global competition. When, by chance, Rimet, encountered in the street Uruguayan diplomat Enrique Buero, who also had been at the Olympics, he stumbled across another key ally. The outcome of this fortuitous meeting was that Uruguay offered, with its centenary celebrations in mind, to stage an international tournament in 1930 – and to cover all travel and hotel costs for countries taking part.

Rimet began his battle to persuade the conservative elements within FIFA that the idea was a good one. Eventually he won, FIFA finally accepted the concept of an international tournament being held every four years, and two years later Uruguay, became the unlikely centre of the football world. For the pioneer entrants from Europe, participation entailed a three-week boat trip and all the unpredictability that went with it.

In the mid-1920s, after professionalism finally achieved widespread acceptance, club football organised itself across international boundaries in Europe. The mother of European two-leg, knockout competitions was the Mitropa Cup, first contested in 1927. The competition was greatly prized in its pre-war heyday and often ferociously contested. The idea belonged to Austrian football administrator Hugo Meisl, later manager of the Austria national team, and embraced clubs from Czechoslovakia, Hungary, Yugoslavia and Italy.

Competition snapped at England's ankles from all corners. With the home countries having set their face against FIFA and withdrawn in a dispute over broken time payments for amateurs, the world had moved on. By the end of the 1920s, teams from the continent were no longer skittles waiting to be

Great Matches

FRIENDLY   **Highbury, 14 November 1934**

England 3   **Italy 2**   **Attendance 56,044**
Brook 2   Meazza 2
Drake

This game has been painted in lurid colours as the great
pre-Second World War, X-certificate international.
Barbarous, though, rather than great is a more apt
description. Sports journalist Archie Ledbrooke called it 'a
disgraceful game. The Italians, goaded on by their fanatical
supporters... and spurred on by the political tendencies of
the time, literally threw themselves into the fray.'

England were 3-0 up at half-
time, then Italy hit back with
two goals by Meazza.

Injuries dictated the selection of no fewer than seven
Arsenal men. The tone was set in the second minute
when one of them, centre forward Ted Drake, collided
with Italy's centre half Luisito Monti, who broke a bone
in his foot. The Italians sought retribution and for more
delicate players the roughhouse was a nightmare. 'The
right wing of Matthews and Bowden... was useless (and it is not wholly a criticism to
say so) in such an affair,' said Ledbrooke.

A deliberate jab of the elbow resulted in captain Eddie Hapgood receiving a broken nose.
By full-time, almost the entire England team were walking wounded. There had been a
memorable performance from wing half Wilf Copping. No matter how much the Italians
threw their weight around, however foul their play, Copping was unmoved. He had two
lethal weapons of his own: a rasping two-footed tackle and a mighty shoulder charge.

Amid the violence came some choice moments. England attacked splendidly in the first
half, going in 3-0 up with two goals from Brook and one from Drake. Italy's goalkeeper
Ceresoli had also made from Brook what Ledbrooke described as the best single save he
had seen in a quarter of a century. In the second half, Italy finally displayed the skills
that had made them world champions. Prompted by the elegant play and sharp finishing
of centre forward Peppino Meazza, they cut the deficit to 3-2 and, but for fine goalkeeping
by Frank Moss, England might not have held out. Amid everything, the feuds continued,
and the match was remembered for blood and bruises rather than as a famous victory.

England: Moss (Arsenal), Male (Arsenal), Hapgood (Arsenal), Britton (Everton), Barker
(Derby County), Copping (Arsenal), Matthews (Stoke City), Bowden (Arsenal), Drake
(Arsenal), Bastin (Arsenal), Brook (Manchester City)

Italy: Ceresoli (Abrosiana Inter), Monzeglio (Bologna), Allemandi (Ambrosiana Inter),
Ferraris IV (Lazio), Monti (Juventus), Bertolini (Juventus), Guaita (Roma), Serantoni
(Juventus), Meazza (Ambrosiana Inter), Ferrari (Juventus), Orsi (Juventus)

knocked down and, while in England team selection continued to be carried out by senior members of various bodies, associations abroad, unfettered by cumbersome structures, grew up more quickly.

The figurehead of coach, someone with real authority, was evolving, and strong individuals such Hugo Meisl and Vittorio Pozzo of Italy asserted wide influence. It seems unimaginable that pre-war England teams, after a brief pep talk from a senior official, were then sent out simply to get on with things. Abroad, in cultures where football was drawn less along class lines, former international players became an important part of the set-up; the value of their expertise recognised.

As the 1930s unfolded, football became an instrument of propaganda for the dictatorships of Europe and the fascist hierarchies set much store on the achievements of the national team. The Italians, arriving to play England at Highbury in 1934, almost seemed to have been sent as emissaries of war; and the Trades Union Congress' (TUC) reaction to the prospect of a home match against Germany one year later threatened a diplomatic crisis.

For Stanley Matthews, destined to be an icon of endurance, this, his second international was a severe jolt to the system. He had won his first cap as a 20-year-old six weeks earlier against Wales, shown great promise, and scored in a 4-0 victory. But the barbarous game against Italy – 'the language and comments made by England players during the interval made my hair stand on end' – was a setback. He was dropped for all internationals in the 1934-35 season. 'I was suffering from nerves and shock of being in such a ruthless match,' he wrote. 'It was the roughest I have ever taken part in. It upset me more than I first realised and it took me quite a time to get back to my normal game.'

Pre-war Politics Mixes Uneasily with Football

If the antics of Italian spectators, who had greeted their heroes at Highbury with the fascist salute, brought home the menace of far right politics, then the visit of Germany in 1935 was viewed as even more inflammatory. Some wanted the game, scheduled for White Hart Lane on 4 December, stopped. The TUC wrote to Sir John Simon, the Home Secretary, stating, 'There will be a grave risk, in view of public opinion in this country, of serious disturbances of the peace if an attempt is made to carry out the programme.'

The government decided to play it down and in reply Simon wrote, 'The match has no political significance whatever… it is a game of football, which nobody need attend unless he wishes.' This was manifestly disingenuous. It was much more than a game of football, as newspaper reports of military preparations for chaperoning the 10,000 visiting Germans, arriving by boat from Dover, Folkestone and Southampton, made clear. The first German trains arrived at Victoria at 5.30am. Drivers of coaches in which the Germans were taken sightseeing were given sealed orders indicating the routes they were to take and the stopping places. The Home Secretary gave an assurance that 'everything was being done... to ensure that there would be no provocative demonstrations or incidents was carried out with thoroughness,' but such oppressive security was not an absolute success as 14 people were arrested for insulting behaviour.

50 Greatest Players

CLIFF BASTIN Outside left

Club: Arsenal

Debut: v Wales, 18 November 1931

Appearances: 21   **Goals:** 12

Arsenal were quick to spot the promise of young Cliff Bastin. They bought him at the age of 17 from Exeter City, an unlikely source of world-class talent, for £2,000. For one so young – quite apart from his speed, directness and powerful shooting from the left wing – Bastin was extraordinarily self-possessed and cool enough to take penalties at the age of 18.

Bastin had joined a team for which greatness beckoned and soon made his own indelible stamp. In 1930 he helped Arsenal to FA Cup victory over Huddersfield Town and in 1930-31 fashioned a potent partnership on the left with Alex James, ever present and scoring 28 goals as Arsenal marched to the League title. Before the age of 20, 'Boy' Bastin had won the League Championship, the FA Cup and been capped for England, a debutant against Wales in the 3-1 victory at Liverpool in November 1931.

The nonchalance Bastin displayed on the pitch disguised a good football brain – he would hug a position unusually close in from the touchline to link up with James, from where he then bore down on goal to devastating effect.

Deafness, which first affected Bastin as a young man, meant he was ineligible for military service. He played more than 200 games for the Gunners during the war, before retiring in 1947, finally forced out of the game by a recurring leg injury.

With political tensions running high in Europe, Germany arrived for a friendly at White Hart Lane in December 1935 with 10,000 fans. Under the Swastika, which flew at half-mast in honour of the late Princess Victoria, England won 3-0 and the game was played out in a marvellous spirit, both on and off the pitch.

50 Greatest Players

EDDIE HAPGOOD Full back

Club: Arsenal
Debut: v Italy, 13 May 1933
Appearances: 30 (*Wartime appearances 13*)

Signed as a skinny 19-year-old from Kettering Town by Arsenal manager Herbert Chapman in 1927, Eddie Hapgood's potential was plain to see. But staying power was another matter. On arrival at Highbury, Hapgood, a frail-looking vegetarian, found himself under orders to eat red meat – and lots of it.

Within two years, he became Arsenal's regular left back, in the minds of some the finest the club has ever had. Hapgood was not only an elegant, assured footballer, but also a courageous one. Carried off the field with a broken nose in the so-called 'Battle of Highbury' in 1934, he returned after half time, clearly handicapped yet with the stomach to carry on the fight.

Old scars were remembered when Italy met England in Milan five years later and, once more in hostile circumstances against one of the world's strongest teams, Hapgood's defensive contribution was outstanding. Yet throwing his weight around was not Hapgood's way. Like all the best footballers he relied on his wits for timely interceptions and averting trouble. Hapgood was living proof that fair play could combine with the uncompromising will to win.

Whether under orders or not, the Germans were model visitors. One party placed a wreath at the Cenotaph in memory of the British soldiers killed in the First World War and the little flags they waved at Tottenham in urging on their team were 'models of discretion'. Nothing was left to chance: hundreds of police flanked the approaches to White Hart Lane and inside the ground they were posted around the pitch at 10-yard intervals.

The atmosphere was amiability itself, notwithstanding that the German teams and fans performed the Nazi salute when their national anthem was played. England won 3-0 and might have had plenty more had they not been thwarted by the heroics of goalkeeper Jacob. It was also the match that marked Stanley Matthews' recall to international duty, following injury to the Middlesbrough winger Ralph Birkett, but by his own admission, the man from Stoke produced another lamentable performance, playing into the experienced hands of the German left back Munzenberg.

As a unit though, England were much the stronger. From the outset Germany had seemed intent on damage limitation, packing their defence although dangerous on the break. England's link-up play between half backs and forwards was far superior. With England 3-0 up halfway through the second period, the contest was over. At full-time, in a display of almost exaggerated good behaviour, the referee congratulated the players on a clean contest and some of the English players left arm in arm with their opponents. It was a singular encounter. Clashes with the Germans thereafter were destined to have a peculiar potency.

The FA's obdurate stand against amateurism, in particular that vexed question of payments made to amateurs as compensation for loss of earnings from regular employment, caused England and the other countries to remain outside FIFA from 1928 until 1946, and meant they missed all three pre-war World Cup tournaments. Yet, from the evidence of matches such as the victory over the Italians in the 'Battle of Highbury', England remained a force in the game; and victory against the English was considered a prize scalp.

There were gentler occasions, however. The 1937 summer tour to Scandinavia, for example, was fondly remembered by FA secretary Stanley Rous. Three victories were recorded – 6-0 against Norway in Oslo, 4-0 against Sweden in Stockholm and 8-0 against Finland in Helsinki – and between matches, the England team cruised the Baltic. 'On the Finnish trip our comfortable ship was becalmed for more than 48 hours in thick fog,' Rous recalled. 'With the boat full of Finnish girls going back on holiday from Stockholm and Uppsala Universities, it was a merry time for all with a number of impromptu dances.'

Just as Mussolini wanted Italian footballers to be emissaries of national strength, so did fascist leaders in Germany. The legacy of England's visit to Berlin in 1938 was a political furore and sense of shame, rather than pride in a 6-3 victory. War was in the air once more. Hitler had just marched into Austria. Britain, although re-arming, was inclined to appeasement and it was usual for Sir Neville Henderson, the British ambassador, to perform a Nazi salute when meeting German officials. Henderson told the FA that players would be expected to do the same during pre-match niceties. 'It carries no hint of approval of anything Hitler or his regime do,' he told FA secretary Stanley Rous. 'If I do it, why shouldn't you or your team?'

England full back Bert Sproston and Stanley Matthews had seen at first hand the feverish cult of personality enveloping Hitler wherever he went.

While out sightseeing in Berlin early on during their visit 1938, Sproston and Matthews were having tea in a cafe when, in a sudden commotion, tables were abandoned as diners scrambled towards the window, jostling for a glimpse of Hitler driving by. 'Everyone was very excited – there was a lot of noise and people performing the Nazi salute,' said Sproston.

That salute, the outstretched arm that was a gesture of faith in Germany yet one of provocation elsewhere, took centre stage on the day of the match.

50 Greatest Players

RAICH CARTER Inside forward

Clubs: Sunderland, Derby County

Debut: v Scotland, 14 April 1934

Appearances: 13   **Goals:** 7

(*Wartime/Victory International appearances 17, goals 19*)

Horatio Carter, known always as Raich, was an ingenious inside forward whose best years were lost to World War II. He made his debut against Scotland in 1934 and played his final match against Switzerland in 1947 – a career spanning 13 years but containing just 13 full internationals. Yet as executioner and tactician, few were his equal. If he had a flaw it was a tendency to become impatient with those who fell short of his own high standards.

Apart from his distinctive prematurely silver-grey hair, Carter's acute awareness of the people and play around him made him stand out. He had a fine understanding, first with Stanley Matthews and later with Tom Finney, setting them up with passes, apparently drifting out of the game while leaving them to perform elaborate sorcery on the wings, and then suddenly ghosting in for the kill once the defence was prised open.

Carter's first game alongside Finney in 1946, a 7-2 win over Northern Ireland in Belfast, showed his ability to adapt to situations and remain one step of the defence, constantly changing tack, feinting and double-feinting throughout the 90 minutes, keeping Finney, Tommy Lawton and anyone else who mattered, well supplied. The ability to see out of the corner of his eye, without apparently looking, and the cold, wicked accuracy of his shooting, made Carter a constant torment to defences and one of the finest players of his type England has ever seen.

The calm before the storm. The England team hesitate to give the Nazi salute in the Olympic Stadium in Berlin in 1938. Moments later they reluctantly complied with the British Ambassador's wish and saluted Herr Hitler. England's revenge came in winning 6-3.

Among the 120,000 in the Olympic stadium on 14 May 1938 were Goebbels, Hess and von Ribbentrop. The day was sweltering; the atmosphere within the stadium highly jingoistic. When Stanley Rous passed down the order to England's players that they, too, should salute during the German national anthem, some, it is said, teetered on the brink of revolt.

Accounts, a few of which may have been revised over time, vary as to the reaction. It was, Matthews recalled, an order issued with a sense of menace – the international situation was so sensitive it needed only a spark to set Europe alight. 'We wondered why we couldn't just stand to attention,' said Bert Sproston. 'A lot of the team weren't happy. But I do think it made us more determined to win.' Yet in his memoir *Football Worlds*, Rous gave a rather more sanitised account of the affair. 'All agreed they had no objection and no doubt saw it as a bit of fun rather than of any political significance.'

So important was the outcome to Germany that the players had been closeted away for special training in the Black Forest. They presented themselves in Berlin looking, in Matthews' words, 'like a bunch of bronzed

50 Greatest Players

STAN CULLIS Centre half

Club: Wolverhampton Wanderers
Debut: v Ireland, 23 Ocober 1937
Appearances: 12 (*Wartime appearances 20*)

The caricature of the pre-war centre half is the beefy stopper with a brief to mark the opposing centre forward and whack the ball clear of danger. But there was no attraction for Stan Cullis, perhaps the most towering individual in the history of Wolverhampton Wanderers, in simply stifling the opposition. He was interested both in attack and defence. He hated wasting the ball and hung on to it like a prized possession, waiting for just the right opening before passing it on.

But before he, and others, could play his game, the ball had to be won. Few were better than Cullis, either at keeping their position, biding their time to seize on a mistake, or, if necessary, committing to a crunching tackle. Then, even as a ball winner near his own goal, Cullis began his constructive work, feeding passes to the flanks, moving upfield, taking the ball again before finally shredding the opposition defence with balls of fatal accuracy.

As with Raich Carter, war robbed Cullis of competitive football at the highest level. Capped 12 times from 1937 to 1939, when, at 22 he became England's youngest ever captain, Cullis made a further 20 international appearances in wartime. There was no other centre half like him. Enlightened and far-sighted, Cullis retired from playing in 1947. Within two years, he was managing Wolves and under his stewardship the club entered its golden age.

Greek statues'; a palpable contrast to the English, pallid and jaded after a hard season. But his team drew heart from their handful of supporters and their exhortation 'to let them have it'. This time Matthews, a little stronger and more seasoned, was the victor in his duel with Munzenberg who, three years on, appeared slower than at White Hart Lane. Matthew's supremacy on the flanks became a crucial factor in England's success. For all their elaborate preparations, the Germans were outclassed.

Even in victory some England players remained troubled by what had occurred before kick-off. 'We were still talking about it,' said Sproston.

'We weren't sure we'd done the right thing. If we'd met them a couple of years later, we wouldn't have stood to attention – we'd have been sticking bayonets into 'em.' The British ambassador, meanwhile, had exacted a modicum of revenge during the match. Sitting alongside Goering, sporting an old pullover and with binoculars slung round his neck, each time England scored, Sir Neville Henderson offered his Nazi host the use of them, saying: 'What wonderful goals. You really ought to get a closer look.'

For Matthews and his teammates, light relief beckoned with their match against Switzerland in Zurich a week later. The game began with high jinks as a pilot flew low over the pitch and dropped the match ball onto the field just before kick-off. The Swiss left back Lehmann was also a band leader, one reputed to keep late hours, but neither he nor his colleagues were anything other than fit and alert, and in the end they proved too much for England, who lost 2-1 to a much disputed penalty.

The England players may have had broader horizons thrust upon them, but in 1939, with the Second World War less than six months away, nothing beat the annual clash with Scotland to get the blood going. As *The Times* reflected, 'The match has a spirit and importance of its own. England have not won in Glasgow since 1927 but there is sound reason for thinking they might do this afternoon. Cullis is one of the outstanding figures in football of the present generation... he has the knack of endowing every clearance with a purpose of its own. Woodley in goal hardly knows what it is to play an indifferent game; Lawton believes that a centre forward should be a distributor of the ball and not merely one who waits for it to be put up to him.'

There was the sense that this England combination had an illustrious future and the result against Scotland bore out the prophesy of 'a grand game', despite wet and blustery conditions. Once Cullis recovered from a shaky start, the half backs were outstanding and Matthews, after a surfeit of over-elaboration early on, became in the closing stages, 'the great player he is'. One-nil down at half-time, England recovered to steal the match two minutes from the end as, from Matthew's perfect centre, Tommy Lawton sent a crashing header past goalkeeper Jimmy Dawson and into the net.

The high morale with which the England camp embarked on its summer tour of Italy, Yugoslavia and Romania, after beating Scotland was tempered by unease at the international situation so acute that the FA had considered cancellation. 'The situation was even worse than it had been the previous year in Germany,' Matthews recalled. 'By now Mussolini was openly talking war.'

But despite Mussolini's bellicosity, the England team was much feted by the locals; their time in Italy blighted only by the bad weather that stopped them

50 Greatest Players

JOE MERCER Half back

Club: Everton
Debut: v Ireland, 16 November 1938
Appearances: 5
(*Wartime/Victory International appearances 27, goals 1*)

Joe Mercer's long and at times heroic career had much in common with that of his partner in the England team, Stan Cullis. Common experiences ranged from playing in the same Cheshire schoolboys side to losing their finest professional years to the Second World War. Yet as personalities there was a sharp contrast, with Mercer's geniality and warmth a contrast to Cullis's puritanical demeanour.

As a wing half – he converted from inside forward as a boy – Mercer, lean and light for his height, was a tireless figure; chasing, covering, harrying and gobbling up ground between both penalty areas with seemingly inexhaustible stamina. He played 32 internationals, five squeezed into 1938-39, and 27 during wartime, when Cullis at centre half and Cliff Britton at right half were his regular partners.

When he damaged a knee in the England v Scotland match of 1946, Mercer's career reached its nadir. After 15 years with Everton, he lost form and confidence, but a transfer to Arsenal revived both his own fortunes and that of the north London club. Although edged out of the international scene, Mercer's career flourished until 1954, until ended by a broken leg. He then excelled as a manager, guiding Manchester City to unparalleled success in the 1960s; in 1974 becoming England's caretaker between the reigns of Alf Ramsey and Don Revie; and, wherever he went, adorning the game with his genial spirit.

from training outdoors. As for the match, played in Milan, the second half had echoes of the Battle of Highbury, and the second Italian goal, redolent of Maradona's 'hand of God' effort 47 years later, was fisted home by the Italian centre half Piola with such force that George Male, who had been contesting the ball, was knocked out. But Joe Mercer, cracking the whip and as indomitable as he had been against Scotland, led the recovery. England laid siege to the Italian goal and equalised through Willie Hall with four minutes remaining.

As a counterpoint to the intensity of international football, the team went sightseeing. These players were unspoiled by money and foreign places had not been made familiar to them through glossy travel brochures or television. Matthews, for one, travelled with his eyes open, sensitive to grotesque inequalities in Yugoslavia where, as the England players were fussed over royally and fed extravagantly, a national food shortage had left the shop shelves almost bare. However, despite the pampering, this party was not given an easy ride on the pitch. Matthews was a passenger, handicapped by hip damage inflicted in the fierce match with Italy, and early into the game Eddie Hapgood tore an ankle ligament. The nine fit men lost 2-1 to an eager and capable team buoyed up by fanatical support. Six days later England redeemed themselves in Romania where the rejigged team won 2-0 in Bucharest.

It was 24 May. Matthews rejoiced when, after a three-day journey by boat and train from Bucharest, he saw the white cliffs of Dover; not knowing that seven years would elapse before England kicked a ball again on foreign soil. Soon many of the team, a unit of strong characters, muscular ball winners, brave and resourceful forwards and, in Stanley Matthews, a fitful genius, would be in battle dress, fated to be deprived of serious competition in their best playing years.

Chapter Three: 1939-50
The War, Recovery and England's First World Cup

It was vital to the morale and sense of well-being for millions in Britain that football should survive during wartime. The sight of men turning out to play the great game and the continuation of competitive fixtures provided pockets of cheer for increasingly exhausted inhabitants. Football affirmed that life should, and indeed was, going on; and a film of an England v Scotland match played at Hampden in May 1940 was shown to the troops to make that point.

During seven years, including the transitional 1945-46 season, England played 37 matches. More than 70 players were called upon, though some were constant figures: Matthews played 29 times; Mercer 27; Lawton 23; Cullis 20; and Carter 17. But caps were not awarded, nor were results credited to a player's account, a state of affairs described by Brian James, author of *England v Scotland*, as a monstrous injustice. 'The years... took great bites out of the career-span of some of the greatest players these islands ever produced and the mere fact of a concurrent world conflict should not deprive them of their credit.'

One benefit of the war was that it sent the selection committee into exile. Although England teams were nominally chosen by a war-time panel, in practice Stanley Rous was the sole selector. There was, said Joe Mercer, a sense of consistency: 'It gave us all the feeling we were being dealt with by someone who knew us, not by a committee of people we might never see.' Moreover, players were constantly together, turning out for their units, regiment or the army. Stan Cullis realised the significance of this, commenting, 'Without quite realising what we were doing, I suppose, we built an international side like a club team. And that was a very important part of the success.'

The Game Goes On

During the war years, the various teams despatched in an England shirt achieved 22 victories, seven draws and suffered eight defeats. No one's appearance could be taken for granted. Obtaining leave from military service was not always a formality. Players had to make their own travel arrangements and cope with a disrupted transport system.

In addition, the Luftwaffe threatened the best-laid plans and, following a German propaganda broadcast, so real was the fear of bombs falling on Hampden Park during England's encounter with Scotland on 11 May 1940 that the RAF refused leave to goalkeeper Sam Bartram. But Scotland football fans were, as ever, ravenous for their entertainment and reckless as to the consequences. Of the 81,000 who had bought tickets, 75,000 turned up, although the 1-1 draw of indifferent quality was poor reward for such spirit.

Nine months elapsed before England's next international, but Scotland, once more, were the opponents. The match, played on 8 February 1941 at St James' Park, Newcastle, resulted in a 2-3 defeat for England but marked a significant stage in the evolution of the English team. A debutant at inside right was Wilf Mannion, a young man conspicuous for his glinting mop of blond hair, ball skills and instinctive understanding, who had been rescued from the beaches of Dunkirk a year earlier. Frank Carruthers, writing for the *Daily Mail*, said, 'Football... will rise majestically again as it continues to produce inside forwards of the distinctive merits of Mannion.'

In two subsequent victories against Scotland, Mannion emerged as tormentor in chief. With the Hapgood, Mercer and Cullis backbone of the pre-war team much in evidence England had firm foundations, while Matthews remained mesmeric and Tommy Lawton, Dixie Dean's successor as Everton centre forward and a debutant against Wales in October 1938, had inherited his mentor's fearsome attacking capabilities.

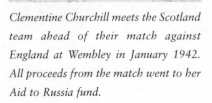

Clementine Churchill meets the Scotland team ahead of their match against England at Wembley in January 1942. All proceeds from the match went to her Aid to Russia fund.

Matches at Hampden were packed to wartime capacity – and sometimes beyond – and if the atmosphere at Wembley was less febrile, football exerted its lure in all conditions. Heavy snow and icy winds for the game against Scotland on 17 January 1942 did not deter 64,000 from turning up to witness, on a snowy pitch delineated with blue markings, England perform with as much domination, cohesion and intent as ever they did in peacetime. They won 3-0, a third victory on the bounce over the

Scots, the proceeds of which were channelled into Mrs Winston Churchill's Aid to Russia fund.

The players themselves only pocketed a paltry proportion of any gate receipts. Stan Cullis recalled Tommy Lawton standing outside Wembley before one international waving a £1 and a 10 shilling note, and shouting: 'Seventy thousand here, and we get only thirty bob for playing. It's ridiculous.' Cullis recalled others grumbling that even turnstile operators were better paid, although he resisted the pressure to ask Stanley Rous for a rise. Cullis was 'blooming glad to be alive and still playing football when millions were giving up everything all over the world'.

Despite being feted for their achievements and lauded in the press, international footballers were still treated like a below stairs class. For their next game against Scotland at Hampden, they were told by the FA: 'Players will make their own travelling arrangements to arrive in Glasgow by 10.00 o'clock on Friday evening. Members of the party are advised to obtain a meal before leaving, and to provide themselves with any refreshments for the journey.' Or, as Lawton put it, 'It was a case of third class travel and your own sandwiches.'

Scottish keeper Crozier saves at the feet of Raich Carter at Wembley in February 1944. However, England went on to win 6-2.

Following their spartan journey, and despite a hat trick from Lawton, England lost 5-4, undone by the clever wing play of Willie Waddell, Billy Liddell and the sharp finishing of centre forward Jock Dodds. But this would be Scotland's final wartime triumph. After a goalless draw at Wembley in October 1942, a series of crushing England victories included an 8-0 annihilation of the old enemy at Maine Road on 16 October 1943, wherein Matthews gave the Scottish defence 90 minutes of nervous strain with his uncanny footwork and body-swerve and Lawton's headed goals hit the back of the net with as much force as many of his ground shots. Cullis, playing at centre half, saw no reason to be modest. 'This was the finest football I have ever seen,' he said.

Cullis had justification for indulging in triumphalism. England's 4-0 victory over the Scots at Hampden in April had been an unpleasant occasion. The crowd had been restricted to 75,000 but thousands more turned up and some stormed the gates. In the crush that followed, more than 60 were injured. The game had long been won when, as Cullis lined up to defend a free kick, Scottish forward Dougie Wallace grabbed at his shorts. As Cullis was left with an agonising injury from which full recovery took a couple of years, a brawl ensued. He was later interviewed by officials from both the English and Scotttish FA and his torn shorts were taken away as evidence.

Excruciating though the assault was, Cullis remained at the centre of things for England's next three games against Scotland: three straight wins, 17 England goals scored. But statistics rarely tell a complete story. While England were 6-2 winners at Wembley on 14 October 1944, at centre half, because of injury to Bill Shankly, Scotland chose to employ Bob Thyne of Darlington, in the early stages of convalescence after being blown up during the Allied invasion of Normandy.

The final wartime encounter re-emphasised the shift in balance of power. England's 6-1 victory at Hampden, much the Scots' worst defeat on home soil, saw Carter and Matthews combining to irresistible effect and Lawton was again uncontainable. However, it was not only a day for the old stagers as Neil Franklin, a young centre half from Stoke City, showed tenacity and concentration during his second encounter with the old enemy, and the excellence of Frank Swift, emerging as number one goalkeeper, manifested itself as he saved a penalty struck by Matt Busby.

Matches against Wales, though considered less a litmus test of international standing, caused England teams more problems. Half England's wartime defeats were inflicted by the Welsh. They won on their first appearance at Wembley on 13 April 1940, a long range shot from Bryn

50 Greatest Players

TOMMY LAWTON Centre forward

Clubs: Everton, Chelsea, Notts County,

Debut: v Wales, 22 October 1938

Appearances: 23   **Goals:** 22

(Wartime/Victory International appearances 23, goals 24)

Tommy Lawton combined brawn and delicacy: a strongly-built centre forward who was capable of executing some manoeuvre of wit or subtlety. 'He was,' said one contemporary, 'the lightest mover of any big man who ever played football'. Another wrote, 'Everything about him was a threat: from his coolness, to the jut of a head on a muscular neck that could flick a heavy ball into goal like a stone from a catapult.'

A restless temperament, not kindly disposed to fools, and with a strong sense of his own worth, Lawton was the complete centre forward – a star who was always news, but one whose abilities usually justified constant attention.

Six feet tall, blessed with a perfect physique, Lawton's trademark style was to gobble up the ground with lithe, feline strides, before unleashing cannonball shots, but he was also notable for hanging in the air, where his uncanny knack of seeming to change direction at the last habitually threw defenders. He scored almost a goal a game in an international career disrupted by the war, including four in the 10-0 annihilation of Portugal in Lisbon in 1947. Many played more full internationals than Lawton, but his place in the pantheon of great English centre forwards is unassailable.

Jones settling the match 1-0. In October 1942, winger Horace Cumner scored both goals as England went down 2-1 to Wales at Molineux. Then in September 1944, while the English had mastered the Scots, the Welsh managed to force a 2-2 draw at Anfield.

Modernising Influences and a Manager

The end of war marked a resumption of games against foreign opposition and the visit to England of Moscow Dynamos in 1945 gave a glimpse of the future, of the meticulous preparations undertaken by totalitarian states for which sporting success was essential propaganda. Tommy Lawton had transferred from Everton to Chelsea and played in their historic

Nearly 85,000 people crammed into Stamford Bridge to watch the first game of the Moscow Dynamos tour of 1945.

encounter against Dynamos at Stamford Bridge, one that drew a crowd of more than 80,000. They saw the Russians take to the field long before kick-off, dressed in tracksuits, indulging in a ten-minute warm up and kicking several balls about – essential preliminaries that the English game was painfully slow to copy. The match was a 3-3 draw. Early on Chelsea were carved apart, saved from ignominy only by Dynamos' inability to shoot.

Indeed, so unstructured was the English game that potential lessons often went unlearned. When Tommy Lawton visited Switzerland in 1946, he found the extent of football coaching at all levels a revelation. In his autobiography, *My Twenty Years of Soccer*, he wrote, 'I said that within five years, we in Britain would be playing second fiddle to the continentals unless something was done quickly. People laughed at me then. But I was only two years wrong.'

However, in one crucial area, England, which in 1946 had finally rejoined FIFA, did belatedly catch up with the likes of pre-war Italy and Russia. A team manager was appointed: Walter Winterbottom, footballer and academic. Rather than pursue a career as a professional, Winterbottom left his grammar school in Oldham to train as a teacher in Chester. There Eddie Lever, a professional with Portsmouth who was studying while recovering from injury, opened his mind to tactics and theories. Winterbottom qualified, went off to teach, and turned out as an amateur

FIFA reconvened after the war in 1945 at the Victoria Hotel in London. England rejoined world football's governing body the following year.

for local teams around Manchester. He was spotted by a Manchester United scout and wooed into the game as a professional on the condition that he had free time to study PE at Carnegie College, Leeds.

When a spinal injury ended his playing career, Winterbottom went to Carnegie as a sports lecturer. He joined the RAF at the outbreak of the Second World War and was seconded to the Air Ministry, where he became head of physical training. He made guest appearances for Chelsea and was called up as a reserve for wartime England internationals. His plans to resume teaching after the war were turned

Walter Winterbottom, England's first 'official' team manager, was appointed in 1946.

upside down, though, when Stanley Rous invited him to take over the national team and develop the game at all levels as FA Director of Coaching. But Rous's vision was not shared by most of the FA councillors. 'They gave Walter the responsibility but saw to it that they retained the power,' he said.

Nevertheless, Winterbottom, a knowledgeable coach and gifted organiser, set to work with a will, introducing the idea of Under 23 and youth team matches, and a summer tour. But he often found his plans throttled by the tortured deliberations of the selection committee and parochial interests of league club chairmen. When Stanley Rous took to the after-dinner speaking circuit, his party piece was a lampoon of the team-picking process. 'A dozen selectors would tug and pull at his nominations like dogs fighting over a bone... with each of the chairmen, retired butchers, greengrocers, builders, motor dealers and farmers, fighting his corner for a player from his own club.'

Rous had attempted to use his own wartime experiences to secure one-man control and sustain the national-team-as-club ethos. He and Winterbottom weren't alone in mourning what might have been. 'It wasn't that they [the administrators] didn't know,' said Stan Cullis. 'They had been told the value of the system we had stumbled across by accident because of the war. It was a great opportunity lost.'

Still, Winterbottom's appointment was progress of a sort and he had had some wonderful raw material with which to work. Emerging from the Royal Armoured Corps was Tom Finney, a young winger of prodigious talent who had joined Preston North End before the outbreak of war. As a soldier Finney exploited every opportunity to develop his technique. 'I got posted to Egypt where I played quite a lot,' he said. 'We had matches against a King Farouk's 11 and a team working on the Egyptian railways. I learned from playing in a hot climate and, on sand pitches, how to bring the ball quickly under control.'

Finney was a man of immense, understated strength, impeccable habits and temperament, and phenomenal skill. He won his first cap in the first official post-war international, against Northern Ireland in Belfast on 28 September 1946, and was one of two new potent elements in an exuberant, free-scoring forward line; the other being Wilf Mannion. They began as they were to continue, combining superbly between themselves and with Raich Carter, Finney scoring once and Mannion a hat-trick in a 7-2 demolition of the home side.

This victory ushered in a mini golden age for England, wherein gifted young blood and talented older hands combined to exhilarating effect. It also triggered the ubiquitous Finney v Matthews debate over which of the maestros should be accommodated on the right wing? Finney, however, as a young boy, had been left-footed, and in one of their wiser moments, the selectors went along with Winterbottom's idea, accommodating both for England's clash with Portugal in Lisbon. This was a bold stroke made easier following injury to the regular outside left, Bobby Langton, who had made his debut with Mannion and Finney. Finney was unperturbed about switching positions: 'Walter said we had a problem with Bobby being injured and told me he wanted me to play outside left. I said I would play left back if necessary!'

Lisbon in May 1947 was a tonic for footballers conditioned to the grind of survival in a post-war Britain that lived by the ration book. It put Matthews, for one, in a near euphoric frame of mind and he described the team's luxurious hotel in Estoril lyrically: 'A blue sky merging into lighter blue sea on the horizon, beautiful snowy white building set amongst exquisite displays of geraniums, dotted with miniature palm trees... I was thrilled with it all.'

Proceedings in Lisbon's monumental national stadium of white marble were delayed by a wrangle over the size of the ball, the Portuguese calling for a size four, smaller than England were used to. It was, in the end, with a size four produced by sleight of Portuguese hand that England set about annihilating their hosts, the game a rout from beginning to end. Both wingers capped virtuoso performances with a goal: Finney in the first half half; Matthews at the death. Lawton and Mortensen each plundered four. The Portuguese slunk away too shame-faced to attend a banquet given in England's honour.

Great Matches

FRIENDLY　　　　　　　　　　　　　　　**Turin, 16 May 1948**

Italy 0　　　**England 4**　　　　　**Attendance 58,000**
　　　　　　　　　　Mortensen
　　　　　　　　　　Lawton
　　　　　　　　　　Finney 2

Outside the stadium business was brisk for the ticket touts. There was pulsating tension in the air and a sense that stakes were high. For the Italians, reputedly on bonuses of £1,000 each to win, they were, but the English appetite for victory was no less keen for being on just £20 a man, whatever the outcome.

Shortly before kick-off torrential rain gave way to dazzling sunshine. The Italians began with an onslaught on England's goal, but within four minutes were in disarray, victims of a sucker punch. The ball was fed out of defence to Matthews who hared down the right, drew Italy's left back, left him for dead and crossed for Mortensen to score from the tightest of angles.

Tom Finney cracks England's fourth goal past a hapless Bacigalupo to seal an emphatic victory.

So much for game plans. England played by instinct, to their strengths, seizing the initiative. Twenty minutes later they were two up, Lawton gobbling up the chance created by Mortensen's thrusting 50-yard dribble and accurate pass.

After half time the Italians responded with sustained pressure. It was the turn of the defence, rallied by Frank Swift, to pull together. But England were not prised open and, with one lethal attack down the left, the contest was over: Mannion bore down on the Italian goal and jabbed a quick pass to Finney, who slammed the ball high into the net.

With Italy's barricades down, England poured forward once more: Mortensen at breakneck speed; another pass to Finney; a brilliant finish that rendered the final 20 minutes irrelevant. This was one of England's proudest days, at the end of which Swift, the team captain, was carried aloft from the pitch on the shoulders of his team-mates.

Italy: Bacigalupo (Torino), Ballarin (Torino), Eliani (Fiorentina), Annovazzi (AC Milan), Parola (Juventus), Grezar (Torino), Menti II (Torino), Loik (Torino), Gabetto (Torino), Mazzola (Torino), Carapallese (AC Milan)

England: Swift (Manchester City, captain), Scott (Arsenal), Howe (Derby County), Wright (Wolverhampton Wanderers), Franklin (Stoke City), Cockburn (Manchester United), Matthews (Blackpool), Mortensen (Blackpool), Lawton (Notts County), Mannion (Middlesbrough), Finney (Preston North End)

The Portuguese were easier meat than anticipated but that could not detract from England's bravura display. Matthews, Mortensen, Lawton, Mannion and Finney were a magnificent act, destined to unhinge sterner opposition over the next two years. Victory over Portugal marked the start of a run of 11 matches unbeaten, in which 43 goals were scored. Four months later England won 5-2 in Belgium and Matthews showed some of the most coruscating form of his England career. A real test of England's true mettle came the following year against Italy in Turin – a fixture between proper heavyweights and one that had acrimonious baggage. Matthews, in a

50 Greatest Players

FRANK SWIFT Goalkeeper

Club: Manchester City
Debut: v Northern Ireland, 28 September 1946
Appearances: 19
(*Wartime/Victory International appearances 14*)

Few players inspired greater affection and respect than Frank Swift. On ability alone he commanded a place in history, but his love of a joke and the irrepressible good humour with which he embraced most situations have made him a legendary figure.

Everything about Swift was remarkable: the much commented upon 12-inch span of his hands, which were compared variously to shovels or hams; his bravery and consistency in goal; and his durability.

For a big man Swift was agile, adept at dealing with low shots as well high ones. He was always distinctive in goal, long arms shooting out, huge hands curling round the ball, which he would then hug to his body; and fearless when it came to flinging himself at the feet of forwards. Tommy Lawton recalls, 'He would chill you to the marrow with his blood-curdling roar of "right" when he thought the ball was his.'

Swift's goal kicks, renowned for length and accuracy, were rarely wasted, and he was forever launching counter attacks with wonderful throws to the wings, using a technique he had learned when watching water polo. A stalwart of the team in wartime internationals, Swift retired in 1950 and was mourned greatly when, eight years later, he died in the Munich air crash, having travelled as a journalist to cover Manchester United's European Cup campaign.

masterpiece of understatement, said, 'I hadn't forgotten the match at Highbury in 1934 or Milan in 1939.'

England's success was built on talent, spirit and continuity. Frank Swift, in particular, was a fine goal keeper, a genial, unifying presence, and was held in universal affection and esteem. 'We won that day in Turin thanks to our wonderful understanding,' said Lawton. 'Probably on sheer football alone, the Italians had the edge, but there was something about our team-work, inspired by that great character in goal, that won us the day.'

But for Lawton the end, at international level, beckoned. By his own admission he played abysmally against Denmark in Copenhagen four months later, a 0-0 draw that left few satisfied. 'After that, I lost my place and never regained it. I wasn't surprised because I had a wretched game,' he said. He was a big loss. No other centre forward in England, good as many were, quite had Lawton's combination of talents and presence.

It fell to Scotland finally to lower England's colour, 3-1 winners at Wembley in April 1949. For the first time in a decade the Scots stifled the destructive threat posed by Matthews, using inside left Billy Steel as a defensive reinforcement. Steel also excelled in attack, his second half goal the culmination of fine team play. England were in transition, the look of the team governed by the whims of selectors and injuries. New defensive pillars Billy Wright and Neil Franklin had emerged and the gifted if idiosyncratic Len Shackleton had come through at inside left along with Jack Milburn at centre forward. But a crop of others came and went, playing one or two matches before being discarded. As 1950 approached, and with it England's debut in the World Cup, there was uncertainty about what constituted the best team.

Matters were complicated by an abrupt departure from the international scene of centre half Neil Franklin who, after a protracted dispute with his club Stoke City, decamped to a new league established in Colombia. Within weeks, though, he was back in Britain, having spent much of his time cooped up in a hotel, his ostensibly fabulous wages eaten up by the astronomical cost of living. On ability alone, Franklin should have been welcomed back to the England fold with open arms, but defection was considered a heinous offence: his negotiations had been secret and he had broken contract to play for a club outside FIFA jurisdiction.

The suspension was lifted in 1951 but, having played 27 consecutive internationals and a further 12 in wartime, Franklin, so commanding in the air, capable on the ground and adept at picking the pockets of opposing forwards, was, to widespread dismay, never picked again. Stanley Rous saw him as 'the nicest of men and a fine player,' but, through dogged preservation of principle, England had lost a player constantly mentioned in dispatches for defensive excellence. No one more than Franklin was responsible for England's 2-0 victory over Scotland at Hampden in 1948 where early on, according to Clifford Webb of the *Daily Herald*, Scottish forwards 'created sheer panic in every England defender save Franklin'. A year later, in Scotland's 3-1 victory at Wembley 'only three England players, Wright, Franklin and Mortensen, produced their best form'. In big matches, against the best, Franklin was conspicuously excellent.

Frank Swift also departed the international stage, his last appearance an undemanding run-out against Norway in May 1949, which England won 4-1. Swift was a fine, brave goalkeeper, a natural clown who bound team-mates together and sustained morale. The England team that travelled to Brazil for the World Cup in 1950 had immense talent but fewer great characters. Moreover, there was no close bond between the players, some of whom were sceptical about the need for coaching and elaborate tactics.

Preparing for Global Competition

The England squad included its two great ball-playing wingers, Tom Finney and, at 35, Stanley Matthews, who had been ignored at international level throughout the season. Matthews was one of those sceptical about Winterbottom. 'You cannot tell star players how they must play,' he said. 'Their minds should not be full of "now I must do this or that" when the ball lands at their feet.' But what was good for Matthews wasn't necessarily good for lesser mortals. Thorough planning, preparation and coaching could produce unexpected results, as another Englishman plotting his campaign for the World Cup would prove.

That man was George Raynor, the manager of Sweden. Raynor was a diminutive, energetic Yorkshireman who, by his own admission, had been a mediocre winger with Rotherham, Bury and Aldershot. He found his metier as a coach during wartime service with the Army Physical Training Corps, where he was quick to spot and rectify a player's weakness. In Sweden, he laid strong foundations by organising coaching courses across the country and regular conventions – what he called his 'stewpot of brains'. Ominously, his team had beaten England 3-1 in Stockholm, a defeat insufficiently explained away by goalkeeper Ted Ditchburn's complaint of being dazzled by the sun in the first half.

Raynor did not have to contend with the absurdities thrust upon Winterbottom when picking a World Cup team, such as a request from Manchester United that their players be ruled out because the club had planned a tour of the United States. In Sweden, the likely candidates were announced early in the year, summoned to training camps and expected to exchange tactical ideas. Raynor ordered featherweight boots from Rio – 'more like carpet slippers' – and had the grass on the training ground cut as short as possible to try to simulate Brazilian conditions. He mocked what passed for preparation by England: 'The attitude of scorning training camps and living together for the shortest possible time – in a luxury hotel if possible'. (The Brazilians by contrast, had been incarcerated in seclusion for four months. Conjugal relations were banned; bed-time, after evening entertainment, was at 10 p.m. sharp.)

It was symptomatic of England's amateurism and lack of intelligence-gathering that the players arrived in Brazil, after a two-day plane journey and without having acclimatised, to discover the local cuisine booby-trapped with spices. Winterbottom felt obliged to stand guard in the hotel kitchen and supervise the cooking himself. George Raynor, on the other hand, had made contact with an exiled Swedish woman living in Rio and recruited her as culinary consultant. Meanwhile, certain players, singled out beforehand in Sweden, were ordered to have daily injections of vitamin C.

England Joins the World Cup Carnival

Nothing prepared England for the culture shock of Brazil. Even Stanley Matthews, a seasoned traveller, was overwhelmed by the chaos and enormity of everything. The England team set out by coach to watch the opening match in the Maracana stadium, which still resembled a building site, but so great were the thronging crowds that the players abandoned their transport and walked the last leg. As the Brazilian team entered the arena, there was a fusillade of fireworks, 'like a miniature blitz', and into the sulphurous smoke thousands of balloons and pigeons were released. Kick-off was preceded by a 21-gun salute. 'I sat down in a daze,' said Matthews. 'In the distance, towering over the ground, was the magnificent figure of Christ, hands outstretched in peace, looking down on the most fantastic scenes.'

The game against Mexico was a limp spectacle, although the Brazilians showed enough flair in their 4-0 victory to impress upon Matthews their fearsome potential. England were in action the following day against Chile. Matthews was not selected. Instead Tom Finney played at right wing. England won 2-0 but laboured, struggling for breath in the oppressive atmosphere. They were made to fend off early pressure, then knocked out of their stride by the bruising Chilean defence. Stan Mortensen's contributions were decisive: his headed goal from Mullen's fine left-wing cross seven

United States goalkeeper Frank Borghi saves from England's Tom Finney in their World Cup group match in Belo Horizonte in 1950 – one of the greatest ever cup shocks in world football history.

minutes before half time; and, in the second half, his powerful surging run past three defenders and his pass to Finney, whose centre was converted with gusto by Wilf Mannion.

Matthews fretted on the sidelines with a sense of foreboding, uncomfortably aware that the entire Chilean team apart from George Robledo, the Newcastle forward, son of a Chilean father and Yorkshire mother, were part-timers – grocers, bookmakers, accountants and engineers. 'We should have done much better against weak opposition,' he said. 'The Brazilians thought we were taking things easy… but I knew different.'

England's next match was against the United States, makeweights in the minds of almost everyone. The venue, Belo Horizonte, was 300 miles away, in a mountainous area where the heat was less oppressive, although the stadium was cramped and the bumpy pitch hemmed in by a cinder track. Nevertheless, it offered agreeable respite from England's raucous billet near the Copacabana beach and the team were guests of the English company that owned the Morro Velho gold mine, where around 2,000 British workers were employed.

The Americans seemed intent on talking down their own chances. 'We ain't got a chance against your boys,' declared their Scottish-born

50 Greatest Players

WILF MANNION Inside forward

Club: Middlesbrough

Debut: v Northern Ireland, 28 September 1946

Appearances: 26   **Goals:** 11

(*Wartime appearances* 4)

Mannion's tally of official caps, like that of Swift, far from tells the whole story of his illustrious career. It neglects games played through the war years; when he arrived on the international scene as a confident, arresting presence with unmistakable class. Mannion's first match against Scotland at Newcastle in February 1941 (a wartime international) epitomised what was to come. 'He played with all the assurance of an established international, holding the ball long enough to create an opening – perhaps too long – moving into surprising positions to the confusion of the opposition, and showing rare craftsmanship in ball play,' wrote Frank Carruthers in the *Daily Mail*.

Tom Finney described Mannion as 'a beautiful exponent of one-touch football... the ultimate players' player, always reading intentions and moving into position'. If he had a weakness, some critics feel it was an over-fondness for the square pass, but as someone who could make things happen in attack, Mannion had few equals.

His understanding with Finney was rarely displayed better than in the 10-0 mauling of Portugal in 1947, where their interplay of short, sharp, witty passes was a joy to watch. Mannion's genius didn't always guarantee victory by such margins, or even at all, but many were delighted merely to have glimpsed it.

manager Bill Jeffrey, 'but we're gonna fight to keep down any cricket score.' As if to convince Winterbottom's men of their casual approach, some of Jeffrey's team, migrants from around the world, went out revelling until the small hours on the eve of the match.

The decision to stick with the men who had struggled to beat Chile caused some surprise, especially as the recent history of selection had been one of vacillation. Even if, at the time, the approach seemed logical – why dismantle a winning team that could go on to develop a greater understanding? – before long, the decision would come to haunt Arthur Drewry, the sole selector. With the wisdom of hindsight came a cacophony of dissenting voices, that of

50 Greatest Players

STAN MORTENSEN Centre forward/Inside right

Club: Blackpool

Debut: v Portugal, 25 May 1947

Appearances: 25   **Goals:** 23

(*Wartime/Victory International appearances 3, goals 3,*
plus 1 Wartime appearance for Wales)

Mortensen's introduction to international football was a glorious
one: the extravagant 10-0 rout of Portugal in which he scored
four times. But along the way he had suffered knock-backs,
including a pre-war vote of no confidence from his club,
Blackpool, and severe injury in the RAF when the Wellington
bomber in which he was training caught fire and crashed.

A head full of stitches did not deter him though, and
Mortensen was soon back playing for services teams where he
began to fulfil his formidable potential. Blessed with a big match temperament,
he worked his magic with admirable economy of effort. The courage he showed in wartime
reappeared in the game against Scotland at Wembley in 1951 when, dazed after a
collision, Mortensen refused to leave the field.

On the pitch Mortensen combined supremely with Stanley Matthews and off it he was
joint master of gags and tomfoolery with Frank Swift. A slight figure, he played to his
strengths: great acceleration; a gift for pulling off the unexpected; and preternatural
powers of anticipation. He was often most dangerous when appearing idle, always liable
to pounce to punishing effect. Eventually injuries robbed him of his speed, but he is
forever remembered as a beacon in England's post-war golden age.

Stanley Rous among them. 'It seemed there was a danger of his [Drewry]
taking America too lightly,' he said. 'Stanley Matthews seemed the ideal man
to undermine a team like theirs, which was clearly long on spirit and short on
skill. I went to see Drewry and urged Matthews' inclusion.'

But Matthews, again, was forced to sit things out, although the team still
had more than enough flair and experience to vanquish so moderate a side
as the United States. There were steady defensive hands such as Alf Ramsey,
Jimmy Dickinson and Billy Wright, while in attack, Tom Finney was capable
of weaving through any obstacle and Wilf Mannion and Stan Mortensen
were old hands at dismantling international defences.

England had played many a match where they pounded the opposition goal and reaped their harvest, but the Americans were not to be pulverised. John Souza at inside left was a clever player and a reminder that the English needed to stay on guard. As the favourites squandered chances by the hatful, the Americans rode their luck. Then, seven minutes before half-time, they struck to calamitous effect. Goalkeeper Bert Williams appeared to have covered an innocuous shot from Bahr, only for Gaetjens, the Haitian-born centre forward, to dart in and deflect the ball into the net with his head.

Four minutes earlier Tom Finney had hit the post. A goal for England might have deflated the Americans once and for all but instead, fortified by the astonishing turn of events, they dug in, throwing bodies behind the ball, harrying England into shooting high and wide, the dreadful playing surface subverting efforts at finer football. England were, perhaps, unlucky when Mullen's header from a free-kick, floated temptingly into the penalty area by Ramsey, appeared to cross the goal line before being scrambled away. The referee, though, gave only a corner. The world seemed against them. Apart from the British miners, the 20,000 crowd had sided with the underdog. At full-time, as hundreds invaded the pitch to carry off the Americans shoulder high, newspapers were set on fire by way of boisterous celebration – or, as commentators with a fondness for metaphor suggested, a funeral pyre.

After the debacle came the recriminations. Rous claimed that the Americans had been fitter, faster and better fighters. Winterbottom's own verdict was that, 'The team played badly, especially the forwards, who were far too eager.' Stanley Matthews felt the will to win was sadly lacking. 'I blame this on the pre-match talk on playing tactics that had been introduced for the first time by our team manager,' he said.

England now faced a match against Spain back in Rio. Matthews was recalled – a prospect he hardly relished – and new caps were awarded to Eddie Baily, the Tottenham inside left, and Bill Eckersley, Blackburn's left back. Back in England, newspapers invoked the spirit of Dunkirk and urged the team to play with 'more devil, less science'. The Spaniards were, it was felt, serious opposition but beatable. With their confidence fragile, the last thing England needed was an aberrant referee, but after 14 minutes, a header from Jackie Milburn, drafted in to replace Roy Bentley, was adjudged offside, despite evidence of a Spanish defender playing him on. That, in itself, was not fatal to morale as Matthews was causing turmoil down the right, but for all the ammunition the forwards were getting, England's shooting – the weapon that so often kept them abreast of technically superior teams – let them down, or else was gobbled up by Spain's goalkeeper Ramallets.

Matthews tells a story of Spanish fouls going unpunished, all the more so when, five minutes after half-time, they took the lead. It came as the England defence failed to deal with a centre slung in from the right, allowing Zarra a free header. This goal killed off England's interest in the World Cup as the Spaniards, 'using their hands freely… they did everything they could to waste time,' held out for victory.

Matthews had left the pitch in Rio, his head 'hung in shame'. Yet while the sense of shock was profound, it failed to effect a revolution. The World Cup was a far smaller tournament than its 21st century counterpart and had taken place thousands of miles away. Consequently, there was a sense of remoteness about it all and no vengeful scrum of reporters and photographers lay in wait for the vanquished when they stepped off the plane.

However, some of Winterbottom's remarks hinted at the scale of the work that needed to be done. 'The 1950 World Cup put our position in the world in sharp perspective,' he said. 'Before the war, most of the South Americans and best European sides were quite unknown. So we went to Rio pretty well unprepared. Arsenal had been to South America… and gave us some indication of what we were going to face. We began to realise what needed to be done… but it was to be a very long time before we could do it.'

The England party arrive back at Heathrow from Rio in July 1950 after returning from their unsuccessful World Cup campaign.

Chapter Four: 1951-57
Upsets and Some Success

The aftershocks from Brazil continued into autumn. Billy Wright, tired and jaded by the burden of captaining his country when so much had gone wrong, was dropped. In November 1950, Yugoslavia almost became the first foreign side to win in England, drawing 2-2 after going 2-0 down. Both England goals were scored by debutant centre forward Nat Lofthouse, who looked a genuine prospect. The selection committee, however, was to persist with its whimsical ways.

In particular, it floundered over a choice of centre half to replace Neil Franklin. Against Wales at Roker Park in November 1950, Les Compton – aged 38 – was called up for his first cap. Against Scotland, six months later, it was the turn of Portsmouth's Jack Froggatt, previously capped twice at outside left. The method behind the selectors' apparent madness was that Froggatt's pace might counter that of the small nippy Scots' forwards. But he had a torrid afternoon, as did Billy Wright, who marked his recall by sending most of his passes astray. These were black marks in a pulsating match, one in which England had to battle with ten men after Mannion fractured a cheekbone. They lost 3-2 but, against the odds, fought valiantly.

Pluck and fighting spirit – these qualities were never in doubt. In most games, and often in adversity, Finney shone. He, and apart from a brief exile, Wright, were two constants in a set-up where selectors quickly jettisoned any player who had an off-day. Winterbottom had other problems, too. The days of postponing League fixtures before international matches were still far away and he had the vested interests of some club managers to contend with, including a reluctance to release key players and disparagement of his efforts to introduce theory and tactics.

Testing Foreign Opposition

Visiting foreign teams continued to rattle the national sense of well-being and threaten in unusual ways. When Austria played at Wembley in November 1951, the challenge was to snuff out their attacking centre half Ernst Ockwirk. England deployed a tactic learned six months earlier from the visiting Argentinians: that of defending deep and picking off attackers in advanced positions. But in a 2-2 draw decided by set pieces, a penalty each and goals from well-rehearsed free kick routines, England frequently looked technically inferior to their opponents.

Yet England's return match against Austria in Vienna six months later was to stir the blood and rekindle patriotic pride. Their 3-2 victory was immortalised by the display of Nat Lofthouse, whose two goals – the second of which saw him knocked out by the advancing Austrian goalkeeper at the end of a brilliant 50-yard run – earned a place in folklore. After treatment Lofthouse had returned to the field in marauding fashion, his tail up, hungry for a hat trick. In the last few seconds he signed off with a ferocious shot that clattered the crossbar.

The victory against Austria came amid a fruitful three years in which England lost only once, to Scotland, in 20 matches. But in *A Century of Soccer*, Terence Delaney claimed the enduring unbeaten home record against foreign opposition had as much to do with unfamiliar conditions and that England's 'long history' gave her a moral advantage. Winterbottom knew that the real test of England's calibre lay in how they tackled the world's best teams abroad. Not surprisingly, he found the home international championship parochial and unsatisfactory. 'The games obviously had less importance than the bigger picture,' he said.

With a football education his mission, in 1953 Winterbottom took England off on a gruelling, bruising summer tour of South America. The game against Argentina was washed out by a cloudburst mid way through the first half; there was a 2-1 victory over Chile; and defeat, 2-1, at the hands of reigning world champions Uruguay. The expedition ended with a game against the USA in New York and, after Belo Horizonte, the hollow consolation of a 6-3 victory.

Any lingering vestiges of complacency about the state of the English game were about to be shattered. On 25 November 1953, Hungary came to Wembley and dispensed an unforgettable lesson. For the purist or neutral it was an exhilarating occasion, but for patriots or anyone with a vested interest in England's fortunes, Hungary's iconoclastic display sent a message far more chilling than any freakish defeat against the United States.

For England, it was as if seven veils had been snatched from them. Tom Finney, who had been dropped and watched from the stands said: 'I came away wondering what we had been doing all those years. The Hungarians were so much better in technique it was untrue. The first thing they did was to come out 20 minutes to half an hour before the game and do all sorts of things with the ball, which was new. We had never done anything like that: it was a question of getting ready and going out five minutes before kick-off.

Great Matches

FRIENDLY

Wembley, 25 November 1953

England 3
Sewell
Mortensen
Ramsey (pen)

Hungary 6
Hidegkuti 3
Puskas 2
Bozsik

Attendance 100,000

Never had the country that gave birth to football been so outpaced, outmanoeuvred and outthought. Hungary, mixing exquisite short passing with the long ball game and showing masterful ball control, dismantled the old order. With a rapier thrust from Bozsik, Zakarias and Hidegkuti, they struck as early as the first minute. Hidegkuti, the deep-lying centre forward with whom this victory is ever synonymous, finished things off, lashing a high, rising shot past Gil Merrick in goal.

Hungary's Sandor Kocsis just fails to beat Merrick and add to England's humiliation.

This was the first flourish of a majestic exhibition. Within 28 minutes, Hungary were 4-1 up; the English bamboozled. And yet Winterbottom's men had their moments, rising fitfully to the occasion. Jackie Sewell's equaliser on 15 minutes was worthy of any international, his low shot the finale of a rapid incisive counter attack from defence through Harry Johnston and Stan Mortensen. The pick of Hungary's four first-half goals was perhaps their third and relished by Geoffrey Green of *The Times*: 'A diagonal ground pass was pulled back by Puskas evading a tackle in the inside right position – sheer juggling this – and finished off with a fizzling left-foot shot inside the near post: 3-1.'

With a dynamic run and finish from a throw-in, Mortensen brought the score to 4-2, but early in the second half the game was laid to rest with a fierce rising shot from the edge of the penalty area by Bozsik and Hidegkuti's volley from Puskas's lob. Alf Ramsey's penalty, scored with half an hour remaining, was of relevance mainly to the statisticians.

England: Merrick (Birmingham City), Ramsey (Tottenham Hotspur), Eckersley (Blackburn Rovers), Wright (Wolverhampton Wanderers), Johnston (Blackpool), Dickinson (Portsmouth), Matthews (Blackpool), Taylor (Blackpool), Mortensen (Blackpool), Sewell (Sheffield Wednesday), Robb (Tottenham Hotspur)

Hungary: Grosics (Honved), Buzanszky (Dorogi), Lantos (MTK Budapest), Bozsik (Honved), Lorant (Honved), Zakarias (MTK Budapest), Budai (Honved), Kocsis (Hoved), Hidegkuti (MTK Budapest), Puskas (Honved), Czibor (Honved)

You would have thought that in international football England would soon have cottoned on to something like that. If you look back, a lot of injuries were caused by the lack of warning up and warming down. We weren't warmed up.

'We had never seen the deep lying centre forward before. Harry Johnston, at centre half, didn't know whether to go with Hidegkuti or not in the first half. But then Walter sized things up – whoever was closest should pick him up. I think it was a great lesson. They were the best international side I have played against.'

England had five months to mull over painful lessons and regroup. For their next outing against Scotland at Hampden Park in April 1954 came wholesale changes, eight in all, and four new caps: right back Ron Staniforth from Huddersfield, left back Roger Byrne from Manchester United, centre half Harry Clarke of Tottenham and inside left Johnny Nicholls of West Bromwich. Nicholls scored with a flying header but had a moderate match and was never picked again. Neither was Clarke. While Byrne made an impressive debut, the star was an old hand, Finney, who linked with Ivor Broadis to devastating effect down the right flank, and whose final passes and crosses shredded the Scottish defence. England won 4-2. After dismemberment by Hungary, and despite being crammed to capacity by 134,000 fanatical Scots, Hampden had proved a place to convalesce.

A World Cup on European Soil

Another World Cup loomed. The venue was Switzerland, where for once England did not risk being undone by fiery food of uncertain origin, a tropical climate or the loss of sleep to beachside revellers. Winterbottom prepared by taking his men on a two-match tour of eastern Europe: a good idea in theory but calamitous in practice. There was a dour tussle with Yugoslavia, which England lost 1-0 at the death; and then another encounter with Hungary, in Budapest. A win would have been miraculous, a draw marvellous, narrow defeat something, perhaps, on which to draw, but nothing had changed. The Hungarians remained, tactically and technically, a world apart, 7-1, victors, carving England to pieces in ruthless fashion. To the echoes of this numbing defeat, England trooped off to Switzerland.

The 1954 World Cup was arranged on a convoluted, almost perverse basis of pools, seeding and knock-out, where the top two teams in each of four pools went into the quarter finals. For all the legendary efficiency of the Swiss, the organisation was, according to football writer Brian Glanville, 'haphazard, and the excesses of the Swiss police sometimes unpleasant... confusion, and sometimes complete chaos, reigned throughout the tournament; stadia were hardly adequate; officials lacked experience in dealing with large crowds.' But, from the standpoint of FIFA officials, what Switzerland lacked in professionalism it compensated for in political neutrality.

The England squad had a curiously lop-sided look. There were seasoned campaigners and pivotal figures: Stanley Matthews, still going strong at 39; Tom Finney; captain Billy Wright; Nat Lofthouse; Jimmy Dickinson; and inside left Ivor Broadis. And then there were the greenhorns: Fulham's centre forward Bedford Jezzard, a hapless debutant in Budapest; and Portsmouth outside right Peter Harris, who had only played two internationals in four years. England, drawn in a pool with Italy, Switzerland and Belgium, played in fits and starts, potent going forward but shaky at the back, where they

badly missed the commanding presences of Frank Swift and Neil Franklin. Their successors, Gil Merrick in goal and at centre half Syd Owen – one of the many permutations at number five – were far less convincing.

England's opening match was an extraordinary 4-4 draw against Belgium, a match that they held in their palm yet contrived to let slip through their fingers. After conceding a goal within five minutes, England took a firm grip, Broadis scoring twice and Lofthouse once, from openings fashioned through orchestrated teamwork and – a familiar story – the ingenious twists and turns of Matthews and Finney. With 15 minutes left, at 3-1 up, and with no sense of Belgian menace, the match looked safe. Then defensive lapses allowed Belgium to strike twice quickly and level the scores. In extra time England again contrived to throw away victory: Lofthouse

Nat Lofthouse (right) scored twice as England drew 4-4 with Belgium in their opening match of the 1954 World Cup.

made it 4-3; yet two minutes later Jimmy Dickinson headed a raking cross into his own net. The English team, lamented *The Times* correspondent, were 'like those rare children of light who can pass through any experience protected by a sheath of impenetrable innocence'.

There was however, one fortuitous benefit. With Owen, who had pulled a muscle, forced to spend the latter stages hobbling on the wing, Billy Wright had slotted in at centre half, where he looked as comfortable and competent as in his usual position. In adversity, one problem was solved: Wright looked the best bet since Neil Franklin at the heart of defence.

Owen's was not the only fitness problem. For the next game, against Switzerland, England had to do without Matthews and Lofthouse. So it was time for another new face, Bill McGarry, of Huddersfield Town, making his debut at right half, and a second outing for Dennis Wilshaw at inside left, who had scored twice in his debut against Wales nine months earlier. Finney replaced Matthews on the right with Jimmy Mullen taking over on the left. Tommy Taylor of Manchester United, who had showed some promise in his three previous matches, deputised for Lofthouse.

Home advantage could not disguise the fact that the Swiss were mediocre opposition. England won 2-0 but the match, played in Berne on a sweltering day, wilted in the heat. Goals in each half from the Wolves left-sided pairing of Wilshaw and Mullen brought victory, Wilshaw's effort a rare tonic in a ponderous match: a clever dribble and fine finishing shot. England had qualified for the quarter finals while, under the cryptic rules of the tournament, Switzerland had to contest a play-off with Italy to determine the other group placing. Against, all expectations, the host nation won.

For England, competitive success had eased the trauma of Budapest, but with teams such as Hungary, Austria, Brazil and Uruguay remaining in the tournament, it seemed implausible they would progress much further. Drawn against world champions Uruguay, the quarter-final was a watershed for Winterbottom's team, a day when the best England had to offer could not carry them at the highest level. They were fit, mobile, passed accurately, tackled hard and gave their all on a blistering day in Basle. But the Uruguayans were trained to other worldly levels of fitness and technical ability which, to their credit, some figures in the English game subsequently took pains to examine and learn from.

There was much to take from defeat. England lost 4-2 yet made a real fight, retrieving an early deficit when Lofthouse equalised after a smart Matthews-inspired attack and then enjoying sustained first-half supremacy. But they were playing at a level where profligacy, errors and the absence of

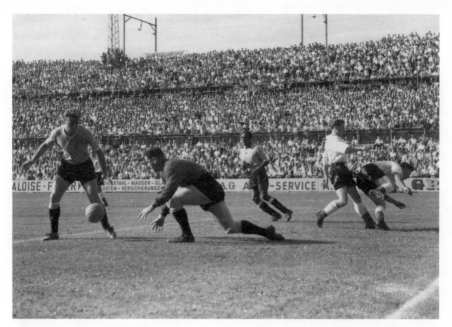

England's hunt for World Cup glory was ended in the quarter-finals by Uruguay.
Uruguayan keeper Maspoli proved difficult to beat and the South Americans won 4-2.

luck were severely punished. No sooner had Wilshaw, following up a
Lofthouse shot beaten away by the Uruguayan goalkeeper, lobbed
agonisingly wide of the net, than Gil Merrick allowed a spectacular long-
range volley shot from centre half Varela to elude him and crash into the net.

A goal down at half time and soon, two – a free-kick against Byrne, a rapid
passing movement and Schiaffino slipped the ball past Merrick, who once
more had appeared flat-footed. Yet England dug into reserves of courage and
determination. They countered and, after scoring through a close range shot
from Finney, made the match retrievable once more. Matthews hit a post,
then forced a fine save from Maspoli in the Uruguayan goal. But the world
champions retained an infinite capacity for speedy retaliation. England were
cut open by another high-speed passing move and Ambrois' diagonal shot
was smartly despatched past Merrick. This, with less than a quarter of an
hour remaining, was the knock-out punch.

Defeat emphasised, rather than disguised, England's problems. Their star
turn, Matthews, was 40 years old. There was a paucity of young blood and
the systematic approach to bringing on young talent, developing an U-23
side, had been implemented too late to bear fruit, although its value would
start to trickle through in a year or two. The brains on England's technical

sub-committee assembled once more and prepared a memorandum on the need for more training grounds and coaches, and team assemblies before international matches. They also called on clubs to allow use of their grounds and provide opponents for practice matches.

Some club managers remained intent on ironing out new methods learned through playing for England. At international level, Tom Finney enjoyed licence to break from deep positions where no marker dare follow him. But back at Preston he was told that England tactics were not wanted and instructed to play forward like a conventional winger. At least one club chairman was hostile to the establishment of U-23 internationals, fearing that they could become a shop window; a magnet for acquisitive scouts.

The Search for a Winning Combination

Winterbottom's vision of the U-23 side providing a stream of graduates to the national team would, in time, become a reality. Meanwhile Tommy Taylor, the young Manchester United centre forward had broken into the team unaided. He was a jinking, dribbling talent, dominant in the air and altogether a forceful presence, but not even Taylor was guaranteed an unbroken run. The World Cup defeat in Switzerland had selectors thrashing about once more.

For England's next match against Northern Ireland in October 1954, seven new faces appeared. But for four, right back Bill Foulkes of Manchester United, right half Johnny Wheeler from Bolton, left half Ray Barlow of West Bromwich Albion and outside left Brian Pilkington from Burnley, this would be their sole cap. Other debutants were Don Revie from Manchester City at inside right, Fulham's Johnny Haynes at inside left, and Manchester United goalkeeper Ray Wood. Gil Merrick's hapless displays in Switzerland condemned him never to be picked for England again.

This England team, assembled from unfamiliar components, laboured to a 2-0 win. Passes often went astray and Northern Ireland looked the better side in the first half. The fact that Foulkes, Wheeler, Barlow and Pilkington were discarded suggested the team was more a reaction, than the beginning of a solution, to England's problems. Against Wales a few weeks later, there were two more new faces: left half Bill Slater of Wolves and outside left Frank Blunstone from Chelsea, as well as the return of an old one, Sunderland's Len Shackleton at inside left.

Shackleton was a big personality and prodigious talent. He first played for England more than six years earlier in Denmark, but had since received only two caps. Shackleton had his own sardonic view – one that could be described as jaundiced had it not been supported by others – as to why: 'I was told off the record that my prolonged absence was caused by selectors' reluctance to play individualists... that it was an unforgivable sin for a player like Stan Matthews or myself to beat an opponent by employing any skill we might possess as ball players.'

Yet England did employ individualists. The selectors had tried, without success, to wean themselves off the ageing Matthews, as if grudgingly forced to recognise a transcendent genius. Finney, too, had been allowed to weave his magic, though both were adept at developing partnerships with inside forwards: Matthews with Raich Carter and Finney with Wilf Mannion and Ivor Broadis. The problem with Shackleton, in an age where deference was expected, was his temperament. He loved playing to the gallery and relished poking fun at people in high places.

England captain Billy Wright (left) jumps with Spanish centre forward Ignacio Arieta during England's 4-1 victory at Wembley in 1955.

According to Maurice Edelston and Terence Delaney, co-authors of *Masters of Soccer*, Shackleton had nearly everything as an inside forward except the ability, or inclination, to 'get stuck in'. He was two-footed, quick when needed and had faultless close control, although was reluctant to tackle back in a hard game. Sometimes he also played with the ball in ways that critics found mockingly self-indulgent, delighting and infuriating in equal measure.

No one was more amazed than Shackleton when, at 33, he was recalled against Wales and then retained for the following match against world champions, West Germany. There, at the highest level, his class shone. For Billy Wright, Shackleton's performance was 'a truly magnificent display of ball control, artistry, positional play – and sheer cheek'. In a sensational, extravagant dribble, he left three defenders in his wake, only for the final touch to let him down, having rounded goalkeeper Herkenrath. Shackleton was unabashed. Before long, he picked up a ball in midfield, bore down on goal and, with two defenders closing in, swerved away from both before chipping the ball into the net as Herkenrath advanced.

50 Greatest Players

DUNCAN EDWARDS Wing half

Club: Manchester United
Debut: v Scotland, 2 April 1955
Appearances: 18   **Goals:** 5

It does scant justice to Duncan Edwards, the Dudley-born boy with a passion for Manchester United, merely to consider him a flame of youthful promise snuffed out by a dreadful accident. By the time Edwards, at 21, perished in the Munich air crash of February 1958, he had become an automatic choice for his country and won two First Division championship medals with Manchester United.

Edwards was described, with justification, as the most complete footballer in Britain. Groomed as a wing half, he turned out for his club – with distinction – at centre half, inside left and centre forward. His power, stamina and skill might have counted for much less had he not also been blessed with a confident and equable temperament. Edwards had seemingly inexhaustible reserves of every precious quality: quick feet; speed of thought; the ability to seize situations by the scruff of the neck and turn events.

As a memorial to his completeness, the winning goal he scored against Scotland at Wembley in 1957 is compelling. With seven minutes remaining and the Scots retreating en masse, Edwards picked up the ball in midfield and charged towards goal with fearsome momentum, leaving defenders spread-eagled, before crashing home a shot of fiendish power from 25 yards.

Of all the talent lost at Munich, Edwards' death was perhaps the most keenly felt and all the more poignant for the fact he clung to life for 15 days before finally succumbing to his injuries.

England won 3-1 at Wembley that day with Bentley and Allen also scoring, but Shackleton's superb performance was ample grounds for wondering why almost a score of inside forwards had been picked ahead of him in the intervening years. It looked as if his renaissance beckoned but, in a final flourish of perverseness, Shackleton was dropped. It was, as his sixth sense had told him, his last outing in an England shirt. For all his abundant talent, he won just five caps.

U-23 Policy Pays Off

However, if selectors had been craven, or foolish, or both, in dispensing with Shackleton, they showed redemptive boldness in picking, for England's next match against Scotland, Manchester United's 18-year-old left half Duncan Edwards. So prodigious and precocious were Edwards' abilities that his claim for a place was irrepressible. He was among the first graduates of the U-23 setup and indisputably the most gifted.

Billy Wright shakes hands with Brazilian captain Santos before their match at Wembley in May 1956. England won 4-2 despite missing two penalties.

As England tucked into an indifferent and uncertain Scotland team, the oldest player and the newest were, in a 7-2 victory, among those who stood out. Matthews, at 41, seemed bent on confounding all received wisdom about the slowing effects of age, causing havoc in short bemusing bursts of speed, while Edwards, indefatigably robust and energetic yet wonderfully light on his feet, offered real optimism – something for England to take on their summer tour.

But any sense of well-being induced by cheerful demolition of the Scots evaporated on the continent. Winterbottom's men lost 1-0 to France in Paris, outplayed, for the most part, by a slicker team; drew 1-1 with Spain in a niggling ill-tempered match; then lost 3-1 to Portugal in Lisbon. It was a dispiriting way to end, and left questions hanging in the air about England's tactical competence and stature as a world force.

England's next outing, in October 1955, against the part-timers of Denmark, brought another sprinkling of new caps: goalkeeper Ron Baynham from Luton, right back Jeff Hall from Birmingham City and inside left Geoff Bradford of Bristol Rovers. A 5-1 victory could not conceal either the indifference of much of England's performance nor the ad hoc nature of team selection – Bradford, even against modest opposition, was hardly international class and was discarded, while Baynham played only two more games.

But graduates were emerging from the U-23 team, among whom Fulham inside forward Johnny Haynes and wing half Ronnie Clayton from Blackburn were starting to look more assured. Meanwhile Roger Byrne of

50 Greatest Players

TOM FINNEY Winger/Centre forward

Club: Preston North End

Debut: v Northern Ireland, 28 September 1946

Appearances: 76   **Goals:** 30

Tom Finney was a player in whom all sorts of skills were condensed within a modest and generous temperament, but this did not mask his unswerving, if unspoken, determination to play his natural game however hostile the attentions of opposing defenders.

Forever associated with Preston North End, Finney, who took what turned out to be the unnecessary precaution of training as a plumber in case he failed as a footballer, was at home on either wing and could also play at centre forward. For England, after some controversial chopping and changing after the war, he moved from right to left so both he and Stanley Matthews could be accommodated on the flanks.

He remained a constant presence when the England team was in its state of flux for much of the 1950s. Twice he was Footballer of the Year, in 1953 and 1957. His sublime skills were partially disguised by a neat, controlled demeanour, subtle changes of pace, ball close to feet, arms by his side; yet he was capable of juggling with the ball and holding on to it until a situation to his liking arose. He was always ready to take or deliver a pass.

For a winger, Finney's scoring rate was remarkable and he was greatly treasured as a team player. The end of his career at international level, which lasted 12 years, was hastened by the cynical attentions of Russian defenders during the 1958 World Cup. However, he had the last word and when England, 2-1 down with five minutes left, were given a penalty, he fired the ball into the net to secure a draw, bowing out with a lesson in how it should be done.

Manchester United had become a mainstay at left back while Billy Wright, amid the shifting sands of players who came and went, had assumed an unflappable and at times heroic indispensability.

In 1956, England not only avoided ignominy but produced some electrifying results. Some positions in the team, notably that of goalkeeper, remained unresolved, but as the year progressed results against serious opposition – Brazil rather than part-timers such as Denmark – were indicators of real progress. Following a 1-1 draw with Wales at Ninian Park in the home international championship in October 1955, England embarked on an unbeaten run of 17 matches that lasted two years.

There was a feast of a match with Brazil at Wembley in May 1956, which England won 4-2 as they rubbed up against some of the finest skills on the world stage. Brazil undid themselves, retrieving a two-goal deficit with panache, yet showed uncontrollable histrionics when two penalties, both of which were missed, were given against them.

A sense of England's star rising was confirmed by the concluding match of their 1956 summer tour, a 3-1 victory against West Germany in Berlin. There was another towering performance from Duncan Edwards – his one-man cavalry charge on the German goal rounded off with a ballistic goal-bound shot; and a display of growing authority from Johnny Haynes, evolving into the pivotal role of play-maker and who, as a passer of the ball, had few peers.

On the World Cup Qualification Trail

English minds began focusing on qualification for the 1958 World Cup, a mission less onerous than it would become as the numbers of pretenders from small nations swelled and standards improved. England had just two other teams in their group: Denmark, and the Republic of Ireland. Denmark, dogged opposition in their first match against England at Molineux in December 1956, were eventually dismantled by familiar combinations: the consummate seniors, Finney and Matthews; the young uninhibited talents, Edwards and Taylor, scorer of a hat-trick in the 5-2 victory. There was more of the same against Ireland at Wembley in May 1957 with a 5-1 win, another Taylor hat-trick, and another incisive performance from Haynes.

A week later, in Copenhagen, Denmark were once more intent on giving England a hard time. At times Winterbottom's team looked jaded after a tough domestic season, but they still had enough reserves to exploit good fortune. With the scores level at 1-1 and 20 minutes left, a Danish player went off injured, swinging a delicate balance decisively England's way. They cashed in with two goals from Taylor and one from John Atyeo.

Three matches and three victories, but a trip to Sweden was not guaranteed. England's durability was tested to the utmost four days later in the final qualifier against the Republic of Ireland in Dublin. Ireland scored in the third minute and led for almost the entire game, dominating for long periods. As full time beckoned, Finney, still composed amid the clamouring pressure and with tricks up his sleeve, weaved down the right, turned Irish

Stanley Matthews (left), Duncan Edwards (centre) and Billy Wright in training at Highbury in April 1956 ahead of the game against Scotland.

defenders inside out and despatched a perfect centre for Atyeo to head home. The spoils of a 1-1 draw entitled England to another quest for the World Cup.

Meanwhile an era had ended. The career of Stanley Matthews, at times so magical as to strain credulity, had concluded in Copenhagen. It had begun in September 1934 against Wales at Ninian Park, when Matthews was 19, and had spanned 22 years and eight months. He was, when recalled amid some controversy to face Denmark, at 42, an unthinkable, almost preposterous age for anyone to contemplate playing international football. But Matthews was Matthews – normal rules had never applied.

England's next meaningful action was in the home internationals, when their long unbeaten run was halted in November 1957 by Northern Ireland, whose 3-2 victory at Wembley was their first on English soil since 1914. But memories of this unexpected jolt were expunged within three weeks when England played France. The team featured an attacking combination of Bryan Douglas of Blackburn Rovers at outside right with Bobby Robson of West Bromwich Albion playing inside him. Douglas, charged with filling the void left by Stanley Matthews, had a fine match and Robson had the pleasure of scoring twice on his debut in a 4-0 win.

50 Greatest Players

STANLEY MATTHEWS Right winger

Clubs: Stoke City, Blackpool

Debut: v Wales, 29 September 1934

Appearances: 54   **Goals:** 11

(*Wartime/Victory International appearances 29, goals 2*)

Almost everything about Stanley Matthews was improbable. His was a life and a talent that ventured into the realms of fantasy: the ball control and body swerve that bamboozled defences around the world; the international career that spanned 23 years. Picture a gaunt looking man on the threshold of middle age rescuing an FA Cup final from the dead. That was Matthews.

He remains a figure of perennial fascination and some controversy. Was he or Tom Finney the supreme winger of his age? Matthews was, undoubtedly, more of a specialist, usually conducting his sorcery down the right wing, caressing the ball with tight-fitting boots, the ball ever close to his feet, feinting, throwing defenders, passing rather than hoofing the ball into dangerous territory where predatory colleagues lurked.

Perhaps more fanatical about fitness than any of his generation, Matthews had, since boyhood, followed a rigorous daily exercise regime. He retained in his forties the capacity to sprint in short bursts and leave young defenders floundering, unable to stop him fairly or otherwise.

Youth and maturity seemed to be gelling nicely. Douglas was among the latest graduates of the U-23 side. Others filtering through were right back Don Howe and inside forward Derek Kevan, both from West Bromwich, who made their respective senior debuts in 1957 against Wales and Scotland. Meanwhile, the half back line looked solid: Wright in its midst, flanked on the left by Edwards, capable of making all things happen, and on the right by Ronnie Clayton of Blackburn Rovers, neat and reliable. Finney, when fit, still demanded selection on the wing as sorcerer and guiding hand; while Taylor had all the presence, muscle, skill, mobility and willingness desirable in a centre forward.

With no international for five months, and with good cause to be buoyant about the future, the players returned to the cut and thrust of club competition. Manchester United, ambitious Championship winners in 1956 and 1957 were also pursuing the European Cup. Their spirit of adventure was to be cruelly rewarded. For club and country, calamity awaited.

50 Greatest Players

BILLY WRIGHT Wing half/Centre half

Club: Wolverhampton Wanderers

Debut: v Northern Ireland, 28 September 1946

Appearances: 105   **Goals:** 3

(*Victory International appearances 4*)

Billy Wright falls into the category of those who achieved greatness. Certainly he was not a juvenile prodigy, far from it, and twice Wolves dispensed with his services as a teenager. But Wright, like many of his generation, had the understated determination to succeed that would not be denied.

As a youth he played centre forward until, in 1941, his manager at Wolves, Major Frank Buckley, decided to try him at wing half. There Wright found his natural home. Under the tuition of Aston Villa's ex-international winger Frank Broome, he learned how to pass and his strong positional sense.

However, there was another setback before Wright's career could gather momentum. He sustained a broken ankle in 1942, but his young bones were able to mend quickly and 17 illustrious seasons lay ahead. One of Wright's strengths was knowing his limitations. He worked at ironing out an early weakness for straying too far upfield, and confined himself to winning and distributing the ball. A solid foursquare figure, he timed tackles immaculately.

At 5 feet 8, Wright was an unlikely centre half but that was the position given to him by England during the 1954 World Cup, when Syd Owen was injured. Wright compensated for his lack of height by timing jumps carefully and consequently won many an aerial contest against bigger men.

In uncertain times, England leaned heavily on figures like Wright. His style was undemonstrative and efficient and, although he had his critics, Matthews among them, he won over most people through graciousness, generosity to other players and belief in leadership by example rather than diktat.

Chapter Five: 1958-62
Rebuilding But Still No Cups

In the wreckage of an Elizabethan airliner that crashed while attempting take-off from Munich airport on 6 February 1958, young footballers for whom wonderful futures beckoned lay dead. Manchester United were flying home in triumph from Yugoslavia, having reached the semi-final of the European Cup after a 3-3 draw with Red Star Belgrade. After the aircraft had stopped to refuel, it struggled, in icy conditions, to become airborne, overshot the runway, ploughed through a perimeter fence and split in two.

The dead included Tommy Taylor, Roger Byrne and David Pegg, who nine months earlier had made his England debut at outside right in the hard-fought World Cup qualifier against the Republic of Ireland. Duncan Edwards' injuries would prove fatal before the month was out. Also among the 23 fatalities was Frank Swift, who had been working as a journalist for the *News of the World*.

When the sense of national trauma subsided, Walter Winterbottom faced having to rebuild, in a hurry, a new team for the World Cup. It had lost, in Edwards, probably its greatest single talent; and in Taylor and Byrne young

Bobby Charlton plays football with some kids in a street in his hometown of Ashington, Northumberland, during his recovery from the Munich air crash. His international career was about to begin.

During the run up to the 1958 World Cup, Brian Clough made a strong case for his inclusion in the squad. Here he is in action against Sweden at Wembley in 1959, a match which England lost 3-2.

men who had matured rapidly to become mainstays. Yet such was the conveyor belt of talent at Old Trafford it could furnish the forward line with a replacement. When England played Scotland at Hampden on 19 April, the first international after Munich, 19-year-old Bobby Charlton, who survived the crash, was called up at inside right. In place of Byrne, Jimmy Langley of Fulham was given a first cap at left back.

It is possible to overstate England's achievement in winning 4-0 – Scotland, on the day were ponderous, unimaginative and given to lumping obtuse high balls towards shortish forwards – but Charlton's debut goal was wondrous. Finney made a shimmering run down the left and put over a delectable centre. Then, from the edge of the penalty area, Charlton seized upon Finney's fine work and whipped a thunderous volley past Tommy Younger in the Scotland goal.

The case for persevering with Charlton seemed overwhelming. As for Langley, *The Times* correspondent noted 'flaws in positional play and adventurous tackling that may yet be punished by a clever winger; but he has a splendidly combative spirit, was lightning quick in recovery and used the ball creatively.'

With little time for experimentation, the selectors picked the same 11 for the friendly against Portugal 18 days later. England won 2-1 and Bobby Charlton, scorer of both goals, suggested the power of his shooting might be a potent, perhaps indispensable, weapon. Less comforting for Winterbottom was the profligacy of Derek Kevan in front of goal and Jimmy Langley's missed penalty. However, with the World Cup finals so close there was a clear need for continuity and England fielded an unchanged team in a post-season match against Yugoslavia.

Whether caused through tiredness or oppressive heat, England's 5-0 defeat by the Yugoslavs in Belgrade was drastically comprehensive. In the view of Maurice Norman, the Tottenham centre half who was Billy Wright's understudy, lack of fitness was part of the problem. 'We weren't really in good shape,' he said. 'In those days, our training was done at the Bank of

England ground in Roehampton. We went through gruelling exercises trying to be fit enough, but after training some players were physically sick. You might expect it pre-season but it was unusual at this time of the season.'

The timing of this heavy defeat was awful and the temptation was to tinker with the side; but in a curious way, England's honourable 1-1 draw with Russia seven days later merely confused matters. Finney and Kevan rediscovered some of their best form, while right half Eddie Clamp of Wolves, one of three new caps, was among the best players on the pitch. The other debutants were Burnley goalkeeper Colin McDonald and Bolton's left back Tommy Banks.

Amid the babble emanating from armchair experts, the selectors had several dilemmas. Did Charlton, for all his gifts, merit automatic selection? After all, his positional sense was sometimes faulty and he tended to leave team-mates bemused with inconsequential crossfield dribbles. Could Brian Clough be ignored as a possible centre forward after scoring 44 goals, albeit in the Second Division, for Middlesbrough? Walter Winterbottom had watched all the potential candidates as carefully as possible, yet even when he had made his mind up, still encountered a peculiarly English complication – Bill Slater, Wolves' powerful left half, was also a PE lecturer at Birmingham University, and it took protracted negotiations to secure his release for the summer.

Before the game against Russia, Winterbottom took soundings from his two senior players, captain Billy Wright and Tom Finney. Kevan, whose bustling rumbustious style divided critics, had played his way into the World Cup squad with a sterling performance on a big stage. Clough, who had played only in practice games on the two-match tour, was frozen out of the 20-man pool. Bobby Smith, whose rugged style was more akin to that of Kevan, was chosen instead as centre forward cover.

Off to Sweden

The squad spent a few days together at Roehampton before departing to Gothenburg and their base for the tournament, the luxurious Park Avenue Hotel. The choice of billet brought scorn raining down on the England party. Rivals such as Brazil, Russia, and others had closeted themselves away in special training camps on the edge of the city. George Raynor, the Swedish coach, was especially scathing and claimed advice he gave to Winterbottom about training quarters long before the World Cup started had been ignored. 'England arrived after everyone else... just 48 hours before their important match with Russia,' he said. 'It was such an amazing choice [of hotel] that England raised sniggers from every training camp in Sweden, and the team was dubbed "The Park Avenue Boys".'

Bill Slater in action in England's opening match of the 1958 World Cup against Russia. Tom Finney scored a penalty five minutes from time to secure England a 2-2 draw.

Billy Wright, palpably a member of the football establishment, rounded on the critics. In his autobiography *One Hundred Caps And All That* he accused them of talking nonsense. 'English footballers come, almost to a man, from places of concentrated population,' he said. 'They are not accustomed to training camps... they are apt to become bored; preoccupied with their own problems.' Nor, he insisted, was the Park Avenue a hedonistic paradise: 'Gothenburg had no more to offer in the way of temptation than many a pleasant but ordinary English town.' Moreover, the training facilities 'were easily accessible'.

For the first game against Russia – opponents fresh in the minds of England camp – there was a logic in sticking with the 11 who acquitted themselves well in Moscow. But this was another day, one on which England, pitifully slow out of the traps, found themselves two goals down at half-time, having hardly ruffled the Russian defence. Russian defenders, meanwhile, busied themselves clattering Douglas and Finney with late tackles and body checks.

Then seemingly from nowhere, and with the match three quarters gone, England snapped into life. A long free kick from Wright was flicked on by Douglas and headed in by Kevan. Finney, despite the savage attention he had received, was suddenly his old self, inducing openings and defensive panic with weaving runs. From one of his centres, Bobby Robson lashed home what all England thought was an equaliser, only for the goal to be disallowed for an alleged foul by Kevan on goalkeeper Lev Yashin. But England pressed on, the Russians buckled and, with five minutes remaining, Haynes latched on to Finney's long through pass and tumbled on the edge of the penalty area. Amid excruciating tension and outbursts of Soviet dissent, Finney's last meaningful act for England in the 1958 World Cup tournament was to plant the spot kick past Yashin and retrieve a draw for his country.

England Line up Against Brazil

Three days later – as Billy Wright's hitherto secret romance with the singer Joy Beverley erupted across the newspapers – England faced Brazil. It was not an inviting prospect: the Brazilians had just beaten Austria 3-0. England, however, the coaching staff buttressed by Tottenham manager Bill Nicholson, did their homework more assiduously than for any previous international. A tactical switch to buttress central defence that entailed Don Howe and Tommy Banks covering Wright, and aimed at repelling the anticipated thrusts of inside left Didi and centre forward Mazzola, worked to perfection. The match ended 0-0; the Brazilians thwarted and outwitted.

These two draws against stiff opposition left England needing a win against Austria to reach the knockout stages. The party took itself away to Boras, a small town 40 miles outside Gothenburg, to take stock, examine injuries and play a full-scale practice match in the small local stadium that would host the game against Austria. Finney was out; Wright had sustained a severely bruised knee against Brazil; but Winterbottom decided to stick with those who had quelled the Brazilians. There was still no place for Bobby Charlton or Ron Clayton, while Bryan Douglas, in indifferent form, was retained.

England's tendency to make life hard by losing early goals was again in evidence. One down after 15 minutes to a thunderous shot by Karl Koller from outside the penalty area, they were forced to chase the game, although they did so energetically, creating a hatful of chances and equalising early in the second half. Alan A'Court of Liverpool, who had been Finney's replacement on the left wing against Brazil, shot fiercely on goal and, as his effort was palmed down by the Austrian goalkeeper Szanwald, Johnny Haynes tapped it into the net.

At this point England looked favourites, but fell victim to a low, long-range, speculative shot from inside left Korner that seemed to leave Colin McDonald in the England goal unsighted. They bounced back within two minutes, though, when Kevan seized upon Haynes' clever reverse pass from the right and thumped the ball past Swanzald. And it was in accord with England's luck generally that the possible winner, a close range shot from Bobby Robson, was disallowed for handball. Robson claimed the ball had hit his stomach.

Three matches and three draws – qualification for the quarter finals hung on a play-off with the Russians two days later. For this, there were three changes in the England side: a recall for Clayton in place of Clamp; and first caps for Peter Broadbent of Wolves at inside right and Peter Brabrook of Chelsea at right wing. If nothing else, the unfamiliar pairing of Broadbent and Brabrook would give Russia something new to deal with. Suspense in the England camp centred around the state of Tom Finney's knee. How badly the team could have done with him to resume his torment of the Soviet defence, but the cloggers had done their work just well enough. Despite a rapid improvement, Finney was not fit enough to be risked. Haynes, whose feet were badly blistered after the match against Austria, had been doubtful but played.

For most of the first half, two tired teams put on a desultory display. Then England sprang to life. Yashin made a smart save from Broadbent; then Brabrook missed a chance at the far post created by Broadbent's fine pass. After half-time, England continued in similar vein, working openings down the flanks, their pressure growing relentless. Twice Brabrook hit the post. Yashin, it seemed, was all that stood between England and an avalanche.

But all the good work was to count for nothing. Russia, overrun and outplayed, delivered a sucker punch 20 minutes from time. A misdirected goal kick from McDonald allowed them a scent of blood and the England defence suddenly found itself by-passed and Illyin, unmarked on the edge of the penalty area, rolled a shot past McDonald, against the post and into the net. It seemed a grotesque contrast of fortune. England rallied furiously and Yashin fended off what would have been an almost instant riposte, a fierce rising shot from Kevan, but this was a match they were destined to lose. England were, without any cause for embarrassment, out of the World Cup.

Questions Are Asked

Another failure, another inquest, and all the more pointed as Northern Ireland and Wales had reached the quarter finals. Heated debates centred on the constant omission of Bobby Charlton and the selections of Clayton and Douglas, both drained by a season in which Blackburn Rovers had contested a long league season and an FA Cup run that went all the way to Wembley. It was easy to overlook the intelligence with which England had stifled Brazil and their wretched luck, but George Raynor, whose condemnation of England's preparations had been so fierce, might well have considered himself vindicated. Sweden, with their training camp culture, plotted a passage to the final, although ultimately they succumbed to the Brazilians, who, 5-2 winners, were on a level of their own as surely as had been the Hungarians of 1953.

It was almost the end for Tom Finney. If he had been fit throughout the World Cup, he might have tipped the delicate balance in England's favour. His final game would be a friendly against the Russians at Wembley four months later, which England won 5-0; a modicum of revenge for the failure in Sweden when the stakes had been high. At 35, Finney, perhaps mindful of Matthews' longevity, still had the appetite to go on, but he was a realist. 'It was disappointing not to be picked again but there were young players coming into the game. I had had quite a few injuries,' he said.

Until Munich, there had, said Finney, been a buoyant spirit within the England setup. 'After Hungary things had changed completely. I think lessons were learned. We had been set in our ways but by 1958, levels of technique and fitness were higher; we had started taking note of dieticians. We were all looking forward to the tournament but then came the Manchester crash. Four or five of those players could have been in the side.'

With the protection of vigilant referees, Finney, who tolerated foul play with astonishing equanimity, might himself have remained in the team. 'You used to get angry at times but not lose your temper,' he said. 'We were always taught at Preston that if you were brought down heavily or felt someone tried to injure you, that you accepted the referee's decision and two wrongs don't make a right. That always stuck with me.'

England's first game after the World Cup was a 3-3 draw with Northern Ireland in Belfast, who, on current form and achievement, could scarcely be regarded as underdogs. Two prodigious goals scored from long range by Charlton revived questions about the wisdom of his exclusion in Sweden. A month after Finney's swansong against Russia, came Nat Lofthouse's, in a 2-2 draw with Wales at Villa Park. In the final match of the 1958-59 home international championship, Billy Wright was awarded his 100th cap and took England to a 1-0 win against Scotland. The end of his career beckoned also. Wright bowed out six weeks and five matches later as England concluded their summer tour of America with an 8-1 victory over the USA in Los Angeles.

Wright's was a career of undemonstrative capability, but he had his critics even among those well disposed to him. Maurice Norman, another graduate of the

England U-23 setup, was one who thought Wright had hung around a little too long. Stanley Matthews, the great individualist, was lukewarm about Wright's captaincy. 'He never inspired me when I played with him in international matches,' he said. Wright on Matthews was far more generous: 'The easiest man in the world to play with… probably the greatest footballer of all time.'

As the decade ended, new faces appeared; some soon discarded; others destined to be vital components of the England team for five years or more. Winterbottom recognised that England's future lay in developing its best young players, but he still had to battle the selectors. The team picked to play Wales at Cardiff in October 1959 brimmed with new faces: Tony Allen of Stoke City at left back; Trevor Smith of Birmingham at centre half; John Connelly of Burnley at outside right; Brian Clough, finally given a chance at centre forward; Clough's Middlesbrough team mate Eric Holliday at outside right. Also in was Jimmy Greaves of Chelsea, who appeared to have cemented his position at inside right on England's dispiriting summer tour of South America, in which they lost to Brazil, Peru and Mexico.

Any policy of continuity seemed to have been jettisoned. A month later, out stepped four more debutants against Northern Ireland at Wembley: goalkeeper Ron Springett of Sheffield Wednesday; centre half Ken Brown of West Ham; centre forward Joe Baker of Hibernian; and inside left Ray Parry of Bolton Wanderers. Nine new faces in two matches, of whom Brown would be capped just once; Clough, Parry and Smith twice; Holliday and Allen three times. Even though England had its U-23 nursery, there was a sense, in the wake of bad results, of selectors thrashing around, latching on to whomever might be doing well for his club; of being seduced by form rather than class. Yet it was on Winterbottom that the pressures of under-achievement fell. In October 1959, the FA felt compelled to assemble an England team and issue an official denial to rumours that the England coach was going to be sacked.

The South American tour showed that England's forward planning was still ramshackle. Jimmy Greaves complained of appalling organisation; having to train in the midday sun for a match kicking off four hours later; of an insalubrious hotel in Mexico where players were crammed three or four to a bedroom; of players being badly burned while relaxing out doors, ignorant of the dangers of strong sun in a rarified atmosphere; of being given insufficient time to acclimatise. Conversely, Greaves found Winterbottom himself had an academic's attention to detail in matters of coaching, something that the young striker, whose game was based on intuition and instinct, found bemusing and comical.

World Cup defeat had knocked the stuffing out of England. In the two years that followed elimination by Russia, the chopped-and-changed team won only four out of 16 matches. Yet Winterbottom understood the need for continuity, even if his masters did not. The team he selected for the 1-1 with Scotland at Hampden in April 1960 was the one he intended to play against Yugoslavia at Wembley in May, and then on the summer tour of Spain and Hungary. The selectors had other ideas. They met for three hours, chewing over various possibilities, only to announce that no touring party would be named until after Easter. Winterbottom, naturally, was the fall guy chosen to publicise their procrastination. With customary self-restraint he told the press: 'I can't now give you a single name for the tour – it is the committee's decision and I have nothing more to say.' It was not hard to imagine his frustration.

Jimmy Armfield, right back at Blackpool, broke into the England side in 1959 and linked up well with Huddersfield's Ray Wilson.

In the event, England lost 3-0 to Spain in Madrid and 2-0 to Hungary in Budapest. Perhaps of greatest significance was the choice, for the first time, of Johnny Haynes as captain. Then, as 1960 drew to a close, Winterbottom's men enjoyed an unexpected purple patch, one in which the opposition, albeit often mediocre, was not merely beaten but annihilated. It began with a 5-2 win over Northern Ireland in Belfast in October 1960 – a score that disguised England's plentiful luck – and lasted into the spring of 1961, during which time they beat Luxembourg 9-0 in a World Cup qualifier, Spain 4-2, Wales 5-1, Scotland 9-3 and Mexico 8-0.

This was more than a tale of Greaves, Charlton, Haynes et al suddenly getting their eye in. England were starting to look more solid at the back. Eddie Hopkinson, whose hapless display in goal during the 3-2 defeat by Sweden in October 1959 was his last for England, had made way for Ron Springett. Right back Jimmy Armfield, from Blackpool, who broke into the team during the torrid tour of South America, seemed assured and composed at the top level, with the intelligence to link well; Ray Wilson, a young left back from Huddersfield Town appeared sturdy and vital; Ron Flowers of Wolves at left half combined elegance with industry, energy and stamina; and Peter Swan of Sheffield Wednesday replenished the centre half position with some welcome authority. The appointment as trainer of Harold Shepherdson, a friendly popular figure and something of a counterpoint to Winterbottom, did much to forge team spirit.

The romp against Luxembourg, while yielding precious World Cup points, hat-tricks for Greaves and Charlton and a fine opportunity for target practice, did not in itself constitute a revival. But success did fortify

50 Greatest Players

JOHNNY HAYNES Inside left

Club: Fulham
Debut: v Northern Ireland, 2 October 1954
Appearances: 56   **Goals:** 18

Johnny Haynes was a diminutive 15-year-old who joined Fulham as an office boy and became Britain's first £100 a week player. Within four years of arriving at Craven Cottage, he made his debut for England. In an era when players fell in and out of favour with bewildering speed, even the most whimsical selectors could see Haynes had gifts that were indispensable to the national team.

Haynes was one of those rare footballers who could control events. Only the most gifted can take possession, appraise the state of play, then unleash the ball calculated to inflict maximum defensive damage, all within a few seconds. He belonged to a small elite of play-makers able to constantly bisect defences with long passes hit from the deep. But he was also a predator, a master of seizing on loose balls in the penalty area, often simply passing them into the net.

He became the motor, then captain of the England team, yet captaincy was perhaps one pressure too many for Haynes, and in the ill-fated World Cup campaign of 1962, amid the vagaries of officialdom and unwelcome surprises thrown up by life touring Chile, neither he nor his team did themselves justice. His misery that year was complete when he was injured in a car crash in Blackpool, after which, and following a change of England team manger, he was never picked again.

Winterbottom's campaign for the side not to be meddled with. The team responsible for so bountiful a run of results was much more settled and talent could express itself. The Spaniards were still a force in the world game yet swept aside by a vibrant self-confidence, one long absent in England's make-up. The nature and scale of victory against the Scots, the fruit of switching to a more attacking 4-2-4 system, moved some journalists to euphoria. 'There was no suspicion of a weak link anywhere in England's ranks,' wrote Ian Wooldridge in the *Sunday Dispatch*. 'Johnny Haynes was a magnificent general probing every weakness in Scotland's defence before deluging it with a stream of passes; Jimmy Greaves, a spritely genius who gave a Stefano-class performance of ball control which made 100,000 fans gasp in disbelief.'

From being briefly in with a chance at 3-2 in the second half, Scotland were flattened by five goals in 11 minutes. They succumbed to some of the most ruthless finishing ever produced by an England team: another hat-trick for Greaves; two each for Bobby Smith and Haynes: voracious form sustained for the encounter with Mexico at Wembley four weeks later. Greaves, Haynes, Charlton, Kevan and Armfield were survivors of the team that toiled to a miserable defeat in Mexico City two years earlier. It was a faded, if unpalatable memory: the here and now was England's momentum, one that brought a swaggering 8-0 victory, conspicuous for fluid team work and dynamic individual displays from the likes of Haynes and Charlton, who scored a hat-trick. The power of Charlton's shooting – and his appetite for doing so – had given England a cutting edge.

The games that mattered, perhaps inevitably, brought with them inhibiting tensions. England could rely on beating Luxembourg in World Cup qualifiers but Portugal were a different matter. Eleven days after the Mexican feast, Winterbottom's team men found themselves in Lisbon, embroiled in a battle that ended the run of turkey shoots. The 1-1 draw could be regarded as a point won, for England had equalised with just eight minutes remaining, Flowers crashing home a shot from a short free kick rolled to him by Johnny Haynes. It was a display redolent of the 1958 World Cup campaign and a match retrieved.

A 3-2 victory over Italy in the Olympic stadium three days later showed England were in good heart; while fatigue and ill fortune did much to explain an end of tour defeat, 3-1, by Austria. There were first – and last – caps for the Burnley duo, John Angus at right back and Brian Miller at right half. By late October England had qualified for the World Cup through a laborious 4-1 victory over Luxembourg at Wembley, captained for the first time by Jimmy Armfield in the absence of the injured Haynes; and a 2-0 home win over

Portugal, a match robbed of its edge after Ray Pointer, playing his third international, and John Connelly put England 2-0 up in the first ten minutes.

A Trip to Chile

The choice of Chile for the 1962 World Cup finals, a rough and ready country recovering from an earthquake, said more for geopolitical even-handedness than for logic. If England were to thrive they needed better-laid plans than in previous campaigns. The England squad had talent and experience: Johnny Haynes, Bryan Douglas, Jimmy Greaves, Bobby Charlton, Jimmy Armfield, Ray Wilson, Ron Flowers and Ron Springett were all bedded into the side. Selectors still liked to fiddle, to indulge their weakness for picking a goodish man playing above his station, but graduates from the U-23 side, their football education enhanced by competing against fine young teams around Europe, were imposing themselves.

One such was Bobby Moore, a 21-year-old right half from West Ham, drafted into the squad for Chile having achieved a record number of youth caps. When Bobby Robson cracked his ankle in a training match, Moore seized his chance and never looked back. Another was Tottenham centre half Maurice Norman who, at 28, had always been the perennial understudy.

There would be no luxury hotel for England on this expedition. After warming up with a 4-0 win over Peru in which Moore and Norman made their debuts, the England party retreated to a remote village in the mountains around 8,000 feet above sea level, where the sense of isolation exerted a strong grip. 'Everywhere was dusty,' said Maurice Norman. 'There was just one train in and one train out every day. We were stuck up the mountain with just one little pitch. For relaxation we just had a bowling alley and a picture palace. It wasn't good preparation for a World Cup game.'

Coya also left an indelible impression on Jimmy Greaves: 'To have our meals we had to walk from barrack-style quarters across a rickety wooden bridge with a 500 foot drop on either side. It was great for building up an appetite.' Officials had, at least, taken the precaution of hiring a specialist British cook and on the food front itself, it was safety first. Yet Peter Swan, in Viña del Mar, was to pick up a stomach bug, be given the wrong treatment and fall violently ill. 'Can you imagine a World Cup like that today?' Ray Wilson wondered rhetorically some years later.

England's first match was against Hungary in Rancagua, a provincial town whose humble stadium reinforced a sense of being in the outback. Fewer than 8,000 turned up to witness Hungary outwitting Winterbottom's men by the simple ploy of man-marking Haynes, through whom so much – too much –

was expected to flow. Despite the continuous presence of Charlton and Greaves, the England attack lacked its ruthless incisiveness of the previous year, while Hungary had the cutting edge that mattered. Springett had been caught cold by Tichy's shot from outside the penalty area, giving the Hungarians a 1-0 half-time lead. England had to haul themselves back – the familiar story – which they did when Flowers scored a penalty given against Sarosi for handball. But when Flowers let in Albert, allowing him to bear down on goal, round Springett and score from a tight angle, the contest was over.

England faced an uphill journey in every sense. Argentina were their next opponents: powerful, talented, invariably physical and prone to malevolence. 'The whole team seemed big, hungry and determined to win,' said Norman. Such was the rudimentary state of the Chilean railways that England turned up at Rancagua with just 40 minutes to spare, having been marooned on the line behind a stationary goods train. Yet whenever an obstacle was thrown in their path, the players came out fighting, and their show against Argentina was one of the best they had given in any World Cup.

On the theory that Argentina could be roughed up by aerial power, Alan Peacock of Middlesbrough was drafted in at centre forward in place of Gerry Hitchens, formerly of Aston Villa but who, unlike Jimmy Greaves, had made a contented transfer to Italy, playing for Inter-Milan. Hitchens had made his debut in England's gluttonous victory against Mexico in 1961 and won five caps since, but events vindicated the wisdom of choosing Peacock. In his 17th minute of international football, he rose to a cross from Charlton, only for his goal-bound header to be handled by centre half Navarro. Flowers despatched the penalty and England grabbed the initiative, doubling their lead before half-time with a crisp shot from Charlton from 20 yards. Greaves stole a third midway through the second half and Argentina's only riposte, aside from manhandling their opponents, was a goal four minutes from time.

Collectively, England had been livelier, sharper and far more robust with performances gratifyingly typical of players at their best: Moore, Flowers and Norman covering and tackling superbly; Armfield, too, contributing with dynamic forward runs in support of the attack. There then followed an insufferably tedious 0-0 draw with Bulgaria that left England, as group runners-up to Hungary, facing Brazil, the World Champions, in the quarter-finals.

England had subjugated the Brazilians before, though it was not an exercise they would have chosen to repeat. One thing, however, seemed to favour them: Brazil had lost the talismanic Pele, victim of a torn thigh muscle, in the group qualifier against Czechoslovakia. But yet another tormentor lay in the wings and this time it was to be Garrincha, 'the little bird', although others,

Ray Wilson (right) tries to get to grips with Brazil's Garrincha in the 1962 World Cup quarter-final. But England had no answer to the 'little bird's' free kicks and lost 3-1.

Didi and Vava had moments when they were uncontainable.

Warily, though by no means devoid of confidence, England squared up to Brazil in the coastal town of Vina del Mar. Brazil scored first on the half hour – for England, going behind had become a ritual – when Garrincha, five feet seven, out-jumped Norman, six inches taller, to head a corner firmly beyond Springett. Eight minutes later, England were level, with Greaves heading Haynes' free kick against the crossbar and Hitchens gobbling up the rebound.

At half-time, England went in level. Fifteen minutes later, they were out of the World Cup, felled by Garrincha. On 53 minutes his wicked long-range free kick bounced off Springett's chest and Vava pounced to accept the gift. Six minutes later, Garrincha struck unaided, with a shot from 25 yards of fiendish power and swerve that left Springett stranded. The contest was over. England had been beaten by a weapon against which they had no protection. Maurice Norman, like his team-mates, had been a bemused spectator of Garrincha's free kicks. 'We'd never seen anything like it. Springett didn't move: you could not believe anyone could bend a ball so far,' he said.

In three successive World Cups the pattern had emerged of England having much – but not quite enough – to offer. Too often they had fought to extricate themselves, not always successfully, from difficult positions. Only rarely had they been commanding as they were against Argentina. Greaves felt that the side had peaked in 1961 and was in slow decline when it mattered most. The loss through injury of Bobby Robson, who worked so well in tandem with Haynes, had weakened England, notwithstanding the composure and assurance shown by Moore, Robson's replacement.

Greaves, inadvertently, had been part of the problem. His ill-fated departure to AC Milan, along with that of Gerry Hitchens to Inter, disrupted the forward line and World Cup team building because both Italian clubs had been reluctant to release them. Inter, eventually, relented before the World Cup finals, and Greaves had been rescued from his Italian misadventure by Tottenham Hotspur, but the uncertainty had taken its toll and Greaves was far from the flashing blade he had been in 1961.

This World Cup seemed to matter to the English press much more than others. The nation, fattened up by earlier achievements, expected and deserved better, or so said many an unforgiving sports editor. Scapegoats in chief were the figureheads: Johnny Haynes, who for some time had had a spiky relationship with journalists; but above all Walter Winterbottom, about whom the press had long hedged its bets. 'Walter is a nice man but too donnish to get the best out of the team. His head is in a cloud of football theory,' declared the *Daily Mail* in May 1959. 'Walter Winterbottom – this is our man of football miracles,' wrote the *Daily Herald*, gushingly, 18 months later.

Winterbottom Pays Price of Failure

Failure in Chile ended his reign as England manager. Shortly after the team returned home, Winterbottom stepped down after 16 years in the job. Few were surprised. He had given everything to his dual role as England team manager and FA director of coaching, but he was at the mercy of the capricious selectors, frequently had to battle the vested interests of League club chairmen, and it was a role that probably asked too much of any individual.

Despite the constraints, Winterbottom had made efforts to move with the times. He had preached tactics and created a national network of coaches. He had seen the need to develop young players and he strove for continuity. His personal manner was exemplary and he afforded irresponsible critics far more courtesy than they deserved. Winterbottom seemed ideal for the job as Secretary of the Football Association, vacant following Stanley Rous's appointment as president of FIFA, but the FA turned its back on all he might have brought to the job. Instead it favoured Denis Follows, whose knowledge of football, whatever his administrative gifts, bore no comparison.

Opinions about Winterbottom were divided. Stanley Matthews was never reconciled to Winterbottom's efforts to assimilate lessons from abroad: 'The England manager has brought some radical changes... and I by no means agree with many of them. Play a natural game, in your native natural style, that is what I believe.' The star witness for Winterbottom's defence was Billy Wright: 'Walter is a visionary; a man of action yet an idealist; a teacher yet a student. His motives and ability are unquestioned.' If Wright had any criticism it was that, 'He could have been more emphatic with erring players... if he had been blunter he would have lent far greater weight to his points.'

Under the circumstances the lack of a scramble to fill Winterbottom's shoes was hardly surprising. The England job was not given added lustre by money as Winterbottom had been paid around £2,000 a year, a modest professional rate at the time. Jimmy Adamson of Burnley, Winterbottom's assistant in Chile, was first choice but still playing and Burnley were reluctant to let him go, so the FA turned to Alf Ramsey, who had served England with distinction at full back, winning 32 caps between 1948 and 1953, and who had worked a minor miracle by managing Ipswich Town to the First Division championship in 1962. Shocks lay in store for the FA grandees when the extent of Ramsey's single-mindedness and lack of deference became apparent. Meanwhile, he insisted on honouring his contract at Portman Road, so Winterbottom, with the good grace that was his hallmark, held the fort.

It was a curious interregnum. Winterbottom remained in charge, yet not in charge, for three more matches, including England's debut in the European Nations Cup, a forlorn, disjointed 1-1 draw with France played at Hillsborough in October 1962. It was an experimental occasion that brought to light almost an entirely new forward line; new caps for outside right Mike Hellawell of Birmingham, the Wolves inside right Chris Crowe, Blackpool centre forward Ray Charnley and Wolves' outside left Alan Hinton. Only Jimmy Greaves survived the cull. For the Home International against Northern Ireland, out of the tombola came three more new caps: centre half Brian Labone of Everton, inside right Fred Hill of Bolton and, on the left wing, Mike O'Grady of Huddersfield Town. Two matches, seven new faces, but only Brian Labone would forge an international career of any substance.

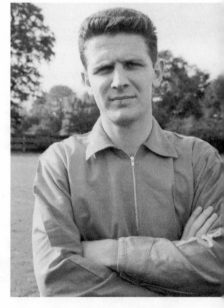

The swansong for Winterbottom and the selectors was another tepid occasion: just 27,500 turned out at Wembley to watch England's 4-0 win over Wales. To Bobby Tambling, Chelsea's outside right, went the curious distinction of being the last England player to be capped by committee. Late on that cold November night, as the floodlights were extinguished, the Winterbottom era flickered to a muted end.

Brian Labone of Everton made his England debut against Northern Ireland at Windsor Park, Belfast in October 1962. England won the match 3-1.

Chapter Six: 1963-66
Triumphant at Last

Alf Ramsey was not the first new manager to preside over a disastrous opening night. But although Ramsey had stipulated, on accepting the job, that sole responsibility for picking players should lie with him, he was still embroiled in the day to day running of Ipswich Town and knew too little about potential internationals to make an informed choice. The England side that ventured to Paris on 27 February 1963 for a European Nations Cup qualifier with France resembled a collection of individuals who were hardly acquainted, even though the only new cap was Ron Henry of Tottenham at left back. England lost 5-2 and so wretched was Ron Springett's performance that it cost him pole position as England's first choice goalkeeper.

Ramsey was a practical, methodical man who liked to build on firm foundations. He had been an excellent full back, his game based on intelligence, anticipation and constructive use of the ball rather than pace and brute force. Small wonder that Bobby Moore caught his eye. Ramsey was not, though, one of soccer's romantics: people grew to admire his teams rather than to love them, in the same way that they came to respect his achievements rather than warm to his chilly, dismissive persona. At Ipswich he had moulded a squad of moderate players into a tight efficient 4-3-3 unit, where everyone knew his role, and in six seasons achieved the improbable feat of leading the Suffolk team from the Third Division South to the First Division championship.

Ramsey's next match, in April, was the annual bout of civil war against Scotland.

Alf Ramsey replaced goalkeeper Ron Springett with Leicester City's Gordon Banks who immediately impressed people with his confidence and agility.

In goal it was time to look beyond Ron Springett, who had often served England well but had too many susceptibilities, especially to shots from long distance. In for his first international came Leicester City goalkeeper Gordon Banks, a change of profound importance.

Out stepped Ramsey and his men – and it was his team this time – but they were soon to find themselves on the wrong end of newspaper headlines once again. Scotland, for most of the game reduced to 10 men after left back Eric Caldow broke his leg in a crunching tackle with Bobby Smith, won 2-1. Any world class players on show that day looked to be Scottish – Denis Law and the swaggering Jim Baxter.

Apart from Bryan Douglas's purposeful display on the right wing, Ramsey would have noticed, as England's most conspicuous redeeming feature, the confidence of Gordon Banks. He was blameless for the two goals and nor had he hesitated in castigating his captain Jimmy Armfield for passing across the penalty area and presenting Baxter with Scotland's first goal. 'There was no way I was going to allow myself to be overawed by the star names around me,' Banks said.

Ramsey took pains to boost the goalkeeper's confidence before England's next international against Brazil. Banks arrived at Wembley in low spirits after Leicester's 3-1 defeat by Manchester United in the FA Cup final. Ramsey made a point of telling him how well he had played, though by half-time he was heaping blame on Banks for his failure to save Pepe's viciously swerving free kick. Brazil were lacking some magical talents, Pele and Garrincha among them, but nonetheless were manifestly superior. England though, through perseverance, saved the day with an equaliser from Douglas five minutes from time. It was a turning point. A 4-2 victory over Czechoslovakia, the first match of their summer tour, was England's most ebullient display abroad for some time. This success, England's first under new management, resulted, says Banks, 'in laying foundations for the club-style spirit that prevailed throughout Alf Ramsey's reign'.

Rest of the World Conquered

England's match against the Rest of the World at Wembley in October 1963, held to mark the FA's centenary, followed a brief purple patch that recalled the intoxicating days of 1961: an 8-1 win in Switzerland; a 4-0 victory over Wales. In the interim, and out of keeping with his avoidance of public proclamations, Ramsey declared at a press conference: 'England will win the World Cup in 1966. We have the ability, strength, character... and players with the right temperament.' In a luxury item of a match resplendent with exhibition football, England beat the Rest 2-1, with Jimmy Greaves no less a star than exalted figures such as Di Stefano, Eusebio, Gento and Denis Law. The more easily swayed in Fleet Street began to talk of England as world beaters.

But the big question – how Ramsey's team would fare in matches with most at stake – remained unanswerable until the next World Cup. Meanwhile, he continued with pragmatic experiments aimed at making England more solid, but he also made some imaginative moves, for instance, promoting Bobby Moore captain in Czechoslovakia in Jimmy Armfield's absence. The match was one of conspicuous achievement for Moore individually and the team as a whole.

While England had beaten the Rest of the World and subjected Northern Ireland to an 8-3 mauling, Scotland brought them down to earth, winning 1-0 at Hampden and, for the first time in 80 years, completing a hat-trick of victories against their old enemy. An intense, rather than an exuberant match, played in rain and swirling wind, had as its keynotes the creative superiority of Baxter and Law, and Moore's sturdy, intelligent defending in the role of sweeper.

An incident before the close season friendly against Portugal in May 1964 reinforced Ramsey's unyielding attitude to discipline. Seven of England's freer spirits had succumbed to the delights of a late night bar in the West End, and on returning to their hotel in Lancaster Gate, each found his passport waiting for him on the bed. Ramsey let the culprits stew until the end of the final training session in Lisbon, and then uncorked his acidulous displeasure. 'If I had enough players here with me, none of you would be playing in this match,' he said. 'Just learn that I will not tolerate the sort of thing that happened in London before we left.' Banks, one of the guilty party, received a further lesson that with Ramsey nothing should be taken for granted. In his own mind, he had performed well in England's 4-3 victory over the Portuguese. Ramsey begged to differ, blamed Banks for two of the goals and dropped him for England's next match against the Republic of Ireland.

Strict Regime

But not everyone was cowed by Ramsey's reaction to late night drinking. Less than three weeks later, as England set off to tour the United States and Brazil, Moore and others broke bounds in New York. When confronted by his manager, Moore stood his ground and made it clear that some of the squad disliked army-style discipline. Relations between the two remained strained for some time.

England enjoyed some target practice at the USA's expense, winning 10-0, before they left for Brazil to take part in a gruelling four-team tournament to mark the 50th anniversary of the Brazilian FA. The expedition led them into scrapes with wildly partisan fans and exposed them to the sorcery of Pele, but the education it offered mattered more than results. Brazil beat England 5-1, having been at 1-1 with half an hour remaining; and it became the turn of Blackpool's Tony Waiters, replacing Gordon Banks, to incur Ramsey's displeasure for allowing free kicks to hurtle by him.

England then drew a fiery game with Portugal 1-1 on a wretched pitch in São Paulo; and lost 1-0 to Argentina, often outclassed and looking leg weary. Even when relaxing on Rio's Copacabana beach before this finale, Ramsey's men had no escape from the inexhaustible reservoir of Brazilian talent. 'A group of scruffy little beach urchins challenged us to a game of football,' Banks recalled. 'They produced the sort of ball tricks that few of our most talented players could match. We really struggled to beat them.'

One English talent with ball tricks had shone on the tour: Peter Thompson, the versatile Liverpool winger, although was fated to have his gifts discarded as Ramsey's preparations for the World Cup advanced and specialist wingers became redundant. Injury to Jimmy Armfield meant the right back spot need re-thinking and of the contenders, Fulham's George Cohen, a debutant when England beat Uruguay 2-1 at Wembley before travelling to America, would monopolise the position for almost four years. Cohen was a confident personality and a disciplined, speedy defender who liked joining the attack. He was of great value to Ramsey because of his willingness to conform to a team plan.

Liverpool's Roger Hunt was less gifted than Jimmy Greaves, but he had explosive pace and was also a regular goalscorer.

Thompson's Liverpool team-mate Roger Hunt at inside forward was also coming to the fore. At international level, Hunt was a slow burning fuse, appearing fitfully after scoring in his debut against Austria in April 1962. In the next two years he was called up only twice. Less gifted than Jimmy Greaves, he was also less of a maverick and had a conspicuous work ethic of which Ramsey approved. He was also a formidable scorer who, within sight of goal, could burn off most defenders with his strength and menacing bursts of pace.

Ramsey would probably have plugged away with his full back pairing of Cohen and Ray

Wilson but for a groin injury that forced the ebullient left back to miss most of the 1964-65 season. It was Wilson's misfortune to return for England's 2-2 draw with Scotland at Wembley in April 1965, only to strain muscles in his side, but this injury proved surmountable. He was back – for good – when England played Hungary the following month. The more significant casualty was West Ham inside left Johnny (Budgie) Byrne who, like Hunt, had flitted in and out since 1962, winning 11 caps. Byrne, invariably garrulous, often brilliant, occasionally undisciplined, hobbled away from Wembley with damaged ligaments never to play for England again.

Confident Build-up

The Scotland match became a landmark in shaping the England team. One lesson learned from the likes of Argentina was that matches were always winnable if the opposition could be shut out. One man to whom a 'they shall not pass' culture was familiar was Leeds United centre half Jack Charlton, linchpin of the least compromising defence in the First Division. And if creative players were to flourish, an aggressor was needed to win the ball on their behalf. The reputation of Manchester United was that of flamboyant entertainers, but at their core was the fearsome hustling presence of Nobby Stiles. Ramsey had taken note of both players. If, with modifications, they could transplant their style from club to country, he saw them fitting into a master plan: Charlton as secure cover if Bobby Moore ventured upfield; Stiles replicating his invasive attacking runs and role as supplier to Bobby Charlton.

Jack Charlton was well versed in the 'they shall not pass' school of football at Leeds United.

Maurice Norman had been a regular first choice centre half for two years but had, by his own admission, lost form towards the end of 1964, but Jack Charlton was an unlikely choice as replacement. Gangling, awkward and headstrong, four years earlier Charlton had been muddling along with Leeds in the lower reaches of the Second Division, sometimes more hindrance than help in their battle for survival. He might have gone nowhere had not his manager, Don Revie, taken him in hand. The ageing dog learned new tricks. A month before his 30th birthday, Jack,

Fulham's George Cohen was a pacy full back who liked to join the attack whenever he could.

against all odds, took his place alongside brother Bobby in the England team.

Both Stiles and Jack Charlton, choices derided by some of the press, impacted on a match where England were down to nine fit men. Brian James of the *Daily Mail* thought Stiles the outstanding player: 'More skilled... than I had rated him; his tackles on club mates Crerand and Law proved that for him, England's cause was paramount.' Of Jack Charlton's performance, James wrote: 'This lanky streak from Leeds was suitably tough and predictably calm in a first-cap situation that would have tested the most experienced international.' Ramsey was not to know it at the time but he had stumbled upon the defensive permutation that would make history: Banks, Cohen, Wilson, Stiles, Charlton and Moore.

Yet he continued to fiddle with the team almost as much as had Winterbottom's selection committee. Some changes were forced by injury or, in the case of Jimmy Greaves' prolonged bout of jaundice, illness; others were the result of not knowing who or what would work best. Ramsey was once described by Jackie Milburn, his successor as manager at Ipswich Town, as a good chicken farmer manager : 'A good chicken farmer, if a hen doesn't lay, he wrings its neck.' This brutal analogy was not wholly accurate, however, as Ramsey sometimes picked up players for another chance long after they might have thought themselves banished forever.

There was, during the rest of 1965, one other debut of real significance: that of Blackpool midfielder Alan Ball, picked for the 1-1 draw with Yugoslavia in Belgrade a month after the first appearances of Stiles and Jack Charlton. Ball provided a taste of what was to come: constant running and an effervescence so essential to the World Cup team's chemistry. He took the eye not so much by what he did but by how much: quality defined by quantity. He was also an important element of an evolutionary process, that of Ramsey's retreat from deploying conventional wingers. Bobby Charlton was being groomed into a roaming midfield role that demanded extra stamina. The winger that could shred defences by a mercurial dance down the flank was a precious commodity, but, in Ramsey's eyes, he was devalued if he shied away from prosaic duties such as tackling back and covering. It was more by default than antipathy from Ramsey that the international careers of wingmen such as Peter Thompson, Terry Paine of Southampton and Manchester United's John Connelly became strangled.

Yet the winger's fate did not become clear until almost the eve of the World Cup. Through 1965 and early 1966, England's results were reliable only for inconsistency. Ramsey's statement that England would win the World Cup looked plausible enough after they beat Spain 2-0 in Madrid in December 1965 but much less so in January 1966 after a lumbering a 1-1 draw with Poland at Goodison Park. The match against Spain though, played on melting snow, signified much. Ramsey adopted a 4-3-3 formation that had Bobby Charlton, Stiles and George Eastham in midfield with Ball dropping back from the front three to lend support when needed: a team without conventional winners that became a template for England's tactical approach. The personnel who operated so well that night were: Banks, Cohen, Wilson, Stiles, Jack Charlton, Moore, Ball, Hunt, Baker, Eastham and Bobby Charlton. Ramsey was inching towards the 11 that would become household names.

But the problem of insufficient width created by 4-3-3 became apparent in the dreary draw with Poland. Ramsey would have been heartened by the energy and aggression provided by Stiles and Ball, qualities that made England less frail and harder to beat. The second game of 1966, World Cup year, was another cagey, low-key affair squeezed into the middle of the park. The opponents were West Germany, but of more importance was Ramsey's latest recruit at centre forward, West Ham's *The fearsome presence of Nobby Stiles* Geoff Hurst. England won 1-0 through *was crucial to Manchester United and,* a goal from Nobby Stiles. *thought Alf Ramsey, to England.*

England stuck with their formation for the annual duel with Scotland. The match was, by turns, untidy and exciting, dominated largely by England's better organisation, though Keith Newton, in for his second cap at left back for Ray Wilson, was tortured by Jimmy Johnstone, a mercurial winger the likes of which Ramsey, within his formulaic system, would have struggled to accommodate. England won 4-3; Charlton had a fine game roaming midfield while Hunt and Hurst ran tirelessly in search of good positions. Hurst's reward was a first goal in England colours. Hunt scored twice and Bobby Charlton got the other.

Indecision on Wingers

Johnstone had sent a reminder as to how potent and destructive a world class winger could be. Possibly it coloured Ramsey's thinking, because for England's next match, a 2-0 victory over Yugoslavia at Wembley, and with the World Cup only two months away, he fielded two conventional wide men, Terry Paine at outside right and Bobby Tambling of Chelsea on the left. That both played well may only have served to confuse him. There was also a debut for the young West Ham midfielder, Martin Peters; and a sparkling return, after a seven months absence through illness, for Jimmy Greaves.

Alf Ramsey kept the squad at a training camp at Lilleshall in Shropshire for 18 days before heading down to London for the first match.

Ramsey, however, was determined to dampen down complacency within the camp, as Gordon Banks recalled. With no reason to think he had put a foot wrong in the game against Yugoslavia, Banks, by way of casual farewell to the England manager, said, 'See you Alf.' At which, says Banks, 'Those cold eyes of his visibly widened and all he said in return was, "Will you?"'

One player destined not to return was Maurice Norman, despite recovering international form. 'I was playing so well it was unbelievable,' he said. 'I'd lost a stone in weight and was quite fast again. But playing against a Hungarian eleven at White Hart Lane in November 1965, I broke my left leg. It was a compound comminuted fracture. I was three years away from football. Otherwise I would have gone to the 1966 World Cup – I was told that by Alf.'

For a World Cup on home soil there would be no lack of preparation. There were no luxury hotels or dislocated compounds in the high mountains. Instead, the squad spent 18 days closeted in a training camp at Lilleshall, Shropshire,

The England squad out to dinner at the Hilton Hotel just ahead of the opening match against Uruguay.

where Ramsey and his lieutenant, Leeds United trainer Les Cocker, ran the show along military lines. After the near catastrophe involving Peter Swan during the 1962 World Cup, there was even a team doctor, Alan Bass, a Harley Street man who served Arsenal. Players used to training two hours a day and relaxing for the rest of the time found themselves behind locked gates, the village pubs out of bounds. They were organised from nine in the morning until nine at night.

The claustrophobic atmosphere that fostered the bonding process also allowed tensions to fester and Ramsey was forced to intervene when a spat between Nobby Stiles and Jack Charlton threatened to get out of hand. The manager, however, was pleased to see he was putting fire in the bellies of his squad. The press was kept strictly at arm's length, allowed restricted access by pre-arrangement.

Transgressors who escaped to seek out a pint at a nearby golf club were warned that any repetition would lead to automatic exclusion from the squad. 'Mornings were virtual non-stop training sessions,' Jack Charlton recalled. 'At times Lilleshall seemed like an exercise in pushing the human mind and frame to the utmost limit of endurance... a test of stamina, skill and the mental ability to cope with things.'

Five of the 27 who had been incarcerated were fated to be dropped: Thompson, the most naturally gifted flank player available to Ramsey but with a tendency to over-elaborate on the ball; Byrne; Tambling; Gordon Milne, the Liverpool wing half; and Keith Newton. The future lay in the hands of late arrivals such as the bustling Hurst and his versatile club-mate Martin Peters.

Pre-tournament Tour

With his squad, if not a team resolved, Ramsey took England on a testing four-match tour of Scandinavia and Poland. The party included three wingers: Connelly, Paine and Ian Callaghan of Liverpool, of whom the latter two were more at home fulfilling midfield duties. There was little to cheer Ramsey in England's scratchy 3-0 win over Finland in Helsinki; but much more in the 6-1 demolition of Norway, where Greaves, fully rejuvenated, gave a comprehensive exhibition of the striker's art by scoring four goals; and Bobby Moore struck a spectacular long-range goal. Greaves though, to everyone's disappointment, appeared lacklustre and disengaged in the 2-0 win over Denmark.

The most severe test, absurdly close to England's first game in the World Cup, lay in Poland. Ramsey's men had first to endure a long, wearisome journey by rail, then face opponents who, backed by a huge and hostile crowd, had much to prove after failure to qualify for the finals. Jack Charlton, in his book *For Leeds and England*, reflected the dilemma that England players experienced. 'Despite the close proximity of the World Cup, there could be no hiding or pulling out of tackles. Every man-jack of us was still playing for his place in that first game; every man-jack of us had to risk injury… or risk being dropped at the final moment.'

The game hung on a sound defensive performance and Roger Hunt's powerful shot that delivered England a 1-0 victory. It perhaps told Ramsey new things about Martin Peters, too, whose roving, roaming display in midfield much impressed Gordon Banks. 'He was a drifter; all smoothness and style – a real players' player.'

Commentator Kenneth Wolstenholme kicks off the BBC's World Cup coverage at Television Centre.

The World Cup Kicks Off

One goal scored, none conceded and no wingers. Yet it was not the formula Ramsey chose for England's first World Cup match against Uruguay on 11 July. John Connelly was recalled for what would be his last cap in a 20-match England career spanning more than five years. Uppermost in Ramsey's mind may have been the notion that trickery on the flanks could prise open one of the world's most obdurate defences. But Connelly, as did everyone with attacking credentials, failed miserably that evening. No one found the wit, craft or imagination to breach an eight-man rearguard or beat one of the world's best goalkeepers, Ladislao Mazurkiewicz.

50 Greatest Players

JIMMY GREAVES Centre forward

Clubs: Chelsea, Tottenham Hotspur
Debut: v Peru, 17 May 1959
Appearances: 57   **Goals:** 44

Judged by statistics alone, the record of Jimmy Greaves hardly reads like one of unfulfilled promise. His talent for the job of scoring goals was peerless and England never had a sharper, cannier striker. His gifts – just some of them – were a quick brain, good control and the ability to hold his nerve, which sometimes gave an impression of impudence.

On the field and in the dressing room, Greaves lived off his wits. He played with good humour and brought with him an air of irreverence to the England camp. The fact that he did not believe in being made to sweat for the sake of it – 'I was never the most enthusiastic of trainers,' he once said with trademark understatement – masked an innate seriousness. A dilettante would not have achieved half the things that Greaves did.

His England career, although lasting eight years, peaked early, and ended not by any falling out or debilitating injury but by an evolutionary process where hard-running front men became the cogs of Ramsey's master plan.

Greaves played a different, more subtle game that could be exasperating to onlookers, apparently disappearing from the action for long periods, yet his antennae for the half chance rarely let him down. Brian Glanville wrote of him: 'His turn of speed was extraordinary; his confidence more remarkable still; his left foot a hammer; his instinct for being in the right place near the goal almost psychic.' Yet too rarely in matches that mattered was Greaves at his best. For a near genius, he never made quite the imprint on football history that his talents merited.

John Connelly watches Uruguayan keeper Mazurkiewicz tip his shot over the bar. The opening match of the 1966 tournament ended in a 0-0 stalemate.

Yet Ramsey regarded this as a point won rather than lost and saw virtue in the fact that England had not conceded a goal. Nor had they lost any ground. The two other group contenders, France and Mexico, fought out a drab 1-1 draw that contained little to alarm Ramsey's men. Between facing Uruguay and Mexico, the England party enjoyed their best day's amusement for some time, as honoured guests of the Pinewood film studios, rubbing shoulders with the likes of George Segal and Sean Connery. Light relief was needed after the tart headlines England had woken up to following the stalemate with Uruguay.

For half an hour, England's second group game threatened more of the same: Mexico, their opponents, had every reason to believe that Ramsey's team could be smothered by a blanket defence. A magical twist was needed to transcend the mediocrity and this came when Bobby Charlton gathered the ball deep in midfield and jinked towards the retreating Mexican defence. At the first tempting sight of goal, Charlton set his sights and crashed a high velocity shot past goalkeeper Calderon and into the net.

From the stands and terraces came a tumultuous outpouring of relief. With Mexico seemingly devoid of attacking initiatives, England could consolidate, clinching victory 15 minutes from time as Calderon palmed Greaves' cross shot into the path of Roger Hunt. England may have been pedestrian but Bobby Charlton was a weapon against which no defence could legislate.

Alan Ball had been dropped and Martin Peters recalled, along with Terry Paine. While neither had a dramatic match, it set the career paths of Paine and Peters in diametrically opposite directions. For Paine, the winger, a dying species under Ramsey, this was the last of 19 caps. Peters, meanwhile, after what was just his fourth international, became a first choice component of the side.

The end beckoned for the flank player. Ian Callaghan, Peter Thompson's less extravagant but more compromising Liverpool team-mate, was recalled to play at outside right for the final group match against France, only to fade away and reappear in an England shirt 11 years later. The game was won by two smart goals, one in each half, from Roger Hunt, victory made easier by an early injury to one of France's more creative players, Robert Herbin. But for followers of England, a greater preoccupation was an injury to Jimmy Greaves, who left the pitch with a badly gashed leg that needed six stitches and put him out of the quarter final against Argentina.

Another legacy of the French game was Nobby Stiles' assumption of the role of bête noire. Stiles earned widespread vilification for a gruesome tackle late in the game on Jacques Simon that left the French forward in an agonised heap. With France in disarray, Greaves picked up possession and fed Callaghan, from whose cross Hunt had scored the second, decisive goal. Stiles' detractors accused him of brutality; his suporters were quick to point out his short-sightedness, that he had merely mistimed a full-blooded challenge. Some FA officials joined the call for Stiles' head, while Ramsey, famously stubborn and pragmatic, called everyone's bluff by announcing that if Stiles went, he would go too.

England won their group, gaining five points out of six without conceding a goal; yet a flatness persisted about their play that the inclusion of wingers failed to solve. Ball, who played against Uruguay but not against France or Mexico, was recalled for the quarter-final against Argentina that set a collection of fiery temperaments on a collision course. Geoff Hurst, meanwhile, was brought back in place of Jimmy Greaves.

Bobby Charlton unleashes a thunderbolt to open the scoring against Mexico in England's second group match.

Through to the Next Round

Ramsey's pre-match talk stressed that England should not rise to the bait of Argentinian foul play. The South Americans, perennially talented, had already displayed their capacity for cynicism, doling out rough stuff to Spain in the first of their group matches and more of the same to West Germany in their second, a vicious goalless draw in which Albrecht, after successive outrages, had exhausted the referee's patience and been sent off. Yet they

West German referee Rudolph Kreitlein is escorted from the pitch after the controversial quarter-final against Argentina.

were resplendent with talent, admired by, among others, Bobby Charlton: 'Onega, a super midfield player with a great left peg... Oscar Maz, a devilish little left-winger... and, of course, there was Rattin.'

Indeed there was. The name of the ineffable Argentinian captain, centre half Antonio Rattin, 'tall, straight-backed, strong and unhurried, and supremely confident on the ball,' would reverberate long and loud. Against England, Rattin behaved as if the role of team captain also bestowed upon him the right to referee, and so inevitably was drawn into conflict with the official nominated by FIFA, Rudolf Kreitlein. Their difference of approach was irreconcilable. Rattin seemed to think a blind eye should be turned to elbows, trips and shirt-tugging on the part of Argentina. Kreitlein, on the other hand, wanted the game played according to international rules.

A small balding figure prone to fussiness, whom the aristocratic Rattin harried with palpable disdain, Kreitlein strove to control events. Almost from kick-off the Argentinians began doing their worst. Before long Rattin tripped Bobby Charlton on the half-way line and was booked. But he carried on undeterred and, while England traded their fair share of fouls, the Argentinians kept Kreitlein much busier.

A fateful juncture arrived ten minutes before half-time. When Kreitlein booked Luis Artime for dissent, Rattin, anxious to determine who was boss, impressed upon Kreitlein the error of his ways so emphatically that no knowledge of Spanish was needed to gain an understanding. His authority so brazenly violated, Kreitlein ordered Rattin from the field. What happened next – Rattin's implacable refusal to depart – was beyond everyone's experience. Almost ten minutes elapsed before Rattin gave up the ghost and flounced off.

The pity was that Rattin and his fellow pantomime gangsters had a great gift for football. They were no easier to break down with just ten men and could slice through England's ranks when the mood took them. Ramsey's re-jigged side was still spluttering, short of the craft to break through an artful massed defence. But, with less than quarter of an hour remaining, the lock was finally picked. Martin Peters despatched a prime near post cross towards Geoff Hurst, who was starting to exploit the space vacated by Rattin, and Hurst's soaring header looped over Roma, sailing triumphantly into the net – a moment of rare beauty in an ugly match.

Alf Ramsey was furious at the Argentina players' behaviour and tried to prevent George Cohen (right) swapping shirts with Alberto Gonzalez.

There was an inimical finale. Ramsey would not let his players swap shirts at full time; a posse of Argentinians descended on the English dressing room spoiling for a fight; and the England manager caused diplomatic turbulence by describing his bellicose opponents as animals. Amid the ramifications, it was easy to overlook that England had made history by reaching the World Cup semi-finals for the first time.

On to the Semi-finals

Their opponents were Portugal, a team capable of brilliance but with a dark side. A Portuguese, Morais, had perpetrated one of the most cynical acts of the tournament, an abominable foul on Pele in a group match that sent the Brazilian genius limping out of the competition. Meanwhile, Portugal's defensive frailties unexpectedly came to light in the quarter-final when their opponents, North Korea, nimble and deft, though ultimately destined to wilt before a greater power, had raced into a three-goal lead before losing 5-3.

The Koreans' nemesis, one blessed with the brilliance to punish defences far less naïve, was Eusebio, a combination of muscularity, supreme ball control and with a ravenous appetite for goals. As memories of Pele faded, Eusebio emerged as the exotic figure of the 1966 World Cup. How he might fare against England became the most absorbing question of the semi-final. For Ramsey, the question was uncomplicated: stop him playing at all costs.

In a great exhibition of man marking, Eusebio's footsteps were to be dogged assiduously by Nobby Stiles. But Stiles versus Eusebio was just one element of a match so rich in skill, played in so wholesome a spirit, that it might have constituted an act of atonement not only for the rancour of England's brawl with Argentina but all the unsavoury confrontations by which the 1966 World Cup had been left pockmarked.

The brilliance of Bobby Charlton, rather than that of Eusebio, divided the teams on a night of controlled passions. Charlton had embellished his first goal on the half hour, a shot hit sweet and firm from the edge of the penalty area, with what looked to be England's crowning glory 12 minutes from time: he converted Hurst's cross pulled back from the by-line into a strike of screaming velocity that scorched through the floodlit night and into the Portuguese net.

But the appeal of the match, its dramatic tension, lay in the sense of menace that lurked in Portugal's attack. Such were England's accomplishments in midfield and defence that this merely smouldered until England attained their two-goal cushion. Nine minutes remained when Torres, the giant centre forward, won supremacy in the air and sent a header goal-bound, only for Jack Charlton to handle on the line. Eusebio's penalty goal energised the final few minutes as the Portuguese, driven on by midfield inspiration Coluna, poured forward in search of an equaliser. But England clung on to their 2-1 lead. For Portugal, there was honour, dignity and Eusebio's tears in defeat; while for England, the style of the achievement was also a glorious feat of self-discovery.

It was the first England performance to receive universal acclaim. Gone were dissenting voices about the lack of wingers. In its most important match the team had played as a coherent unit. But the fact that Ramsey felt no temptation to tinker against fellow finalists West Germany crushed the spirits of Jimmy Greaves, whose gashed leg became the curse of his life. 'It would be an understatement to say I was disappointed,' he wrote later. 'I had always anticipated I would be part of the greatest day in the history of our game. Alf came round to me at around midday and said, "I've decided on an unchanged team. I know you'll understand."'

A disconsolate Eusebio is escorted from the pitch in tears after Portugal's semi-final defeat.

Great Matches

WORLD CUP FINAL   **Wembley, 30 July 1966**

England 4   **West Germany 2**   **Attendance 96,924**
Hurst 3   Haller
Peters   Weber

Ramsey's boast, was not, after all, vainglory. On a day drenched in patriotism and tension, in an epic match of shifting fortunes too pitted with errors, too grinding, ultimately, to merit description as a classic, England won the World Cup. As drama it was stupendous, rendered all the more so through the imperfections and controversies that chafed against its fitful glinting brilliance.

Mentally and physically, Ramsey's men were at a peak. In high morale, the fervour of the home crowd acting as an elixir, they were severely tested early on by Germany's opening goal, the opportunity of a crisp strike presented to Haller by Wilson's uncharacteristically feeble header.

A goal down within 13 minutes but on terms six minutes later as Moore, with great speed of thought, launched a long, perfectly weighted free-kick towards Geoff Hurst, who timed his arrival impeccably and sent a delicious glancing header arcing over Tilkowski and into the net.

Restoration of parity ushered in some fine football: both sides fluid and full of energetic rhythm; probing for, and finding, openings that brought near misses, examples of forward profligacy and fine saves at either end.

For a period after half-time the match lost impetus, as if both teams were gripped by the fear of losing everything. Hustlers such as Stiles and Ball came into their own, and thanks to Ball's indefatigable chivvying, the stalemate was broken 13 minutes from the end, as he

Hurst opens the scoring with a header from Bobby Moore's free kick.

(continued overleaf)

bundled Tilkowski over the goal line for a corner. Ball took it. Hurst's shot ballooned off Weber into the path of Martin Peters and, with typical efficiency, Peters fired the ball into the net.

At this point, the German reputation for durability was born. With most of Wembley against them and time ebbing away, the timing of their final thrust could not, for England, have been more cruel. A minute remained when Jack Charlton was penalised for his part in an aerial duel with Held. Emmerich's driven free kick from the left caused disarray, rebounding to Held who swung the ball across goal. It squirted into the path of Weber who rammed it home.

After Alf Ramsey's pep talk, England waded into extra time the more invigorated, with Ball in particular a miracle of perpetual energy. He pursued a long through ball from Stiles down the right flank and crossed for Geoff Hurst to crash the ball against the underside of the bar. Over the line or not? The doubts of Herr Dienst, the Swiss referee, were swayed in England's favour by his Russian linesman, Bakhramov. So a goal forever to be dissected by analysts was born.

Germany went in frenetic pursuit of an equaliser, while England's job was to remain cool. Fittingly, the imperturbable Bobby Moore was the mainspring for a glorious crescendo as, eyes and wits still about him, he launched a ball upfield for Hurst to chase. The German defence was spread-eagled, its bolt shot, as the West Ham centre forward thumped the ball with his left foot high past Tilkowski. The World Cup belonged to England.

Hurst hammers the ball against the bar, and then the ground, for England's controversial third goal.

It's all over now as Hurst completes his hat-trick and England win the World Cup.

England: Banks (Leicester City), Cohen (Fulham), Wilson (Everton), Stiles (Manchester United), J. Charlton (Leeds United), Moore (West Ham United), Ball (Everton), Hunt (Liverpool), R. Charlton (Manchester United), Hurst (West Ham United), Peters (West Ham United)

West Germany: Tilkowski (Borussia Dortmund), Hottges (Werder Bremen), Schnellinger (AC Milan), Beckenbauer (Bayern Munich), Schulz (SV Hamburg), Weber (FC Cologne), Haller (Bologna), Overath (FC Cologne), Seeler (SV Hamburg), Held (Borussia Dortmund), Emmerich (Borussia Dortmund)

50 Greatest Players

GEOFF HURST Centre forward

Club: West Ham United
Debut: v West Germany, 23 February 1966
Appearances: 49   **Goals:** 24

That Geoff Hurst should have had so illustrious a career says much for his quiet determination, but also for Alf Ramsey's ability to look beyond the obvious. As the 1966 World Cup beckoned, Ramsey was beset with uncertainties about front line players. Hurst was a less obvious choice to the outside world than, for instance, the manifestly brilliant Peter Osgood; yet on closer inspection he had much to recommend him.

Tall, solidly built and superb in the air, he also had a powerful shot. These were the classic attributes of the English centre forward, but Hurst had something extra – a cool, mature temperament and the ability to soak up punishment without fuss.

Hurst is forever associated with games versus West Germany, against whom he made a low-key debut. He is remembered principally, of course, for his hat-trick in the 1966 World Cup final and the theatrical last minute goal that said as much for his stamina as for dramatic timing, but in England's ill-fated 1970 World Cup quarter-final against the Germans he was also a commanding figure, often too much for his markers. His final appearance, too, was against West Germany, an anti-climactic occasion that led to England's exit from the European Nations Cup in April 1972.

Hurst was still playing well and might, with luck, have been recalled to a side experiencing turbulent times. Some, Jimmy Armfield among them, reckoned Hurst the best centre forward England ever had – not bad for the ex-wing half who once looked destined only for obscurity.

The outcome of events more than justified Ramsey's decision. The team had belatedly gained an understanding that perhaps had its roots in those intense days at Lilleshall, all the rigorous practice matches and the pre-World Cup tour. Certainly Alan Ball thought so. 'We had built up a perfect understanding with each other,' he said. 'I could find Geoff Hurst with a pass in the dark, we had worked on moves so often together. Ramsey knew exactly what we were capable of doing.'

Chapter Seven: 1967-74
Defending Champions

For the mother of football nations, victory in the World Cup final was the yardstick by which all other achievement would be judged. The team may have exceeded the sum of its parts, yet Ramsey seemed intent on sticking with his winning formula. England kept the side that beat Argentina, Portugal and West Germany for a further three internationals, against Northern Ireland, Czechoslovakia and Wales. Only when the team squared up to play Scotland in April 1967 did he recall Jimmy Greaves in place of Roger Hunt.

For the second time in nine months, Wembley went berserk with a sense of national pride. But it was Scottish supporters indulging in uproarious jingoism. Their side won 3-2 – the first to beat the world champions and the first victors over England since Austria in October 1965. Potent the Scots were, but for most of the match they had played a handicapped side. Jack Charlton broke a toe on the quarter hour; Greaves too became handicapped by injury; but many of the able-bodied had no such excuse. Scotland fans felt able to believe they were the best in the world. Some dug up the Wembley pitch in memory of a great battle won.

Jim Baxter (right) and Billy Bremner celebrate getting one over the old enemy as Scotland beat England 3-2 in the first match at Wembley after the World Cup final.

The time had arrived to test a few understudies. When England played Spain at Wembley a month later, there were five changes: a debut for Chelsea midfielder John Hollins and recalls for Chelsea's Peter Bonetti in goal, Keith Newton of Blackburn Rovers at left back, Alan Mullery of Tottenham at right half and Brian Labone at centre half. Banks, whose reliability in goal was unsurpassed, nevertheless had an indifferent game against the Scots and conceded a bad goal, allowing Jim McCalliog to squeeze in a shot at the near post.

Greaves, who scored in England's 2-0 win, looked livelier than for some time and was retained for a friendly against Austria three days later, but neither he nor fellow striker Roger Hunt impressed in a laborious 1-0 victory. For Greaves, it was a last chance squandered: he never played for his country again, despite a clamour for his recall in 1968-69, when his game had recovered its old swagger. By then, communications between Ramsey and Greaves were fractured. 'Ramsey revealed, much to my surprise, that I had asked not to be considered,' said Greaves. 'What I actually said is that I didn't want to be called up if I wasn't going to get a game. He had been calling me up for training with the squad and then not picking me.'

European Nations Entry

For some time Hurst and Hunt remained England's familiar pairing up front. Meanwhile, England's new focus became the European Nations Cup, which they had entered for the first time and for which the qualifying games were the home internationals. As Ramsey plotted the future, Mullery, who had as an adjunct to his role as grafter the knack of bursting forward and scoring spectacular goals, became a regular in place of Stiles; and Keith Newton the familiar stand-in for Ray Wilson.

Ramsey realised the 4-3-3 formation with which England had won the World Cup could not be a template forever. Nor was he blind to the impact a singular talent could have. England's lack of width could not be ignored and so Ramsey recalled Peter Thompson for the home international against Northern Ireland in November 1967 and a friendly in West Germany six months later. But, as Thompson recalls, what Ramsey wanted appeared a contradiction: to play as he did for Liverpool yet not hold the ball. For Thompson this diktat was 'like tying my legs together'. Against West Germany, he 'had a shocker' and did little better against Northern Ireland. Ultimately Ramsey obtained width by grooming new full backs who overlapped as Cohen and Wilson, both near the end of their international careers, had done.

However, he still experimented with a winger or two, aware that even fine defenders such as Ray Wilson could be made to look silly by a magician working the flank. When England drew their friendly with the USSR at Wembley in December 1967 2-2, Wilson – and others – floundered in the wake of the visitors' outside right Chislenko who, apart from displaying mesmerising skill on a snow covered pitch, scored both his team's goals. As England progressed to the quarter final stages of the Nations Cup in spring 1968, Mike Summerbee of Manchester City was tried on the right against Spain at Wembley. It was the second of his three appearances but none matched the bravura displays to which he treated fans at Maine Road. Old habits served England well in the return at Madrid: a classic hard-running backs to the wall 4-3-3 show where Ball and Mullery excelled; and Bobby Moore once more thrived in adversity. England, 1-0 winners of the cagey home leg, were 2-1 victors at the Bernabeu.

The semi-final against Yugoslavia, England's biggest match since becoming world champions, was played in Italy: theoretically neutral territory, yet where a hostile press and public awaited Ramsey's team. Gordon Banks recalls sustained abuse in the newspapers, '...accusing us of being animals and saying we had hacked our way to the World Cup.' It was a harbinger of the battering they would get on the pitch. Often the game resembled warfare conducted with a nod to Association rules. The outcome turned on the exposure of Bobby Moore's occasional inability to command the air. Just four minutes remained when Moore missed a dipping cross and allowed the ball to fall to the sharp Yugoslav winger, Dzajic. His punishing low shot zipped past Banks and into the corner of the net. A miserable ending became ignominious when Alan Mullery, one of many buffeted throughout, was fouled once too often, lashed out in retaliation, and became the first England player dismissed in a full international.

It showed what the mighty could expect from ruthless opponents away from Wembley, where all England's World Cup matches had been won, but also exposed England's inability to pierce obdurate defences. As the press campaign to reinstate Greaves gathered momentum, Roger Hunt became a target for malcontents following two drab drawn games against Romania. 'Roger was particularly depressed by the hammer he was having to take,' said Banks. 'He never received the appreciation and credit he deserved for his dedicated and unselfish work.' By January 1969, after a second ineffectual display against Romania, Hunt's confidence was so undermined that he asked Ramsey not to be picked again. Some agreed with Banks, that Hunt had indeed been unappreciated, but while Geoffrey Green of *The Times* acknowledged that Hunt was a 'doer of good by stealth' he felt also that the Liverpool man was no more than a workhorse of moderate ability.

New faces and a vibrant 5-0 victory over France at Wembley two months later reined in the critics. Terry Cooper of Leeds United, a converted winger making his debut at left back, provided a sparky presence, while another Leeds man, Mike O'Grady, last capped against Northern Ireland in October 1962 when with Huddersfield, added further impetus down the left and scored with a searing volley from Hurst's headed knock-down. Yet O'Grady was discarded after his stirring performance.

Manchester City's Colin Bell linked up with team-mate Francis Lee in England's midfield in the aftermath of the European Nations Cup in 1968.

One livewire with whom Ramsey did persevere was Manchester City outside right Francis Lee, capped three months earlier in the 1-1 draw with Bulgaria. Lee was an effervescent figure, a confident, direct runner given to unnerving defenders; a master at creating turbulence and winning penalties by whatever means. He would find himself in partnership with club colleague Colin Bell, a splendidly versatile footballer full of hard running and sharp shooting – a classic Ramsey player. Meanwhile, as extravagant praise was showered upon Lee, Ramsey warned that if any went to his head, he risked being dropped. There was no compromising the England manager's determination to squash the superstar cult, the unmanageable ego.

Big heads were not his only problem: there were the old equivocations of successful club managers about releasing players. 'Niggling injuries' caused Jack Charlton to drop out of several internationals. 'In other circumstances, they might not have been enough to stop me playing. But if we [Leeds United] had a big match coming up, it was very much in the interests of the manager to say "You'd better pull out".'

Victory against France marked a turning point in England's form. Ramsey's men made a clean sweep of the home international championship, in which Bobby Charlton rediscovered his best form, Lee underlined his potential and left for a summer tour of South America buoyed by a 4-1 victory over the Scots at Wembley. There, away from familiar opponents and the comforts of a temperate climate, sterner tests awaited.

Journey to Latin America

The idea of a Latin American tour made perfect sense. Mexico were hosting the 1970 World Cup and there were lessons to be learned about playing in heat, humidity and at altitude. The team would also benefit from exposure to everything the opposition might offer, from technical genius to gamesmanship. But a tough expedition was made needlessly uncomfortable by the rudeness Ramsey displayed towards the locals and the media. On arrival in Mexico he complained about the lack of a motorcycle escort to the stadium, about a band that played through the night outside the team's hotel, about a hostile reception when players inspected the pitch. In Guadalajara he shooed away journalists who followed the England team down to a dressing room following a civic presentation.

England beat a representative Mexican eleven 4-0; drew 0-0 with the full Mexican side; beat Uruguay 2-1 in Montevideo the day after a gruelling 24-hour trip via Peru; but lost their biggest challenge, beaten 2-1 by Brazil in Rio. They were not always appetising to watch. Indeed, there were increasing signs of Ramsey's move from 4-3-3 to 4-4-2, an even more defensive formation. However, no one could detract from the teamwork that was so decisive in beating Uruguay and, but for the heat and their collective exhaustion, England might have conquered Brazil instead of succumbing to two late goals.

Five months elapsed before England's next game, against Holland in Amsterdam. There was a first cap for Liverpool's Emlyn Hughes at left back and a 1-0 victory with little to commend it. Five minutes remained when Peter Thompson was brought on for Francis Lee, almost a postscript to Ramsey's affair with orthodox wingers. One month later England managed another pedestrian 1-0 victory, at home to Portugal. So ended the 1960s, with England, on the threshold of defending the World Cup, inculcated with habits that made them tough, yet with a sterility about their play that left supporters uneasy.

Ramsey remained haughtily indifferent towards public opinion. The first match of 1970, another fixture with Holland, goalless and played with a much changed side, had Wembley registering displeasure with a slow handclap. Asked by a reporter for his reaction, Ramsey took refuge in facetiousness, remarking, 'But surely they were slow handclapping the Dutch?' Unfamiliar faces included Leeds United centre forward Mick Jones, who had last played against West Germany and Sweden in 1965 when with Sheffield United; and on the left flank, debutant Ian Storey-Moore of Nottingham Forest. Neither would play for their country again.

Sections of the press wondered what the England manager was up to. Donald Saunders in the Daily Telegraph wrote: 'Ramsey... should now be in a position to add and subtract from the team without throwing it so utterly out of its stride as it was last night.' Yet Gordon Banks felt critics had ignored the quality of the opposition, 'a team that was to emerge as one of the best in the world with the likes of Cruyff, Krol, van Hanegem and Keizer...'

The Dutch, who had failed to qualify for Mexico, would go one way and England another, inching unadventurously through the home internationals towards a 4-4-2 system rooted in caution rather than exuberance. The World Cup draw pitched them in with Czechoslovakia and Romania, challengers of sorts, and Brazil, opponents of quite another calibre. Ramsey's party of 27 flew out for acclimatisation and warm-up matches 29 days before the tournament began. They would be ostentatiously well prepared.

With Mexico City more than 7,000 feet above sea level, it took Ramsey's players a fortnight of acclimatisation before they could train properly. Sunbathing was rationed to half an hour a day: 15 minutes each side, back and front. Meanwhile, the England party offended local sensibilities by bringing their own bus, food and water. As Ramsey continued to give the hungry local news media short shrift, Brazilians players visited sick children in hospital and bore gifts of flags, badges and autographed books, their battle for local hearts won game, set and match.

England's warm-up included matches in Colombia and Equador. Ramsey, meanwhile, had to prune his squad from 28 to 22. Under pressure from Sunday newspaper journalists with deadlines to meet, the England manager, much out of character, confided in them his choice of men before any of the players had been told. Ramsey swore the press corps to secrecy, but was betrayed by a sports editor in Manchester pursuing family reaction to news that Manchester United central defender David Sadler had been dropped – a fate Sadler learned not from his manager, but from his wife, phoning from England.

It was Peter Thompson's misfortune to be omitted for the second successive World Cup. Yet the victors of 1966 were still there in force: Alan Ball, Bobby Charlton, Bobby Moore, Geoff Hurst, Martin Peters and Nobby Stiles. The defence, though, had been substantially rebuilt. Gordon Banks had no serious challenger but Cohen and Wilson made way for Keith Newton of Everton and Terry Cooper of Leeds. Alan Mullery was first choice over Stiles and Brian Labone of Everton now preferred to Jack Charlton. New strikers included Leeds United's predator in chief Allan Clarke, West Bromwich Albion's talismanic centre forward Jeff Astle and Peter Osgood from Chelsea, a man perhaps too mercurial for his own good.

Mexico Here We Come

Having got to grips with Mexican altitude, England flew off on their pre-tournament tour for a first ever match with Colombia in Bogota. It was, in the minds of several players all of whom were appalled by the poverty they saw, a doubtful privilege. But the game showed England had reaped the value of rigorous training as they were superior in every department. They cruised to a 4-0 win, quite able to deal with 90 minutes at 8,500 feet.

However, football achievement was eclipsed by a charade involving Bobby Moore and the alleged theft of a bracelet from a shopping area by the

*Looking confident and relaxed during their time at Lilleshall, the England squad prepare
to leave for Mexico and their defence of the World Cup title.*

Tequendama Hotel where England were staying. The likelihood of it being a
shabby little fit-up emerged only after Moore had been engulfed in lurid
headlines. He was released after questioning and took part in England's
game in Ecuador, but arrested and detained for four days when England re-
entered Colombia on the return journey to Mexico. After diplomatic
pressure, and with the case against him unravelling, Moore finally departed,
with composure and dignity.

England had learned much. In Ecuador, they had played at more than
9,000 feet, 'chests frighteningly tight, hearts pounding, our lips flecked with
foam', said Bobby Charlton, yet still they had won 2-0. Pain barriers were
overcome and fears conquered; players grew used to the ball swerving in the
air 'like a boomerang'. But the pantomime involving Moore turned Mexican
opinion even more vehemently against Ramsey's team and Guadalajara, base
camp for the group matches, was unwelcoming territory, with local
newspapers brazenly libelling the players as thieves and drunks.

England's first game against Romania was a test of temperament against
opponents preoccupied with defence and inclined towards cynicism – Wright
and Lee, in particular, received vicious attention from the defender Mocanu
that went unpunished. The moment was sweet when, on 65 minutes, Hurst
controlled a cross to the far post from Alan Ball, skipped round a defender
and scored from a tight angle. Of many pleasing performances, none surpassed
that of Terry Cooper, a zestful attacking force overlapping on both flanks.

Brazil also won their opening match in extravagant, if careless, fashion, 4-1 victors over Czechoslovakia. Their clash with England was beautifully teed up, a heavyweight encounter between champions past, rediscovering their soul, and the pragmatic World Cup holders. The capricious Mexicans did their bit to disrupt England. On the eve of the match, they joined the Brazilian throngs outside the team hotel, chanting, waving flags, blaring horns, even attempting to break in. 'The streets around were alive with hatred,' wrote Bobby Charlton. 'There wasn't as policeman in sight.'

England took to the field having endured successive nights of broken sleep, all too aware that Brazil could threaten from all angles. Newton, kicked out of the match against Romania, was replaced at right back by Tommy Wright. Mullery was charged with stifling Pele, much as Stiles had subdued Eusebio four years earlier, but Pele was just one of Ramsey's worries. He was apprehensive also about Brazilian free kicks and the capacity of Jairzinho and Rivelino to rip up defences along the wings.

After mutual embraces and exchanges of fine words, England still had to qualify for the quarter-finals. Their final group match against Czechoslovakia was an anti-climactic spectacle in which Mexican persecutors bombarded Gordon Banks' goal with coins and rubbish. Jack Charlton was reinstated at centre half; Keith Newton at right back; Geoff Hurst was rested; and Allan Clarke awarded his first cap. It was a significant debut: Clarke, the pre-match volunteer to take penalties in Hurst's absence, had his bluff called four minutes into the second half when a Czech defender handled in the penalty area. With singular coolness, Clarke hit the ball crisply for the single, decisive goal.

In so inelegant a fashion, England became quarter-finalists, drawn against West Germany. They decamped to Leon for a fixture that would brim over with the elements of tragedy: a contest between the victors of 1966 and the vanquished with much to prove; one in which England were often superb but were undermined by misfortune, events and Achilles heel weaknesses.

The first blow was delivered before kick-off: Gordon Banks, laid low by a stomach bug, made way for Peter Bonetti of Chelsea, a goalkeeper of talent and agility yet unproven in big internationals. For an hour, though, the absence of the world's greatest goalkeeper mattered little. England were fluid, decisive, enterprising, often given the run of the park. Franz Beckenbauer, pegged back, struggled to contain 32-year-old Bobby Charlton. After 30 minutes, Mullery and Newton sliced open the German defence, a flowing move crowned by Mullery's imperious shot past Sepp Maier in the German goal. Within four minutes of the second half, England were 2-0 up,

Great Matches

WORLD CUP GROUP MATCH

England 0   **Brazil 1**
Jairzinho

Guadalajara, 7 June 1970

Attendance 70,950

This was a very English outcome: glory extracted from defeat, defenders emerging as legends from a monumental match; a pinnacle almost, but not quite, scaled. As a close contest and a study in contrasting styles, there was no more satisfying match in the 1970 tournament.

The milestones were many. There was the supernatural moment in the 11th minute when Gordon Banks catapulted himself across goal to flip Pele's downwards header over the bar, a chance created, as Ramsey had feared, by Jairzinho's knack of making lacerating runs down the right. There was Bobby Moore, in the tumult of battle, defying Pele and others with tackles so perfect as to be beautiful. And there was the agonising miss by substitute Jeff Astle, who scuffed a feeble shot wide of a gaping goal; then Alan Ball hitting the bar.

The genius that ran through the Brazilian team undid England on the hour. Tostao, an elegant centre forward with as complete a range of skills as any, worked space for himself and floated over a centre. It fell for Pele, who did the simplest, most destructive thing, sliding the ball square for the on-rushing Jairzinho who lashed the ball high into the net. By so fine a margin, the great and the good were separated.

England: Banks (Stoke City), Wright (Everton), Cooper (Leeds United), Moore (West Ham United), Labone (Everton), Mullery (Tottenham Hotspur), Ball (Everton), R. Charlton, (Manchester United), Peters (West Ham United), Hurst (West Ham United), Lee (Manchester City)

Substitutes: Astle (West Bromwich Albion) for Charlton R, Bell (Manchester City) for Lee

Brazil: Felix (Fluminense), Carlos Alberto (Santos), Everaldo (Gremio), Clodoaldo (Santos), Brito (Flamengo), Piazza (Cruzeiro), Jairzinho (Botafogo), Paulo Cesar (Botafogo), Tostao (Cruzeiro), Pele (Santos), Rivelino (Corinthians)

Substitute: Roberto (Cruzeiro) for Tostao

The imperious Franz Beckenbauer was a major influence as West Germany deposed the World Champions in that fateful quarter-final in Leon in 1970.

Newton once more instrumental, latching on to Hurst's pass, galloping forward and despatching a long cross to the far post that was headed in with gusto by Martin Peters.

Then both managers embarked on a crucial deployment of substitutes. Helmut Schoen replaced Lubuda with Grabowski, a winger capable of tormenting any defender wilting in the heat. Events started turning against England when Beckenbauer's own shot rebounded back to him off Francis Lee and, despite all the strictures from Alf Ramsey, the German was allowed to get the ball to his right foot. His second shot, from an acute angle, was a powder puff but grotesquely misjudged by Bonetti, who dived too soon and over the ball.

Ramsey tried to bolt the stable door, to revive midfield and stiffen the defence, replacing Charlton with Bell and Peters with Hunter. Charlton, though, was by no means done and his departure freed Beckenbauer to adopt a more attacking role. Time ticked away; the match thundered on. In the 78th minute, Colin Bell crossed and a low diving header from Hurst dropped past the far post to Lee, who, had he been more alert, might have followed up to score. Punishment was almost instant. A weary clearance

50 Greatest Players

GORDON BANKS Goalkeeper

Clubs: Leicester City, Stoke City
Debut: v Scotland, 6 April 1963
Appearances: 73

'Of all the players to lose, we had to lose him.'
The enforced absence of Gordon Banks had caused
Alf Ramsey's state of dejection after England's defeat by
West Germany in the 1970 World Cup quarter-final.
As Ramsey muttered the words over and over again, he
acknowledged that Banks was priceless.

It was not only spectacular saves such as that against
Brazil in the qualifying group that illustrated Banks'
class. It was his consistency, the result of enormous
dedication. Ever alert, agile and with remarkable powers
of concentration, he was a source of confidence that helped make a great defence
around him.

No one becomes the world's best by accident. Banks spent hours each day studying
angles, practising catches and shot-stopping. As brave and tough as any in the
business, he regarded broken bones and concussion as an occupational hazard.

At his peak in 1970, Banks was admired by the great managers around the world,
including Helmut Schoen of Germany and Mario Zagalo of Brazil. He was Footballer of
the Year in 1972 and would probably have remained a long-term fixture in England's
goal but for a car crash in October that year which cost him an eye, brutally cutting
short a magnificent career.

from Brian Labone fell to Schnellinger. His deep cross was met by Seeler,
who leaped with startling energy and contrived a back header that Bonetti,
stranded in no man's land, could not reach.

It was 2-2 with extra time to be played and the echoes of 1966
were uncanny. But this time the force was with West Germany. In the
110th minute, Grabowski whipped past Cooper on the flank and Lohr
headed down his centre to the feet of Gerd Muller, against whom Bonetti,
at close range, had no ghost of a chance. The indestructible spirits had
pecked away at the frailties of the better team. England were no longer
world champions.

50 Greatest Players

BOBBY CHARLTON Inside forward

Club: Manchester United
Debut: v Scotland, 19 April 1958
Appearances: 106   **Goals:** 49

Despite being thrown from the plane still strapped to his seat, Bobby Charlton survived the Munich air crash which killed so many young Manchester United talents such as Duncan Edwards, Tommy Taylor and Roger Byrne. Yet although jolted into England colours more abruptly than anyone anticipated, Charlton's potential was clear from the day he took the international stage and volleyed a stunning goal at Hampden Park.

He still had much to learn. Early on, his positional sense without the ball could be faulty. Sometimes he crowded other forwards and was accused of not tackling hard enough in defence. But set against that, he had a catalogue of gifts: neatness on the turn, the body swerve that deceived so many defences, delicate footwork and forceful running.

Charlton was disinclined to waste energy, preferring to conserve himself for decisive short sprints, but under Alf Ramsey he was given a deeper roaming role, one that required a greater work rate. It never compromised him as a player.

England's World Cup semi-final against Portugal showed Charlton at his peak: as opportunist, as sharpshooter, forever moving intelligently and passing the ball with beautiful care. The flowing run, his residual hair flopping, the feint, the punishing burst into space and explosive shot – such a combination can only conjure the image of Bobby Charlton in full cry.

His substitution against West Germany in the World Cup quarter-final of 1970 was a traumatic watershed for player and country. But if Charlton's form was fitful in the intervening years, it distorts history to suggest there was a long slow decline. Even in the blistering heat of Mexico, he was still about his business, playing with authority and fire, his fulminating shots a perpetual threat to all-comers.

Ramsey Unrepentant

Ramsey, defensive and prickly even in victory, became more so in defeat. His tactics against West Germany and others were dissected and accusers concocted a lengthy indictment. He was too slow to bombard the Brazilian defence with high balls; he used Lee on the right when he was better on the left; he didn't risk Peter Osgood who was in the form of his life; and he played keep-ball instead of pressing harder when German heads were down. There were also those fateful substitutions: withdrawing Charlton; replacing Peters with Hunter; persisting with Terry Cooper who was being roasted by Grabowski.

Whatever, Ramsey took the blame himself rather than reproaching individuals, all of whom, he said, with a tinge

The unstoppable Gerd Müller is hauled to the ground by Peter Storey during England's European Nations quarter-final defeat against West Germany in 1972.

of defiance, he would pick again. Such loyalty bound players to him, as did his discretion with anyone whose standards slipped. 'If you did something wrong, he'd just take you aside and tell you,' said Maurice Norman.

Nevertheless, some were embarrassed by Ramsey's deplorable public relations. 'His view of the press was that they know nothing about football, so why should I talk to them?' said Norman. His preoccupation was, as ever, the team, one that needed rebuilding. The West Germany game marked the end of internationals for the Charlton brothers: Bobby, in amassing 106 caps, had beaten Billy Wright's record, while Jack finished with 35, all but one collected after the age of 30.

More than five months elapsed before England's next match. Their 3-1 win over East Germany at Wembley in November 1970 brought a debut in goal for Peter Shilton, Banks' former understudy at Leicester City. Competitive football resumed in the shape of European Championship qualifiers against Malta, Greece and Switzerland, and the home internationals. Throughout 1971 Ramsey's teams, populated by several new faces, produced more scratchy performances than fluent ones. In May 1972, West Germany once more became the rock on which English ambition foundered, 3-1 winners at Wembley in the European Championship quarter-final. The Germans, on a night when Bobby Moore had a poor match, were powerful and incisive, while England were ponderous and too inclined to play innocuous square balls. Two weeks later, English interest was extinguished in a goalless draw in Berlin.

50 Greatest Players

BOBBY MOORE Left half

Clubs: West Ham United
Debut: v Peru, 20 May 1962
Appearances: 108   **Goals:** 2

When playing the world's best, on the biggest stages, Bobby Moore excelled. Gifted with the temperament and talent to lead men, Bobby Moore learned quickly, matured rapidly and was seemingly possessed of a sixth sense that entitled him to take command.

Within a year of his debut, Alf Ramsey made Bobby Moore captain of the England team. Their relationship was not always easy: Moore had an independence and fondness for enjoying life that was sometimes a cause of tension. Yet by 1966, having recovered from testicular cancer, Moore remained as skipper. It was hard to imagine anyone else telling him what to do.

His football intelligence allowed him to snuff out danger before it arose. He could rob opponents either with the deftest nick or with wholesome, full-blooded tackles. Timing was everything – and his antidote to a lack of pace. He was a master of possession, advancing steadily from deep then, with an appraising upward glance, delivering a perfect ball, long or short.

Moore's defiance of the Brazilian forward line in 1970 and the coolness and vision he showed through 120 emotional minutes of the 1966 World Cup final eclipse many other imperious performances. Moore was, said Pele, the finest defender in the world. And Pele knew at first hand because Moore, with unfailing elegance, had stopped him in his tracks in a way that few could.

After his playing days were over, Moore tried management with Southend United and a variety of business ventures, but none were a real success and his gifts went to waste. He was working as a radio summariser when cancer once again took a grip. His untimely death in February 1993, aged 51, was mourned throughout football.

Quest for Qualification

Qualification for the 1974 World Cup in West Germany depended on beating Wales and Poland. The first match, at Ninian Park against Wales in November 1972, was Ramsey's 100th in charge of the national team. Only Bobby Moore remained from the earliest days. A few weeks earlier Gordon Banks had been involved in the road crash that cost him an eye and ended his career. Trojans such as Ball, Hunter and Bell were still going strong, but the new key figures were men such as Liverpool defender Emlyn Hughes and Derby County centre half Roy McFarland. According to Alan Ball, 'The new boys were leaning heavily on the older players whereas it was time the older players should have been able to lean on the new ones a bit.'

The game against Wales marked a first cap for Kevin Keegan, along with Liverpool team-mate Ray Clemence. Neither Keegan nor any English player distinguished themselves on the night, but Ramsey's England banked two qualifying points with a 1-0 win. It looked like the start of a formal procession to the World Cup finals. However, all England's failings, the lack of creative midfield power, an attack that misfired and a defence prone to basic errors, were evident in the return at Wembley in January 1973. Wales battled to a 1-1 draw, scoring when Roy McFarland failed to catch the Welsh forwards offside, allowing Leighton James and John Toshack a clear run on Clemence's goal.

Keegan, so vibrant for Liverpool, had another anonymous game and was dropped. Other attackers such as Rodney Marsh of Manchester City, at club

Mick Channon fires at goal but doesn't manage to score on a tragic night at Wembley as England drew 1-1 with Poland and failed to qualify for the 1974 World Cup finals.

The 'clown' Tomaszewski celebrates his magnificent match-winning performance for Poland that heralded the end of Alf Ramsey's term as England manager.

level full of showman's tricks and improvisation, and centre forward Martin Chivers, so potent for Tottenham, failed to gel. Of the new forwards, Mick Channon showed most promise, combining spirit and skill in a way that too often his colleagues lacked.

The stakes were raised for England's match against the Poles in June. As ever, Ramsey laid his plans: solidity in defence, containment the priority. Within seven minutes of taking the field in Katowice, these were in disarray. A poorly defended free kick bounced off Bobby Moore, Peter Shilton fumbled and England were 1-0 down. Two minutes after half-time, Moore attempted a dribble out of defence and lost possession to the Polish forward Lubanski, who fired a low show past Shilton.

The score was bad, but more disturbing was England's inability to respond. Ramsey's team, locked in a pattern of sterile play, then became sucked into ill-tempered exchanges. After defender Cmikiewicz aimed a kick at Martin Peters, at the time lying on the pitch, Alan Ball saw red, grabbed the Pole by the throat, and became the second England player sent off in a full international.

Ramsey, contrary as ever amid apoplectic headlines, insisted the team had played well. But the visit of Poland to Wembley in four months' time became weighted with expectation. Only victory would do. Between times, England won 2-1 in Russia, lost 2-0 in Italy and thrashed Austria 7-0 at Wembley. With just three weeks to go before the Poles arrived, England showed more fluency and sharpness against the Austrians than for ages with Tony Currie of Sheffield United displaying a command in midfield that had long been absent.

England began against Poland with pace and confidence – but a night of outrageous fortune and misfortune unfolded, where Poland's goalkeeper Tomaszewski, portrayed with gusto by Brian Clough as a clown, confounded all those who had made jokes at his expense. Sins of commission and omission in previous matches caught up with England. Individual blunders – those of Moore in Katowice and, on that angst-filled October evening at Wembley, of Norman Hunter – left the team holed beneath the waterline.

Why, on the hour, Hunter failed to clear an undemanding ball that fell to him on the halfway line and set up the Poles to score their killer goal, caused as much mystery as it did trauma. Why Ramsey brought on Kevin Hector of

Great Managers – 1962-74

ALF RAMSEY

Ramsey, free from the burden of craving public acclaim, was the man who got on with the job and made England world champions. Born in Dagenham, where his father traded in hay and straw, army service in wartime delayed his entry into League football. As a soldier, Ramsey made guest appearances for Southampton, where, aged 26, his professional career began.

Ramsey made his debut for England in December 1948, still with Southampton, but then transferred to Tottenham, for whom he excelled. He won 32 caps between 1948 and 1953 and, after leaving Spurs, became manager of Ipswich Town in 1955. With great astuteness, he devised a disciplined 4-3-3 system that exploited the talent available to him and by 1962 had taken Ipswich from the Third Division South to the League Championship.

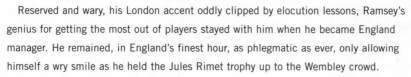

Reserved and wary, his London accent oddly clipped by elocution lessons, Ramsey's genius for getting the most out of players stayed with him when he became England manager. He remained, in England's finest hour, as phlegmatic as ever, only allowing himself a wry smile as he held the Jules Rimet trophy up to the Wembley crowd.

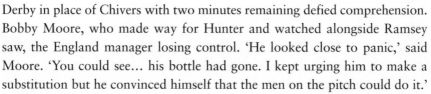

Derby in place of Chivers with two minutes remaining defied comprehension. Bobby Moore, who made way for Hunter and watched alongside Ramsey saw, the England manager losing control. 'He looked close to panic,' said Moore. 'You could see… his bottle had gone. I kept urging him to make a substitution but he convinced himself that the men on the pitch could do it.'

Allan Clarke's penalty equaliser was too little to save England; too little, ultimately, to save Ramsey. Two internationals and six months later, Ramsey's detractors got their way. On 1 May 1974, the man who had moulded England into world champions was summoned to FA headquarters at Lancaster Gate and sacked. Ramsey's enemies finally had their scalp.

Those who had served him regarded Ramsey's dismissal as brutal and short-sighted. In Ball's view, Ramsey was 'a true knight… always a hero in my eyes'. Jimmy Greaves, who had less to thank Ramsey for than Ball, felt the England manager was shabbily treated and, apart from winning the World Cup, that his greatest achievement was bringing to heel 'the amateurs who had

129

50 Greatest Players

MARTIN PETERS Midfielder

Clubs: West Ham United, Tottenham Hotspur
Debut: v Yugoslavia, 4 May 1966
Caps: 67 **Goals:** 20

Ron Greenwood's description of Martin Peters as 'ten years ahead of his time' had something of the epitaph about it. Yet although open to ridicule on Peters' off-days, it captured the essence of his protégé; the wit and anticipation that featured so strongly in Peters' game.

Peters was schooled in the best West Ham tradition. He had, like England team-mates Bobby Moore and Geoff Hurst, an ideal temperament. He went about his work elegantly, moving fluidly about the pitch, striking superb passes and finishing moves with crisply taken goals. The word 'thoroughbred' was commonly used in connection with Peters.

His knack of throwing defences by arriving late and unseen to seize on a scoring opportunity was unrivalled: 'Martin Peters... ghosting in' became a commentator's catch-phrase. Indeed, Peters timed his late run from England hopeful to indispensable member of the 1966 World Cup winning team with just that precision.

For a time, Peters' rise signalled the demise of conventional wingers under Ramsey's management, but whatever his position, Peters' talents were gifts no manager would sacrifice lightly. He was, quite simply, the right player at the right time.

mismanaged English football for so many years'. Alan Mullery, while conscious Ramsey bothered very little with analysing the opposition, felt he was 'without any football weakness... brilliant... very clever tactically'.

He did have tactical triumphs, but latter Ramsey teams appeared inflexible, unable to respond to events, and his use of substitutes was often maladroit. Uncertainty caused him to chop and change. His last match, against Portugal in Lisbon, brought a shoal of six new caps, of whom West Ham midfielder Trevor Brooking and Sunderland centre half Dave Watson would have prolonged England careers. Once ousted though, Ramsey's principal anxiety, having pushed back FA officialdom, was that the tide of functionaries in blazers might roll in again. 'The sad thing is,' he said in his parting shot to journalists, 'that the bloody amateurs are back in command.'

Chapter Eight: 1974-82
Managerial Change

After the gloom, light relief. Temporary charge of England was entrusted to Joe Mercer, who had managed Manchester City with great distinction and whose genial style made him universally popular. Untrammelled by the cares of long-term responsibility, Mercer's mission was to cheer everyone up. It was the shortest of interregnums: five weeks; seven matches. 'We're all going to have a laugh and a joke,' he told the players at their first get-together.

They did, though Mercer's short reign had its hiccups. He recalled Kevin Keegan, whom he had then to extricate from an ugly incident in Belgrade on England's summer tour. Keegan, among a group of players larking around by the luggage carousel, was singled out by airport police, marched off and roughed up. It took Mercer's diplomatic intervention to rescue things and prevent England players walking out on their match with Yugoslavia.

One unhappy member of Mercer's band was Stan Bowles who, substituted in the home international against Northern Ireland and dropped against Scotland, walked out. Another maverick was unearthed to take his place: Frank Worthington, a centre forward of prodigious talent but sybaritic habits. Like many an errant talent, Worthington's appearances in an England shirt were to be limited.

Under Mercer, some newish names became props for England's future: Keegan; Colin Todd of Derby County, a supremely elegant defender; Emlyn Hughes; Mick Channon; and Dave Watson. Those looking to the future went about their business competently, winning three, drawing three and losing only to Scotland in an error-strewn match at Hampden.

Genial Joe Mercer's tenure as England manager was brief but lightened the spirits of the players.

The future, for England, was Don Revie. Steeped in theory since his earliest days as a junior footballer in Middlesbrough, his birthplace, Revie had performed miracles with Leeds United, transforming the Yorkshire club from a rudderless shambles drifting towards the Third Division into League Champions. Unlike Ramsey's Ipswich, Leeds had stayed at the top. They were, in every sense, fearsome, battle-hardened in Europe and packed with footballers as bruising as they were brilliant. Shortly before Ramsey's demise, they won their second League title in five years. Their football could be sublime, or, when desperate, resemble a street fight.

Don Revie signed a five-year deal as manager in 1974 and set about the job in his own unique way.

Revie Pitches for the Job

It was Revie who sought out the FA, and FA Secretary Ted Croker, although mindful of Leeds United's disreputable past, felt the team had, in part, reformed its character. Sir Andrew Stephen, the FA chairman, was enthusiastic. Things moved swiftly and on 4 July 1974 Revie was in charge, armed with a five-year contract.

The first footballing challenge, a European Championship qualifier against Czechoslovakia, was three months away. One of Revie's first acts was to embrace an extraordinary number, 81, of present and potential England players, all of whom he invited to a bonding get-together in Manchester. He negotiated a better financial deal, securing, in addition to their £100 appearance fee, a further £100 for a draw and £200 for a win. He courted journalists, laying on drinks and sandwiches at press conferences. He began battling his old adversary Alan Hardaker, secretary of the Football League, to try to get fixtures postponed the Saturday before an international match. And, his antennae always sensitive to the benefits of the populist gesture, he introduced 'Land of Hope and Glory' as the team's anthem before matches.

Alan Ball, with whom Revie later fell out irreconcilably, had mixed feelings about this first flush of activity. Ball believed the preoccupation with a better financial deal was ill-conceived. 'Every minute of every match in which we wore a white shirt, we were England,' he wrote in his memoir, *It's All About A Ball*. 'Revie acted as though he thought every extra quid... would

Alan Hudson (left) and Alan Ball both benefited from Don Revie's appointment.

ensure players tried just that bid harder.' Ball was, however, much stirred by 'Land of Hope and Glory'. 'I could feel a new upsurge of English pride. The crowd sang as if they meant every word,' he said.

Revie's era started soundly with a 3-0 win over Czechoslovakia, the catalyst a double substitution that brought on Trevor Brooking and, for his first cap, Dave Thomas of Queens Park Rangers. Thomas's team-mate Gerry Francis was also given his international debut. The next European Championship qualifier, against Portugal, an arid 0-0 draw, was less satisfactory. Five months elapsed before England were in action again, at home to West Germany.

By then, Revie had evolved his own way of doing things. Shortly before the game, in March 1975, he made Alan Ball captain in place of Emlyn Hughes, suddenly shunted aside, though recalled in a crisis two years later. Ball's appointment fomented controversy in the light of his poor disciplinary record. Revie also gave a debut to Chelsea midfielder Alan Hudson, whose extravagant talent had long begged testing at the top level. West Germany, albeit with depleted ranks, were rigorous opposition and Hudson played superbly in England's 2-0 win. A month later England beat Cyprus 5-0 in their next European Championship qualifier and Newcastle centre forward Malcolm MacDonald created a post-war record by scoring all the goals. Revie, it seemed, had chosen well from the talent at his disposal.

Yet his mind moved in strange ways. While he sought to replicate the cosy 'family' atmosphere he created among his close-knit bunch at Leeds, complete with parlour games and curfews, Revie mystified players by dropping some without warning. Hudson, so commanding against the

Germans, was discarded, never to be recalled. Keegan was so annoyed at being left out without explanation for a game against Wales that he packed his bags and stormed off. Some managers might never have picked him again but Keegan, though he didn't know it, was a firm favourite. When Revie caught up with him, it was to say he had wanted to rest Keegan so he would be fresh to play Scotland.

Soon Ball was in the camp of the bewildered. Fresh from England's 5-1 rout of the Scots at Wembley in May 1975, the England captain had every reason to be in high feather. Ball, along with Colin Bell and Gerry Francis, had played masterfully, departing for the summer break in high optimism. Yet the 1975-76 season was barely underway when Ball's wife was called by a journalist asking for a reaction to her husband being dropped. Only the following day did Ball receive official notification from Revie's office that Gerry Francis was replacing him as captain, the tone apologetic yet without explanation.

Ball was furious. 'I cherished that England captaincy,' he said. 'I was still convinced that I was as good as any midfield player he had available.' He wondered if it was Revie's riposte to an episode during England's three-day get together at West Park Lodge, when some players went out drinking and broke the midnight curfew. 'If he'd called me in next morning and laid the law down, I'd have stood for it,' said Ball. 'But he said nothing to make me believe, on the strength of that incident, that my international career was over.'

England and Revie Start to Falter

Revie had made a sworn enemy. And England's performance against Scotland would be the last highlight of his managerial reign. Through the season, England looked increasingly disjointed and toiled against mediocre opposition. With poor results against Czechoslovakia and Portugal, Revie's men failed to qualify for the finals of the European championship. New players were tried by the half dozen: the friendly with Wales at Wrexham in March 1976 brought debuts for defenders Trevor Cherry of Leeds United, Phil Neal and Phil Thompson of Liverpool and Mick Doyle of Manchester City. New in attack were Phil Boyer of Norwich and Ray Kennedy of Liverpool, while as substitutes there were Dave Clement of Queens Park Rangers and Peter Taylor of Crystal Palace.

Two months later, as England joined Italy and Brazil for America's bicentennial tournament, four more new faces came in against the Italians: Arsenal goalkeeper Jimmy Rimmer; Chelsea midfielder Ray Wilkins; Manchester United outside left Gordon Hill; and, as substitute for Rimmer, Joe Corrigan of Manchester City. Ted Croker, once a Revie enthusiast, was having second thoughts. 'He was changing his mind all the time... it changed my whole outlook on the sort of person who was a good England manager,' Croker said. 'Alf Ramsey never asked a player to do a job he didn't do for his club. But Don, because at Leeds he had tremendous success playing one or two people in different roles, rather got the impression he could do it at England... Alf judged a player by international appearances.'

Revie's allsorts happened to prosper against Italy in America, overturning a 2-0 deficit to win 3-2. However, much more serious business with the Italians beckoned in the autumn, when World Cup qualification would be contested. By then, life for Revie, already pathologically uncertain about who played best and where, was further complicated by the need to shore up a midfield left threadbare by injuries to Colin Bell and Gerry Francis.

The first World Cup qualifier, against Finland in June 1976, went according to plan: a 4-1 win on a bumpy pitch illuminated by the intelligent scheming of Trevor Brooking and Francis, and the vigorous forward play of Channon and Keegan. But in the return three months later, England appeared infected by self-doubt and alarmingly vulnerable to counter-attacks. Revie's team won 2-1, yet left Wembley to growls of discontent: a gloomy omen for the heavyweight encounter in Rome four months later. There, Revie picked a team that showed timidity at work in his mind. Emlyn Hughes and Stan Bowles – the latter by popular demand – were recalled from exile and Brian Greenhoff was pitched into midfield. The outcome was dismally predictable: England overrun; Bowles isolated; the attack a blunt instrument. Italy's 2-0 win crushed England's ambitions of joining the World Cup throng in Argentina.

In February 1977, Holland, their ranks blessed with Cruyff, Neeskens, Rep and van de Kerkhof, came to Wembley for a friendly and played Revie's men off the pitch with a 2-0 victory that was frighteningly stylish and incisive. The world was on Revie's back. Mick Channon, the player most capped by Revie, had a clear view of Revie's failings. 'He went overboard with tactics,' Channon said. 'Eventually your mind was full of too much... you could end up a nervous wreck. Players aren't really that intelligent. They just want to play football. He was so enthusiastic and wanted everyone to have the same enthusiasm. I think he felt frustrated that everyone didn't feel the same.'

Revie's passion for parlour games and boarding school rules was mocked by a group of players who met up only occasionally. 'He wanted the England team to be his boys like at Leeds,' said Channon. 'He was trying to do everything right but just having the mickey taken out of him. You sensed his

England's team to face Argentina in Buenos Aires in June 1977 was unaware of Revie's impending departure. England earned a hard-fought 1-1 draw.

frustration. He was a very nervous man... he would sweat through nerves. I don't think he could trust anyone... he thought everyone was going to do him. If you analyse it, you have to say he lost control.'

Channon's diagnosis of paranoia was borne out by events. Revie sensed a conspiracy to oust him and began plotting his escape. An offer of the financial security he craved had come from the United Arab Emirates, where he had been approached to take over the national team. World Cup qualification hung by a thread; the critics became deafening after dismal defeats against Wales and Scotland in the home internationals. By early summer, Revie's mind was made up.

He began choreographing his defection during England's summer tour to South America. Les Cocker was put in charge during the early stages as players were told Revie had flown to Helsinki to watch the Italians in their World Cup qualifier against Finland. What no one knew was that he had first been out to Dubai to cement a deal with the Emirates.

When Revie finally arrived in Buenos Aires, he approached Dick Wragg, chairman of the FA International Committee, and asked for his contract, along with that of Les Cocker, to be paid up for the two remaining years. Revie said he was convinced that the FA was about to sack him. Wragg was astounded, as was Ted Croker, who told the England manager to see the job through. 'To say he was leaving England in the lurch and that he wanted paying off for the privilege was laughable,' said Croker.

Under the circumstances, the tour, three hard-fought draws against Brazil, Argentina and Uruguay, was a surprising success. Far from being sacked, Revie was approached about renewing his contract. At the time, he was non-committal. On 12 July 1977 the world found out why. 'Nearly everyone in the country seems to want me out. So I'm giving them what they want,' Revie announced.

50 Greatest Players

ALAN BALL Midfielder

Clubs: Blackpool, Everton, Arsenal
Debut: v Yugoslavia, 9 May 1965
Caps: 72 **Goals:** 8

Ball, one of a select band to be capped before the age of 20, combined energy, commitment and talent to miraculous effect. Few in England's history have been blessed with greater stamina. He was a motor, a galvanising force, and the sight of Ball flagging, whatever the conditions, was almost unknown.

His arresting display of running, passing and tackling over 120 minutes helped drive England to victory over West Germany in the 1966 World Cup final. Alf Ramsey, rarely given to hyperbole, told Ball afterwards: 'Young man, you will never play a better game of football than you did today.'

Ramsey was right, although Ball did give many other stirring performances, and in England's 5-1 win over Scotland at Wembley nine years later he showed that his fire was undimmed as he and Gerry Francis bestrode midfield to thrilling effect.

With so passionate a temperament, some of Ball's encounters were bound to end in acrimony. As, indeed, did his England career, after he was mysteriously ditched as captain by Don Revie, when manifestly he still had more to give. Yet inauspicious though this swansong was, Ball's credentials stand alongside the best. He made the most of his gifts and rarely was potential more fulfilled.

His defection to the United Arab Emirates was a terrific scoop for Jeff Powell of the *Daily Mail*, a long-standing confidant, who had travelled with Revie from Britain to the Middle East. But few applauded at Lancaster Gate, where formal notice of Revie's resignation arrived after it was front page news. The ex-England manager's deal with the Arabs amounted to £340,000 over four years: small wonder he was portrayed as a soccer mercenary.

A messy legal wrangle ensued. Revie was accused of bringing the game into disrepute on four counts, one being that, through breach of contract, he had set a bad example to all. After a hearing that began in December 1978, the FA Commission banned Revie from any involvement in English football for ten years. It took another year, following a high court hearing spread over

18 days, for Revie to get the ban overturned. But the damage was done and his reputation was tarnished forever.

England, meanwhile, were left with the near hopeless task of trying to qualify for the World Cup. There was a sense of immediacy, verging towards crisis, about the need to fill the breach. The FA turned to former West Ham manager Ron Greenwood, 55 and semi-retired, initially on a caretaker basis. 'I had to help restore faith in the game and prove we could still play,' said Greenwood. 'Revie's defection damaged the reputation and morale of our game and that was unforgivable.'

Greenwood was a disciple of Walter Winterbottom, 'who opened my eyes to a brave new world of coaching and changed the whole direction of my life.' He coached the England youth and U-23 teams and in 1963 was considered as Winterbottom's possible successor. Greenwood differed from his two predecessors in caring 'more about purity and the finer values of football than about winning for winning's sake'. He attempted to practise what he preached while managing West Ham, but in 1974 he had retreated to the role of general manager at Upton Park and, cut off from daily contact with players, had grown increasingly depressed. However, a clarion call from Sir Harold Thompson, the gruff, often abrasive chairman of the FA, unexpectedly propelled Greenwood back to the heart of the game.

A man with a cerebral, mild-mannered air, Greenwood was formally appointed on 17 August 1977. He was a strategist and, once established, persuaded the FA to let him appoint a team of managers and coaches to run the international side at all levels, giving the set-up a continuity it had always lacked. Meanwhile, for his first game, he drew heavily on players from Liverpool, hoping that club success – Liverpool had just won the European Cup – would be replicated. Six were picked against Switzerland at Wembley in September: Ray Clemence, Phil Neal, Terry McDermott, Emlyn Hughes, Ray Kennedy and, for the first time in 11 years, Ian Callaghan. Kevin Keegan, now playing in Hamburg, was in, too, but the team failed to spark. The Swiss defended cannily, English forwards often got in each other's way and the game ended 0-0.

England's next two matches were the last rites of their ailing campaign to qualify for the World Cup. Goal difference was everything, but away to Luxembourg in October, they managed only two in a pallid display. Italy came to Wembley in November with qualification almost a formality, but that did not detract from England's best display for more than two years. It was a 2-0 win stamped with colour and conviction, in which new caps Peter Barnes of Manchester City and Steve Coppell of

Manchester United roamed spiritedly down the flanks, and Brooking and Keegan combined superbly.

Victory for Italy over Luxembourg put England out of her misery. Greenwood, or whomever would get the job permanently, could start afresh. The FA selection committee sat in December to make its choice. Greenwood's rivals were Brian Clough of Nottingham Forest, Bobby Robson of Ipswich, Dave Sexton of Manchester United, Jack Charlton of Sheffield Wednesday and Lawrie McMenemy of Southampton. Clough was the choice of the masses but the job went to the incumbent. He was, in Jimmy Greaves' view, 'the right man at the wrong time', his appointment, after Revie, 'like inviting a village vicar to take over from a foot-in-the-door salesman'.

Greenwood Restores Order

Greenwood's reign proper began with heavyweight friendlies against West Germany in Munich and Brazil at Wembley. England, pepped up by a tireless, invigorating performance from Kevin Keegan and astute midfield contributions from Wilkins and Brooking, might have extracted an honourable draw from Germany but for losing concentration near the end and allowing Bonhof to score with a rasping free kick. Two months later, the Brazilians displayed the dark, cynical side that sometimes overcame them, their creative talent rarely visible as they kicked England players with impunity, gouging out a 1-1 draw.

A clean sweep of victories in the 1978 home internationals suggested Greenwood had restored order in the ranks. There followed an electrifying 4-1 victory over Hungary at Wembley with what Greenwood regarded as his best side: Shilton, Neal, Watson, Hughes, Mick Mills of Ipswich, Wilkins, Brooking, Keegan, Coppell, Trevor Francis of Nottingham Forest and Barnes. It was a team full of pace and invention, one that, in playing with a sense of enjoyment, fulfilled a Greenwood credo.

England then set out to qualify for the European championships. The first match, against Denmark in Copenhagen, quivered with mistakes, fierce tackles, fine goals and inspired moments, particularly those that flowed from Brooking, for whom Keegan was so obliging an outlet. Victory against the Danes was a happy omen: England worked their way undefeated through a qualifying group that included Northern Ireland, the Republic of Ireland and Bulgaria. New figures emerged: Kenny Sansom, the Crystal Palace left back, capped in a dour goalless draw against Wales in May 1979; Tottenham midfielder Glenn Hoddle, whose first game was England's 2-0 defeat of Bulgaria in November 1979; and West Bromwich midfielder Bryan

Ron Greenwood's appointment to replace Don Revie was like 'inviting a village vicar to take over from a foot-in-the-door salesman' according to Jimmy Greaves.

Robson, a debutant in February 1980 when England beat the Republic 2-0 at Wembley.

England departed for the European Championship in Italy having won 20 and lost only three games under the Greenwood regime. Their first opponents, in a group that also included Italy and Spain, were Belgium, against whom the finer things – Wilkins' inspired outwitting of an offside-trap and deftly lobbed goal and Ceuleman's ferocious equaliser from a corner poorly cleared – were obliterated by hooliganism. The abiding memories were of a match derailed by brawling spectators and clouds of tear gas.

Greenwood, feeling the need for victory over Italy was urgent, surprised many by choosing a strike force that included the rough-cut Garry Birtles of Nottingham Forest alongside team-mate Tony Woodcock. The Italians, with their usual amalgam of wit and thuggery, knew too much for an England team that was solid but, fielding Ray Kennedy in place of Brooking, lacked ingenuity. When Neal sold himself with a tackle on the right and, from Graziani's cross, Tardelli scored the only goal of a tight game, England's prospects of advancement looked bleak. A 2-1 victory over Spain, for all the co-ordinated neatness in midfield and Clemence's penalty save from Tardi, was too little to keep them in the tournament.

An arduous season for Hamburg had left Keegan with ligament trouble that blunted his pace. Keegan's verdict was, 'We failed abysmally in our group, but now we have a gauge for the World Cup.' Four months later, the long qualifying preamble got underway but without Keegan, by now a Southampton player, whose season was to be plagued by injury.

The pleasure of England's 4-0 victory over Norway in September 1980 – a result more emphatic than the performance – was soon dissipated by a 2-1 defeat in Romania. Injuries that left Greenwood with a makeshift midfield, and a dubious penalty in favour of the home team, conspired against him. But a 2-1 victory over Switzerland at Wembley, with Brooking restored and Bryan Robson increasingly authoritative, revived England's campaign to make it to the 1982 World Cup in Spain.

As the year turned, though, form and fortune dipped miserably. England endured six matches without victory, losing at home to Spain, Brazil and Scotland, and, crucially, 2-1 away to Switzerland in another World Cup qualifier. The knockers gradually got to Greenwood. 'I could sense people looking at me as if I had committed some crime,' he wrote later. 'We had been badly hit by injuries but they were still my teams, playing my way, which had been failing.'

Greenwood to Go?

Within minutes of the final whistle in Basle, Greenwood felt the time had come to quit. Ted Croker and Dick Wragg tried, without success, to dissuade him, but an announcement was delayed as England remained in Switzerland to train for their next qualifier in Hungary a week later. Greenwood prepared with unaccustomed vigour, working tirelessly at the basics. He chose a combination that could both press back the Hungarians and pull apart their defence with dummies and runs. At the heart of things, once more, were Keegan and Brooking, who scored all the goals in England's 3-1 win. The result was a triumph of tactics and England's recuperative powers.

Yet Greenwood remained determined to quit. A statement was due at Luton airport after the plane landed, but during the flight home Greenwood told the players. There was, he said, general disbelief followed by an impromptu campaign to change his mind. It worked. 'What counted most of all was the players' attitude,' Greenwood said. 'They were the best bunch of lads a manager ever had.'

And so it was business as usual – with knocks still in store. Defeat in Norway, 2-1, after taking the lead, was unpalatable and looked to have snuffed out hopes of World Cup qualification. As the press revived calls for his head and accused players of being more interested in money than

50 Greatest Players

PETER SHILTON Goalkeeper

Clubs: Leicester City, Stoke City, Nottingham Forest,
Southampton, Derby County
Debut: v East Germany, 25 November 1970
Appearances: 125

Who but Peter Shilton would have enabled Leicester City to
contemplate selling Gordon Banks, the world's best
goalkeeper? When just 13, Shilton, with his precocious
talent, had caught Banks' eye. 'This lad's a good 'un,'
he said laconically to Leicester trainer George Dewis.
'He'll be having you out of the team soon,' replied
Dewis prophetically.

Shilton observed and aped all Banks' best habits: the
extra practice at stopping shots, the fanatical dedication to
fitness. He had magnificent reflexes and agility and a great
command of his area. He started shouting at fellow international
defenders in 1970 and was still at it 20 years later, aged 40, signing off in 1990 after
England's splendid World Cup campaign in Italy. 'He liked making a noise,' said Ron
Greenwood. 'It reassures the defenders that there is someone behind them.'

His flaws were few. In Greenwood's eyes these were a weakness at the back post and
an occasional failure to extend his arms to their full extent, but on other days his
singular defiance of forward lines, his large frame an insuperable obstacle, suggested,
if anything, he was superhuman.

national pride, Greenwood was entitled to think that resignation might, after
all, have been a better option.

But miraculously, other group results went his way. Greenwood's
benefactors were the Swiss – 'bless all their mountains, cuckoo clocks and
financial gnomes' – who contrived to beat Romania in Bucharest, lose in
Hungary and draw the home return with Romanians. The convoluted
arithmetic meant England only needed to draw with Hungary at Wembley to
get to Spain. Greenwood opted for solid, in-form players: Peter Shilton was
preferred to Clemence in goal; West Ham's Alvin Martin to Ipswich's Russell
Osman in central defence; Brooking for the unpredictable Hoddle in
midfield; and Steve Coppell, who had served him so well down the right, for

Trevor Francis. Coppell's return, though, was ill-starred and harsh treatment from Hungarian defenders precipitated the knee trouble that, in time, would force him out of the game.

The force was with Greenwood and his men. A crowd of 92,000 packed Wembley on the night of 18 November 1981 with a will for England to win. They did so comprehensively against a Hungarian team that had already qualified and had a blunted appetite. A goal from Ipswich Town's Paul Mariner divided the teams. England were, for the first time in 12 years, back at the World Cup finals.

Spanish Adventure

In planning, even in public relations, England went well prepared. The team made its base near Bilbao, having beguiled the locals by playing a testimonial

50 Greatest Players

RAY CLEMENCE Goalkeeper

Clubs: Liverpool, Tottenham Hotspur
Debut: v Wales, 15 November 1972
Appearances: 61

But for Peter Shilton, Ray Clemence might have been unchallenged in the England goal for a dozen years or more. Whatever problems England had outfield, managers from Ramsey to Robson had two of the world's finest goalkeepers at their disposal.

Greenwood couldn't decide who was best and so alternated them. He picked Shilton for the 1982 World Cup in Spain, principally because of his club form. For Clemence, his England career must, at times, have seemed like being second among equals. Yet in some ways Greenwood thought him superior: 'The speed and understanding with which he went to the source of any trouble... Ray was like a third back.' Gordon Banks put Clemence, 'no more than a fingertip behind Shilton when it comes to class and consistency'.

Bobby Robson, who eventually committed himself to Shilton, admitted that at one time there was nothing between the two. Clemence was a tall commanding figure with long arms, good on corners and crosses, with an agility that enabled him to make vital saves. 'The country was lucky in the extreme to have them both,' said Robson.

Bryan Robson scored twice in England's World Cup opener against France in Bilbao in 1982. Paul Mariner added a third in a 3-1 victory.

against the city's club team Athletic Bilbao. It paved the way for England to use Athletic's splendid training facilities, ten miles from their hotel, where Greenwood began plotting his course and choice of personnel.

He had long alternated Clemence and Shilton in goal, whom he regarded of equal calibre. The events of 1970, where an inexperienced Peter Bonetti was thrust into the Guadalajara cauldron, lodged in Greenwood's mind. He had brought both keepers but, after much soul-searching, plumped for Shilton, who was relentlessly dedicated and, on club form, the more confident. But if spoiled for choice in goal, injury had deprived Greenwood of his two diamonds, Keegan and Brooking. For the first game against France, he built the team around Mick Mills; central defenders Phil Thompson and Terry Butcher of Ipswich Town – 'still growing in authority'; and, in midfield, Robson and Wilkins. His strike force would rely on the pace of Trevor Francis and the honest toil and opportunism of Ipswich's Paul Mariner.

On a sweltering day in Bilbao, England had a sensational start, with Bryan Robson scoring after 27 seconds, exploiting French defensive lethargy after Butcher knocked down a throw-in from Steve Coppell. France regrouped, gathered their wits and equalised in 25 minutes through Soler, after Francis conceded possession. England made midfield tactical adjustments at half time and regained the lead on 66 minutes as Robson

50 Greatest Players

KEVIN KEEGAN Inside forward

Clubs: Liverpool, SV Hamburg, Southampton
Debut: v Wales, 15 November 1972
Appearances: 63   **Goals:** 21

The incandescent effect Keegan had as soon as he joined
Liverpool from Scunthorpe did not transfer immediately to
England. He made his debut alongside team-mate Ray
Clemence but, in a faltering side, struggled to make an
impact in early games. No matter. Before long he would hit
his stride. Keegan was never a man to be kept down.

He was a classic self-made footballer, less a natural than
many whose comparative achievements pale into
insignificance, but ferociously competitive against himself
and the world. He constantly demanded practice,
dedicating himself to the difficult things, such as hitting crosses on the turn
or the defender's art of man-marking.

Keegan yearned to be the complete footballer, to make an impact everywhere he could.
For his height, he was abnormally good in the air, directing goal-bound headers with power
and precision. Sometimes he would astonish as a last line of defence, once appearing, as if
by magic, in a European championship qualifier against Bulgaria to clear a goal-bound shot
off the line.

One of the pleasures of watching England was the handsome understanding Keegan
struck up with Trevor Brooking, based on the former's willingness to run and the
latter's ingenuity. Both would have graced a sustained assault on the World Cup; both
were fated with less than half an hour's action, against Spain in 1982. In another era,
the glittering prizes might have come their way.

hurtled forward from nowhere to head home Trevor Francis' right wing
cross. England's third, and Mariner's fifth goal in as many internationals,
sealed an impressive victory.

The same 11 players ground out a 2-0 win over Czechoslovakia. This was
a scrappier match, but it ensured progress to the next group stages. Keegan,
his back still a problem and frustrated at having to kick his heels, stole away
to see his specialist in Hamburg, while Greenwood grappled with other
injury concerns – to Clemence and third choice goalkeeper Joe Corrigan, and
Bryan Robson's groin strain. Hoddle was Robson's replacement in the third

50 Greatest Players

TREVOR BROOKING Midfielder

Club: West Ham United
Debut: v Portugal, 3 April 1974
Appearances: 47   **Goals:** 5

In the lexicon of adjectives attached to footballers, 'cultured' is commonly applied to Trevor Brooking, one of six players capped in what became Alf Ramsey's last match as England manager.

Brooking was a distinguished graduate of the West Ham academy that habitually produced creative footballers with an optimistic side to their game. Small wonder he flourished under Ron Greenwood's management of England or that he should combine so well with Kevin Keegan, a kindred spirit in many ways. Keegan felt Brooking was a luxury 'every team ought to afford'.

Blessed with the brain and technique to create time and space, if not great pace, he could, for someone so seemingly benign, inflict untold damage on opposing defences, striking long, perfect passes. This was a key part of his act with Keegan, though sometimes they reversed the roles with Keegan turning provider and Brooking becoming the breaking forward. Rarely did the two perform better in tandem than in England's European Championship qualifier against Denmark in September 1978, a 4-3 thriller – the apotheosis of Brooking's appetizing style of football.

group match against Kuwait, a dour encounter enriched only by a fine goal from Francis that concluded his long incisive run.

Flashes of such quality would be essential if England were to break down the European champions West Germany, their opponents in the second stage, and Spain, the hosts. England moved camp to Madrid and, against the Germans, Greenwood despatched those who had beaten France and Czechoslovakia. The match, for all that was at stake, was a stultifying 0-0 draw, the triumph of caution over ambition.

Under the convoluted competition rules, England had to beat Spain, who had made spluttering progress throughout, by two goals to reach the semi-final. Greenwood watched Spain's 2-1 defeat by the Germans and 'saw nothing to fear'. Brooking and Keegan, meanwhile, were edging closer to full fitness. A bolder spirit might have gambled on them. 'I was definitely fit and so was Trevor,' Keegan claimed in his autobiography. 'Leaving us on the bench was Ron Greenwood's biggest mistake. We were his two best players; we were very influential.'

But Greenwood had too many doubts. What happened has become part of England folklore. His team played with purpose yet failed to pierce an inferior side until, with 27 minutes left, he threw on his 'two trumps' for their first – and last – taste of World Cup action. They caused havoc, yet Keegan missed an open goal, heading wide from Robson's cross, and Brooking, surging through Spanish lines, might have scored but instead forced a fine save from goalkeeper Arconada. Once again, England had a match by the throat but failed to win. They drew 0-0. England's interest in this World Cup was at an end.

Greenwood – and this time he meant it – announced his retirement. The verdict on his reign was mixed. 'Simply not bright or good enough,' according to Brian Glanville, who also issued a backhanded compliment to coach Don Howe's 'careful negativity'. While many appreciated the dignity Greenwood restored to the post of England manager, the word 'negative' became inextricable from judgements of his World Cup campaign. It was a charge Greenwood denied. 'Never, not once, did we take to the field with defence in mind. England, in my five years... were always sent out to win.'

With only a few minutes left, Kevin Keegan heads wide of the Spanish goal. The match ended 0-0 and England went out of the 1982 World Cup in the Second Round.

After Greenwood departed – Bobby Robson was anointed successor before the World Cup campaign had finished – he vented his feelings about the impossibility of the job. 'In England, the clubs rule,' he said. 'In the fattest and oldest professional league in the world… tournaments fill a ten-month season to the limit. A handy package of improvements would include… a firm acceptance that England's needs take priority over those of the clubs and a commitment to new ideas, enlightened coaching and serious study on the continent by our managers.' Greenwood's *cri de coeur* in retirement could so easily have come 30 years earlier from his old mentor, Walter Winterbottom.

Great Managers – 1977-82

RON GREENWOOD

In the wake of Don Revie's defection to the United Arab Emirates, the England set-up was rudderless and morale was low. Greenwood's restoration of stability and a sense of self-respect to the England international camp fell short of greatness, but should not be underestimated.

Steeped in theory and a dedicated coach – there was none finer, according to Geoff Hurst – some criticised him for a lack of charisma and inspiration. Greatly removed by age from his players (Greenwood was 55 when called out of semi-retirement) he would never keep them all happy. But he did command respect.

Greenwood joined Chelsea just before the outbreak of the war. He served in the RAF, re-joined the London club briefly after war ended, then transferred to Bradford Park Avenue, where he played wing half. He switched to centre half, eventually returning via Brentford to Chelsea, where he won a League Championship medal in 1955.

He was a constructive, strong tackling player and a deep thinker about the game, inspired, like others, to learn more after Hungary's demolition of England at Wembley in 1953. He coached England U-23s and took over as West Ham manager in 1961, where he remained in charge until 1974.

Chapter Nine: 1982-90
The Robson Years

Bobby Robson, once critical of Greenwood from the sidelines, was quick to show humility after exposure to the heat of the job. 'When I took over, I was a million miles away from understanding the unique demands,' he said. 'The problems come in all shapes and guises.' After the intimacy of Suffolk and the trustworthy patrician directors at Ipswich, Lancaster Gate, with its plots and politics, was a foreign land.

Before long, Robson waded into controversy, dispensing with Kevin Keegan, who had won 63 caps and been described by Greenwood as 'a rare and brilliant little chap'. Keegan's indignation was intense. 'I had to learn from the press,' he said. 'That was so hurtful. I had captained England for 30-odd games and twice been voted European Footballer of the Year. The players saw me as a figurehead.'

Robson was also to rebuild without Trevor Brooking, for whom 1982 was the finale of a fine career. The new England manager had less than three months to mould his first side for a European championship qualifier against Denmark in Copenhagen. Ray Wilkins, playing his 53rd international, was made captain, but there was no drastic dismantling by Robson of his inheritance. The only new cap, as substitute, was Luton Town midfielder Ricky Hill. A last-minute equaliser from Jesper Olsen made the score 2-2 and denied Robson his first victory. For the Danes that would have been rough justice, as they were often only kept at bay by Peter Shilton. On the terraces, hooligans performed their oafish rituals, a miserably commonplace feature of England's travels abroad.

England's first match at Wembley under Robson, against West Germany, showed the crucial importance of top class attackers. Germany, 2-1 winners, had them in Karl-Heinz Rummenigge and Pierre Littbarski, whereas England did not. Robson, though, drew

Bobby Robson was quick to realize the enormity of the England manager's job.

50 Greatest Players

RAY WILKINS Midfielder

Clubs: Chelsea, Manchester United, AC Milan
Debut: v Italy, 28 May 1976
Appearances: 84   **Goals:** 3

Ray Wilkins was more appreciated by managers and fellow professionals than by the man in the crowd. He was a connoisseur's player of precocious ability, though he often infuriated fans by playing innocuous short, square balls instead of taking a more adventurous option.

Ron Greenwood, however, saw Wilkins not as a negative figure but as 'a composed mature innovator who draws others into the game, slows things down or quickens them up to order and takes on responsibility.' Wilkins was a natural leader – not a clenched fist ranter but a man with a broad vision of the game, who valued possession and hated wasting the ball.

And he was capable of dazzling moments of inspiration. His goal in the 1980 European Championships, when he first lobbed the ball over Belgian defenders and then over the goalkeeper, showed technique of the highest order and uncharacteristic impudence. Perhaps the only shame of Ray Wilkins' career is that the world would have liked to have seen more of this flamboyant side of his football.

satisfaction from an assured debut by Tottenham defender Gary Mabbutt, who also hit the post with a powerful cross shot in the first half.

The next European qualifier, against Greece in Athens, went better. A makeshift team reshaped by injury, in which Bryan Robson was made captain for the first time, set to with gusto on a rain-soaked pitch. Robson, who had grown in stature and profile since transferring from West Bromwich to Manchester United, excelled in midfield alongside Liverpool's Sammy Lee and Mabbutt, auxiliary replacements for Wilkins and Hoddle. England won 3-0, and then a month later thumped Luxembourg 9-0 at Wembley.

Soon Robson would be reacquainted with the fickleness of those who, on good days, sang his praises. The return against Greece at Wembley in March 1983 was a 0-0 draw of unspeakable dreariness, though atoned for in part when England bounced back with a 2-0 win over Hungary. Experiments in selection came thick and fast and with them the sense that Robson, like Revie and occasionally Ramsey, was flailing around. The grim fare of summer 1983, the indifferent players passing through a revolving door, honed Fleet Street's desire for excoriation. The European championship qualifier against Denmark at Wembley in September – only group winners would progress to the finals – assumed a terrifying significance. 'Robson... knows his credibility will be on the line,' intoned the *News of the World*. There was, as Robson later admitted, something fearfully defensive about his pre-match team talk, which accentuated the talents of the opposition. 'I think it made them freeze... I should have given our lads more confidence by talking them up,' he said.

The vibrant Danes were, indeed, too much. They constantly pulled England apart, though the match was settled by a 37th minute penalty from Allan Simonsen. Bryan Robson, absent injured, was badly missed, but the absence of one man alone could not explain away England's deficiencies. The critics pounced. 'Robson did so pathetically little with pathetically little,' wrote Brian Glanville. 'He sticks to bad players, leaves out good ones and seems to listen to dubious advice.'

More vilification came in 1984 as the tabloids sought to out-do one another after defeats in France, 2-0, Wales, 1-0, and at home to Russia, 2-0, the last of which triggered a 'Robson out' demonstration. An escape route beckoned – Barcelona had made an offer for his services – but, with three years on his contract left to run, Robson felt obliged to tough things out. In this respect, he was made of sterner stuff than Don Revie.

The bedrock of his side comprised players such as Shilton, Sansom at left back, Wilkins and Robson in midfield, and Woodcock, in striking partnership with various others. Perhaps only Shilton and Robson were emphatically world class, but there was young talent alongside journeymen stopgaps. John Barnes, the Jamaican-born winger playing for Watford, who made his debut in May 1983

Allan Simonsen's penalty nestles in the back of Peter Shilton's net, putting England's qualification for the 1984 European Championship in serious doubt.

151

50 Greatest Players

GLENN HODDLE Midfielder

Clubs: Tottenham Hotspur, Monaco
Debut: v Bulgaria, 22 November 1979
Appearances: 53   **Goals:** 8

'Hoddle's case was the classical one in the history of English football: the brilliant unorthodox footballer who worries the mediocrities.' The judgement of Brian Glanville could be an examination question.

When Hoddle made his debut against the Bulgarians, a brilliant future seemed to beckon. His mastery of midfield passing and his ability to strike stunning goals from distance were in evidence. But the great Hoddle debate revolved around inconsistency: why could he not do it more often? Ron Greenwood felt his control was of 'Brazilian quality' but that he drifted into bad positions, failed to take a game by the throat and was over-fond of the long ball.

Hoddle then became thwarted by Bobby Robson's preferences in midfield. When the centre was dominated by Bryan Robson and Wilkins, Hoddle, if he were to be accommodated, was pushed out wide, where he was far less effective. When injury to Robson and the suspension of Wilkins forced changes during the 1986 World Cup, Hoddle assumed his favoured territory and was much improved.

The judgement of his peers is interesting. Gary Lineker described him as 'a striker's dream... I would make runs that were never seen by most people but always seen by him.' He was, though, conspicuously absent from Bobby Robson's dream team. Long will the Hoddle debate continue.

during England's 0-0 draw against Northern Ireland in Belfast, had extravagant gifts. The 1-1 draw with Scotland at Hampden in May 1984 – the match that laid to rest the long-ailing home international championship – brought a first appearance, as substitute, by Leicester City striker Gary Lineker. It did not, however, mark Lineker's inexorable rise to fame and a further nine internationals elapsed before he had his first full 90 minutes in a friendly against the Republic of Ireland in March 1985.

With his reputation in shreds, yet sticking to his task, Robson took England on a summer tour of South America. There, as if sunlight had punched through a blanket of cloud, his team – and John Barnes in particular – found themselves bathing in superlatives. Set against all that preceded it, a score of Brazil 0, England 2, took some swallowing.

The crowning moment was, of course, Barnes' mesmerising serpentine dribble and audacious goal. But Barnes, then just 20, kept it in more perspective than most, claiming that in a more competitive game, one Brazilian defender or another would have dispossessed him. Yet England had, collectively, been more solid and confident that for some time. Other young players, such as Mark Chamberlain of Stoke City on the right flank and Portsmouth centre forward Mark Hateley, whose imperious header clinched victory, played with heart and poise. The radiance of so deliciously unexpected a win did much to mitigate defeat in Uruguay and a sterile 0-0 draw in Chile.

The campaign to qualify for the 1986 World Cup in Mexico began four months later. England's group contenders were Finland; Northern Ireland; Turkey and Romania. Suddenly goals came more easily, even if the opposition was modest: five, without reply, against Finland at Wembley in October 1984; within four weeks, eight against the Turks in Istanbul. England then extracted a 0-0 draw from Romania in May 1985; and despite scratchy draws against Finland in Helsinki (1-1) and the Romanians at Wembley (also 1-1), results elsewhere went in Robson's favour. On October 16 1985, Northern Ireland, whom England had conquered 1-0 at Windsor Park, beat Romania 1-0 in Bucharest. This meant England had qualified for Mexico 86 without the ordeal of some last minute scramble. Later that day they celebrated with a 5-0 hammering of Turkey, topped with a hat-trick from Lineker.

A summer tour of Mexico and the USA had given Robson and his hopefuls a taste of heat, altitude, and what may lie ahead. Rising stars such as Barnes, Lineker, Hateley – whose move to AC Milan made him a connoisseur of unyielding defences – and Chris Waddle of Newcastle United sometimes misfired but had skills that would serve England well. Lineker showed signs of evolving into that most precious commodity, a reliable goalscorer.

But by then, perceptions of England were inextricably linked to the conduct of its football fans. The behaviour of Liverpool supporters before the 1985 European Cup final against Juventus in the Heysel stadium, Brussels, had ended with the deaths of 39 fans, mainly Italians. Robson's dismay was sharpened by a more pragmatic concern: that a ban on English clubs from European competition might restrict the development of his players. Yet despite being saddled with the notoriety of pariah football state, England headed for Mexico in good heart and reasonable form, unbeaten in

50 Greatest Players

JOHN BARNES Winger

Clubs: Watford, Liverpool
Debut: v Northern Ireland, 28 May 1983
Appearances: 79   **Goals:** 11

John Barnes' virtuoso goal against Brazil so early in his international career became something of a curse. Spectators came to expect the same magic in every game, but football is never that simple; certainly not for Barnes, one of England's more complex, enigmatic talents.

Whatever the status of the Brazilian encounter, it proved that Barnes' ball skills were of the highest calibre, yet such moments were not easily replicated and, as an eager-to-please young man, he would embark on other mazy dribbles but lose possession, often making him the first target for fickle fans.

For all his unhurried air, Barnes was, he says, as committed to England as anyone, though he was frustrated not to be deployed in a more central role. When, free from injury, things clicked and everyone was on the same wavelength, Barnes was a glorious sight – a powerful runner with electrifying pace yet graceful; his spectacular shots the stuff of schoolboy fantasy. England would have been the poorer without him yet, too often, his genius lay fallow.

11 matches. Glenn Hoddle's potential had been unlocked with a move from wide to central midfield. In defence, Sansom and Butcher were steady and resourceful. Lineker looked as good a finisher as any, with Trevor Steven of Everton a neat, intelligent prompter on the left flank. Yet there were problems: a knee operation had blunted Hateley's edge and Bryan Robson's often dislocated shoulder was by no means right.

The Cauldron of Mexico 1986

So much for good omens. Mexico 1986 began with the most dismal of defeats, with England vanquished 1-0 in Monterrey by a mediocre Portuguese side. Almost unimaginably, things looked set to worsen against Morocco when, in seven mad minutes before half-time, Robson ended a brave forward

With mounting pressure on manager Robson, Gary Lineker scored three goals against Poland in their last group game, the win putting England through to the second round.

run goal by falling over and damaging his shoulder yet again, while Wilkins was dismissed for dissent, registering disgust at an offside decision by throwing the ball towards the referee. Mercifully for England, Morocco, like many a moderate side, could not milk numerical advantage. They retreated, allowing Glenn Hoddle to command midfield and pull strings.

England grasped the lifeline given by a 0-0 draw. Among productive changes made for the match against Poland was the replacement of Hateley by Peter Beardsley of Newcastle United. Beardsley and Lineker hit it off beautifully; the latter scoring a hat-trick within 26 minutes that displayed sharpness, anticipation and neat execution. Poland were sunk. England's 3-0 win and results elsewhere in the group delivered them to the second round. Meanwhile the popular press was in pendulous form. After Portugal, England were 'World Cup Wallies'; but after Poland, it was a case of 'Robson Lionhearts are on the March'.

In Mexico City, a match against Paraguay awaited; trial by skill and provocation. But English tails were up; the change to a four-man midfield had made all the difference. After nervous opening exchanges – Shilton excelled in mopping up sloppy defensive errors – they went in 1-0 up at half time, Lineker in close attendance to round off an attack constructed by Hoddle and Steve Hodge of Aston Villa. Early in the second half, Lineker fell victim to a savage elbow in the throat dealt by Paraguay defender Delgado. However,

50 Greatest Players

PETER BEARDSLEY Striker

Clubs: Newcastle United, Liverpool, Newcastle United
Debut: v Egypt, 29 January 1986
Appearances: 59   **Goals:** 9

There are few greater delights than seeing potential realized to the maximum. Peter Beardsley's was – and he was among the most satisfying players of his era. Apart from pace, control and an excellent shot, Beardsley was perpetually alert, sharp, quick-witted and worked for the benefit of the team.

Few appreciated Beardsley more than Gary Lineker. They complemented one another because their strengths were quite different, with Beardsley dropping deep, taking defenders with him, creating space and aware of the bigger picture. Signs that the two would click came in their first international together, a 1-0 victory over Russia, in May 1986 and were underlined in the crucial last World Cup group match against Poland that brought Robson one of his most exhilarating victories as England boss. Beardsley was everywhere, linking, prompting and unleashing splendid passes in a match of high stakes.

If Bobby Robson had a complaint, it was that Beardsley didn't score enough himself, rarely thrusting into the penalty area as the second striker. However, in every other sense he was the model international: willing, modest, the sort of man who made a happy camp and the last to make any manager lose his sleep.

returning to the field after treatment, Linker repaid Delgado and co with interest, sweeping home a cross from Tottenham defender Gary Stevens.

Adios Paraguay, bienvenido Argentina. England were on the up. Tabloid journalists salivated over the potential for conflict, invoking memories of the Falklands War. Security at the Aztec stadium in Mexico City was immense. For Bobby Robson, the outcome boiled down to one thing alone: shackling Diego Maradona, the world's best footballer. 'I've got 24 hours to devise a way,' he said. 'Other teams have already tried everything… to no avail.'

No-one could legislate for Maradona: not for his skill, nor his effrontery. In a tight first half, England kept him bottled up. Five minutes into the second half, the genie escaped. As Maradona ran at the heart of the English defence then lost possession, Steve Hodge hooked the ball over his head

50 Greatest Players

CHRIS WADDLE Midfielder/Winger

Clubs: Newcastle United, Tottenham Hotspur, Marseille
Debut: v Republic of Ireland, 26 March 1985
Appearances: 62   **Goals:** 6

He didn't always look the part – in fact sometimes he looked the slouch – yet Chris Waddle was a football purist who had much in common with his soul-mate John Barnes, including inconsistency. He presented Bobby Robson with the problem an unconventional talent often poses: how best to exploit it?

Robson preferred playing Waddle wide, to use his skill and pace in getting beyond full backs. When this worked, Waddle was wonderful to watch, although his apparent anonymity in some games had the Wembley crowd on his back. In others though, such as against the Italians at Wembley in November 1989, Waddle crowned a fine run of games with a display that, according to Bobby Robson, left the Italian defender Maldini 'a broken man'.

Waddle also played wonderfully well at times in Italia 90. He ran the Belgians ragged during England's second round victory and excelled in the semi-final against West Germany, though that match would long cause him agony as he blazed England's final penalty over the bar in that apocalyptic shoot-out.

Some felt he still had more to give his country, but Waddle was discounted early in Graham Taylor's regime. As with Barnes, when Waddle departed the international scene, many were left wondering what might have been.

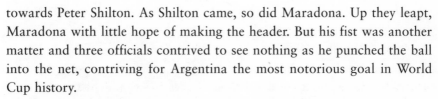

towards Peter Shilton. As Shilton came, so did Maradona. Up they leapt, Maradona with little hope of making the header. But his fist was another matter and three officials contrived to see nothing as he punched the ball into the net, contriving for Argentina the most notorious goal in World Cup history.

Maradona had done his dirty deed. With England knocked out of kilter, he then worked magic: a scintillating epic run past defender after defender, leaving Stevens, Butcher and Fenwick in his wake, with Shilton drawn and beaten. A wicked double blow, yet England still had the spirit for retaliation. What Maradona could do, John Barnes, on the bench and itching to be given

Diego Maradona proves that it was his hand and not God's that scored Argentina's first goal in the titanic World Cup encounter with England in Mexico.

his head, might imitate. Robson pitched him on with 15 minutes left and immediately Barnes zipped into overdrive, tormenting defenders. From his run and delicious cross, Lineker pulled a goal back. Three minutes remained when the same combination almost contrived an equaliser, Lineker missing Barnes' centre by a whisker.

Few turned on Robson afterwards. The villains were the feeble Tunisian referee and the diabolical Maradona himself. 'We were too angry for tears,' said Chris Waddle. 'We'd been cheated by a player with such skill that he had no need to cheat.' England returned home with pride intact, Bobby Robson still in a job and Gary Lineker, whose six goals made him top scorer in the tournament, awarded the Golden Boot. Soon Robson's thoughts turned towards the European Championship, which in 1983 had almost been his nemesis. But the team was now more solid and the qualifying group of Turkey, Northern Ireland and Yugoslavia only moderate contenders.

To Europe Again

In October 1986 Bryan Robson returned for the first group match, a 3-0 win at Windsor Park over Northern Ireland. The team cruised through 1987 winning the return at Wembley 2-0, drawing 0-0 with the Turks in Izmir, on whom, in October they dealt a repeat of the 8-0 thrashing inflicted three years earlier. Lineker had left Everton for Barcelona, yet his sharpness seemed enhanced. He scored a hat trick against the Turks and all four when England beat Spain 4-2 at the Bernabeu in February.

Great Managers – 1982-90

BOBBY ROBSON

Robson had been profoundly successful at Ipswich Town, sustaining them as a genuine force among bigger and richer clubs. The son of a Durham miner, he had his first break as a professional with Fulham, where he formed a vibrant forward partnership with Johnny Haynes and Bedford Jezzard in the 1950s.

He was sold to West Bromwich Albion for £25,000, flourishing as an attacking midfielder, and won 20 England caps between 1958 and 1962 before – unluckily many thought – losing his place to Bobby Moore. He returned to Fulham where he began learning his trade as a coach under, among others, Ron Greenwood.

Robson entered management at Craven Cottage in 1968, but the capricious board at Fulham sacked him within nine months. The west London club's loss was Ipswich's gain, though. In January 1969 Robson got the manager's job at Portman Road, survived early rough times and created a side of flair and talent on limited resources. Ipswich's achievements – and their style – were testimony to a man who loved the game.

Victory in Spain, which showed how formidable England were when the abilities of Hoddle, Waddle and Beardsley were welded, brought a debut for Arsenal central defender Tony Adams, another in the mould of raw, passionate defenders beloved of Robson. By November, England had stormed to certain qualification for the European championships, overrunning Yugoslavia 4-1 in Belgrade. 'It was one of the best displays and results in my entire eight years, but sadly, underestimated by the critics, who wrote off the Yugoslavs as a bad team,' said Robson. 'They never were: for 25 minutes we were unplayable. Beardsley, Barnes, Robson and Adams all scored in that glorious opening spell. At the time, I thought we had the best forward line in Europe.'

Hostile critics were back in their barracks, but not for long. When the 1988 European Championships proper came along, England lost their head of steam, undermined through injury and illness to key players. Butcher broke a leg; Waddle failed to recover full fitness after a hernia operation; Lineker, unknown to everyone, had hepatitis. Beardsley and Barnes had lost their sharpness after a hard season with Liverpool. As in 1961, England peaked one year too early before a big competition.

In England's group were the Republic of Ireland, Holland and the USSR: all beatable. But, after a 1-0 defeat by the Irish, things went from bad to worse. The match against Holland marked Shilton's 100th cap, yet it was his miserable duty to pick the ball out of England's net three times, his team carved open by the likes of Ruud Gullit and Marco van Basten. In both games England had shown some style and fighting spirit, but it was the finale, a 3-1 defeat to the USSR when already out of the running, that Robson found unforgivable. 'I had asked them to play for pride and give a performance for their country, but we capitulated,' he said.

The media sought Robson's blood once more – it was the worst summer of his life – but the FA stood by him and, knowing that 'every match from that point on was dynamite', Robson felt compelled to examine good new

50 Greatest Players

KENNY SANSOM Left back

Clubs: Crystal Palace, Arsenal
Debut: v Wales, 23 May 1979
Appearances: 86   **Goals:** 1

The ambition of several talented left backs to play for England foundered on the consistency of Kenny Sansom. There was little – apart from height – that he lacked. Greenwood and Robson both made Sansom their first choice. In Greenwood's eyes, 'He was full of good habits... unafraid of work, with a skill on the ball that meant he was rarely caught in possession.' Robson rated him world class, 'with a dextrous left foot that could cuddle and cosset the ball'.

Like most of the very best, Sansom relied on technique; the timing of a tackle, rather than brute force. He had many outstanding games; his performance in Brazil in 1984, when England and Robson were at a low ebb, a fine example of his accomplishments.

Inevitably the occasional defensive error lingers in the memory. One of Sansom's few nightmares was a horribly miscued clearance against Ireland in England's opening European Championship match of 1988, and it set the tone for a miserable campaign. By then Sansom's career had reached its twilight stage and a worthy successor, the redoubtable Stuart Pearce, was at hand to carry on the good work.

players as he attempted to reach the 1990 World Cup in Italy. Consequently, he tried out defenders such as Queens Park Rangers full back Paul Parker; the Nottingham Forest pairing of Des Walker and Stuart Pearce; Tony Dorigo of Chelsea; Gary Pallister of Middlesbrough; and in midfield an ebullient talent from Newcastle United, Paul Gascoigne.

Of his senior players, Robson was baffled by John Barnes' inconsistency and wondered also whether Glenn Hoddle 'was a luxury; whether we could afford to play him'. Barnes, in turn, never saw himself as the out and out winger of common perception. 'I felt inhibited,' he said. 'Right backs are better at international level, and if I did trouble my marker, the opposition simply put two defenders on me.'

Dutchman Marco van Basten ran England ragged in the European Championship match in 1988. Holland won the match 3-1 and went on to win the tournament.

England's first qualifier against Sweden at Wembley, in October 1988, was goalless; the crowd and the press quick to vent their spleen. More invective followed a stuttering 1-1 draw in Saudi Arabia a month later that brought debuts for David Seaman of Arsenal in goal; Sheffield Wednesday right back Mel Sterland; Arsenal midfielder Michael Thomas; and, as substitutes, the Arsenal pair Alan Smith and Brian Marwood. Gascoigne, also on the bench, had made his debut in September during England's 1-0 win over Denmark, a limp affair watched by fewer than 26,000.

A 2-0 victory in Albania yielded precious World Cup points and gave Robson respite. When the Albanians came to Wembley on 26 April 1989, England was mourning those who died at Hillsborough before Liverpool's FA cup semi-final with Nottingham Forest. The atmosphere, sombre at first, was relieved by a 5-0 victory, eagerly accepted at the expense of Europe's poorest relation. When England beat Poland 3-0 at Wembley in June, Lineker once more was sharp; Barnes and Waddle resurgent on the flanks. 'It was,' Robson reflected wryly, 'virtually the same side that had returned from Germany in disgrace.'

In Sweden, two defensive icons helped steer England to a point: Shilton, although approaching 40, seemingly inextinguishable; and Butcher, who played bandaged and bloodied after a clash of heads. England were inching towards qualification but still needed grist from Poland, who in Katowice, were far more assertive than at Wembley, supporting three strikers with attacking wide men. Overrun in midfield, Shilton and stalwart defenders Butcher, Pearce, Walker and Gary Stevens of Glasgow Rangers fended off the onslaught, allowing Robson's men to escape with a 0-0 draw. It was enough. Italia 1990, and a chance of redemption for the European Championship fiasco, beckoned.

World Cup Run-up

Pretenders came and went in friendly matches running up to the World Cup finals. David Platt of Aston Villa made the squad late, deputising with authority for Bryan Robson as England beat Brazil 1-0 at Wembley on 28 March 1990. Paul Gascoigne, sometimes a chaotic presence and at others an irresistible force, went showboating in England's 4-2 victory over Czechoslovakia a month later.

Then in May, Robson became engulfed in another crisis not of football's making. Suddenly, he found his private life being mauled by the popular press. Amid his efforts to refine England's preparations for Italy, the *News of the World* whipped up a salacious souffle about Robson's alleged extra-marital affairs. Moreover, and in curious circumstances, it had been resolved that Robson would quit after the 1990 World Cup. The process had began in March, the result of unguarded remarks made to journalists at Heathrow airport by FA chairman Bert Millichip. 'What happens in Italy will affect our decision about Bobby's contract,' he said. Pressed on possible replacements, he added, 'I have some names in mind. There are three candidates.' All of which was news to Robson himself who, before long, was contacted by a reporter and informed that Graham Taylor of Aston Villa had been lined up as his successor.

By the end of April, as a result of the press reports, Robson received a lucrative offer to coach the Dutch club PSV Eindhoven – good enough to provide financial security for the rest of his life. On 3 May, Robson met Millichip, who refused to give any guarantees about his future with England, but when Robson formally accepted the job in Holland, the press took it as another stick with which to beat him. 'I was accused of being greedy, unpatriotic, a cheat, a liar and of running out on England,' he later wrote in his autobiography *Against the Odds*. 'What a way for us to go to Italy.'

In the interests of confining hooligan followers, all England group matches were to be played in Sardinia, where the capital, Cagliari, bristled with security police. Ten days before going into action, Robson and his team were once more skewered by the press after an inept 1-1 draw in a friendly with Tunisia, made all the more lamentable by Terry Butcher butting one of his opponents.

Italia 90

England's first match in the tournament was another lumpen 1-1 draw with the Republic of Ireland. The match, played in a howling gale, had few satisfying moments save for Lineker's smart early goal: he gathered a fine pass from Waddle on his chest, ran on and prodded the ball past Pat Bonner. The Irish played in primitive style, their preferred method aerial bombardment. Shilton was brave enough and good enough to repulse them, but was let down in the second half when Steve McMahon, on as substitute, conceded possession to Kevin Sheedy whose fierce left foot shot was unstoppable.

As a spectacle it was excruciating. 'Have you ever witnessed a more embarrassing exhibition of wasted energy?' wondered Ian Wooldridge in the *Daily Mail*. Things did not bode well for England's next match against Holland, but the Dutch, so often a superior race in football terms, had also experienced first match embarrassment, held to a draw by Egypt. England abandoned their usual 4-4-2 system, deploying Mark Wright as a sweeper to counter Holland's attacking threat. It proved an effective modification. The match was a goalless draw, but England were enterprising and accomplished, the defence played with poise and concentration and Gascoigne looked worthy of a world stage.

England had only to beat Egypt to reach the knock out stages. But Bryan Robson, having injured his toe fooling around with Gascoigne, also had Achilles tendon trouble. The Egyptians were manifestly limited in attack yet stubborn and hard to break down. England were 1-0 winners of a turgid encounter enhanced by a rare moment of class, when Gascoigne's probing free-kick was met by a regal header at the far post by Mark Wright. Yet Robson's relief was tempered by the perplexing loss in form of Waddle and Barnes. Meanwhile, so extreme was Bryan Robson's despondency about his injuries that, to the glee of the popular press, he summoned a faith healer from England.

The show in Sardinia was over and the football circus decamped to Bologna, where England faced Belgium. The match was absorbing, often pulsating, yet without a goal after 90 minutes. Then, in extra time, England summoned inspiration when it most mattered. Gascoigne, wonderfully commanding, unlocked a tiring defence two minutes the end. When his run though midfield was curtailed by a foul, he swung a free kick into the penalty area where Platt,

David Platt (second left) celebrates his extra-time winner against Belgium in the World Cup second round match at Italia 90.

on as substitute, found space and lashed a scintillating volley into the net.

This theatrical flash catapulted England into the quarter finals. From Bologna to Naples they went, to face Cameroon, conquerors of Argentina in the group stages. It was a fixture ripe for the unexpected. Platt, starting for the first time, found his opponents 'physically intimidating... they all seemed built for boxing rather than football.' Among their ranks was the venerable centre forward Roger Milla, of indeterminate age and, in the role of substitute, capable of inflicting great damage.

England drew first blood, Platt connecting with Stuart Pearce's deep cross after Lineker had drawn defenders with a near post run. But Cameroon were not easily brushed aside. After half-time, Milla took the stage and started orchestrating. He was bundled over in the penalty area by Gascoigne in the 56th minute and Kunde just beat Shilton with the spot kick. Three minutes later, Milla, with a wily through ball, put through substitute Ekeke to give Cameroon the lead.

It was time for radical measures. In Terry Butcher's place, Robson threw on Trevor Steven, who injected new energy down the right. But then Mark Wright cut his eye and had to go off. Bandaged and re-deployed in midfield, his heroic return revived English spirits. Gascoigne began to play, but from his brilliant though ball Platt shot wide instead of scoring. Lineker, though, was irrepressible. Eight minutes remained when he was chopped down near goal and, with fabulous coolness, struck a penalty to equalise. It was England, despite their exhaustion, whose morale seemed higher. In extra time, Lineker effected an action replay of his dash into the danger area: another penalty; another goalkeeper outwitted by England's finest striker. Waiting in the wings were some old adversaries.

Gary Lineker scores from the spot against Cameroon to put England into the semi-finals.

Great Matches

WORLD CUP SEMI-FINAL		**Turin, 4 July 1990**
England 1	**West Germany 1***	**Attendance: 62,628**
Lineker	Brehme	

* West Germany won 4-3 on penalties

This was a poignant addition to England's collection of noble defeats. In a sense, they didn't lose at all, thwarted only by a fiendish penalty shoot-out. The unnerving finale was preceded by two hours of intense, often fluid football, played in an admirable spirit.

Much of the action was absorbing rather than brilliant, though punctuated with vignettes of emotion. England's thrust was remarkable after enervating matches against Cameroon and Belgium: Gascoigne obeyed orders not to wander and not to let Lothar Matthaus rampage towards goal; Waddle did a fine job deeper in midfield; and Walker and Wright marshalled the defence.

After a vibrant first half, the Germans struck first – a free-kick tapped to Brehme whose shot deflected wickedly off Paul Parker's boot and over Shilton's head. Once more Robson refreshed the side to great effect, abolishing the sweeper, replacing Butcher with Steven and moving Hoddle wide. As the attack pepped up, Parker made amends, his searching ball food for Lineker, who exploited chaos in the penalty area and stabbed home a momentous goal.

Lineker scores again, to send the semi-final into extra time.

(continued overleaf)

In extra time, play ebbed and flowed. Gascoigne, booked for a rash tackle on Berthold, wept as the world looked on, aware his transgression would cost him a place in the final. But while each side hit the post, no mortal blow was landed. And then came those penalties: the agony of Pearce; the desolation of Waddle; the end, amid such melodrama, of England.

Chris Waddle is disconsolate as he watches the West German players celebrate their place in the World Cup final after his missed penalty.

England: Shilton (Derby County), Parker (Queens Park Rangers), Pearce (Nottingham Forest), Walker (Nottingham Forest), Butcher (Rangers), Wright (Derby County), Platt (Aston Villa), Gascoigne (Tottenham Hotspur), Beardsley (Liverpool), Lineker (Tottenham Hotspur), Waddle (Marseille)

Substitutes: Steven (Rangers) for Butcher

West Germany: Illgner (FC Cologne), Kohler (Bayern Munich), Augenthaler (Bayern Munich), Berthold (Roma), Buchwald (Vfb Stuttgart), Thon (Bayern Munich), Matthaus (Inter Milan), Hassler (Juventus), Brehme (Inter Milan), Klinsmann (Inter Milan), Völler (Roma)

Substitutes: Reuter (Bayern Munich) for Thon, Riedle (Lazio) for Völler

Paul Gascoigne is reduced to tears as England's World Cup dream ends in failure.

Chapter Ten: 1990-94
The Taylor Era

Exit the second most successful manager in England's history. With legendary endurance Bobby Robson had suffered sour criticism from Alf Ramsey, persecution by the tabloids and saloon bar sniping from Brian Glanville, who disparaged the England manager's 'lack of intelligence'. Yet as a football man, Robson had few peers. He had done the lot, and in a new millennium, in his late sixties, he would still be at it, a knight of the realm, rescuing and reviving Newcastle United.

He handed over to Graham Taylor without bitterness. Taylor was on a rising tide. He had made, if not a silk purse, at least unexpectedly fine material from the sow's ear he had inherited at Watford. He graduated to Aston Villa and did much to restore their fortunes. Although his playing experience was confined to that of a workaday defender in the lower divisions with Grimsby and Lincoln City, he knew about the press and its ways and his manner was, for the most part, open and engaging.

Opinions were divided. John Barnes, whom Taylor had nurtured at Watford, was 'excited', especially when told that the role of out and out winger would no longer be forced upon him. But Jeff Powell in the *Daily Mail* feared for Taylor. 'The giant leap... will be more hazardous and unsighted than any attempted by his predecessors,' he said. Taylor requested Lawrie McMenemy, the former Southampton manager, as his assistant and to look after the England U-21s. He shed Don Howe as coach, replacing him with Steve Harrison, who was devoid of experience at the top level.

One of Taylor's first acts was to appoint Gary Lineker as captain. While no one doubted Lineker's talent, his motivational skills were far from apparent. But different players are stirred in different ways. 'The sleeves-rolled, clenched-fist style of some

Graham Taylor's performance as England manager was frequently criticised by the media.

players, like Bryan Robson and Terry Butcher, never influenced me,' John Barnes said. After Italia 90, Taylor lost, through injury or retirement, Butcher, Robson and Shilton, all tough campaigners with big personalities. 'Looking at the squad there wasn't a captain in their mould,' he said. 'Lineker... represented everything you wanted football to be represented by at that difficult time. He had a very good image and handled the press very articulately.' It was hard to imagine then how strained the relationship would become; the thoroughness and speed of its dissolution.

Hopeful Start

The Taylor era began without calamity. There were no defeats in 1990 and three European championship qualification points from a 2-0 victory over Poland at Wembley, although just one from a hustling 1-1 draw against the

---

50 Greatest Players

TERRY BUTCHER Central defender

Clubs: Ipswich Town, Rangers
Debut: v Australia, 31 May 1980
Appearances: 77   **Goals:** 3

Occasionally bloodied but never bowed, Butcher sat at the heart of the England defence for almost a decade, much of the time as captain. He epitomised the quintessential English battler, tough-tackling and roaring encouragement, yet had more skill than is often appreciated.

Butcher, a strong though not disruptive personality, had some grim experiences fighting for various causes, once almost bleeding to death after smashing his nose in a League match; and famously completing a game for England against Sweden after his head had been cut open and bandaged.

His versatility and willingness to slot in anywhere were tested to the maximum in the 1990 World Cup, where he was played as sweeper, right back, centre half, sometimes in the team and sometimes substituted.

Commanding in the air, a capable passer with his left foot, Butcher was, above all, brave and never shied away from the ball. True, he was slow on the turn and sometimes his passion led to uncontrolled outbursts, but overall he served England nobly.

50 Greatest Players

BRYAN ROBSON Midfielder

Clubs: West Bromwich Albion, Manchester United
Debut: v Republic of Ireland, 6 February 1980
Appearances: 90   **Goals:** 26

What manager would not crave a player willing to run
forever, win the balls that mattered, spray accurate passes,
long or short, score vital goals and sacrifice personal safety?
Such were the attributes of Bryan Robson, a comic book
hero – Captain Marvel – who, according to Bobby Robson,
was 'the bravest, most committed and the strongest player
I ever had'.

Brave or reckless? Chief among the statistics when
discussing Robson are his injuries, which cost him 30
international caps and required a succession of
operations. He was involved in three World Cup tournaments but saw out
neither of the last two. The former Manchester City manager and pundit Malcolm Allison
said he should have played 'with more common sense'.

But more agreed that Robson's bravery gave him a special dimension. He was one of
England's most inspiring captains, not just a runner but a strategist. He was three
players in one: defender, midfielder and phenomenal scorer. All these functions were
displayed marvellously in one of his finest games, a 3-1 win over France in the 1982
World Cup finals, in which he scored twice. Bobby Robson's devotion to his namesake
knew no bounds. 'I could see no failings,' he said.

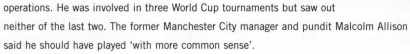

Irish in Dublin from which Gascoigne was dropped 'for tactical reasons'.
Then, his Achilles tendon apparently healed, Robson was reinstated as skipper
for England's home matches against Cameroon and the Republic of Ireland in
1991. This catalysed a peculiar, complex series of exchanges, private and
public, involving Taylor, Lineker, and Lineker's agent, Jon Holmes, chronicled
in Colin Malam's biography, *Gary Lineker: Strikingly Different*. Lineker
rebutted any suggestion from Taylor that he had taken offence at being made
to stand down for Robson, but Linker did identify the Ireland match as the
source of his problems. Afterwards he wrote a newspaper article saying he had
been 'tired' during the game. Taylor was unimpressed and told the newspapers
so. Their divisions had become public property.

Unbeaten though undistinguished, England motored on. But suddenly Taylor faced problems more material than poor relations with Lineker. In the 1991 FA Cup final, Gascoigne, playing for Tottenham against Nottingham Forest, thundered into a mad, bad challenge on Gary Charles that wrecked his knee ligament and left him out of football for more than a year. The 1991-92 season would be blighted by injury for John Barnes, robbed of his pace by a ruptured Achilles tendon. Chris Waddle meanwhile, who had transferred to Marseille and was producing some of the best football of his career, found himself a bit-part player. 'We were reverting to 4-4-2 and the long early ball. I don't think I ever fitted into Graham's plans,' Waddle said. Yet despite his predilection for the long-ball game, one reliant for effectiveness on a big target man, Taylor continually overlooked Mark Hateley, then with Glasgow Rangers and in excellent form.

England ground another European point from their encounter with Ireland at Wembley in March 1991, drawing 1-1; then three from a 1-0 victory over the Turks in Izmir six weeks later. It was progress but plaudits were few, and a second 1-0 win against Turkey in October induced more catcalls than cheers. England could thank Chris Woods of Sheffield Wednesday, Shilton's successor in goal, for sparing them further embarrassment. Taylor, like Robson before him, was now in Alf Ramsey's sights, England's eminence grise stating that the team 'could not possibly play together... that it was a selection mistake by the manager'. It also marked Waddle's last appearance for England, one in which he looked a bereft figure, ordered out wide, yet starved of service.

A clutch of new caps came and went during a meaningless summer tour of Australia, New Zealand and Malaysia, although Taylor's hand was, in part, forced by clubs reluctant to release players. Three more fresh faces, midfielders Andy Gray of Crystal Palace, Andy Sinton of Queens Park Rangers and Tony Daley appeared for the European Championship qualifier in Poland, a match salvaged late on by Lineker's inspired turn and volleyed goal as he seized on a knocked down corner. With that 1-1 draw, Taylor surmounted his first

Graham Taylor during an England training session with star pupil David Platt.

50 Greatest Players

DES WALKER Central defender

Clubs: Nottingham Forest, Sampdoria, Sheffield Wednesday
Debut: v Denmark, 14 September 1988
Appearances: 59

'You'll never beat Des Walker'. Such was the gleeful refrain sung by his fan club. Walker was a defender who knew his trade and his own mind. His trade was thwarting the world's best forwards and his mind was not to talk about it.

Walker was rarely a constructive player. Once he had done his job, he liked to off-load the ball as soon as possible. That job, his full time occupation, was sealing up cracks at the back: wherever, whenever.

He was fantastically quick and, at his peak, almost impossible to beat for pace. Like the best of his peers, he saw trouble before it came. Or, when it did, Walker was the last line of resistance, the man who would head balls away to safety, clear off the goal-line and nick the ball of a forward's toe when catastrophe threatened. He stuck to what he knew and did it brilliantly.

---

competitive hurdle: England would contest the 1992 European Championship in Sweden.

Linker found it a curious reward to be dropped, at short notice, from the starting line-up for England's next game, a friendly against France at Wembley in February 1992, though he did get on as substitute. 'I've got no divine right to play,' he said later. 'But it was the day before and left me in a tricky position with the media. He [Taylor] didn't give me any time to think about it.' Then, in England's game against Brazil at Wembley in May, Lineker formed an experimental spearhead with David Platt for which Taylor, conspicuously, praised only Platt's role in a post-match press conference. Taylor went further in undermining Lineker, who missed a penalty against the Brazilians, by saying to a Sunday newspaper, 'When someone [Lineker] is a national institution, it's almost as if you can't touch them. We could perhaps argue that we played Brazil with ten men.'

But whichever of Taylor's problems were self-inflicted, there was no legislating against the wretched timing of injuries to Barnes and right back

Gary Stevens, in a pre-European championship friendly with Finland in Helsinki. Both would be lost to the cause. In a squad where true international quality was thinly spread, Platt, scorer of both goals in England's 2-1 win, had emerged as a vital force.

European Championship in Sweden

England were in a group with the hosts, Sweden, France and Denmark, last minute entrants because Yugoslavia, in the throes of civil war, had been thrown out by UEFA. The Danes, summoned from assorted holiday destinations, were first up to play England, and gave them a hard time. England laboured, the defence creaked, Tony Daley got sent off, yet Taylor's men scraped a 0-0 draw. A fundamental problem lay at right back: besides Gary Stevens, Lee Dixon of Arsenal, and Rob Jones of Liverpool had also pulled out through injury. Against Denmark, Keith Curle of Manchester City filled in. Andy Sinton did the job against France and for the Sweden game David Batty of Leeds United was called upon.

England, although in less disarray, were scarcely more creative when playing the French. Another 0-0 draw, besmirched by defender Boli butting Stuart Pearce, created a general neurosis around England's inability to score. It meant that Sweden had to be beaten if England were to progress. This critical situation seemed to concentrate minds. Within three minutes, England were a goal up: neat work by Batty, a centre from Lineker, a streaky

Tomas Brolin (left) scores the winner for Sweden in the final group match of the 1992 European Championship, sending England home at the first hurdle.

shot from Platt. Showing more energy and purpose than for some time, England seized the game and, had Daley been sharper near goal, might have finished off Sweden by half-time.

But the interval proved fateful. Sweden's switch to a more attacking formation, introducing the tall, quick Johnny Ekstrom, altered the balance of power. After 51 minutes, the Swedes equalised. Then, in the context of a game needing to be won, Taylor effected a baffling substitution: that of Lineker for Arsenal's Alan Smith. Ultimately, Sweden's brighter football prevailed: a slick, swift interchange of passes, followed by Tomas Brolin's goal driven past Woods, signalled England's sorry exit.

50 Greatest Players

GARY LINEKER Striker

Clubs: Leicester City, Everton, Barcelona, Tottenham Hotspur
Debut: v Scotland, 26 May 1984
Appearances: 80   **Goals:** 48

With a wonderful economy of effort, sense of purpose and dedication to his craft, Gary Lineker became England's most effective striker of modern times. He knew which causes to chase and which to leave alone, a knack honed in his time with Barcelona. Everything was in equilibrium: fitness, intelligence and an astoundingly even temperament.

Lineker was the most adept in the business at losing defenders, running one way then another, creating a yard of space in a chaotic penalty area – the place where he came alive – and then pouncing. His trade required bravery. Sometimes he was brutally dealt with, yet he turned the other cheek with preternatural self-control.

What made Lineker indispensable for almost a decade was his speed off the mark and instinct for the half chance, as well as his technical ability as executioner. Rarely flashy, he more often went for the punishing low, unreachable shot.

He was not perfect. His passing sometimes went astray and he didn't always hold up the ball to his manager's satisfaction, but in the biggest theatres, such shortcomings usually mattered little: for Lineker, above all, could be relied upon to strike the telling blow when most needed.

When the hanging judges came to assess Taylor's career, his treatment of Lineker was a damning indictment. It was suggested that, apart from being tactically inept, there was an element of spite; that taking off Lineker robbed him of the chance of equalling, or even breaking, Bobby Charlton's all-time record of 49 goals for England. 'Only he [Taylor] knows,' said Lineker. Yet Taylor felt he had justification. He told the *Sunday Times*, 'Gary would admit he had not been as sharp as we would have liked. In training his shots were hitting the bar or rebounding off a goalkeeper. I got it into my head he was in a rut.'

This unhappy affair ended Lineker's international career. At 32, with 80 caps, he left Tottenham for Japan, for a lucrative swansong as an icon for Grampus Eight. Taylor's new captain was Stuart Pearce, a member of the bulldog breed. Some new, potentially convincing, figures emerged as the England manager began rebuilding for World Cup qualification: Alan Shearer, then with Blackburn Rovers, was a razor-edged striker; and Paul Ince, of Manchester United, a midfielder with bite and passion.

Early milestones in England's bid to qualify for the 1994 World Cup, to be held in the USA, were an unsatisfying 1-1 draw with Norway at Wembley (though marked with a heartening return by Gascoigne); a 4-0 victory over Turkey, with Gascoigne again prominent; and a 6-0 demolition of San Marino that, for all its clout, left critics bemoaning the ineffectiveness of star players. Not, however, that of David Platt, to whom, with Pearce injured, the captaincy had passed – he celebrated with four goals and a missed penalty.

Optimism that England would get to America increased after their 2-0 victory in Turkey, one achieved in hostile circumstances and in which Tony Adams enhanced his reputation as an international defender. But this was the last high water mark of Taylor's era. World Cup points were not prised easily from Holland, with whom England drew 2-2 at Wembley, surrendering their lead with four minutes left; nor Poland, where substitute striker Ian Wright salvaged a point with a fine equaliser on 84 minutes. But defeat in Norway, 2-0, jolted England's equilibrium. Graham Taylor was pilloried for his methods: a cloak and dagger refusal to name the team in advance and an ill-conceived stratagem of having three tall defenders to nullify the aerial threat of Norway's six feet four striker, Jostein Flo. Platt admitted there had been too little time to refine things in training. 'It was the worst performance by an England team I have played in,' he said. 'When we lost the ball, we were defending so deep we invited them to play the ball to Flo.'

The 1993 summer tournament in America, designed to test the host nation's appetite for football, rekindled an old English nightmare. Some 43 years after defeat at Belo Horizonte, England again suffered humiliation at the hands of the Americans, losing 2-0 in Boston, their performance abject. There was a clamour for Taylor's head but England were not yet in inexorable decline. Needing three wins from their last three qualifying games, they set about Poland with uncharacteristic zest and came out 3-0 winners. Gascoigne was back to his best, striking sparks, and centre forward Les Ferdinand of Queens Park Rangers was man of the match. But it was typical of Taylor's luck that, for the crucial match with Holland in Rotterdam, Gascoigne would be suspended and Ferdinand and Stuart Pearce injured.

Qualification Failure

In an atmosphere made combustible by swarms of battling fans, the gods scowled upon England. Taylor's men soaked up early pressure, found their

---

50 Greatest Players

DAVID PLATT Midfielder

Clubs: Aston Villa, Bari, Juventus, Sampdoria, Arsenal
Debut: v Italy, 15 November 1989
Appearances: 62   **Goals:** 27

Rejection need not be the end of the world. Manchester United released David Platt as a youngster. He then found his way to Crewe, but far from being a dead end, under Dario Gradi's management, Crewe was an academy for receptive talent; and Platt one of its most eminent pupils.

Once in the big time with Aston Villa, Platt's career blossomed. Had Manchester United kept faith, they might have been blessed with a replacement for Bryan Robson because Platt, with his accomplishments in defence, midfield and attack, was in that mould. When given his head in the 1990 World Cup, Platt responded superbly. His capabilities extended from man-marking the Dutch creative genius Ruud Gullit to scoring the sensational volleyed goal at the death against Belgium that pushed England on to the quarter-finals.

Platt had tremendous stamina, worked constantly at his game and took responsibility – as good in the air as on the ground. He was a natural choice for captain; though his misfortune was to peak when many fine players were being lost through injury and retirement; or else would dip out of favour under Graham Taylor's management.

composure and by half-time landed blows of their own. A good goal by Rijkaard was discounted for offside, but this was the extent of England's good luck. On 57 minutes, the match turned horribly. Platt, running in on the Dutch goal, was felled by captain Ronald Koeman on the edge of the penalty area. No penalty was given, though there was every justification for sending off Koeman, as the Dutchman later admitted, but he was merely booked and England's free kick came to nothing. Within two minutes of his transgression Koeman struck a stupefying blow at the other end. From a free kick, given after an uncannily similar infringement, Koeman, of all people, clipped the ball over the English wall and into the net.

The moment shattered England's hopes and Graham Taylor's career, his moments of pathetic consternation captured by TV documentary makers. Dennis Bergkamp scored a second ten minutes later but by then, said Platt, 'Our morale had been knocked out of us.' The last rites of England's qualifying campaign, in November 1993, descended into low farce when, within moments of kicking off against San Marino, Pearce under-hit a back-pass to David Seaman and England's beleaguered first eleven lost a goal within seven seconds. They dusted themselves off and won 7-1 but Denmark, 3-1 victors in Poland, qualified as runners-up behind Norway.

The media bayed for his resignation and this time there was nothing else for it: Taylor, harried, derided and caricatured as a turnip after defeat by Sweden, obeyed. But his players, with a few exceptions, were more generous. Several acknowledged Taylor's care and preparation, his bad luck and their own shortcomings. No one could have given more. But at the highest level, his best was not enough.

Who next for the poisoned chalice? In the end, it was a man of many parts, perhaps too many. Terry Venables, accomplished coach, streetwise man about town, whose life had more angles than a dodecahedron, needed work after an acrimonious divorce from Tottenham Hotspur. Never had a an appointee to the England job come so baggage-laden. Venables was a contradiction: seemingly fly, yet a football man of substance; a wheeler-dealer with a hinterland of distractions, yet focused, clear thinking and positive. His appointment was announced on 28 January 1994. Colourful days lay ahead.

Chapter Eleven: 1994-99
Venables and Hoddle

With England having no interest in the 1994 World Cup, the next big set piece occasion was the European Championship. As hosts, the onus to perform well was enormous, but the country's capacity to organise and to throttle hooliganism was also on trial.

Venables brought with him a dragnet of tangled business affairs. These had already been scrutinised by the BBC programme *Panorama*, and another beckoned, relating to how Venables raised money to invest in Tottenham. The FA had, in appointing Venables, hoped all litigation would be sorted out within six months. In the event, it dragged on interminably. He was appointed on a two-year contract, with the title of coach rather than manager, and with an escape clause for his employers should his affairs prove too much of an embarrassment.

A Tactical Brain in Action

He brought back Don Howe and engaged Bryan Robson, now managing Middlesbrough, as coach. Ray Wilkins and Dave Sexton joined forces to look after the England U-21s. Players found Venables a shrewd coach with original ideas and he was big enough to make unpopular decisions. David Platt, who retained the captaincy, said, 'Everyone realised Terry had a very good technical mind. Working in Barcelona helped in the same way that playing in Italy helped me.'

There was no better way to fend off hostile coverage than by winning matches. Venables did his credentials considerable good, first by beating Denmark, 1-0 at Wembley; then Greece, 5-0. Immediately he gave the press something on which to chew, having devised, against the Danes, a 4-3-2-1 formation, his self-styled 'Christmas tree'. He risked unpopularity by recalling Barnes for a home match against the USA in October 1994, but also embraced bright new players, such as Liverpool winger Steve McManaman and his midfield team-mate Jamie Redknapp, as well as Manchester United right back Gary Neville. Venables' various teams went undefeated for 15 months before losing 3-1 to champions Brazil at Wembley in the Umbro summer tournament.

But Venables was powerless to grapple with the thugs who dogged England wherever they played. Orchestrated by right-wing trouble-makers, they

Matthew Le Tissier never came good for England despite his undoubted talent.

brought terror to England's match against Ireland in Dublin on 15 February 1995, forcing abandonment of the game in the first half with the score at 1-1 and begging questions about England's fitness to stage Euro 1996.

Venables began experimenting though, as ever, his efforts were subverted by untimely injuries. He tried, mostly as a substitute, Matthew Le Tissier of Southampton. Le Tissier was a goalscorer and playmaker of ineffable talent, but too often appeared languid and disengaged. Venables also gave Tottenham's Nick Barmby a chance. He was a lively versatile creator, who in England's 0-0 draw with Colombia at Wembley in September 1995 showed great aptitude for linking midfield and attack.

The Colombia game marked the end of John Barnes' chequered international career, a frenetic encounter in which he hardly had a kick.

Alan Shearer had become the focal point of attack, preferred, even when goals dried up, to Ian Wright of Arsenal or Tottenham's Les Ferdinand. A solid looking defence was evolving with Tony Adams partnered in the middle by the composed and intelligent Gareth Southgate of Aston Villa. Neville was a phlegmatic, competent right back and Pearce, full of vim, was a durable presence on the left, a spot contested by Graeme le Saux of Chelsea, a defender with an attacker's spirit, neat on the ball and able to deliver excellent crosses. In midfield, Platt, when fit, had alongside him the fitful genius of Gascoigne. Teddy Sheringham, playing behind Shearer, operated in cunning, distracting fashion.

Football Comes Home

The first major tournament in England for 30 years began for the hosts, as in 1966, with a downbeat draw at Wembley. Shearer gave them a first-half 1-0 lead against Switzerland but, seven minutes from time, Stuart Pearce conceded a penalty for handling a shot at point blank range. Venables, however, was philosophical: 'We have a point; we're unbeaten; we can go on from here.'

For England, Euro 96 exploded into life in the second group match against

Scotland. After a cagey first 45 minutes, England made tactical adjustments and McManaman, switching sides, began shredding Scotland's right flank. The defining dramatic moments came 13 minutes from the end with Adams' foul on Gordon Durie in the penalty area; Seaman fisting Gary McAllister's penalty over the bar; and, from the corner, the

Paul Gascoigne celebrates in his own special style after scoring against Scotland at Euro 96.

start of a flowing move that had as its climax Gascoigne's sublime improvisation, when he flicked the ball over Hendry with his left foot and volleyed with his right past the helpless Andy Goram.

The nation was captivated: England's anthem 'Three Lions on the Shirt' was bellowed out with increasing volume and fervour. A feverish tide was set to engulf Holland, England's next opponents.

The quarter final, against Spain, was of a different complexion, a tense, more inhibited spectacle drawn out over 120 minutes in which neither team scored in open play, though the Spaniards had a good goal erroneously disallowed for offside. The penalty shoot-out beckoned. Stuart Pearce, showing immense nerve, atoned for his miss of six years previously; Spain hit the bar; and when Seaman saved Nadal's spot-kick, England were through.

The dramatists had been at work again. Once more England faced Germany. It was, ultimately, of scant consolation that the match was as fine as in 1990, electrified within two minutes as Shearer headed England into the lead, seizing upon Adams' flick from Gascoigne's corner. The euphoria was dampened within a quarter of an hour when England were found wanting at right back – Neville was suspended – and, from a raking cross, Stefan Kuntz equalised. The match simmered eventfully through the rest of the 90 minutes before, in extra time, erupting into a magnificent yet inconclusive climax: Anderton hit the post and then, from his cross, Gascoigne failed by a whisker to toe the ball over the line. For the Germans, Kuntz had a golden goal disallowed.

Once more, came the torture of penalties. England had, in part, exorcised Italia 90 by dispatching the Spaniards, but few opponents were less likely than Germany to buckle under pressure. In went the kicks, one after

Great Matches

EUROPEAN CHAMPIONSHIP GROUP MATCH		Wembley, 18 June 1996
England 4	**Holland 1**	**Attendance: 76,798**
Shearer 2 (1 pen)	Kluivert	
Sheringham 2		

This match laid to rest so many failures and gave its audience leave to indulge in dreams. England had established command by half-time when Ince's cleverness in the Dutch penalty area was rewarded with a penalty, converted by Shearer. It was but an appetizer – the feast was to follow.

There followed 12 gorgeous minutes. Sheringham headed a goal from a corner then, in a move born of exultation and confidence, McManaman passed to Gascoigne and Gazza went on a driving run. He cut a short, square ball to Sheringham who dummied to shoot, yet instead flicked on for Shearer to sweep the ball into the net. Rampant at 3-0 up, England poured forward again, Anderton shot and Sheringham picked up the pieces.

When Patrick Kluivert finally scored for Holland, it was irrelevant to England, though fatal to Scotland, who were edged out of the contest on goal difference. For the English nationalists this was a perfect night.

England: Seaman (Arsenal), G. Neville (Manchester United), Adams (Arsenal), Southgate (Aston Villa), Pearce (Nottingham Forest), McManaman (Liverpool), Ince (Inter Milan), Gascoigne (Rangers), Anderton (Tottenham Hotspur), Sheringham (Tottenham Hotspur), Shearer (Blackburn Rovers)

Substitutes: Platt (Arsenal) for Ince, Barmby (Middlesbrough) for Shearer, Fowler (Liverpool) for Sheringham

Holland: Van der Sar (Ajax), Reiziger (Ajax), Blind (Ajax), Bogarde (Ajax), Winter (Lazio), de Boer (Ajax), Seedorf (Sampdoria), Witschge (Bordeaux), Jordi (Barcelona), Bergkamp (Arsenal), Hoekstra (Ajax)

Substitutes: Kluivert (Ajax) for de Boer, de Koch (Roda JC Kerkrade) for Witschge, Cocu (PSV Eindhoven) for Hoekstra

Alan Shearer sweeps home his second goal of the match.

another. It was 5-5, not a chance fluffed. Then up stepped Gareth Southgate, so steady throughout the tournament, but not a man for this ordeal. His timid shot was saved by Kopke and England's glorious vision had ended.

The fate of Venables had been decided six months earlier, following his decision to stand down and concentrate on his legal battles with Tottenham chairman Alan Sugar and various libel actions. In May, before Euro 96 kicked off, Glenn Hoddle, at just 38, had been appointed his successor. But he wasn't the only

Shearer scores after two minutes in England's Euro 96 semi-final against old foes Germany.

50 Greatest Players

PAUL GASCOIGNE Midfielder

Clubs: Tottenham Hotspur, Lazio, Rangers, Middlesbrough
Debut: v Denmark, 14 September 1988
Appearances: 57   **Goals:** 10

Gazza. Two rasping syllables that evoke a swirl of images: lager, juvenile pranks, emotional excesses, moments of genius. When on his game, Paul Gascoigne's speed of thought, timing of runs, brilliant execution of passes and sheer dominating presence were enthralling.

He was fit to walk into any world eleven and the same temperament that inspired mad moments also begat moments of extravagant skill: witness the sublime goal that sunk Scotland in Euro 96. Yet Gascoigne was, for all his nonsense, a good squad man, attractively devoid of ego.

Bobby Robson gave him his chance and Gascoigne came on strong in the 1990 World Cup. It famously ended in tears, as did things eight years later when Glenn Hoddle dropped Gascoigne for the 1998 tournament. His football, like events in his life, came in fits and starts, the results of his brilliance being perhaps too much for his temperament to bear.

Great Managers – 1994-96

TERRY VENABLES

The opaque world that surrounded Terry Venables could not obscure the fact that, behind the banter and his jack-the-lad air, he was a first rate football coach, able to motivate through knowledge and understanding.

As an inside forward and midfielder with various London clubs, including Tottenham and Chelsea, Venables won two England caps in 1964 before cutting his teeth as a coach with Queens Park Rangers and Crystal Palace. He came to international prominence after taking over at Barcelona in 1984, winning the Spanish League championship in 1985 and reaching the European Cup final a year later.

Venables was appointed manager of Tottenham in 1987, where he stayed six years and became chief executive before, amid much legal wrangling, his relationship with club chairman Alan Sugar unravelled in 1993. Few doubt that, had he not become enmeshed in the long aftermath, Venables could have built an England team capable of thriving for years to come. He subsequently managed Middlesbrough and in July 2002 was appointed as David O'Leary's replacement at Leeds United.

contender. Jimmy Armfield, the former England captain turned sports journalist, had been hired to trawl for possible successors when Graham Taylor quit and was called into action once more. Armfield's first approach was not to Hoddle but to Manchester United manager Alex Ferguson. However, the board at Old Trafford insisted Ferguson honour his contract.

Hoddle Takes Control

Hoddle, who left behind his job managing Chelsea, signed a four-year deal and brought with him his trusted assistant, John Gorman. Hoddle's credentials were promising. As player-manager he had got Swindon Town into the Premier League before being lured to Stamford Bridge. He inherited a squad that pulled together admirably in Euro 96, though its biggest talent, Paul Gascoigne, would cause his biggest headache. In November 1996,

Gascoigne publicly admitted to beating his wife. It raised questions about his state of mind and the politics of selection, yet despite the outcry, Hoddle picked him for his squad to play in England's World Cup qualifier in Georgia. The trip went without mishap but further difficulties with Gascoigne lay over the horizon.

Victory over Georgia, 2-0, was the third in England's qualifying campaign. Hoddle's team had also won 3-0 in Moldova and beaten the Poles 2-1 at Wembley. The real battle, though, was with Italians, notoriously unyielding in big games, and the first reverse of Hoddle's reign came in February 1997 when Italy travelled to Wembley and won 1-0, a fierce strike by Gianfranco Zola deflected off Sol Campbell.

Glenn Hoddle employs touchline telepathy to communicate tactics to his players.

Hoddle's difficulties had been manifold: Seaman, Adams and Sheringham absent injured; Shearer only half fit; and England scarcely made a chance. Any surprise element of picking Le Tissier dissipated when the Southampton player let it leak that he had been selected. Hoddle never chose him again.

'Had my most experienced players been available, we would have won it,' Hoddle said afterwards. Further victories against Georgia, 2-0, at Wembley and Poland, 2-0, in Katowice put things back on track, but now all hung on the return with Italy in October. Meanwhile, Hoddle had begun picking the best young players around. Manchester United's prodigious youth team of the early 1990s had come of age: David Beckham made his debut against Moldova in September 1996; Nicky Butt his against Mexico in March 1997; while Paul Scholes was capped against South Africa in April 1997. Sol Campbell, Tottenham's colossal young central defender, whose first England game, a 3-0 home victory over Hungary in May 1996 had been under Venables, would also become a regular.

50 Greatest Players

STUART PEARCE Left back

Clubs: Nottingham Forest, West Ham United
Debut: v Brazil, 19 May 1987
Appearances: 78   **Goals:** 5

The nickname 'Psycho' tends not to be a term of endearment, but in the case of Stuart Pearce it was a back-handed compliment, one in which he revelled. He was fierce rather then brutal; in a tradition of conspicuously patriotic defenders such as Terry Butcher and Tony Adams who wore their hearts on their sleeves and felt it their job to gee up everyone around them.

Pearce's game was about pace, thunderous tackling, the thrust down the flank, the adventure of taking a pot-shot at goal. Few hit a dead ball with more venom. He was, like Sheringham, a late developer and did not make his league debut until he was 22, after a football apprenticeship with non-league Wealdstone. Within three years he was in the England team.

Pearce's willingness to put his head on the block made him ideal captain material. Lesser men might not have recovered from their penalty shoot-out miss during Italia 90, yet Pearce was unflinching under similar pressure at Euro 96. The country rejoiced with him as he laid the old ghost.

In summer 1997, England took part in Le Tournoi, a four-team tournament in France, and produced skilful, convincing football against serious opposition: France, Italy and Brazil. By the time of the big game in Rome, Italy's group results left England needing just a draw to ensure automatic World Cup qualification. Hoddle got his tactics spot-on, packing midfield with solid ball-winners such as David Batty, Gascoigne and Paul Ince, captain for the night, who battled on courageously after cutting his head. England shut out the Italians with consummate efficiency: a 0-0 draw ensuring their passage. The night, marred only by the ruinous behaviour of England's barbaric supporters, was a reward for attention to detail. Indeed, Hoddle's preoccupations extended from diets, to mattresses, to the ministrations of his faith healer, Eileen Drewery. Some thought he went too far. 'He wanted to know what you were doing in your own time,' said Seaman. Players also grew bored by Hoddle's attempts to curb their recreational activities. Yet despite the intermittent tensions, there was, Seaman said, a good team spirit in the run-up to France 1998, one that survived even the exclusion of Paul Gascoigne.

Whilst many despaired over Gascoigne's antics and fitness, his selection was considered inevitable. But his fitness was just one problem for Hoddle, along with that of Ian Wright, Darren Anderton, Les Ferdinand, Jamie Redknapp and Tim Flowers. France 1998 was a watershed: the end of a regular England place for Stuart Pearce, while that of Michael Owen, the young Liverpool striker, would bloom magnificently. As for Gascoigne, Hoddle had agonised up until England's last warm-up game against Belgium in Casablanca. Gascoigne lasted 55 minutes before being taken off with a dead leg and a cut on the head. 'After all I'd seen of him physically and mentally, I knew deep down he had run out of time,' said Hoddle in his World Cup diary. 'At the airport it kept coming to me that I couldn't take Gazza to France.'

Many applauded Hoddle for his bravery. The rest of the players were, according to Seaman, 'knocked back for the day, but only for the day.' Soon thoughts were concentrated on England's first group match in Marseille, against Tunisia, for which England supporters, the genuine and the rabble-rousers, had gathered en masse.

Forward for France 98

Expectations were high. A fine header by Alan Shearer from a set piece just before half-time and, near the end, a beautiful curling shot from Paul Scholes, set up by Paul Ince's driving run, gave England victory. Hoddle made one change for the next match against Romania in Toulouse, replacing Gareth Southgate, who had an ankle injury, with Gary Neville. But the buoyancy created by victory over Tunisia was punctured by the Romanians, who controlled the first half and snatched a lead two minutes after the interval. Although Owen equalised after substituting for Sheringham, England let the match slip at the death, with Graeme le Saux's challenge too little to prevent Dan Petrescu slipping a shot through Seaman's legs.

All hung on the final group match against Colombia in Lens. Beckham came in for Batty, to spice up midfield, and Owen for Sheringham, to run at a cumbersome defence. The day would belong to players previously much criticised: Darren Anderton, excellent throughout, who scored with a spectacular volley; and Beckham, getting his first goal for England with a blistering free-kick. Two-nil up at half-time, England coasted through the

Paul Scholes surges forward during England's group match with Tunisia.

second half towards a second round clash with their old foes, Argentina.

And so to St-Etienne. No pep-talk required; no need to invoke the hand of God. The same England team as beat Colombia was urged by Hoddle to go for the throats of the Argentinians. Yet within five minutes they were on the back foot, a goal down after Simeone fell over Seaman and Batistuta scored from the penalty spot, the England keeper almost, but not quite, managing to fend the ball away.

Whatever Simeone did, Michael Owen could match, bursting into the Argentinian penalty area, brushing a defender, tumbling down and, from the spot, came Shearer's riposte to Batistuta. Perhaps two wrongs had made a right. There was, however, no funny business about the next telling action: Owen zipping from the half-way line past Argentinian defenders, cutting a wonderful shot across goal and into the net: a flash of the blade that made

Michael Owen gives England a 2-1 lead against Argentina with one of the most famous goals in England's footballing history.

A red card for David Beckham and both he and the nation are devastated.

the 18-year-old Liverpool striker an international star.

The match became an emotional switchback. Scholes missed a chance to make it 3-1 when, just on half-time, Argentina were awarded a free kick. Ortega disrupted the England wall and Zanetti scored a clever equaliser through the gap. Then shortly after the interval David Beckham's momentary petulance caused a national trauma. Fouled by Simeone and dumped to the pitch, Beckham flicked out with his boot and was sent off for violent conduct. Hoddle's worst fears about his temperament were borne out. And yet, through adroit tactical adjustments,

50 Greatest Players

TEDDY SHERINGHAM Striker

Clubs: Tottenham Hotspur, Manchester United, Tottenham Hotspur
Debut: v Poland, 29 May 1993
Appearances: 51   **Goals:** 11

The best players always have something extra to offer. Sheringham was a late developer, serving a long apprenticeship at Millwall before playing at the top level. He wasn't capped until he was 27, but this long apprenticeship taught him a great deal.

He has a complete understanding of what goes on around him, playing at a canter rather than a gallop, though his reactions are sharper than most. He has excellent control, a taste for the unexpected and the ability to perform it.

Sheringham excels when playing behind the main striker, pulling away in disruptive directions, creating space for himself or others. He has combined well with a variety of partners and, because he has looked after himself physically, remained a strong contender for his England place when well into his thirties.

50 Greatest Players

ALAN SHEARER Striker

Clubs: Southampton, Blackburn Rovers, Newcastle United
Debut: v France, 19 February 1992
Appearances: 63   **Goals:** 30

Angular, combative, single-minded – few players ever looked the more complete centre forward than Alan Shearer. He had a lust for goals that drives all top strikers, willing and able to shrug aside anything standing in his way.

Shearer was the first striker to score 100 goals in the Premiership. By then he was long established as an international: quick, fearless, commanding the air with beautifully timed jumps; usually nerveless in front of goal; his combative presence forever the bane of defenders.

He was at his peak during Euro 96 and the sight of Shearer celebrating, arm aloft after scoring against Holland, captures the essence of the man enjoying his work. If anyone could be relied upon to give England a kick-start on the big occasion, it was Shearer. He did it against Germany in the Euro 96 semi-final, against Tunisia in the 1998 World Cup, back leading the line after a terrible ankle injury, and – his swansong – against the Germans in Euro 2000. England then were frail and lacking direction but Shearer remained indefatigable.

England held firm, the Argentinians unable to break through the middle and disinclined to run at the flanks. Campbell's thumping header might have stolen it ten minutes from time but for a foul given against Shearer on the goalkeeper, Roa.

Extra-time blew itself out. England had held firm, but the curse of the penalty shootout, for which England had not practised, loomed again. After Ince missed, all weighed upon Batty who had never taken a penalty in a senior match. He missed, too – the shoot-out ended 4-3 to Argentina.

'Put your chest out, your chin up and walk out with pride,' Hoddle said. Yet within six fluctuating months Hoddle himself would be made to walk out, and scarcely with pride. 'Who would have thought,' asked FA chief executive Graham Kelly rhetorically, 'that... a woman, a book and a couple of bad results would conspire to remove the England coach?' The book was Hoddle's World Cup diary, which left sports journalists indignant that the

England manager had plotted to conceal Southgate's lack of fitness in France, and derisive when Hoddle declared his biggest mistake was having Eileen Drewery, his faith healer, join the party too late. 'A lot of the players wanted and needed to see her,' he wrote. 'There was both physical and mental healing to be done.'

Judgement Questioned

Had results gone for Hoddle after the World Cup, much might have been forgiven, but in early September efforts to qualify for Euro 2000 got off to the worst possible start, with England losing 2-1 in Sweden. Defeat was made the more sour by its circumstances: Ince sent off; Anderton injured once more; Shearer's second-minute goal wiped out by a rapid double strike from the Swedes around the half hour; crowd trouble. An abysmal 0-0 draw at Wembley with Bulgaria on 10 October added further strain, but four days

50 Greatest Players

DAVID SEAMAN Goalkeeper

Clubs: Queens Park Rangers, Arsenal, Manchester City
Debut: v Saudi Arabia, 16 November 1988
Appearances: 75

The sight of David Seaman, inconsolable after being beaten by Ronaldinho's free kick that despatched England from the 2002 World Cup, may become the enduring image of a goalkeeper who rarely let his country down. Soon after, the horrible misjudgement of a corner in the Euro 2004 qualifier against Macedonia effectively ended a 14-year international career.

To judge Seaman by his high-profile blunders is to distort history. While perhaps he tempted fate by signing himself 'Safe Hands', his usually were. He had to wait until Peter Shilton's retirement to claim a regular place but through most of the 1990s saw off those who would oust him. He was a steady reliable presence, often working with defenders he was used to from Arsenal: Lee Dixon, Tony Adams and Martin Keown. But whatever the line-up in front of him Seaman could usually be relied upon. He excelled at reaction saves, was brave at the feet of attackers, and, until the twilight of his career, usually commanded in the air. Ultimately Seaman's durability, an indicator of true value, should be the talking point.

later, albeit in an mediocre performance, England collected maximum points in Luxembourg, 3-0 winners. In November, Hoddle's team looked much more the part, beating the Czech Republic 2-0 at Wembley, although the selection of Paul Merson, Ian Wright and Dion Dublin, their combined ages adding up to more than 90, was scarcely looking to the future.

Yet Hoddle would seal his own fate in the most bizarre way, lanced by an injudicious interview in *The Times*, wherein he seemed to suggest that people who were born disabled were paying for sins in a previous life. The article appeared on 31 January 1999. Soon everyone, even the Prime Minister, leaped on the bandwagon of condemnation. Hoddle floundered for 48 hours before deciding to quit, acknowledging in a terse statement that he had made 'a serious error of judgement'.

It became open season on all Hoddle's judgements: selections for group matches in the World Cup finals; publicly stating that Beckham was 'unfocused' coming into the tournament. Publication of his diary made players wary. 'It made you suspect that if you'd gone to him with a problem, the details would also have gone into the book,' said Seaman. But Phil Neville felt that 'on football matters' Hoddle deserved to keep his job. 'I don't think he ever completely lost the respect of the players,' he said. He had lost the respect of the press, though, which needed better management if it were not to store up grievances and embark on acts of vengeance.

Howard Wilkinson took temporary charge. The England team he sent out at Wembley on 10 February against France lost 2-0 and looked tactically inept. Exit Wilkinson. The people's choice was Kevin Keegan, who had turned Newcastle United into a vibrant force before walking out and was now in charge at Fulham. Two days after defeat by France, David Davies, FA director of communications, was on the phone to Craven Cottage and, shortly afterwards, slipping into Harrods, courting Fulham's chairman Mohamed Al Fayed, hoping the Egyptian entrepreneur would permit Keegan to answer his country's call.

Chapter Twelve: 1999-2002
Keegan and Eriksson

It was, of course, an irresistible temptation. Keegan had written in his autobiography that a part of him would 'always be tempted by the idea of coaching the England football team', but there was an odd choreography. Keegan accepted the job on 17 February but only, he said, for four matches, vowing to return to Fulham after England played Bulgaria in June. As a concept it was hard to fathom and in practice it worked out differently, only to end with a familiar Keegan motif, that of him walking out when he felt he could do no more.

After Hoddle's mind games and red herrings, Keegan's engagement with the press stood him in good stead, at least for a while. He got a fine start, a Euro 2000 qualifying victory, 3-1, against Poland on 27 March, achieved in invigorating style and with a hat-trick from Paul Scholes, now becoming an indispensable part of the England setup. A month later, for a friendly in Hungary, Keegan gave the squad his own stamp by introducing Leicester City's foursquare young striker Emile Heskey; the free-scoring Kevin Phillips of Sunderland; Jamie Carragher of Liverpool; Manchester United's mobile central defender Wes Brown; and Sunderland full-back Michael Gray.

Mr Motivator Takes the Job

It was then that Keegan announced he wanted the England job full time. Soon he was assailed by its uncomfortable realities. For England – and Scholes – the sense of a job well done against Poland was erased by a dismal 0-0 draw with Sweden at Wembley on 5 June, Scholes sent off for a reckless tackle. There was little improvement in Bulgaria four days later, as they failed to capitalise on an early lead given by Alan Shearer on 14 minutes. With a man sent off, the Bulgarians were there for the beating, but the match ended 1-1, its redeeming feature a splendid debut by the young Leeds United central defender, Jonathan Woodgate.

Four European points dropped in two matches with, in September, Luxembourg at Wembley and Poland in Warsaw to come. Luxembourg were not the problem. Victory arrived on demand, 6-0, but five days later England managed only a goalless draw against the Poles. For England to steal into Euro 2000 via the play-offs, Sweden had to beat Poland. They did: a single goal from Freddie Ljungberg gave England their lifeline.

Two battles with the Scots would settle who would go to the finals in Holland and Belgium. On 13 November, England played at Hampden. They won 2-0, the job almost done it seemed, victory secured by two goals inside the first half-hour from Scholes. The Scots were, for the most part, ineffectual and a makeshift England team, with Sol Campbell at right back and Redknapp on the left, able to survive. But the same eleven performed atrociously at Wembley and when Don Hutchison headed Scotland ahead just before half-time, Keegan's ragged team struggled to survive. They lost 1-0 but had, after all, qualified: 'The only good thing to come out of the match,' Keegan said.

No one could doubt Kevin Keegan's passion for football or for the English national side.

The draw for the European championships pitched England against Germany, Portugal and Romania – none an easy ride. Three months elapsed before England's next match, a friendly with Argentina. Two fresh faces were drafted into the squad: Aston Villa defender Gareth Barry and Liverpool's prodigious midfield talent Steven Gerrard. The match was a 0-0 draw, but an honourable one, from which Keegan and his players could draw sustenance. Heskey, accompanying Shearer up front, surprised many with his power, pace and skill.

After the Argentina match Shearer announced he would retire from international football following Euro 2000. Meanwhile, one left-sided player after another was getting crocked: Graeme le Saux, Jason Wilcox, and then, for a friendly against Brazil on 27 May, Heskey and Adams pulled out with back trouble. Owen scored in the 1-1 draw, looking as sharp and confident as of old, though the defence was suspect. Following a 2-0 win over Ukraine four days later, Keegan announced his squad, leaving the media to froth over the absence of Andy Cole and wondering whether to swallow the official line, that along with Redknapp and Arsenal midfielder Ray Parlour, injury cost him his place.

England's final warm-up was a turgid 2-1 victory in Malta, secured by goals from Keown and Heskey. Keegan and his players travelled to their base, the Balmoral Hotel at Spa, in Belgium, on 8 June. With their opening match against Portugal in Eindhoven five days away, Shearer was struggling with an injury to his left knee that he had been carrying for weeks.

The match against Portugal was richly entertaining but England, having taken an early 2-0 lead with resplendent football, then showed a laxity that was brutally exposed by adroit technicians. Scholes scored on three minutes, McManaman in the 19th, but all too soon Luis Figo pulled back a goal, having been allowed to advance and send a flying shot past Seaman from long range. Rui Costa and Joao Pinto wrested the initiative, and Pinto scored with a diving header shortly before half-time When Nuno Gomes struck on the hour, the Portuguese revival was as complete as the English sense of loss. Yet Keegan seemed disconcertingly upbeat. 'I do not regret the system I used,' he said. 'If only we could have held them for another 10 minutes and made them more desperate.'

It invited the accusation that Keegan was more cheerleader than tactician, but a 1-0 win over the Germans at Charleroi five days later restored hope.

Alan Shearer scores the winner for England against Germany in their European Championship group match in Charleroi.

The bogeymen were at last beaten and the joy within the England camp knew no bounds, especially that of Alan Shearer whose 53rd minute header delivered victory. But the Belgian town became synonymous less with celebration than with the misery visited upon it by brawling supporters. The following day the FA was warned by UEFA that a repetition would see England expelled from the tournament – a shocking blow to morale and a devastating for England's bid to stage the 2006 World Cup with the FIFA vote on a venue just three weeks away.

In the end, the Romanians, rather than drunken thugs, despatched England home. Keegan's men needed just a point but contrived to lose the match 3-2, despite having led at the interval following a penalty from Shearer on 41 minutes and a goal from Owen on the stroke of half-time. But English deficiencies extended beyond the error of Nigel Martyn, replacing Seaman, for gifting the Romanians a quick equaliser; and the inept challenge from Phil Neville that supplied their match-winning penalty so near the end. Keegan's post-match critique said it all: 'Can't pass; can't keep possession; can't carry out instructions and give the ball away too much... I wasn't able to get my team to do what I wanted.' Meanwhile, thanks in part to the hooligans, Germany, rather than England, were awarded the 2006 World Cup.

Before long, myriad cares were pressing down upon Keegan as he began scheming qualification for the 2002 tournament to be held in Japan and Korea. Ahead of the first group match against Germany, he baffled many with his tactic of deploying Gareth Southgate as a midfielder. Rumours of dissent among the players took hold. The match, the last before Wembley was demolished and rebuilt, became the most miserable of wakes. On a wet gloomy October day, England were undone in 14 minutes as Scholes fouled Ballack 35 yards out, England dithered in the wall and Hamann's long-range free kick squirted past Seaman.

Keegan Quits Again

England were overrun, outfought and out-thought. Keegan left the pitch to an angry noise from the crowd. He had reached the end of the road. After the final whistle, he went to the dressing room and told the players he was going to quit, saying he had taken the team as far as he could. 'People's eyes were wandering round the room, not knowing where to look,' said Gary Neville. 'There was a feeling of "this can't be real."' The obituaries were no less damning for being compassionate. In *The Times*, Oliver Holt observed: 'The game he loves, that he had once conquered with his spirit and hard work, had turned on him and taunted him with its complexities.'

With Keegan's dramatic disappearance through the trap door, Peter Taylor and Howard Wilkinson were entrusted with temporary charge. Under Wilkinson, England extracted their first World Cup qualifying point from Finland in a 0-0 draw and might, with luck have won, as three minutes from time Arsenal midfielder Ray Parlour saw his shot strike the bar and bounce down goal side of the line.

One World Cup point out of six amounted to a meagre deposit for Keegan's successor. Various names swirled the airwaves but possibles such as Alex Ferguson of Manchester United and Arsene Wenger of Arsenal were not to be prised from their clubs. The FA chief executive Adam Crozier had been busy looking elsewhere and the man in his sights was Lazio coach Sven-Goran Eriksson.

A Foreigner Takes Over the National Team

The appointment of Eriksson, who brought a urbane charm to the job that was foreign in every sense, was announced on 31 October. Little Englanders were appalled. Jack Charlton, the Geordie who had thrived as manager of the Ireland team, regarded it as 'a terrible mistake', while for Gordon Taylor, chief executive of the Professional Footballers Association, it was 'a very sad day for English football... a terrible indictment of our national association.'

Eriksson, who recruited as right hand man his chief scout from Lazio, Tord Grip, did not arrive immediately. He intended honouring his contract with Lazio until the end of the season. Peter Taylor took his turn in charge for a friendly with Italy in November and made some imaginative selections, including the quick energetic Kieron Dyer from Newcastle and Derby County's abrasive young midfielder Seth Johnson. Moreover, he made David Beckham, now wearing the mantle of plutocratic superstar with unexpected grace, captain. Although England lost 1-0 in Turin, there were good signs, particularly the composure of Rio Ferdinand, who had learned much since transferring from West Ham to Leeds, and, able both to defend and work the ball upfield, gave England a dimension they had lacked.

As Lazio's form began creaking, Eriksson's position in Italy, his loyalties divided between present and future, became untenable. Early in the new year he was installed as England manager and launched himself into the job, scrutinising likely players wherever, whenever. For his first game in charge, a friendly against Spain at Villa Park on 28 February, Eriksson gave a debut to Chris Powell, the Charlton left back, who, at 31, seemed an unlikely long-term bet to balance the left side. England won 3-0 with goals from

50 Greatest Players

MICHAEL OWEN Striker

Club: Liverpool
Debut: v Chile, 11 February 1998
Appearances: 60 **Goals:** 26

For a striker to be called to England colours aged 18 is phenomenal. The world marvelled at Owen before it came to marvel at Wayne Rooney. Each achieved an international reputation within months of making his debut. Owen's goal in the 1998 World Cup against Argentina told the world that no occasion would leave him overawed.

England have in Owen a top-drawer striker for the foreseeable future. The speed of his runs, the punishing assurance of his finishing; the sniffer's instinct for the half chance – all make him a terrifying opponent. But the rate and intensity at which he plays inevitably strains his body; and Owen's achievements have been checked by injury. Yet Eriksson stuck with him when the fickle started having doubts; and was vindicated when Owen scored a goal against Portugal in Euro 2004 stamped with genius. It was a reminder that injury-free, there are few more alarming prospects for any defence than Owen on top of his game.

Emile Heskey, Nick Barmby and Aston Villa central defender Ugo Ehiogu in a game that, after a slow start, England dominated.

The need for World Cup points was pressing and when Finland came to Anfield on 24 March tension deepened as Gary Neville's own goal put England 1-0 down after 24 minutes. Fine strikes, though, from Owen and Beckham, either side of half-time, brought victory on a night when Eriksson learned much: that by leading through example Beckham confirmed his fitness for captaincy; that Scholes, Campbell and Owen were keystones; and that Ferdinand probably was as well, if sometimes still careless.

Three more points were bagged in March as England beat Albania 3-1 in Tirana, though they had to probe the Albanian defence for more than 70 minutes before Owen finally struck. The match was a landmark for Ashley Cole, the young Arsenal left back making his debut who was more convincing at international level than Chris Powell; and for Andy Cole who, almost on full-time, scored his first goal in 13 internationals.

Great Matches

WORLD CUP QUALIFIER   **Olympic Stadium, Munich, 1 September 2001**

Germany 1   **England 5**   **Attendance: 63,000**
Jancker   Owen 3
                         Gerrard
                         Heskey

Six minutes were gone in England's biggest game under Eriksson and uncertainty in England's central defence let in Jancker to score. The Germans rarely sacrificed a lead easily, and England's task seemed monumental, but no-one could have imagined how they would respond.

It was essential to strike back quickly. Owen, first to react to Barmby's header, put England level on 13 minutes. The game kept its balance until the stroke of half-time when Gerrard latched on to the ball outside the penalty area and hit a

Michael Owen lashes in his second goal of the match.

shot with ballistic pace past Kahn, the timing as perfect as the spectacle.

England seized full control on 48 minutes: Beckham's cross, Heskey's header, Owen, sharp as a tack to finish the job. Suddenly England's midfield looked invincible, with Beckham, Scholes and Gerrard challenging, probing and ripping the defence apart with pinpoint passing. On 66 minutes Owen raced through once more and lashed a shot high into the net. The players could scarcely believe it. Their ascent into dreamland became complete on 74 minutes as Heskey burst clear and planted the ball once more past the hapless, helpless Kahn.

Germany: Kahn (Bayern Munich), Worns (Borussia Dortmund), Nowotny (Bayer Leverkusen), Linke (Bayern Munich), Rehmer (Herta Berlin), Hamann (Liverpool), Deisler (Hertha Berlin), Ballack (Bayer Leverkusen), Bohme (Schalke 04), Jancker (Bayern Munich), Neuville (Bayer Leverkusen)

Substitutes: Asamoah (Schalke 04) for Worns, Klose (Kaiserslautern) for Ballack and Kehl (Freiburg) for Neuville.

England: Seaman (Arsenal), Gary Neville (Manchester United), Campbell (Arsenal), Ferdinand (Leeds United), Cole (Arsenal), Beckham (Manchester United), Scholes (Manchester United), Gerrard (Liverpool), Barmby (Liverpool), Heskey (Liverpool), Owen (Liverpool)

Substitutes: McManaman (Real Madrid) for Barmby, Hargreaves (Bayern Munich) for Gerrard, Carragher (Liverpool) for Scholes

All the good things that England had started achieving came together in Athens in June, where England beat Greece 2-0 with goals from Scholes and Beckham, a match full of crisp passing and intelligent moves, and in which Robbie Fowler, so unsettled at Liverpool, had one of his best international outings. It was, with hindsight, no bad thing that England were jolted out of their stride in August, collectively out of sorts as they lost 2-0 to Holland in a friendly at White Hart Lane. They had missed another driving force, Steven Gerrard, injury-prone but arrestingly dominant in midfield when fully fit. Meanwhile, Owen Hargreaves, aged 20, Canadian born, of British parentage and playing impressively with Bayern Munich, made his debut, willing but raw. As a return battle with Germany loomed on 1 September, Eriksson had much to address and ordered England not to show fear; not to afford Germany the exaggerated respect shown to Holland.

There was no cold water to douse a performance of this magnitude; only a jittery performance against Albania at St James' Park, which England won 2-0, although relied on Fowler's goal to settle things two minutes from time. A draw with Greece on 6 October at Old Trafford would automatically book England's place in the World Cup finals. Defeat, even with Owen absent injured, was unthinkable.

But the Greeks, rather than bearing gifts, came to snuff out the attacking potential of wing backs Ashley Cole and Gary Neville. A collective malaise descended: Cole's mistake allowing Charisteas to score on 36 minutes; and Ferdinand ill-positioned as Nikolaidis squeezed a shot past Martyn on 69. For England, the game centred on ten ordinary players and one phenomenon – Beckham, playing as if for his life, devouring the work of four men. He it was who placed a free kick on Sheringham's head, whose first act after coming on as substitute in the 68th minute was to put England momentarily level. And then, amid excruciating tension, with injury time running down, Beckham commandeered a free kick within firing range of the

David Beckham celebrates his heroic performance against Greece.

Greek goal and sent it arcing, like some miracle, into the top corner of the net.

Eriksson had now to find his best squad for Japan. Some problems, such as finding suitable left-sided players seemed intractable. Of his goalkeepers, David Seaman, at 38 the oldest and frequently written off by critics, still looked the best bet as Nigel Martyn of Leeds had spilled a few shots too many and David James of West Ham lacked international experience.

As the season reached its climax, injuries wrought havoc with Eriksson's squad. Beckham broke a bone in his left foot playing for Manchester United against Deportivo la Coruña, followed by Gary Neville in United's European Champions League semi-final with Bayer Leverkusen. The forecast was that neither would play in Japan. Kieron Dyer, scythed down in Newcastle's last Premiership game at Southampton, looked doutbful. No less critical than Beckham's injury was that to Steven Gerrard, who pulled up with a groin strain in Liverpool's final league match against Ipswich. Injuries to Dyer and Beckham turned out less serious than at first feared, but Gerrard's was insuperable and England was robbed of a match winner.

Danny Mills of Leeds United, robust, with attacking instincts but a long history of misdemeanours, became the beneficiary of Neville's misfortune. Wayne Bridge of Southampton, widely touted as possible cover at left back, strengthened his claim with a lively debut against Holland in Amsterdam in February 2002. Less predictable was the second half impact made by another debutant, Darius Vassell, the young Aston Villa striker, whose scissor-kick equaliser on 61 minutes and thrusting energy on the flanks took everyone by surprise. Two months later, as England beat Paraguay 4-0 at Wembley, Vassell restated his case with another goal, hard work and unsettling speed. Such was the state of flux in some positions that West Ham winger Trevor Sinclair, originally on stand-by, found himself shuttling to and from Japan and, eventually, following injury to Hargreaves, making an unexpected impact.

The Sun Rises on 2002 World Cup

For the tournament, England had an island base near Kobe, Japan. Their first business was two friendlies: a 1-1 draw with South Korea in Seogwipo and a 2-2 draw with Cameroon, salvaged at the death. These matches provided comfort to anyone who harboured fears that England might peak too early, but the team's sterility in their first group match against Sweden alarmed everyone, especially the failure to capitalise on a 1-0 lead when the momentum was with them. Campbell's pounding header from Beckham's corner on 22 minutes and the first half assertiveness of Hargreaves and Scholes in midfield had promised so much better. Beckham, not fully fit, was

Making up for past misdemeanours, David Beckham slots home the penalty that gave England victory over Argentina in their 2002 World Cup group match.

taken off on the hour but Dyer, his replacement, was also convalescing and his impact negligible. Swedish substitutions, the replacement of Magnus Svensson by his namesake Andreas, had, by contrast, a galvanising effect. Just before the hour, a mistake by Mills, failing with a chest pass to reach Seaman and fluffing his clearance, set up Alexandersson for a firmly driven equaliser. England had Seaman to thank for salvaging a point; the old failures of conceding possession and losing shape depressingly obvious.

Next up, a clash with Argentina. Few fancied England. Eriksson gave his men a pathologist's breakdown of his opponents then sent them out on a bonding session. The sense of collective failure against Sweden brought a collective will to improve. England's 1-0 victory was a triumph for their all-for-one one-for-all spirit and glorious atonement for Beckham who, after Owen was felled by Pochinetto, scored the winning penalty just before half-time. Mills, fighting for his international reputation, drove forward and covered at the back like a demon, while Ferdinand and Campbell were ubiquitous, mopping up and second-guessing correctly. When Hargreaves was injured, Butt and Scholes, who moved into the centre, bonded like glue and Sinclair provided unexpected penetration down the left. Near the end, England defended desperately deep, but clung on for a victory no less delicious than their 5-1 annihilation of Germany.

Michael Owen gives England the lead against Brazil in their World Cup quarter-final and raises the hopes of the nation. But it was not to be as Brazil came back to win 2-1.

A cautious goalless draw against Nigeria gave England the point needed for progress to the knockout stages. Argentina, to worldwide astonishment, had been drummed out. In the second round, England faced Denmark. Now good fortune was with Eriksson's men as the Danes had a whiff of vulnerability about them. On four minutes, Beckham whipped over a corner, needlessly conceded, and Ferdinand's forceful header at the far post squirmed through Danish keeper Thomas Sorensen and over the line. Denmark were on the ropes early and England summoned their knockout punches: a low centre flicked on by Butt for Owen to steer the ball into the far corner; and then, on half-time, collective Danish frailties were punished by Heskey, whose smart shot put the match beyond reach.

England's opponents in the quarter-finals, Brazil would not be so supine. Even when misfiring they could carve any team apart. Back in England, the monumental encounter of 1970 was endlessly replayed, a match that stirred the senses for most of its 90 minutes. Thirty-two years later, England fans were left only with an overwhelming sense of what might have been – and then of disillusion.

For almost all the first half things went well. Owen's smartly taken early goal on 23 minutes gave England a priceless lead and, a tactical battle won, the Brazilians were well-smothered, unable to launch lethal counter-attacks until a fatal loss of possession on half-time. Beckham leaped high near the touchline to avoid being sandwiched by two Brazilians, Scholes missed a midfield challenge and, with incisive passes, Brazil cut through for Rivaldo to score.

50 Greatest Players

DAVID BECKHAM Midfielder

Club: Manchester United, Real Madrid
Debut: v Moldova, 1 September 1996
Appearances: 72   **Goals:** 13

He was not, in the end, undone either by celebrity status, a penchant for the ridiculous or his petulance. The great talent who became a hate figure after his idiocy against Argentina in the 1998 World Cup finally grew up.

Doubts about whether Beckham was more concerned for his image than his football were expunged once he became captain. Everyone knew about his long-range passing; his divine talent when striking a dead ball; but Beckham's ferocious refusal to be beaten may not have been fully understood until his heroic performance against Greece at Old Trafford in October 2001.

He is undoubtedly a great player. But is he a great captain? Some critics questioned his tactical awareness and ability to motivate during England's worst moments in Japan, where he was far short of his full, formidable fitness. Since then Beckham has retained the talisman's knack of turning games with a free kick or majestic pass. Yet his emotional side still causes rushes of blood to the head, and during Euro 2004, England would have profited from a cooler approach to taking penalty kicks.

But it was neither Rivaldo nor Ronaldo but Ronaldinho on whom the outcome turned: the devilish free-kick on 50 minutes that contrived to make a fool of Seaman and then his sending off a few minutes later, which England were so pitifully unable to exploit. When it came down to 11 against ten, it looked as though England had only the ten.

In the heat, against the best opposition, on the grounds of lack of fitness and tactical inability to press home an advantage, England were found wanting. Owen, Beckham and Scholes were shadows of themselves and Eriksson admitted that when they ran out of steam, the game was up. But, he said, he had learned 'who is a tournament player and who is not' and accepted 'personal blame' for England's loss of form. With luck, time is on the side of most of his squad – for the Coles, Ashley and Joe; for Ferdinand, Owen and Vassell; and for Gerrard, the prodigy so sorely missed.

Chapter Thirteen: 2002-04
Sven's Nearly Men

The defeat against Brazil, the first conquerors of Eriksson's England in a heavyweight contest, left much to ponder. Yet defeat against ten men did not demand drastic reconstruction of a team most felt still capable of high achievement: age favoured many; though one icon over whom, at 39, murmurs of doubt swelled to a chorus, was David Seaman. If withstanding Argentina's siege showed indomitable spirit, the question raised by the Brazilians was Eriksson's ability to adapt and inspire in unpredictable circumstances. One player was heard to remark that 'when things were going wrong, the players needed Winston Churchill but got Iain Duncan Smith'.

But it was time to move on. The new goal was qualifying for Euro 2004. A friendly against Portugal, the host nation, at Villa Park in September 2002 contained one real bonus: the potential – on ability if not always on temperament – of Alan Smith as an international. His thumping header, gilding a fine cross from Leeds United team-mate Lee Bowyer, was significant in itself but more so his energy, control, constant harassing of the defence with powerful runs and ability to take knocks: a true target man's display. 'Not within living memory has an England manager been able to call on a forward whose presence is so threatening to opposing players when they are in possession,' said Richard Williams in the *Guardian*.

David James in goal also impressed, despite some indecision at corners. Lee Bowyer, making his debut in place of the injured Beckham, had rocky moments but blossomed after fashioning the bullet for Smith to fire. In the second half Eriksson made his usual plethora of substitutions. Amid players less familiar with each other Portugal gained ground and equalised after 79 minutes when Costinha was allowed a free header from a corner. England's weakness at set pieces would become a feature of the next two years.

The policy of giving fringe players a 45-minute run-out became a topic of fractious debate. As a spectacle, friendlies tended to die but Eriksson was unapologetic. 'In my job, to see 11, 12 players today and win ... is that more important than to see Dunn, Woodgate, Hargreaves play for 45 minutes? For me, no.' Pundits disagreed. Gary Lineker was scathing. 'Both sides made so many changes that the thing was meaningless ... it left a very bad taste in the mouth.'

The Euro 2004 qualifiers pitched England in a group with Slovakia, Macedonia, Liechtenstein and Turkey. This division was perceived as a straight fight between Eriksson's men and the Turks; and the runners-up would have to face a play-off. The volatility of Turkish fans, and deaths two years earlier in Istanbul of two Leeds United supporters, added a combustible edge.

A month after the Portugal game, serious business was underway with matches in five days against Slovakia in Bratislava and Macedonia at Southampton. Victories were expected; but most small nations were well enough organised to pose problems. If the result was all, then England's 2-1 victory over the Slovaks was a job well done. But, on a vile night with wind and rain gusting across the primitive Tehelne Pole stadium, the first half football was dismal; while crowd violence and racial abuse by home supporters of England's black players recalled a darker age.

Yet Eriksson showed the wherewithal to salvage a performance that, after 45 minutes, had been very poor. At 1-0 down he freed the team from its 4-4-2 formation, moving Paul Scholes to link up with strikers Owen and Heskey. As England began to pass and move, things improved – not least their luck: on 65 minutes, from a foul harshly awarded, Beckham's fluky 35-yard free kick deceived the goalkeeper. As England pressed again, a smart cross to the near post from Scholes enabled Owen to head a winner eight minutes from time.

Eriksson had also to endure a pre-match inquisition from reporters hungry for details about his recently exposed affair with the TV personality Ulrika Jonsson. With three points bagged and a reputation for dignity intact, he rushed headlong into a match with Macedonia at Southampton – a stumbling block where English discomfiture was caused needlessly, through glaring individual errors. It was a watershed for David Seaman. His maladroit positioning against Brazil had had more momentous consequences, but the spectacle of him beaten directly by a corner from Macedonia's Sakiri on 11 minutes was more shocking, seeming confirmation that age had at last robbed him of the legs and reactions to deal with whipped-in aerial deliveries. Seaman's aberration, in what would be the last of his 75 caps,

Gary Neville and Paul Scholes celebrate David Beckham's equaliser against Slovakia.

triggered a half of lurching fortunes. Beckham, in fiery mood, equalised two minutes later, taking Scholes' through pass, chesting down the ball, and lifting it past the goalkeeper. But then Campbell hashed clearing Sakiri's shot, squirting the ball to Trajanov who beat Seaman from the edge of the penalty area. At 2-1 down against a team ranked 90th in the world, it took another stalwart, Gerrard, to restore parity, controlling on his chest Beckham's backward header before shooting home from 20 yards nine minutes from half-time.

The score stayed 2-2 but that wasn't the end of the story. Gerrard was taken off injured on 55 minutes after stretching for the ball. Chances were created but either saved or missed before, in a fit of pique, Smith was ordered off for a second needless bookable offence near full-time. So much for the hope that he had matured. The abiding memory of this match was England's startling lack of emotional and technical control. The Turks meanwhile had swept aside smaller fry: they had three wins from three, latterly a 5-0 workout against Liechtenstein.

England's need to sustain a run of victories against Turkey was imperative. But it would be almost six months before they met, after Eriksson's team had played Liechtenstein on 29 March 2003. Time for further experiments; for David James finally to claim his place as England's number one goalkeeper; for fresh tremors and doubts to surface: about individuals and the ritual mass substitutions to give outsiders some taste of the action.

A New Talent Arrives

In that time a phenomenal talent burst from nowhere on to the big stage. One minute few people unconnected with Everton had heard of 16-year-old Wayne Rooney. The next, he was performing schoolboy comic stuff – a thunderous late winner against Arsenal at Goodison made him the youngest scorer in the Premiership; two weeks later, driving like a dagger through the heart of Leeds United's defence, he shot a low guided missile that secured three more points. As substitute he was a fearful weapon. But such was Rooney's precocious confidence and ability to shrug aside older bruisers, he was game for 90 minutes. Eriksson gave Rooney his debut in a friendly against Australia at Upton Park on 12 February 2003. England's woeful display that night was not down to Rooney but to Australia's talent – Harry Kewell, Mark Viduka et al – prevailing over soft-centred, slow-witted opponents with little appetite for the contest. The first team, culprits in chief, went in 2-0 down at half-time; the young guns – Rooney, Jermaine Jenas of Newcastle and Ledley King of Tottenham among them – showed more pride though could not prevent a 3-1 defeat. All eyes had focused on Rooney, at

17 years 111 days England's youngest ever international – each flick, sharp little pass and goal-bound dash noted.

In March serious competition resumed with England's qualifier in Liechtenstein. Rooney, an 80th-minute replacement for Emile Heskey, had little time to illuminate another mundane show in which victory was fashioned by old hands – Owen's goal on 28 minutes and Beckham's on 53, another sublime free kick. But too much hung on the captain working miracles. Beforehand Gareth Southgate had complained about a lack of passion among England's newer recruits and afterwards Gary Neville bemoaned 'sloppy things right through the team … things were happening that just didn't look good.'

It took the match against Turkey to fire them up. The game, played at Sunderland on 2 April 2003, was one to savour though England's hooligan rabble managed to concoct a truculent atmosphere. Eriksson's boldness in starting with Rooney, despite the divided opinion of his coaches, was rewarded. The ponderous 4-4-2 that could leave midfield and attack dislocated was jettisoned in favour of a diamond formation, anchored by Butt and with Scholes as its attacking point. There was greater penetration and flexibility, with Rooney, like an electric eel, covering, chasing, unhinging the Turkish defence with piercing runs, nothing so potent at his lack of fear.

The goals came late. Darius Vassell, often more effective for England than Aston Villa, had replaced Owen on 57 minutes and on 76 minutes broke

Wayne Rooney cuts through the Turkish midfield with pace and directness.

through. A ball in from the left by Wayne Bridge, a shot from Ferdinand saved by goalkeeper Rustu and Vassell pounced to drive the ball home. This was enough to win the game but few in the 47,667 crowd felt secure until the final moments when Dyer, Rooney's replacement, fell in the penalty area after a challenge from Ergun and Beckham scored from the spot.

England were top of their group. The talk was no longer of 'how good is Rooney?' but of nurture and protecting him from a surfeit of expectation and exploitation. Many felt him to be the obvious successor to Emile Heskey, an unselfish toiler as a target man, but whose recent performances belied an ability displayed only in flashes. Yet in a limp close season friendly against South Africa on 22 May in Durban, Heskey's aerial dominance, rare goal in the 2-1 victory, and ability to hold up the ball underlined what he had to offer. Eriksson made clear his determination to stick with him. 'It's difficult to find his qualities in other attackers in England,' said the England manager. 'Heskey has always been important for us, even if he is not at his best every game.'

With Beckham having fractured a scaphoid bone in his foot and ruled out of the next qualifier against Slovakia, Frank Lampard, thriving since a move from West Ham to Chelsea, advanced his cause with a vigorous second-half showing against the South Africans. His talent for playing the intelligent ball, then moving and thinking quickly, was emphasised soon after in England's friendly against Serbia & Montenegro at Leicester, a 2-1 victory in which the midfield diamond formation appeared fluid and inventive. Joe Cole, from a free kick, and Gerrard finishing an excellent team move, were the scorers.

But a week later against Slovakia at Middlesbrough on 11 June 2003, poise and confidence were absent. Instead there was the familiar story of England going a goal down to modest opponents, a poor goal too – Janocko's 31st-minute free kick from the left touchline was allowed to curl over every player and bounce past David James. With England alarmingly susceptible to Slovak incursions down the flanks, Eriksson re-shuffled at half-time, putting Gerrard at the base of his midfield diamond and bringing on Owen Hargreaves for Danny Mills. But Michael Owen's knack of chasing into the penalty area and collapsing under contact proved fruitful again, Marian Zeman adjudged to have fouled him. Owen scored the spot-kick and, as England gathered momentum, scored a handsome winner, heading home Gerrard's teasing cross.

Good and Bad

A 3-1 victory over Croatia at Ipswich shortly before the next qualifier in Macedonia amply illustrated England's strengths and defects: doziness and a lack of concentration in defence, alongside decisive shafts of class – Owen's

50 Greatest Players

STEVEN GERRARD Midfielder

Club: Liverpool
Debut: v Ukraine, 31 May 2000
Appearances: 28   **Goals:** 4

At his peak Steven Gerrard is the urgent, driving engine that every major international side should have. Early in his career he passed an enormous test: thriving in a World Cup qualifier on which so much hung, instrumental in the 5-1 destruction of Germany at Munich. Gerrard's display, seizing the midfield by the scruff of the neck, scoring a crucial goal and performing party tricks near the end, will be long remembered.

His failure to make the 2002 World Cup finals through a groin injury was a critical loss for England, for Gerrard combines ferocity and finesse; defends to the death; can bore through the heart of a defence himself or take defenders out with a sweeping pass. It is a priceless combination, and all of England was thankful to have him fit for Euro 2004. There he did much fine work, though too often was on the back foot helping an overworked defence, never quite imposing himself in the manner predicted.

instinctive close-range header on 50 minutes; Lampard's emphatic goal from outside the area ten minutes from time. Events in Skopje against Macedonia were to resemble an anthology of the good and the bad that had characterised the team's passage thus far: an inept first 45 minutes with England going in a goal down; then a reinvigoration with canny substitutions that led ultimately to victory. There was also a miserable recurrence of the racial abuse black players had been forced to withstand in Slovakia.

In a first half best forgotten, passes were misplaced and defenders often outmanoeuvred before Campbell slipped in the 27th minute when trying to head clear. The ball fell to Hristov whose shot went in off David James's legs. Eriksson's response was to bring on Heskey for Lampard, giving a third striking option alongside Rooney and Owen. This looked a sound move: Beckham launched a cross into the penalty area, Heskey headed down and Wayne Rooney, at 17 years 317 days, became England's youngest scorer, striking a crisp right foot shot into the corner of the net. Heskey became a perpetual distraction and Beckham cranked himself up for one of those typical sleeves-rolled-up performances, driving home a decisive penalty in the 63rd minute after Chelsea's John Terry was fouled.

Terry was to mature rapidly, for which Eriksson would have cause to give thanks. Solid and committed, efficient and brave, he was an old-fashioned type of centre-half, out of the Tony Adams mould, whose priority was defence rather than seeking to impress with passing skills. Victory in Macedonia meanwhile had strengthened England's hand. Assuming a home victory over Liechtenstein on 10 September, a draw in Turkey would suffice to qualify. The omens were good: the Turks had never beaten England. But there were forebodings about crowd trouble. The FA, which declined its ticket allocation, the Home Office and Eriksson all entreated England fans to stay at home.

Liechtenstein were dealt with in the customary manner: England spluttering through a first 45 minutes best forgotten and being transformed after half-time. A familiar combination fashioned the breakthrough: a quick-witted Gerrard, having spotted Owen's run, crossed impeccably for his Liverpool colleague to head a wonderful goal. The exaltation had barely subsided before England's best talents combined again, Gerrard redirecting Beckham's drilled pass to Rooney who smashed the ball for 2-0.

These players had adorned a modest performance, even though all three were substituted by the 70th minute. With England three more points to the good the pressure on Turkey would intensify. And yet with qualification in their grasp England's own preparations faced being derailed through the players' unimaginably militant reaction to Rio Ferdinand's suspension for missing a routine drugs test.

The chain of events had begun on 23 September when, through what he claimed was a memory lapse, Ferdinand failed to report for the test at Manchester United's training ground. The outcome, in December, was an eight-month ban, a heavy blow to Ferdinand whose form and fitness had dipped since 2002 and leaving Leeds. However, before his punishment had been determined, the FA, on 6 October, ruled that Ferdinand should not be considered for the game in Istanbul.

Rio Ferdinand was banned from playing for 8 months after missing a drugs test.

The next day, senior players threatened to strike. Their climb-down 24 hours later was somewhat lame, though they remained defiant, and said in a statement: 'The organisation we represent [the FA] has not only let down one of our team-mates but the whole of the England squad.'

Hostility in Istanbul

If the press had been hostile to this pantomime, it was nothing compared with what awaited England in Istanbul on 11 October. There were no English voices among the frenzied 42,000 – Turkey's border had been closed to England supporters; a handful of infiltrators detained at the airport were sent home. Had any defied the odds by slipping through, 5,000 Turkish police were on hand.

England's defence, with Butt anchoring the midfield diamond, soaked up everything thrown at it – provocation and skill in equal measure. Shortly before half-time when Tugay was judged to have fouled Gerrard in the box, Beckham, losing his footing as he ran up to take the penalty, ballooned the ball grotesquely over the bar. This began acrimonious exchanges which led to a scuffle in the tunnel involving Beckham, Turkish defender Alpay, and others.

Having lectured Beckham during the interval about the need to calm down, Pierluigi Collina endured a further searching examination of his refereeing

Turkish defender Alpay taunts David Beckham for his missed penalty.

talents in a second half of feuds. But apart from gamesmanship, Turkey had little to offer. They were stifled and under constant threat from England's raids, Rooney always a lacerating force. The game ended 0-0, ensured qualification for England, and marked one of Eriksson's finest achievements.

He had nine months to mould a squad capable of challenging Europe's best. France remained the yardstick, alongside whom England were drawn in the group stages with Switzerland and Croatia. Many of his XI seemed automatic choices – the world-class talents of Beckham, Gerrard, Scholes, Campbell, and now Rooney. If the core stayed fit and in form, England could prosper. But during the next few months new doubts about the make-up of the team's central defence were raised – Ferdinand was suspended, Woodgate injured and Southgate's fitness in doubt. There were anxieties too about England's ability to score if Owen were blunted.

Then there was uncertainty about Eriksson himself. Having done the hard work of qualifying, it seemed fair to assume he would see the job through. But close to Soho Square lay temptation. Chelsea FC, driven by chief executive Peter Kenyon for Russian billionaire owner Roman Abramovich, seemed to operate on the basis that every man had his price. While the incumbent manager Claudio Ranieri had steered his team towards unparalleled success, Chelsea appeared to fancy the England manager, the biggest bauble in town; and Eriksson seemed willing to be courted.

Ordinary mortals were bemused. After the triumphant 0-0 draw in Turkey, journalists pressed him over his intentions. 'Do you not understand me … is it bad English? Yes, I will be manager at the European Championship,' Eriksson had replied. But by March 2004, five months later, things were less clear-cut.

Yet the World Cup draw for 2006, which pitched England in a qualifying group with Wales, Northern Ireland, Austria, Poland and Azerbaijan, looked a probable passage to qualification. Moreover, there was no doubting the FA's keenness to keep Eriksson – it had offered an extension on his contract that had three years to run. Eriksson, though, had moved clubs regularly during his career. 'If we don't do well in the European Championship, who wants me in 2006?' – was his somewhat plaintive rhetorical question.

Meanwhile the new strain of star militancy resurfaced as Alan Smith, called up for the friendly against Denmark on 16 November 2003, was stood down instantly when news emerged of his arrest for throwing a plastic bottle back into the crowd during Leeds' home match with Manchester United. Players, incensed that Smith had been punished before any proof of guilt, demanded a meeting with the FA chief executive Mark Palios. It marked a nadir in relations between the FA and the players. Eriksson, too, was unimpressed. 'I believe a footballer should be allowed to play until he is charged,' he said. 'We should deal with the football side and let justice take care of justice.'

Smith was never charged. England lost 2-3 to Denmark at Old Trafford where the best memories were of attacking contributions from Joe Cole, Frank Lampard and Wayne Rooney. The shakiness of Matthew Upson in defence, however, was some cause for concern. Rooney and Cole each scored in the first nine minutes but Denmark came back from 2-1 down to win with a goal from Tomasson eight minutes from time.

For England's next outing, a friendly against Portugal in Faro on 18 February 2004, Eriksson, true to his word, recalled Alan Smith. The squad

Great Managers – 2000-

SVEN-GORAN ERIKSSON

After the charismatic motivator came the thinking man, and one with a formidable array of achievements. Eriksson did not have a particularly distinguished career as a player, but as a manager he has won championships in three countries: with Gothenburg, Benfica and with Lazio in Italy.

Eriksson's success is based on sheer industry – never have players been more thoroughly scrutinised – but he also treats them like adults. He tries to encourage leadership in his players; not to make them fearful; not to complicate matters. In Italy he was nicknamed 'Il Gentilmano'.

He rescued the bid to qualify for the 2002 World Cup; reached the quarter-finals; and, but for England's defeat and tactical outmanoeuvre by Brazil, would have been hailed as a national saviour. Questions still surround his powers to respond to the unexpected; also the instinct of his teams to defend too deep when leading against strong opposition. This was to cost England dear against France and Portugal in Euro 2004.

was taking on the air, if not of a closed shop then certainly of a clique hard to break into. Eriksson, like Alf Ramsey and unlike Don Revie, stuck with those who served him well, unswayed by patchy form at club level. Yet Owen apart, his strike force – Smith, Vassell, Heskey and Rooney – had, before the Portugal match, scored just 20 Premiership goals combined. What caught the eye in a fluid 1-1 draw was the excellent understanding between Rooney and Owen, both industrious, mobile and canny. Ledley King gave England the lead two minutes after half-time; Pauleta equalising with 20 minutes to go.

These were grounds for optimism on the field; but in March, confusion about Eriksson's intentions intensified. Tales of a possible defection to Stamford Bridge were buttressed by photographs taken by the *Sun* of Eriksson emerging from the flat of Chelsea chief executive Peter Kenyon – fire that had created the smoke of rumour. When it emerged that Eriksson had also talked to other European clubs, jingoists started re-examining the Swede's fitness for the post, deploring too the FA's decision to throw so much money at it (£2 million a year after tax). Others condemned what they saw as the concealed hand of Roman Abramovich. Eriksson finally signed a contract that, according to FA chief executive Mark Palios, gave a 'cast-iron guarantee' that Eriksson would remain until after the 2006 World Cup and, in theory, tied him to the job until 2008. It also gave him an extra £500,000 a year.

No one emerged with credit apart from the beleaguered Claudio Ranieri, dignified throughout. Eriksson's equivocation struck a sour note. 'I haven't let anyone down by listening to anyone else,' he said. 'I never talked about money or a contract to a club. I only ever talked about whether there were possibilities if I left the FA. I'm staying on because I wanted the job... although I would not deny that what came out made me take the decision sooner than maybe otherwise I would have done.'

All this was poor preparation for a mediocre friendly against Sweden in Gothenburg on 31 March, the last before Eriksson picked his squad for Portugal. A final cast of the net brought in a couple of fresh faces: Aston Villa defender Jlloyd Samuel; and Manchester City's ebullient attacking midfielder Shaun Wright-Phillips, though neither ended up playing. Another outsider, Tottenham striker Jermain Defoe, was England's beacon during a dismal 1-0 defeat, a livewire for the 80 minutes he spent on the field after replacing the injured Darius Vassell. England made and squandered chances in the first half; then a neat flicked goal by Ibrahimovic on 53 minutes saw Sweden wrest the initiative and win the match.

The debate about Defoe's suitability was one of a few contentious areas. Another centred on Heskey when, arguably, Alan Smith offered all that Heskey did and more. Smith's first touch was often surer; no target man was more willing to harry defenders. Yet Heskey was called up; Smith and Defoe left on stand-by. The absence of Ferdinand and Woodgate, and doubtful fitness of Southgate, another stand-by, thrust John Terry to the fore as a first choice defender. Liverpool's Jamie Carragher and Ledley King were also called up. Eriksson retained some stalwarts not necessarily on form or first choice for their club, such as the Manchester United duo Nicky Butt and Phil Neville. The biggest cause for celebration was the confidence and fitness of Steven Gerrard. It looked, on paper, a fitter, stronger England than in 2002.

Eriksson used a triangular warm-up tournament in Manchester featuring Iceland and Japan to experiment. On the theory that one can learn from mistakes, the match against Japan, drawn 1-1, was a valuable education: a diamond midfield with Frank Lampard at its base proved too porous, inviting dangerous incursions from adroit opponents. There was a reversion to 4-4-2 against Iceland, who proved easy meat. England won 6-1: Lampard, relieved of his role as defensive linchpin, attacked and linked with gusto, opening the scoring with a 20-yard shot. Scholes' passing and movement recalled his best days; Vassell's two goals sustained his high standards. Inevitably the most vivid moment came from Rooney, a superlative strike with minimal back-lift from 25 yards that scorched into the net.

High Drama in Portugal

That key players were in good shape was, perhaps, too good to last. A hamstring problem ruled John Terry out of the first game of Euro 2004, against France. Pundits were divided over who should replace him: Jamie Carragher, useful in central defence or at left back; or Ledley King, sufficient an all-rounder to have been deployed in midfield by Tottenham. Eriksson went for King.

The blunders of hands more experienced than King were responsible for England unravelling, so exasperatingly, in added time. The game against France was flecked with drama, its outcome pure soap opera. Early on, England were out-passed and out-classed, Zinedine Zidane pulling strings, a shimmering force. But Beckham, even if below par, could change things with one sweet strike of a dead ball. And so it was, seven minutes before half-time: a foul out on the right, a flat ball whipped in by the England captain for Frank Lampard, showing marvellous athleticism and strength, to head England into the lead.

But the game plan was hard to determine. In the second half, England's firefighters, fetchers and carriers grew overworked as France, seemingly by invitation, pressed for an equaliser. Then, like some jack-in-the-box, Wayne Rooney gathered possession inside the French half and bore down on the penalty area only to be felled by Mikael Silvestre. Was Beckham, though, too pumped-up as he fired a respectable but less than deadly shot at reachable height for Fabien Barthez, an old colleague in the French goal, being more familiar than most with Beckham's repertoire?

Everything turned on Barthez's admirable save. Added time had arrived when Emile Heskey, on for Rooney, made a hash of challenging Makelele, catastrophically, for England, within Zidane's shooting range. One strike later, with David James a spectator, France were level.

Frank Lampard (centre) beats Silvestre to the ball and puts England 1-0 up against France in Lisbon.

Worse would follow as Gerrard, epitomising his team's traumatic state, hoisted a back pass into the path of Thierry Henry. Out rushed James; down went Henry; Zidane's penalty was unerring and true.

England had five days to recover before facing Switzerland in Coimbra. Terry would be fit but Nicky Butt had twisted a knee and would miss the rest of the tournament. Expectations that England would be allowed to convalesce in this match were scotched early on as the Swiss exploited space and assaulted the England goal with driven corners and free kicks. Then on 23 minutes Beckham lofted a ball from the right to Owen in the penalty area who, fashioning his own space, dinked up the ball for Rooney to head a close-range goal.

For ten minutes, England played as if liberated. But jitters returned during the second half. The Swiss, still organised, and with Hakan Yakin's set-piece skills at their disposal, were not finished. It took a helping hand from the referee on 59 minutes to swing the balance: Bernt Haas was booked for a second innocuous offence and sent off. Switzerland kept tight for ten more minutes before Rooney, finding space down the left, struck a venomous shot that hit the post, struck goalkeeper Stiel on the back of the head and bounced into the net. Switzerland sagged; England started carving them open freely. On 79 minutes, Beckham found the overlapping Neville on the right, who crossed deep for Gerrard, bursting through on the left, to shoot high into the net.

Post-match talk was of the result being all; also of the phenomenal Rooney. Optimists believed England's best players would show their true colours as the tournament progressed. They could feel vindicated after England's final group match against Croatia in Lisbon in which Rooney simply carried on where he left off.

Yet for most of the first half, the outcome, a 4-2 victory, was unforeseeable. Vulnerability at set pieces recurred to costly effect in the sixth minute after Beckham conceded a cheap free kick near the corner flag. A ball whipped in by Rapaic caused sufficient chaos for Ashley Cole to head

Wayne Rooney heads England's first goal against Switzerland and starts the first wave of Rooneymania.

goalwards, James to save, the ball to squirt off John Terry and Kovac to plunder a close-range goal. England then came to dominate possession, though often looked laboured before a sharp move eight minutes from half-time prised open their opponents. Rooney's brilliant improvised headed pass inside the penalty area was met with similar elasticity by Paul Scholes, whose header ended a three-year scoring drought for his country.

If that brought relief, Rooney, single-handed, brought exultation. As half-time beckoned, he received a squared pass from Scholes 25 yards from goal, and drove, with minimal back-lift, a ferocious shot across the Croatian goalkeeper Butina and into the net. England, though, remained vulnerable to Croatia's raids down the flanks. Then in the 68th minute, Rooney, running from midfield, took a short pass before thrusting into the space before him and driving the ball with breathtaking assurance past the goalkeeper's right hand side. England were 3-1 up, needing only a draw to qualify. Yet Croatia, seeking three goals to turn the group upside-down, stuck at it, Tudor's scoring header on 74 minutes exposing a flat-footed and static defence. But with the game stretched, England landed a knockout punch five minutes later, Lampard gathering the ball on the edge of the Croatian area and showing neat footwork to score his second goal of Euro 2004, a smart, low shot.

It was a better day for the big names: James, whose positional sense against France was poor, and who had looked bemused as high balls whistled around him against Switzerland, made some smart saves. Scholes was nearer his fizzing best; though Beckham, despite his industry, was only a moderate force out on the right flank. Owen ran hard and prompted, but goals, and that touch of lethal sharpness, still eluded him.

With France beating Switzerland 3-1 and winning the group, England would take on Portugal in the quarter-finals. Cue a return to form for Owen, his early goal the summit of achievement for Eriksson's team. It was a marvellous piece of improvisation, combining the elasticity and speed of thought some feared had deserted him. On three minutes, as a dreadful back header from Costinha came Owen's way, he met it with a balletic leap, extended his right foot, and flicked the ball delicately past the advancing goalkeeper, Ricardo.

England, despite having had one day less to prepare, were pepped up for the next 20 minutes. Then came the twist that would undermine them: Rooney, contesting a long ball with defender Andrade on the edge of Portugal's penalty area, suddenly peeled away minus his boot, hobbling. It looked bad and it was: Rooney had broken his foot. Vassell, despite running and foraging with good spirit, was no real substitute – Rooney, with his nerveless finishing, strength and gift of linking up the play, left a vacancy no one could fill.

As Portugal dominated the midfield and England conceded possession too cheaply, free kicks were given away that might have done irreparable damage had Luis Figo's sights been better set. Defenders became heroes: Sol Campbell a human blockade. The duel between Ashley Cole and the Manchester United winger Cristiano Ronaldo was one of wits and indefatigable athleticism, Ronaldo's intricate footwork nullified by Cole's

Sven-Goran Eriksson looks down at the injured Rooney and appears to know that England are at the end of the road.

impeccable, crisp tackling. This was without doubt the Arsenal full back's finest game for England.

With Gerrard and Beckham pinned back and Rooney gone, England's creative thrust was absent. As the second half unfolded, Portugal substitute Simao gave his team a telling incisiveness. Seven minutes from time, he was given two chances to cross from the left and from the second, Helder Postiga, unmarked in the penalty area, flashed a header past David James.

Whatever England's deficiencies, these did not include any shortage of character. On full time, the team wound itself up for a final assault. Up went the heavy artillery, as from Beckham's free kick, Owen hit the bar and Campbell and Terry piled in. Goalkeeper Ricardo flapped beneath Terry's challenge, fell and Campbell headed home emphatically. Swiss referee Urs Meier, some distance behind the play and without consulting the linesman, joined the list of bogeyman officials by ruling that Ricardo had been fouled.

In extra time the force was back with Portugal. Their second goal, five minutes into the second half, was a resounding strike from Rui Costa, one that seemed to have a finality about it as it crashed in, with James helpless. Yet England, however disjointed and overrun, were not finished. Lampard latched on to a knockdown by Terry from Beckham's corner, swivelled and fired a superb equaliser, displaying a control and wit that had eluded him for most of the night.

50 Greatest Players

WAYNE ROONEY Striker

Club: Everton
Debut: v Australia, 12 February 2003
Appearances: 17   **Goals:** 9

A 16-year-old unknown to football during the World Cup of 2002 would be an English icon in the European Championship two years later. An extraordinary talent giving his all with drive and energy: such is Wayne Rooney. He became England's youngest debutant at 17 years 111 days, barely six months after his first game for Everton, his ability to inflict damage on illustrious opponents already well-known. In his first real test, the Euro 2004 qualifier against Turkey, he was electrifying.

By the end of Euro 2004, everyone knew that Rooney was an agent of the spectacular. But he was ingenious too, with an instinctive positional sense. His rapid thought, instant control and quick passing were sometimes too good for everyone. Older hands helped keep his temper in check. Rooney looked the most complete young international since Duncan Edwards. But for an injured foot, he might have driven England to the Euro 2004 final.

Stalemate, therefore, and a penalty shootout. Three potential candidates, Rooney, Gerrard and Scholes, had been substituted. As turf around the penalty spot appeared to crumble, Beckham, his expression suggesting grim determination rather than the composure needed, screwed his shot over the bar. In the tit-for-tat battle of nerves, Vassell, ultimately, became the fall guy, his low shot saved by Ricardo. It was fitting, in a game of infinite twists, that Ricardo should determine the outcome, his penalty, possibly the smartest of all, scorching past James's right hand to make Portugal 6-5 victors.

In the aftermath, questions old and new were raised about England's calibre, tactics and preparation. Four crucial penalty shootouts lost in major tournaments since 1990: bad luck or technical deficiency? Some figures expected to dominate – Gerrard, Beckham and Scholes – fell short. Were England, when in a winning position, too ready to retreat against opposition who, in time, would surely punish them? Euro 2004 was far from a humiliation yet left a nation crestfallen.

THE ESSENTIAL HISTORY OF
ENGLAND

STATISTICS

The England Directory

The Football Association

- Founded 1863

Honours

- World Cup winners 1966

- Home International Championship winners
  (outright) 1888, 1891, 1892, 1893, 1895,
  1898, 1899, 1901, 1904, 1905, 1909,
  1911, 1913, 1930, 1932, 1938, 1947,
  1948, 1950, 1954, 1955, 1957, 1961,
  1965, 1966, 1968, 1969, 1971, 1973,
  1975, 1978, 1979, 1982, 1983;
  (shared) 1886, 1890, 1903, 1906, 1908,
  1912, 1927, 1931, 1935, 1939, 1952,
  1953, 1956, 1958, 1959, 1960, 1964,
  1970, 1972, 1974.

- Rous Cup winners 1986, 1988, 1989

- Overall international record:
  Played 815, Won 457, Drawn 200, Lost 158,
  Goals for 1833, against 837 (record does not
  include result of drawn matches decided by
  penalty shoot-outs)

- Number of countries, organisations and
  representative teams played against 72

Opponents most faced

- Scotland P110 W45 D24 L41 F192 A169

- Wales P97 W62 D21 L14 F239 A90

- Northern Ireland P96 W74 D16 L6 F319 A80

- France P26 W16 D4 L6 F65 A32

- Germany (including West Germany) P25 W11
  D5 L9 F44 A 31

- Italy P22 W7 D6 L9 F28 A26

- Brazil P21 W3 D8 L10 F18 A29

- Belgium P20 W14 D5 L1 F69 A25

- Hungary P20 W13 D2 L5 F51 A28

Top Tens

CAPS

- Peter Shilton 125
- Bobby Moore 108
- Bobby Charlton 106
- Billy Wright 105
- Bryan Robson 90
- Kenny Sansom 86
- Ray Wilkins 84
- Gary Lineker 80
- John Barnes 79
- Stuart Pearce 78

GOALSCORERS

- Bobby Charlton 49
- Gary Lineker 48
- Jimmy Greaves 44
- Tom Finney 30
- Nat Lofthouse 30
- Alan Shearer 30
- Vivian Woodward 29
- Steve Bloomer 28
- David Platt 27
- Michael Owen 26
- Bryan Robson 26

HIGHEST SCORES

- 13-0 v Ireland 1882
- 13-2 v Ireland 1899
- 11-1 v Austria 1908
- 10-0 v Portugal 1947
- 10-0 v USA 1964
- 9-0 v Ireland 1895
- 9-0 v Luxembourg 1960
- 9-0 v Luxembourg 1982
- 9-1 v Ireland 1890
- 9-1 v Wales 1896

HEAVIEST DEFEATS

- 1-7 v Hungary 1954
- 2-7 v Scotland 1878
- 1-6 v Scotland 1881
- 0-5 v Yugoslavia 1958
- 1-5 v Scotland 1882
- 1-5 v Scotland 1928
- 1-5 v Brazil 1964
- 3-6 v Hungary 1953
- 2-5 v France 1931
- 2-5 v France 1963

Youngest player

- Wayne Rooney (17 years 111 days)

Oldest player

- Stanley Matthews (42 years 103 days)

Players sent off

- Alan Mullery v Yugoslavia 1968
- Alan Ball v Poland 1973
- Trevor Cherry v Argentina 1977
- Ray Wilkins v Morocco 1986
- David Beckham v Argentina 1998
- Paul Ince v Sweden 1998
- Paul Scholes v Sweden 1999
- David Batty v Poland 1999
- Alan Smith v Macedonia 2002

The famous twin towers of Wembley Stadium. Wembley saw its last international in October 2000 when England lost 1-0 to Germany in a World Cup qualifier. Since then the team has played at a variety of grounds all over the country. Currently under construction on the same site, the new Wembley is due to be ready in 2006.

England's oldest enemy on the football field is Scotland – there have been 110 meetings between the two teams.

Bobby Moore and Peter Shilton, England's two most-capped players, relax in the Wembley tunnel.

50 Greatest Players

This list is not intended to be definitive. Not many fans would agree on exactly the same choice of the greatest players ever to have donned an England shirt. The 50 listed here are the author's choice, taking into consideration their respective performances, their achievements as players and their dedication to the cause. Whether or not you agree with the selection, it shows what a great variety of incredible talent has represented England over the years.

No 1 Stanley Matthews (Right winger) – 54 appearances, 11 goals. A footballing legend, Matthews' international career lasted 23 years; he served his clubs, Blackpool and Stoke, for even longer (see page 75).

No 2 Bobby Moore (Left half) – 108 appearances, 2 goals. Superb tackler and a master of possession, Moore is rightly regarded as one of the world's greatest ever defenders (see page 126).

No 3 Bobby Charlton (Inside forward) – 106 appearances, 49 goals. An inspirational player, Bobby Charlton remains England's top ever goalscorer (see page 124).

No 4 Tom Finney (Winger/Centre forward) – 76 appearances, 30 goals. Modest, but fast and skilful winger, Finney maintained a phenomenal scoring record for Preston North End and England (see page 72).

No 5 Duncan Edwards (Wing half) – 18 appearances, 5 goals. Powerful, skilful, confident with quick feet and speed of thought, Edwards was a regular for Manchester United and for England when he was killed in the Munich air crash (see page 70).

No 6 Stephen Bloomer (Inside forward) – 23 appearances, 28 goals. Whipcord thin, pale faced, Bloomer was a classic goal poacher for Derby, Middlesbrough and England (see page 16).

No 7 Gordon Banks (Goalkeeper) – 73 appearances. Ever alert, agile and consistently difficult to beat, Banks is without doubt England's finest ever goalkeeper (see page 123).

No 8 Gary Lineker (Centre forward) – 80 appearances, 48 goals. Always able to create space, Lineker also had an instinct for goalscoring and remains England's most effective striker of the modern era (see page 173).

No 9 Bryan Robson (Midfielder) – 90 appearances, 26 goals. Known as Captain Marvel, Robson was often in the right place at the right time. He was also rather injury prone (see page 169).

No 10 Paul Gascoigne (Midfielder) – 57 appearances, 10 goals. The most exciting English player of modern times, Gascoigne on song was thrilling to watch. However, his brilliance only came in fits and starts (see page 181).

No 11 Stan Cullis (Centre half) – 12 appearances. Elegant ball winner who hated to waste it once he'd got it. Had a magnificent career with Wolves both as player and manager (see page 39).

No 12 Alan Ball (Midfielder) – 72 appearances, 8 goals. His endless stamina and passionate temperament made Ball a combative motor at the heart of the England team (see page 137).

No 13 Jimmy Greaves (Centre forward) – 57 appearances, 44 goals. Fast, agile with a hammer shot, Greaves was a magnificent player but rarely performed well for England when it mattered (see page 103).

No 14 Ernest Needham (Half back) – 16 appearances, 3 goals. 'Nudger' Needham of Sheffield United was the finest half back in England before the First World War (see page 20).

No 15 Peter Shilton (Goalkeeper) – 125 appearances. With his huge frame and marvellous agility, Shilton was the perfect person to take over from Gordon Banks (see page 142).

No 16 Tommy Lawton (Centre forward) – 23 appearances, 22 goals. Combining brawn and subtle delicacy, Lawton was the complete centre forward. He starred for Everton, Chelsea and a number of other sides (see page 47).

No 17 Geoff Hurst (Centre forward) – 49 appearances, 24 goals. Tall, strong, superb in the air and with a powerful shot, Hurst was the perfect English player. Appropriate that he scored a hat-trick in England's greatest victory in 1966 (see page 112).

No 18 David Beckham (Midfielder) – 72 appearances, 13 goals. World superstar Beckham single-handedly got England to 2002 World Cup Finals. Brilliant striker of a dead ball. Has the potential to become an England legend (see page 202).

No 19 Frank Swift (Goalkeeper) – 19 appearances. Frank Swift's huge hands and agility made him a stalwart for Manchester City and England. Tragically killed in the Munich air crash in 1958 (see page 52).

No 20 Michael Owen (Striker) – 60 appearances, 26 goals. Became a world superstar with his goal against Argentina in France in 1998. Owen remains a quick and deadly finisher for Liverpool and England (see page 196).

No 21 Johnny Haynes (Inside left) – 56 appearances, 18 goals. One of England's finest ever playmakers, Haynes also scored regularly himself (see page 86).

No 22 Stan Mortensen (Centre forward/Inside right) – 25 appearances, 23 goals. Lightening-fast striker, combined beautifully with club colleague Stanley Matthews for Blackpool and England (see page 58).

No 23 Trevor Brooking (Midfielder) – 47 appearances, 5 goals. Creative and elegant, Brooking was said to have 'brains in his boots' (see page 146).

No 24 Kevin Keegan (Inside forward) – 63 appearances, 21 goals. Player with a wholehearted approach to the game. Full of running and brilliant in the air (see page 145).

No 25 Eddie Hapgood (Full back) – 30 appearances, 0 goals. Elegant and courageous defender for Arsenal and England renowned for his fair play (see page 35).

No 26 G.O. Smith (Centre forward) – 20 appearances, 11 goals. Public schoolboy and amateur footballer with Corinthians, Smith was a brilliant passer with a deadly shot (see page 11).

No 27 Billy Wright (Wing half/Centre half) – 105 appearances, 3 goals. Solid and dependable defender. Quiet progress saw him rack up 105 caps for England as well as a long career at Wolves (see page 76).

No 28 Alan Shearer (Striker) – 63 appearances, 30 goals. Quick, fearless and cool in front of goal, Shearer maintained a lust for goals that made him the complete centre forward (see page 188).

No 29 David Platt (Midfielder) – 62 appearances, 27 goals. Equally effective all over the pitch, Platt was the perfect replacement for Bryan Robson (see page 175).

No 30 Wayne Rooney (Striker) – 16 appearances, 9 goals. An extraordinary talent, full of drive, energy and goals. Became a national hero for his performances at Euro 2004 (see page 218).

No 31 Terry Butcher (Central defender) – 77 appearances, 3 goals. The heart of the England defence for almost a decade, Butcher epitomised the bulldog spirit but possessed no little skill (see page 168).

No 32 Martin Peters (Midfielder) – 67 appearances, 20 goals. An even-tempered, elegant player, Peters was an alternative to a conventional winger (see page 130).

No 33 Raich Carter (Inside forward) – 13 appearances, 7 goals. Energetic and tricky inside forward. Enjoyed long careers with Sunderland and Derby (see page 37).

No 34 Peter Beardsley (Striker) – 59 appearances, 9 goals. Quick-witted and always sharp, Beardsley was the perfect team player and the perfect provider for Gary Lineker (see page 156).

No 35 Wilf Mannion (Inside forward) – 26 appearances, 11 goals. The ultimate players' player, Mannion was a legend in Middlesbrough, he would have won more caps but for the war (see page 57).

No 36 Cliff Bastin (Outside left) – 21 appearances, 12 goals. Cool under pressure, fast and with a powerful shot, Bastin starred for the great Arsenal sides of the 1930s (see page 33).

No 37 Ray Clemence (Goalkeeper) – 61 appearances. Tall and commanding, Clemence was superb at dealing with crosses and corners (see page 143).

No 38 Dixie Dean (Centre forward) – 16 appearances, 18 goals. Prolific scorer for both Everton and England, particularly with his head (see page 26).

No 39 Stuart Pearce (Left back) – 78 appearances, 5 goals. Fierce player with a powerful shot, Pearce was a lion-hearted defender who was never afraid to put his head on the block (see page 184).

No 40 Joe Mercer (Half back) – 5 appearances. Actually played 27 times for England (22 during wartime). Tireless box-to-box player with Everton and later with Arsenal (see page 41).

No 41 Vivian Woodward (Centre forward) – 23 appearances, 29 goals. A prolific scorer, Woodward had the complete armoury of attacking skills (see page 19).

No 42 Chris Waddle (Midfielder/Winger) – 62 appearances, 6 goals. When on form Waddle was a skilful, flying winger. But he never quite fulfilled his international potential (see page 157).

No 43 Teddy Sheringham (Striker) – 51 appearances, 11 goals. Sheringham excelled when playing behind the main striker. Combined well with a number of different partners (see page 187).

No 44 Steven Gerrard (Midfielder) – 28 appearances, 4 goals. A tower of strength in midfield, Gerrard's performances are essential for England to do well at the highest level. One for the future (see page 208).

No 45 Kenny Samson (Left back) – 86 appearances, 1 goal. Skilful on the ball and a great timer of tackles, Samson was first choice at left back for both Ron Greenwood and Bobby Robson (see page 160).

No 46 Ray Wilkins (Midfielder) – 84 appearances, 3 goals. A players' player, Wilkins had a broad vision of the game and was able to organize things and draw the best from other players (see page 150).

No 47 John Barnes (Winger) – 79 appearances, 11 goals. Elegant and unhurried, Barnes in full flight was an exciting sight for England fans (see page 154).

No 48 Glenn Hoddle (Midfielder) – 53 appearances, 8 goals. A master of the midfield and scorer of magnificent goals (see page 152).

No 49 Des Walker (Central defender) – 59 appearances. Fantastically quick, Walker had the ability to see trouble before it came (see page 171).

No 50 David Seaman (Goalkeeper) – 75 appearances. Commanding in the air, brave at the feet of attackers, Seaman rarely let his country down between the posts (see page 189).

Results 1872-2004

The following pages include details of every official match played by England since 1872 with the number of caps attained by each player in a specific game in brackets and the captain in bold type. Dates, venue, result and goalscorers are also featured. Attendance figures are compiled from official and unofficial sources and there are Fact Files sprinkled throughout as complements to the overall statistics.

In the early years, Scotland provided England's only opposition but with Wales and then Ireland adding to the friendly fixture list, the need for a competitive touch to the games grew stronger. So in 1883-84 when all four countries had started to play each other, the first British – known as the Home International Championship – was launched. The formula was simple enough; the four played each other once in a season, home and away fixtures alternating every year. Teams level on points shared the title as goal average did not count. However in 1978-79 goal difference was allowed to determine the winners. The 1980-81 series was abandoned when both England and Wales declined to play in Northern Ireland because of the political situation in the province. But interest in the tournament as a whole was declining apart from the annual fixture between England and Scotland. In fact, the 1983-84 season proved to be the last as England refused to play either Northern Ireland or Wales and the Scots soon followed this lead.

England and Scotland continued to meet each other for a time though there were increasing problems caused by hooliganism. The Rous Cup was introduced to revive the fixture and this was expanded to include foreign visitors in later years but it proved a short-lived experiment and was dropped. Subsequent meetings against the other three home countries were restricted to matches in either the European Championship qualifying competition or the preliminary stages of the World Cup.

Actually England did not participate in the World Cup until 1950, 20 years after the initial tournament in Uruguay. England, in company with Scotland, Wales and Northern Ireland, had quit FIFA, the world governing body, after refusing to be associated with any of the axis countries following the First World War. They left again over broken time payments to amateurs before finally returning to the fold in 1946, having missed the 1930, 1934 and 1938 tournaments.

There had been a gradual move to include foreign countries in England's fixture list and summer tours became part of the scene in the years leading up to the outbreak of war in 1939. Because of the Second World War there was no World Cup competition in 1942 or four years later as Europe was still in recovery. But England had been able to stage numerous international fixtures for wartime charities during hostilities, almost solely against Scotland and Wales. No caps were awarded to the players but these matches were invariably well attended for the worthy causes designated. Figures in italics after the names of the players indicate the number of times played in these unofficial fixtures in both world wars.

England was again slow to enter the European Nations Cup which later became the European Championship but achieved its initial triumph on the global stage when hosting the 1966 World Cup, a feat which remains the only true honour in England's footballing history.

1872

Friendly

DATE	VENUE	OPPONENTS	SCORE	GOALSCORERS	ATTENDANCE	TEAM
Nov 30	Hamilton Crescent, Partick	SCOTLAND	D 0-0		4,000	Barker (1), Greenhalgh (1), Welch (1), Maddison (1), **Ottaway** (1), Brockbank (1), Chenery (1), Clegg JC (1), Smith AK (1), Morice (1), Maynard (1)

FACT FILE

The oldest surviving England shirt is believed to be the one worn by Arnold Kirke Smith in the original match with Scotland in 1872.

At the time of England's first official international in 1872, teams listings in the press began with the extreme outside forward, working back to the goalkeeper. Ironically for this game with Scotland, Barker kept goal in the first half, Maynard in the second.

1873

Friendly

DATE	VENUE	OPPONENTS	SCORE	GOALSCORERS	ATTENDANCE	TEAM
Mar 8	Kennington Oval, London	SCOTLAND	W 4-2	Kenyon-Slaney 2, Bonsor, Chenery	3,000	**Morten** (1), Greenhalgh (2), Howell (1), Goodwyn (1), Vidal (1), von Donop (1), Chenery (2), Clegg WE (1), Bonsor (1), Kenyon-Slaney (1), Heron H (1)

FACT FILE

William Kenyon-Slaney, a two-goal debutant for his country in 1873, was the first England international from outside the British Isles. He was born in India.

Receipts for the first England v Scotland international at The Oval in 1873 were £106.1s.0d (£106.05). The FA made a profit of £73.8s.6d (£73.42) after paying expenses which included £10 for the hire of the ground from the Surrey CCC and £15.l4s.6d (£15.72) to provide the Scottish team with lunch and dinner. The England team paid their own expenses.

1874

Friendly

DATE	VENUE	OPPONENTS	SCORE	GOALSCORERS	ATTENDANCE	TEAM
Mar 7	Hamilton Crescent, Partick	SCOTLAND	L 1-2	Kingsford	7,000	Welch (2), Ogilvie (1), Stratford (1), **Ottaway** (2), Birley (1), Wollaston (1), Kingsford (1), Edwards (1), Chenery (3), Heron H (2), Owen (1)

1875

Friendly

DATE	VENUE	OPPONENTS	SCORE	GOALSCORERS	ATTENDANCE	TEAM
Mar 6	Kennington Oval, London	SCOTLAND	D 2-2	Wollaston, Alcock	2,000	Carr (1), Haygarth (1), Rawson H (1), Birley (2), von Donop (2), Wollaston (2), **Alcock** (1), Rawson W (1), Bonsor (2), Heron H (3), Geaves (1)

1876

Friendly

DATE	VENUE	OPPONENTS	SCORE	GOALSCORERS	ATTENDANCE	TEAM
Mar 4	Hamilton Crescent, Partick	SCOTLAND	L 0-3		16,000	Savage (1), Green (1), Field (1), Bambridge EH (1), Jarrett (1), **Heron H** (4), Cursham AW (1), Heron F (1), Smith CE (1), Buchanan (1), Maynard (2)

1877

Friendly

DATE	VENUE	OPPONENTS	SCORE	GOALSCORERS	ATTENDANCE	TEAM
Mar 3	Kennington Oval, London	SCOTLAND	L 1-3	Lyttelton A	1,200	Betts (1), Lindsay (1), Bury (1), **Rawson W** (2), Jarrett (2), Wollaston (3), Cursham AW (2), Hon. A Lyttelton (1), Wingfield-Stratford (1), Bain (1), Mosforth (1)

1878

Friendly

DATE	VENUE	OPPONENTS	SCORE	GOALSCORERS	ATTENDANCE	TEAM
Mar 2	First Hampden, Glasgow	SCOTLAND	L 2-7	Wylie, Cursham AW	15,000	Warner (1), Hon. E Lyttelton (1), Hunter (1), Bailey (1), Jarrett (3), **Cursham AW** (3), Fairclough (1), Wace (1), Wylie (1), Heron H (5), Mosforth (2)

1879

Friendly

DATE	VENUE	OPPONENTS	SCORE	GOALSCORERS	ATTENDANCE	TEAM
Jan 18	Kennington Oval, London	WALES	W 2-1	Sorby, Whitfield	200	Anderson (1), Bury (2), Wilson (1), Bailey (2), Clegg WE (2), Parry (1), Sorby (1), **Cursham AW** (4), Wace (2), Mosforth (3), Whitfield (1)

FACT FILE

William Clegg, selected to play for England against Scotland in 1879, was a solicitor. He was working on papers for the trial of Charles Peace and had to delay his departure from Sheffield until the Saturday morning. Heavy snowfall meant he did not arrive for the match until it had been in progress for 20 minutes.

The youngest England international, until Wayne Rooney in 2003, was James Prinsep, capped against Scotland in 1879 at the age of 17 years and 252 days.

1879

Friendly

DATE	VENUE	OPPONENTS	SCORE	GOALSCORERS	ATTENDANCE	TEAM
Apr 5	Kennington Oval, London	SCOTLAND	W 5-4	Mosforth, Bambridge EC 2, Goodyer, Bailey	4,500	Birkett (1), Morse (1), Christian (1), Bailey (3), Prinsep (1), Hills (1), Goodyer (1), **Wace** (3), Sparks (1), Bambridge EC (1), Mosforth (4)

1880

Friendlies

DATE	VENUE	OPPONENTS	SCORE	GOALSCORERS	ATTENDANCE	TEAM
Mar 13	First Hampden, Glasgow	SCOTLAND	L 4-5	Mosforth, Bambridge EC 2, Sparks	10,000	Swepstone (1), Brindle (1), Luntley (1), Bailey (4), Hunter (2), **Wollaston** (4), Bastard (1), Sparks (2), Widdowson (1), Mosforth (5), Bambridge EC (2)
Mar 15	Racecourse Ground, Wrexham	WALES	W 3-2	Sparks 2, Brindle	3,000	Sands (1), Luntley (2), Brindle (2), Hunter (3), Hargreaves F (1), Marshall (1), Cursham HA (1), **Sparks** (3), Mitchell (1), Johnson (1), Mosforth (6)

1881

Friendlies

DATE	VENUE	OPPONENTS	SCORE	GOALSCORERS	ATTENDANCE	TEAM
Feb 26	Alexandra Meadows, Blackburn	WALES	L 0-1		3,000	Hawtrey (1), Harvey (1), Bambridge AL (1), **Hunter** (4), Hargreaves F (2), Marshall (2), Rostron (1), Brown J (1), Tait (1), Hargreaves J (1), Mosforth (7)
Mar 12	Kennington Oval, London	SCOTLAND	L 1-6	Bambridge EC	8,500	Hawtrey (2), Field (2), Wilson (2), **Bailey** (5), Hunter (5), Holden (2), Rostron (2), Macauley (1), Mitchell (2), Bambridge EC (3), Hargreaves J (2)

1882

Friendlies

DATE	VENUE	OPPONENTS	SCORE	GOALSCORERS	ATTENDANCE	TEAM
Feb 18	Knock Ground, Belfast	IRELAND	W 13-0	Vaughton 5, Brown A 4, Brown J 2, Cursham HA, Bambridge EC	2,500	Rawlinson (1), Dobson (1), Greenwood (1), Hargreaves F (3), King (1), **Bambridge EC** (4), Barnet (1), Brown A (1), Brown J (2), Vaughton (1), Cursham HA (2)
Mar 11	First Hampden, Glasgow	SCOTLAND	1-5	Vaughton	10,000	Swepstone (2), Greenwood (2), Jones A (1), **Bailey** (6), Hunter (6), Cursham HA (3), Parry (2), Brown A (2), Vaughton (2), Mosforth (8), Bambridge EC (5)
Mar 13	Racecourse Ground, Wrexham	WALES	L 3-5	Mosforth, Parry, Cursham HA	5,000	Swepstone (3), Hunter (7), Jones A (2), **Bailey** (7), Bambridge EC (6), Parry (3), Cursham HA (4), Parr (1), Brown A (3), Vaughton (3), Mosforth (9)

FACT FILE

Howard Vaughton, scorer of five goals against Ireland in 1882, later became a director of the Birmingham firm which manufactured the second FA Cup trophy. Receipts for the match amounted to £9.19s.7d (nearly £10).

1883

Friendlies

DATE	VENUE	OPPONENTS	SCORE	GOALSCORERS	ATTENDANCE	TEAM
Feb 3	Kennington Oval, London	WALES	W 5-0	Mitchell 3, Cursham AW, Bambridge EC	2,000	Swepstone (4), Paravacini (1), Russell (1), **Bailey** (8), Macrae (1), Cursham AW (5), Bambridge AL (2), Mitchell (3), Goodhart (1), Cursham HA (5), Bambridge EC (7)
Feb 24	Aigburth CC, Liverpool	IRELAND	W 7-0	Cobbold 2, Dunn 2, Whateley 2, Pawson	2,500	Swepstone (5), Paravacini (2), Moore (1), **Hudson** (1), Macrae (2), Whateley (1), Pawson (1), Goodhart (2), Dunn (1), Cobbold (1), Cursham HA (6)
Mar 10	Bramall Lane, Sheffield	SCOTLAND	L 2-3	Mitchell, Cobbold	7,000	Swepstone (6), Paravacini (3), Jones A (3), **Bailey** (9), Macrae (3), Cursham HA (7), Cobbold (2), Mitchell (4), Goodhart (3), Cursham AW (6), Whateley (2)

1884

Home International Championship

DATE	VENUE	OPPONENTS	SCORE	GOALSCORERS	ATTENDANCE	TEAM
Feb 23	Ballynafeigh Park, Belfast	IRELAND	W 8-1	Johnson 2, Bambridge EC 2, Cursham HA 3, Bambridge AL	3,000	Rose (1), Dobson (2), Beverley (1), **Bailey** (10), Macrae (4), Johnson (2), Holden (2), Bambridge AL (3), Dunn (2), Bambridge EC (8), Cursham HA (8)
Mar 15	First Cathkin, Glasgow	SCOTLAND	L 0-1		10,000	Rose (2), Dobson (3), Beverley (2), **Bailey** (11), Macrae (5), Wilson C (1), Bromley-Davenport (1), Gunn (1), Bambridge EC (9), Vaughton (4), Holden (3)
Mar 17	Racecourse Ground, Wrexham	WALES	W 4-0	Bromley-Davenport 2, Gunn, Bailey	4,500	Rose (3), Dobson (4), Beverley (3), **Bailey** (12), Forrest (1), Wilson C (2), Holden (4), Vaughton (5), Bromley-Davenport (2), Gunn (2), Bambridge EC (10)

FACT FILE

England scored in 52 consecutive matches from 1884 to 1901. Ernest 'Nudger' Needham then missed a penalty against Wales in the 1902 goalless draw. Afterwards England completed another 32 successive scoring games.

1885

Home International Championship

DATE	VENUE	OPPONENTS	SCORE	GOALSCORERS	ATTENDANCE	TEAM
Feb 28	Whelley Range, Manchester	IRELAND	W 4-0	Bambridge EC, Spilsbury, Brown J, Lofthouse	6,000	Arthur (1), Walters PM (1), Walters AM (1), **Bailey** (13), Forrest (2), Lofthouse (1), Spilsbury (1), Brown J (3), Pawson (2), Cobbold (3), Bambridge EC (11)
Mar 14	Leamington Road, Blackburn	WALES	D 1-1	Mitchell	7,500	Arthur (2), Moore (2), Ward (1), **Bailey** (14), Forrest (3), Lofthouse (2), Davenport (1), Brown J (4), Mitchell (5), Dixon (1), Bambridge EC (12)
Mar 21	Kennington Oval, London	SCOTLAND	D 1-1	Bambridge EC	8,000	Arthur (3), Walters PM (2), Walters AM (2), **Bailey** (15), Forrest (4), Amos (1), Brown J (5), Lofthouse (3), Danks (1), Bambridge EC (13), Cobbold (4)

FACT FILE

In 1885 James Forrest was the first professional to play for England. Scotland protested about his inclusion and he wore a different style jersey from the rest of the team. His wages with Blackburn Rovers were £1 a week. He received £1 playing for England, so Blackburn did not pay him that week!

1886

Home International Championship

DATE	VENUE	OPPONENTS	SCORE	GOALSCORERS	ATTENDANCE	TEAM
Mar 13	Ballynafeigh Park, Belfast	IRELAND	W 6-1	Spilsbury 4, Dewhurst, Lindley	4,500	Rose (4), **Walters PM** (3), Baugh (1), Shutt (1), Squire (1), Dobson C (1), Leighton (1), Dewhurst (1), Lindley (1), Spilsbury (2), Pike (1)
Mar 27	Second Hampden, Glasgow	SCOTLAND	D 1-1	Lindley	11,000	Arthur (4), Walters AM (3), Walters PM (4), **Bailey** (16), Squire (2), Forrest (5), Cobbold (5), Bambridge EC (14), Lindley (2), Spilsbury (3), Brann (1)
Mar 29	Racecourse Ground, Wrexham	WALES	W 3-1	Dewhurst, Amos, Brann	5,000	Arthur (5), Squire (3), Walters PM (5), **Bailey** (17), Amos (2), Forrest (6), Dewhurst (2), Brann (2), Lindley (3), Cobbold (6), Bambridge EC (15)

FACT FILE

N.L. 'Pa' Jackson, prime mover behind the Corinthians, had been the first to suggest awarding caps in 1886. Such headwear was usually worn anyway by players at the time to distinguish themselves from each other. Though the idea of white silk caps with a red rose was not taken up, the original England design was on royal blue velvet with a red rose. Later the date of the match was placed on the peak, then the initials of the opposing country and a silver tassle added. The rose eventually gave way to the three lions, which had appeared on the shirts much earlier.

1887

Home International Championship

DATE	VENUE	OPPONENTS	SCORE	GOALSCORERS	ATTENDANCE	TEAM
Feb 5	Bramall Lane, Sheffield	IRELAND	W 7-0	Cobbold 2, Lindley 3, Dewhurst 2	6,000	Arthur (6), Howarth R (1), Mason (1), Haworth G (1), Brayshaw (1), Forrest (7), Sayer (1), Dewhurst (3), Lindley (4), Cobbold (7), **Bambridge EC** (16)
Feb 26	Kennington Oval, London	WALES	W 4-0	Cobbold, Lindley 2, own goal	4,500	Arthur (7), Walters PM (6), Walters AM (4), Haworth G (2), **Bailey** (18), Forrest (8), Lofthouse (4), Dewhurst (4), Lindley (5), Cobbold (8), Bambridge EC (17)
Mar 19	Leamington Road, Blackburn	SCOTLAND	L 2-3	Dewhurst, Lindley	12,000	Roberts (1), Walters AM (5), Walters PM (7), **Bailey** (19), Haworth G (3), Forrest (9), Bambridge EC (18), Cobbold (9), Lofthouse (5), Dewhurst (5), Lindley (6)

1888

Home International Championship

DATE	VENUE	OPPONENTS	SCORE	GOALSCORERS	ATTENDANCE	TEAM
Feb 4	Nantwich Road, Crewe	WALES	W 5-1	Dewhurst 2, Woodhall, Goodall, Lindley	6,000	Moon (1), Howarth R (2), Mason (2), Saunders (1), Allen H (1), Holden-White (1), Woodhall (1), Goodall (1), **Lindley** (7), Dewhurst (6), Hodgetts (1)
Mar 17	Hampden Park, Glasgow	SCOTLAND	W 5-0	Lindley, Hodgetts, Dewhurst 2, Goodall	10,000	Moon (2), Howarth R (3), Walters PM (8), Allen H (2), Haworth G (4), Holden-White (2), Woodhall (2), Goodall (2), **Lindley** (8), Hodgetts (2), Dewhurst (7)
Apr 7	Ballynafeigh Park, Belfast	IRELAND	W 5-1	Dewhurst, Allen A 3, Lindley	7,000	Roberts (2), Aldridge (1), Walters PM (9), Holmes (1), Allen H (3), Shelton C (1), Bassett (1), Dewhurst (8), **Lindley** (9), Allen A (1), Hodgetts (3)

FACT FILE

It was at Oxford University c. 1888 that 'soc' was taken out of Association Football and turned into 'soccer'. Charles Wreford Brown is thought to have instigated the phrase when asked if he was going to play rugger. He replied: 'No, soccer.'

1889

Home International Championship

DATE	VENUE	OPPONENTS	SCORE	GOALSCORERS	ATTENDANCE	TEAM
Feb 23	Victoria Ground, Stoke	WALES	W 4-1	Bassett, Goodall, Southworth, Dewhurst	6,000	Moon (3), Walters AM (6), **Walters PM** (10), Fletcher (1), Lowder (1), Betts (1), Bassett (2), Goodall (3), Southworth (1), Dewhurst (9), Townley (1)
Mar 2	Anfield Road, Liverpool	IRELAND	W 6-1	Shelton A, Yates 3, Lofthouse, Brodie	6,000	Rowley (1), Clare (1) Aldridge (2), Wreford-Brown (1), Weir (1), Shelton A (1), Lofthouse (6), Burton (1), **Brodie** (1), Daft (1), Yates (1)
Apr 13	Kennington Oval, London	SCOTLAND	L 2-3	Bassett 2	10,000	Moon (4), Walters AM (7), **Walters PM** (11), Hammond (1), Allen H (4), Forrest (10), Brodie (2), Goodall (4), Bassett (3), Weir (2), Lindley (10)

1890

Home International Championship

DATE	VENUE	OPPONENTS	SCORE	GOALSCORERS	ATTENDANCE	TEAM
Mar 15	Racecourse Ground, Wrexham	WALES	W 3-1	Currey 2, Lindley	5,000	Moon (5), Walters AM (8), **Walters PM** (12), Fletcher (2), Holt (1), Shelton A (2), Bassett (4), Currey (1), Lindley (11), Daft (2), Wood (1)
Mar 15	Ballynafeigh Park, Belfast	IRELAND	W 9-1	Townley 2, Davenport 2, Geary 3, Lofthouse, Barton	6,000	Roberts (3), Baugh (2), Mason (3), Barton (1), Perry (1), **Forrest** (11), Lofthouse (7), Davenport (2), Geary (1), Walton (1), Townley (2)
Apr 5	Hampden Park Glasgow	SCOTLAND	D 1-1	Wood	26,379	Moon (6), Walters AM (9), **Walters PM** (13), Haworth G (5), Allen H (5), Shelton A (3), Bassett (5), Currey (2), Lindley (12), Wood (2), Daft (3)

FACT FILE

In the 1890s there were three occasions when England were engaged in two international fixtures on the same day: 15 March 1890, 7 March 1891 and 5 March 1892. This was despite the fact that only three such matches were played each season. England met Ireland and Wales each time and won all six games.

1891

Home International Championship

DATE	VENUE	OPPONENTS	SCORE	GOALSCORERS	ATTENDANCE	TEAM
Mar 7	Newcastle Road, Sunderland	WALES	W 4-1	Goodall, Southworth, Chadwick, Milward	15,000	Wilkinson (1), Porteous (1), Jackson (1), Smith A (1), Holt (2), Shelton A (4), Brann (3), **Goodall** (5), Southworth (2), Milward (1), Chadwick (1)
Mar 7	Molineux, Wolverhampton	IRELAND	W 6-1	Cotterill, Daft, Henfrey, Lindley 2, Bassett	15,231	Rose (5), Marsden (1), Underwood (1), Bayliss (1), Perry (2), Brodie (3), Bassett (6), Cotterill (1), **Lindley** (13), Henfrey (1), Daft (4)
Apr 6	Ewood Park, Blackburn	SCOTLAND	W 2-1	Goodall, Chadwick	8,000	**Moon** (7), Howarth R (4), Holmes (2), Smith A (2), Holt (3), Shelton A (5), Bassett (7), Goodall (6), Geary (2), Chadwick (2), Milward (2)

FACT FILE

At Blackburn in 1891, thousands stayed away from the match with Scotland because there were no Rovers players in the England team. But the second England goal was scored by Edgar Chadwick of Everton, born in Blackburn.

1892

Home International Championship

DATE	VENUE	OPPONENTS	SCORE	GOALSCORERS	ATTENDANCE	TEAM
Mar 5	Racecourse Ground, Wrexham	WALES	W 2-0	Henfrey, Sandilands	4,500	Toone (1), **Dunn** (3), Lilley (1), Hossack (1), Winckworth (1), Kinsey (1), Gosling (1), Cotterill (2), Henfrey (2), Schofield (1), Sandilands (1)
Mar 5	Solitude, Belfast	IRELAND	W 2-0	Daft 2	7,000	Rowley (2), Underwood (2), Clare (2), Cox (1), Holt (4), Whitham (1), Athersmith (1), Pearson (1), Devey (1), **Daft** (5), Hodgetts (4)
Apr 2	Ibrox Park, Glasgow	SCOTLAND	W 4-1	Southworth, Goodall 2, Chadwick	21,000	Toone (2), **Dunn** (4), Holmes (3), Holt (5), Reynolds (1), Shelton A (6), Bassett (8), Goodall (7), Chadwick (3), Hodgetts (5), Southworth (3)

1893

Home International Championship

DATE	VENUE	OPPONENTS	SCORE	GOALSCORERS	ATTENDANCE	TEAM
Feb 25	Perry Barr, Birmingham	IRELAND	W 6-1	Sandilands, Gilliatt 3, Winckworth, Smith GO	10,000	Charsley (1), Harrison (1), Pelly (1), Smith A (3), Winckworth (2), Cooper (1), Topham R (1), Smith GO (1), **Cotterill** (3), Gilliatt (1), Sandilands (2)
Mar 13	Victoria Ground, Stoke	WALES	W 6-0	Spiksley 2, Goodall, Bassett, Schofield, Reynolds	10,000	Sutcliffe (1), Clare (3), **Holmes** (4), Reynolds (2), Perry (3), Turner (1), Bassett (9), Whitehead (1), Goodall (8), Schofield (2), Spiksley (1)
Apr 1	Richmond Athletic Ground, London	SCOTLAND	W 5-2	Spiksley 2, Gosling, Cotterill, Reynolds	16,000	Gay (1), Harrison (2), Holmes (5), Reynolds (3), Holt (6), Kinsey (2), Bassett (10), Gosling (2), **Cotterill** (4), Chadwick (4), Spiksley (2)

FACT FILE

England's most successful sequence of results began in 1890 against Wales and ended against the same opposition in 1896 after 20 unbeaten matches, comprising 16 wins (including nine successive wins) and four draws.

1894

Home International Championship

DATE	VENUE	OPPONENTS	SCORE	GOALSCORERS	ATTENDANCE	TEAM
Mar 1	Solitude, Belfast	IRELAND	D 2-2	Devey, Spiksley	8,000	Reader (1), Howarth R (5), **Holmes** (6), Reynolds (4), Holt (7), Crabtree (1), Chippendale (1), Whitehead (2), Devey (2), Hodgetts (6), Spiksley (3)
Mar 12	Racecourse Ground, Wrexham	WALES	W 5-1	Veitch 3, Gosling, own goal	5,500	Gay (2), Lodge (1), Pelly (2), Hossack (2), Wreford-Brown (2), Topham A (1), Topham R (2), **Gosling** (3), Smith GO (2), Veitch (1), Sandilands (3)
Apr 7	Celtic Park, Glasgow	SCOTLAND	D 2-2	Goodall, Reynolds	45,107	Gay (3), Clare (4), Pelly (3), Reynolds (5), Holt (8), Needham (1), Bassett (11), Smith GO (3), **Goodall** (9), Chadwick (5), Spiksley (4)

1895

Home International Championship

DATE	VENUE	OPPONENTS	SCORE	GOALSCORERS	ATTENDANCE	TEAM
Mar 9	County Cricket Club, Derby	IRELAND	W 9-0	Bloomer 2, Goodall 2, Bassett, Howell, Becton 2, own goal	8,000	Sutcliffe (2), Crabtree (2), **Holmes** (7), Howell (1), Crawshaw (1), Turner (2), Bassett (12), Bloomer (1), Goodall (10), Becton (1), Schofield (3)
Mar 18	Queen's Club, London	WALES	D 1-1	Sandilands	13,000	Raikes (1), Lodge (2), Oakley (1), Henfrey (3), **Wreford-Brown** (3), Barker (1), Stanbrough (1), Dewhurst (1), Smith GO (4), Gosling (4), Sandilands (4)
Apr 6	Goodison Park, Liverpool	SCOTLAND	W 3-0	Bloomer, Smith S, own goal	42,500	Sutcliffe (3), Crabtree (3), Lodge (3), Needham (2), Holt (9), Reynolds (6), **Gosling** (5), Smith S (1), Goodall (11), Bassett (13), Bloomer (2)

FACT FILE

In 1895, Rabbi Howell was probably the only full-blooded Romany ever to play for England. It was said he had been born in a caravan near Sheffield.

1896

Home International Championship

DATE	VENUE	OPPONENTS	SCORE	GOALSCORERS	ATTENDANCE	TEAM
Mar 7	Solitude, Belfast	IRELAND	W 2-0	Bloomer, Smith GO	12,000	Raikes (2), Lodge (4), Oakley (2), Crabtree (4), Crawshaw (2), Kinsey (3), Bassett (14), Bloomer (3), **Smith GO** (5), Chadwick (6), Spiksley (5)
Mar 16	Arms Park, Cardiff	WALES	W 9-1	Bloomer 5, Smith GO 2, Goodall, Bassett	10,000	Raikes (3), Oakley (3), Crabtree (5), Henfrey (4), Crawshaw (3), Kinsey (4), Bassett (15), Bloomer (4), **Smith GO** (6), Goodall (12), Sandilands (5)
Apr 4	Celtic Park, Glasgow	SCOTLAND	L 1-2	Bassett	57,000	Raikes (4), Lodge (5), Oakley (4), Crabtree (6), Crawshaw (4), Henfrey (5), Goodall (13), Bassett (16), **Smith GO** (7), Wood (3), Burnup (1)

1897

Home International Championship

DATE	VENUE	OPPONENTS	SCORE	GOALSCORERS	ATTENDANCE	TEAM
Feb 20	Trent Bridge, Nottingham	IRELAND	W 6-0	Bloomer 2, Wheldon 3, Athersmith	14,000	Robinson (1), Oakley (5), Williams (1), Middleditch (1), Crawshaw (5), Needham (3), Athersmith (2), Bloomer (5), **Smith GO** (8), Wheldon (1), Bradshaw (1)
Mar 29	Bramall Lane, Sheffield	WALES	W 4-0	Bloomer, Needham, Milward 2	5,000	Foulke (1), Oakley (6), Spencer (1), Reynolds (7), Crawshaw (6), Needham (4), Athersmith (3), Bloomer (6), **Smith GO** (9), Becton (1), Milward (3)
Apr 3	Crystal Palace, London	SCOTLAND	L 1-2	Bloomer	37,000	Robinson (2), Oakley (7), Spencer (2), Reynolds (8), Crawshaw (7), Needham (5), Athersmith (4), Bloomer (7), **Smith GO** (10), Chadwick (7), Milward (4)

FACT FILE

Between 1895 and 1899, Steve Bloomer scored in ten consecutive matches notching up a total of 19 goals.

1898

Home International Championship

DATE	VENUE	OPPONENTS	SCORE	GOALSCORERS	ATTENDANCE	TEAM
Mar 5	Solitude, Belfast	IRELAND	W 3-2	Morren, Athersmith, Smith GO	12,000	Robinson (3), Oakley (8), Williams (2), Forman (Frank) (1), Morren (1), Turner (3), Athersmith (5), Richards (1), **Smith GO** (11), Garfield (1), Wheldon (2)
Mar 28	Racecourse Ground, Wrexham	WALES	W 3-0	Smith GO, Wheldon 2	4,000	Robinson (4), Oakley (9), Williams (3), Perry T (1), Booth (1), Needham (6), Athersmith (6), Goodall (14), **Smith GO** (12), Wheldon (3), Spiksley (6)
Apr 2	Celtic Park, Glasgow	SCOTLAND	W 3-1	Bloomer 2, Wheldon	40,000	Robinson (5), Williams (4), Oakley (10), Needham (7), **Wreford-Brown** (4), Forman (Frank) (2), Spiksley (7), Wheldon (4), Smith GO (13), Bloomer (8), Athersmith (7)

1899

Home International Championship

DATE	VENUE	OPPONENTS	SCORE	GOALSCORERS	ATTENDANCE	TEAM
Feb 18	Roker Park, Sunderland	IRELAND	W13-2	Frank Forman, Bloomer 2, Athersmith, Settle 3, Smith GO 4, Fred Forman 2	13,000	Hillman (1), Bach (1), Williams (5), Forman (Frank) (3), Crabtree (7), Needham (8), Athersmith (8), Bloomer (9), **Smith GO** (14), Settle (1), Forman (Fred) (1)
Mar 20	Ashton Gate, Bristol	WALES	W 4-0	Bloomer 2, Fred Forman, Needham	10,000	Robinson (6), Thickett (1), Williams (6), Needham (9), Crabtree (8), Forman (Frank) (4), Athersmith (9), Bloomer (10), **Smith GO** (15), Settle (2), Forman (Fred) (2)
Apr 8	Villa Park, Birmingham	SCOTLAND	W 2-1	Smith GO, Settle	22,000	Robinson (7), Thickett (2), Crabtree (9), Forman (Frank) (5), Howell (2), Needham (10), Athersmith (10), Bloomer (11), **Smith GO** (16), Settle (3), Forman (Fred) (3)

1900

Home International Championship

DATE	VENUE	OPPONENTS	SCORE	GOALSCORERS	ATTENDANCE	TEAM
Mar 17	Lansdowne Road, Dublin	IRELAND	W 2-0	Johnson, Sagar	8,000	Robinson (8), Oakley (11), Crabtree (10), Johnson (1), Holt (10), Needham (11), Turner (1), Cunliffe (1), **Smith GO** (17), Sagar (1), Priest (1)
Mar 26	Arms Park, Cardiff	WALES	D 1-1	Wilson	20,000	Robinson (9), Spencer (3), Oakley (12), Johnson (2), Chadwick A (1), Crabtree (11), Athersmith (11), Foster (1), **Smith GO** (18), Wilson (1), Spouncer (1)
Apr 7	Celtic Park, Glasgow	SCOTLAND	L 1-4	Bloomer	64,000	Robinson (10), Oakley (13), Crabtree (12), Johnson (3), Chadwick A (2), Needham (12), Athersmith (12), Bloomer (12), **Smith GO** (19), Wilson (2), Plant (1)

1901

Home International Championship

DATE	VENUE	OPPONENTS	SCORE	GOALSCORERS	ATTENDANCE	TEAM
Mar 9	The Dell, Southampton	IRELAND	W 3-0	Foster 2, Crawshaw	8,000	Robinson (11), Fry (1), **Oakley** (14), Jones W (1), Crawshaw (8), Needham (13), Turner (2), Foster (2), Hedley (1), Banks (1), Cox (1)
Mar 18	St James' Park, Newcastle	WALES	W 6-0	Bloomer 4, Foster, Needham (pen)	11,000	Kingsley (1), Crabtree (13), Oakley (15), Wilkes (1), Bannister (1), **Needham** (14), Bennett (1), Bloomer (13), Beats (1), Foster (3), Corbett B (1)
Mar 30	Crystal Palace, London	SCOTLAND	D 2-2	Blackburn, Bloomer	35,000	Sutcliffe (4), Iremonger (1), Oakley (16), Wilkes (2), Forman (Frank) (6), Needham (15), Bennett (2), Bloomer (14), **Smith GO** (20), Foster (4), Blackburn (1)

1902

Home International Championship

DATE	VENUE	OPPONENTS	SCORE	GOALSCORERS	ATTENDANCE	TEAM
Mar 3	Racecourse Ground, Wrexham	WALES	D 0-0		8,000	George (1), Crompton (1), Crabtree (14), Wilkes (3), Abbott (1), Needham (16), Hogg (1), Bloomer (15), Sagar (2), **Foster** (5), Lipsham (1)
Mar 22	Balmoral Showgrounds, Belfast	IRELAND	W 1-0	Settle	16,000	George (2), Crompton (2), Iremonger (2), Wilkes (4), Bannister (2), **Forman (Frank)** (7), Hogg (2), Bloomer (16), Calvey (1), Settle (4), Blackburn (2)
May 3	Villa Park, Birmingham	SCOTLAND	D 2-2	Wilkes, Settle	15,000	George (3), Crompton (3), Molyneux (1), Wilkes (5), Forman (Frank) (8), Houlker (1), Hogg (3), **Bloomer** (17), Beats (2), Settle (5), Cox (2)

1903

Home International Championship

DATE	VENUE	OPPONENTS	SCORE	GOALSCORERS	ATTENDANCE	TEAM
Feb 14	Molineux, Wolverhampton	IRELAND	W 4-0	Sharp, Davis H, Woodward 2	24,240	Baddeley (1), **Spencer** (4), Molyneux (2), Johnson (4), Holford (1), Hadley (1), Davis H (1), Sharp (1), Woodward (1), Settle (6), Lockett (1)
Mar 2	Fratton Park, Portsmouth	WALES	W 2-1	Bache, Woodward	4,000	Sutcliffe (5), **Crompton** (4), Molyneux (3), Johnson (5), Forman (Frank) (9), Houlker (2), Davis H (2), Garraty (1), Woodward (2), Bache (1), Corbett R (1)
Apr 4	Bramall Lane, Sheffield	SCOTLAND	L 1-2	Woodward	36,000	Baddeley (2), **Crompton** (5), Molyneux (4), Johnson (6), Booth (2), Houlker (3), Davis H (3), Humphreys (1), Woodward (3), Capes (1), Cox (3)

1904

Home International Championship

DATE	VENUE	OPPONENTS	SCORE	GOALSCORERS	ATTENDANCE	TEAM
Feb 29	Racecourse Ground, Wrexham	WALES	D 2-2	Davis G, Bache	9,000	Baddeley (3), **Crompton** (6), Burgess (1), Lee (1), Crawshaw (9), Ruddlesdin (1), Brawn (1), Common (1), Brown A (1), Bache (2), Davis G (1)
Mar 12	Solitude, Belfast	IRELAND	W 3-1	Common 2, Bache	15,000	Baddeley (4), **Crompton** (7), Burgess (2), Ruddlesdin (2), Crawshaw (10), Leake (1), Brawn (2), Common (2), Woodward (4), Bache (3), Davis G (2)
Apr 9	Celtic Park, Glasgow	SCOTLAND	W 1-0	Bloomer	40,000	Baddeley (5), **Crompton** (8), Burgess (3), Wolstenholme (1), Wilkinson (1), Leake (2), Rutherford (1), Bloomer (18), Woodward (5), Harris (1), Blackburn (3)

FACT FILE

Winger Richard Bond, capped eight times before World War I from 1905, served in the Bradford Pals Battalion during the conflict and was captured by the Germans. Steve Bloomer, who had been coaching in Berlin when war broke out, was interned.

1905

Home International Championship

DATE	VENUE	OPPONENTS	SCORE	GOALSCORERS	ATTENDANCE	TEAM
Feb 25	Ayresome Park, Middlesbrough	IRELAND	D 1-1	Bloomer	21,700	Williamson (1), Balmer (1), Carr (1), Wolstenholme (2), Roberts (1), Leake (3), Bond (1), Bloomer (19), Woodward (6), **Harris** (2), Booth F (1)
Mar 27	Anfield, Liverpool	WALES	W 3-1	Woodward 2, Harris	16,000	Linacre (1), **Spencer** (5), Smith H (1), Wolstenholme (3), Roberts (2), Leake (4), Bond (2), Bloomer (20), Woodward (7), Harris (3), Hardman (1)
Apr 1	Crystal Palace, London	SCOTLAND	W 1-0	Bache	27,559	Linacre (2), **Spencer** (6), Smith H (2), Ruddlesdin (3), Roberts (3), Leake (5), Sharp (2), Bloomer (21), Woodward (8), Bache (4), Bridgett (1)

1906

Home International Championship

DATE	VENUE	OPPONENTS	SCORE	GOALSCORERS	ATTENDANCE	TEAM
Feb 17	Solitude, Belfast	IRELAND	W 5-0	Bond 2, Day, Harris, Brown A	16,000	Ashcroft (1), Crompton (9), Smith H (3), Warren (1), Veitch (1), Houlker (4), Bond (3), Day (1), Brown A (2), **Harris** (4), Gosnell (1)
Mar 19	Arms Park, Cardiff	WALES	W 1-0	Day	15,000	Ashcroft (2), Crompton (10), Smith H (4), Warren (2), Veitch (2), Houlker (5), Bond (4), Day (2), Common (3), **Harris** (5), Wright (1)
Apr 7	Hampden Park, Glasgow	SCOTLAND	L 1-2	Shepherd	102,741	Ashcroft (3), Crompton (11), Burgess (4), Warren (3), Veitch (3), Makepeace (1), Bond (5), Day (3), Shepherd (1), **Harris** (6), Conlin (1),

---

FACT FILE

Stanley Harris, fully capped six times for England, was also an amateur international and scored seven goals in the 15-0 win over France in Paris on 1 October 1906.

Several players capped for England have either previously or subsequently also appeared for other home countries. John Hawley Edwards played for England v Scotland in 1874, despite having been born in Wales. In 1876 he turned out for Wales v Scotland. John Reynolds had already played five times for Ireland when it was discovered that he had been born in Blackburn and appeared eight times for England. Bob Evans played for Wales v England four times in ten internationals and for England against Wales twice in four appearances from 1906. Additionally, Stuart Macrae, born in Bute, Scotland made five appearances for England 1883-84.

1907

Home International Championship

DATE	VENUE	OPPONENTS	SCORE	GOALSCORERS	ATTENDANCE	TEAM
Feb 16	Goodison Park, Liverpool	IRELAND	W 1-0	Hardman	22,235	Hardy (1), **Crompton** (12), Carr (2), Warren (4), Wedlock (1), Hawkes (1), Rutherford (2), Coleman (1), Hilsdon (1), Bache (5), Hardman (2)
Mar 18	Craven Cottage, London	WALES	D 1-1	Stewart	25,000	Hardy (2), **Crompton** (13), Pennington (1), Warren (5), Wedlock (2), Veitch (4), Rutherford (3), Bloomer (22), Thornley (1), Stewart (1), Wall (1)
Apr 6	St James' Park, Newcastle	SCOTLAND	D 1-1	Bloomer	35,829	Hardy (3), **Crompton** (14), Pennington (2), Warren (6), Wedlock (3), Veitch (5), Rutherford (4), Bloomer (23), Woodward (9), Stewart (2), Hardman (3)

1908

Home International Championship

DATE	VENUE	OPPONENTS	SCORE	GOALSCORERS	ATTENDANCE	TEAM
Feb 15	Solitude, Belfast	IRELAND	W 3-1	Woodward, Hilsdon 2	22,600	Maskrey (1), Crompton (15), Pennington (3), Warren (7), Wedlock (4), Lintott (1), Rutherford (5), **Woodward** (10), Hilsdon (2), Windridge (1), Wall (2)
Mar 16	Racecourse Ground, Wrexham	WALES	W 7-1	Wedlock, Windridge, Hilsdon 2, Woodward 3,	8,000	Bailey (1), Crompton (16), Pennington (4), Warren (8), Wedlock (5), Lintott (2), Rutherford (6), **Woodward** (11), Hilsdon (3), Windridge (2), Hardman (4)
Apr 4	Hampden Park, Glasgow	SCOTLAND	D 1-1	Windridge	121,452	Hardy (4), Crompton (17), Pennington (5), Warren (9), Wedlock (6), Lintott (3), Rutherford (7), **Woodward** (12), Hilsdon (4), Windridge (3), Bridgett (2),

Friendlies

DATE	VENUE	OPPONENTS	SCORE	GOALSCORERS	ATTENDANCE	TEAM
Jun 6	Vienna	AUSTRIA	W 6-1	Hilsdon 2, Windridge 2, Bridgett, Woodward	5,000	Bailey (2), Crompton (18), Corbett (1), Warren (10), Wedlock (7), Hawkes (2), Rutherford (8), **Woodward** (13), Hilsdon (5), Windridge (4), Bridgett (3)
Jun 8	Vienna	AUSTRIA	W 11-1	Woodward 4, Bridgett, Bradshaw 3, Warren, Rutherford, Windridge	5,000	Bailey (3), Crompton (19), Pennington (6), Warren (11), Wedlock (8), Hawkes (3), Rutherford (9), **Woodward** (14), Bradshaw (1), Windridge (5), Bridgett (4)
Jun 10	Budapest	HUNGARY	W 7-0	Hilsdon 4, Windridge, Woodward, Rutherford	6,500	Bailey (4), Crompton (20), Corbett (2), Warren (12), Wedlock (9), Hawkes (4), Rutherford (10), **Woodward** (15), Hilsdon (6), Windridge (6), Bridgett (5)
Jun 13	Prague	BOHEMIA	W 4-0	Hilsdon 2 (1 pen), Windridge, Rutherford	12,000	Bailey (5), Crompton (21), Corbett (3), Warren (13), Wedlock (10), Hawkes (5), Rutherford (11), **Woodward** (16), Hilsdon (7), Windridge (7), Bridgett (6)

FACT FILE

Bob Crompton of Blackburn Rovers, capped 41 times by England, was probably the first professional footballer to drive his own car to the ground for training in 1908.

1909

Home International Championship

DATE	VENUE	OPPONENTS	SCORE	GOALSCORERS	ATTENDANCE	TEAM
Feb 13	Valley Parade, Bradford	IRELAND	W 4-0	Hilsdon 2 (1 pen), Woodward 2	28,000	Hardy (5), Crompton (22), Cottle (1), Warren (14), Wedlock (11), Lintott (4), Berry (1), **Woodward** (17), Hilsdon (8), Windridge (8), Bridgett (7)
Mar 15	City Ground Nottingham	WALES	W 2-0	Holley, Freeman	11,500	Hardy (6), Crompton (23), Pennington (7), Warren (15), Wedlock (12), Veitch (6), Pentland (1), **Woodward** (18), Freeman (1), Holley (1), Bridgett (8)
Apr 3	Crystal Palace, London	SCOTLAND	W 2-0	Wall 2	40,000	Hardy (7), **Crompton** (24), Pennington (8), Warren (16), Wedlock (13), Lintott (5), Pentland (2), Fleming (1), Freeman (2), Holley (2), Wall (3)

Friendlies

DATE	VENUE	OPPONENTS	SCORE	GOALSCORERS	ATTENDANCE	TEAM
May 29	Budapest	HUNGARY	W 4-2	Woodward 2, Fleming, Bridgett	10,000	Hardy (8), Crompton (25), Pennington (9), Warren (17), Wedlock (14), Lintott (6), Pentland (3), Fleming (2), **Woodward** (19), Holley (3), Bridgett (9)
May 31	Budapest	HUNGARY	W 8-2	Woodward 4, Fleming 2, Holley 2	13,000	Hardy (9), Crompton (26), Pennington (10), Warren (18), Wedlock (15), Lintott (7), Pentland (4), Fleming (3), **Woodward** (20), Holley (4), Bridgett (10)
Jun 1	Vienna	AUSTRIA	W 8-1	Woodward 3, Warren, Halse 2, Holley 2	3,000	Hardy (10), Crompton (27), Pennington (11), Warren (19), Wedlock (16), Richards (1), Pentland (5), Halse (1), **Woodward** (21), Holley (5), Bridgett (11)

FACT FILE

Vivian Woodward not only played 23 times for the full England team, he appeared in 41 amateur internationals and was in Great Britain's Olympic teams of 1908 and 1912.

1910

Home International Championship

DATE	VENUE	OPPONENTS	SCORE	GOALSCORERS	ATTENDANCE	TEAM
Feb 12	Solitude, Belfast	IRELAND	D 1-1	Fleming	25,000	Hardy (11), Morley (1), Cowell (1), Ducat (1), Wedlock (17), Bradshaw (1), Bond (6), Fleming (4), **Woodward** (22), Bache (6), Hall (1)
Mar 14	Arms Park Cardiff	WALES	W 1-0	Ducat	20,000	Hardy (12), **Crompton** (28), Pennington (12), Ducat (2), Wedlock (18), Bradshaw (2), Bond (7), Fleming (5), Parkinson (1), Holley (6), Wall (4)
Apr 2	Hampden Park, Glasgow	SCOTLAND	L 0-2		106,200	Hardy (13), **Crompton** (29), Pennington (13), Ducat (3), Wedlock (19), Makepeace (2), Bond (8), Hibbert (1), Parkinson (2), Hardinge (1), Wall (5)

1911

Home International Championship

DATE	VENUE	OPPONENTS	SCORE	GOALSCORERS	ATTENDANCE	TEAM
Feb 11	Baseball Ground, Derby	IRELAND	W 2-1	Shepherd, Evans	20,000	Williamson (2), **Crompton** (30), Pennington (14), Warren (20), Wedlock (20), Sturgess (1), Simpson (1), Fleming (6), Shepherd (2), Woodger (1), Evans (1)
Mar 13	The Den, London	WALES	W 3-0	Woodward 2, Webb	22,000	Williamson (3), Crompton (31), Pennington (15), Warren (21), Wedlock (21), Hunt (1), Simpson (2), Fleming (7), Webb (1), **Woodward** (23), Evans (2)
Apr 1	Goodison Park, Liverpool	SCOTLAND	D 1-1	Stewart	50,000	Williamson (4), **Crompton** (32), Pennington (16), Warren (22), Wedlock (22), Hunt (2), Simpson (3), Stewart (3), Webb (2), Bache (7), Evans (3)

FACT FILE

Some time after Bob Crompton passed the record of international appearances held by Steve Bloomer, he was presented with a portrait of himself in oils at a select gathering at Blackburn in 1911.

1912

Home International Championship

DATE	VENUE	OPPONENTS	SCORE	GOALSCORERS	ATTENDANCE	TEAM
Feb 10	Dalymount Park, Dublin	IRELAND	W 6-1	Fleming 3, Freeman, Holley, Simpson	15,000	Hardy (14), **Crompton** (33), Pennington (17), Brittleton (1), Wedlock (23), Bradshaw (3), Simpson (4), Fleming (8), Freeman (3), Holley (7), Mordue (1)
Mar 11	Racecourse Ground, Wrexham	WALES	W 2-0	Holley, Freeman	14,000	Williamson (5), **Crompton** (34), Pennington (18), Brittleton (2), Wedlock (24), Makepeace (3), Simpson (5), Jefferis (1), Freeman (4), Holley (8), Evans (4)
Mar 23	Hampden Park, Glasgow	SCOTLAND	D 1-1	Holley	127,307	Williamson (6), **Crompton** (35), Pennington (19), Brittleton (3), Wedlock (25), Makepeace (4), Simpson (6), Jefferis (2), Freeman (5), Holley (9), Wall (6)

1913

Home International Championship

DATE	VENUE	OPPONENTS	SCORE	GOALSCORERS	ATTENDANCE	TEAM
Feb 15	Windsor Park, Belfast	IRELAND	L 1-2	Buchan	20,000	Williamson (7), **Crompton** (36), Benson (1), Cuggy (1), Boyle (1), Utley (1), Mordue (2), Buchan (1), Elliott (1), Smith (Joe) (1), Wall (7)
Mar 17	Ashton Gate, Bristol	WALES	W 4-3	Fleming, McCall, Latheron, Hampton	8,000	Scattergood (1), **Crompton** (37), Pennington (20), Moffat (1), McCall (1), Bradshaw (4), Wallace (1), Fleming (9), Hampton (1), Latheron (1), Hodkinson (1)
Apr 5	Stamford Bridge, London	SCOTLAND	W 1-0	Hampton	52,500	Hardy (15), **Crompton** (38), Pennington (21), Brittleton (4), McCall (2), Watson (1), Simpson (7), Fleming (10), Hampton (2), Holley (10), Hodkinson (2)

1914

Home International Championship

DATE	VENUE	OPPONENTS	SCORE	GOALSCORERS	ATTENDANCE	TEAM
Feb 14	Ayresome Park, Middlesbrough	IRELAND	L 0-3		25,000	Hardy (16), **Crompton** (39), Pennington (22), Cuggy (2), Buckley (1), Watson (2), Wallace (2), Shea (1), Elliott (2), Latheron (2), Martin (1)
Mar 16	Ninian Park, Cardiff	WALES	W 2-0	Smith (Joe), Wedlock	17,000	Hardy (17), **Crompton** (40), Colclough (1), Brittleton (5), Wedlock (26), McNeal (1), Simpson (8), Shea (2), Hampton (3), Smith (Joe) (2), Mosscrop (1)
Apr 4	Hampden Park, Glasgow	SCOTLAND	L 1-3	Fleming	127,307	Hardy (18), **Crompton** (41), Pennington (23), Sturgess (2), McCall (3), McNeal (2), Walden (1), Fleming (11), Hampton (4), Smith (Joe) (3), Mosscrop (2)

1919

Victory Internationals

DATE	VENUE	OPPONENTS	SCORE	GOALSCORERS	ATTENDANCE	TEAM
Apr 26	Goodison Park, Liverpool	SCOTLAND	D 2-2	Turnbull, Puddefoot	45,000	Hardy (*1*), Longworth (*1*), **Duckworth** (*1*), Fleetwood (*1*), McCall (*1*), Grimsdell (*1*), Turnbull (*1*), Shea (*1*), Puddefoot (*1*), Joe Smith (*1*), Martin (*1*)
May 3	Hampden Park, Glasgow	SCOTLAND	W 4-3	Grimsdell 2, Puddefoot 2	80,000	Hardy (*2*), Longworth (*2*), **Duckworth** (*2*), Fleetwood (*2*), McCall (*2*), Grimsdell (*2*), Turnbull (*2*), Shea (*2*), Puddefoot (*2*), Joe Smith (*2*), Martin (*2*)
Oct 11	Ninian Park, Cardiff	WALES	L 1-2	Puddefoot	20,000	Williamson (*1*), Ball (*1*), **Knight** (*1*), Voysey (*1*), Hilditch (*1*), Grenyer (*1*), Hendren (*1*), Buchan (*1*), Puddefoot (*3*), Barnes (*1*), Brooks (*1*)
Oct 18	Victoria Ground, Stoke	WALES	W 2-0	Whittingham, Joe Smith	19,765	Hardy (*3*), Smith J (*1*), **Hudspeth** (*1*), Bagshaw (*1*), Parker (*1*), Watson (*1*), Turnbull (*3*), Whittingham (*1*), Cock (*1*), Joe Smith (*3*), Hodkinson (*1*)

Home International Championship

DATE	VENUE	OPPONENTS	SCORE	GOALSCORERS	ATTENDANCE	TEAM
Oct 25	Windsor Park, Belfast	IRELAND	D 1-1	Cock	30,000	Hardy (19), Smith J (1), **Knight** (1), Bagshaw (1), Bowser (1), Watson (3), Turnbull (1), Carr (1), Cock (1), Smith (Joe) (4), Hodkinson (3)

1920

Home International Championship

DATE	VENUE	OPPONENTS	SCORE	GOALSCORERS	ATTENDANCE	TEAM
Mar 15	Highbury, London	WALES	L 1-2	Buchan	21,100	Hardy (20), Clay (1), **Pennington** (24), Ducat (4), Barson (1), Grimsdell (1), Chedgzoy (1), Buchan (1), Elliott (3), Smith (Joe) (5), Quantrill (1)
Apr 10	Hillsborough, Sheffield	SCOTLAND	W 5-4	Kelly 2, Cock, Morris, Quantrill	40,000	Hardy (21), Longworth (1), **Pennington** (25), Ducat (5), McCall (4), Grimsdell (2), Wallace (3), Kelly (1), Cock (2), Morris (1), Quantrill (2)
Oct 23	Roker Park, Sunderland	IRELAND	W 2-0	Kelly, Walker	22,000	Mew (1), Downs (1), Bullock (1), Ducat (6), **McCall** (5), Grimsdell (3), Chedgzoy (2), Kelly (2), Walker (1), Morris (2), Quantrill (3)

FACT FILE

One of the oldest teams to represent England was the 1920 team which faced Scotland. The average age was 30 with six of the side over that age.

1921

Home International Championship

DATE	VENUE	OPPONENTS	SCORE	GOALSCORERS	ATTENDANCE	TEAM
Mar 14	Ninian Park, Cardiff	WALES	D 0-0		12,000	Coleman (1), Cresswell (1), Silcock (1), Bamber (1), Wilson (1), Bromilow (1), Chedgzoy (3), Kelly (3), **Buchan** (3), Chambers (1), Quantrill (4)
Apr 9	Hampden Park, Glasgow	SCOTLAND	L 0-3		100,000	Gough (1), Smart (1), Silcock (1), Smith B (1), Wilson (2), **Grimsdell** (4), Chedgzoy (4), Kelly (4), Chambers (2), Bliss (1), Dimmock (1)

Friendly

DATE	VENUE	OPPONENTS	SCORE	GOALSCORERS	ATTENDANCE	TEAM
May 21	Brussels	BELGIUM	W 2-0	Buchan, Chambers	25,000	Baker H (1), Fort (1), **Longworth** (2), Read (1), Wilson (3), Barton (1), Rawlings A (1), Seed (1), Buchan (4), Chambers (3), Harrison (1)

Home International Championship

DATE	VENUE	OPPONENTS	SCORE	GOALSCORERS	ATTENDANCE	TEAM
Oct 22	Windsor Park, Belfast	IRELAND	D 1-1	Kirton	30,000	Dawson (1), Clay (2), Lucas (1), Moss (1), **Wilson** (4), Barton (2), Chedgzoy (5), Kirton (1), Simms (1), Walker (2), Harrison (2)

FACT FILE

Benjamin Howard Baker, the Chelsea goalkeeper who first played for England in 1921, was an Olympic standard high jump and pentathlon athlete, Wimbledon tennis player, club cricketer, water polo international and accomplished swimmer.

1922

Home International Championship

DATE	VENUE	OPPONENTS	SCORE	GOALSCORERS	ATTENDANCE	TEAM
Mar 13	Anfield, Liverpool	WALES	W 1-0	Kelly	30,000	Davison (1), Clay (3), Titmuss (1), Smith B (2) **Woosnam** (1), Bromilow (2), Walden (2), Kelly (5), Rawlings W (1), Walker (3), Smith WH (1)
Apr 8	Villa Park, Birmingham	SCOTLAND	L 0-1		33,646	Dawson (2), Clay (4), Wadsworth (1), Moss (2), **Wilson** (5), Bromilow (3), York (1), Kelly (6), Rawlings W (2), Walker (4), Smith WH (1)
Oct 21	The Hawthorns, West Bromwich	IRELAND	W 2-0	Chambers 2	20,173	Taylor (1), Smith J (2), Harrow (1), Moss (3), Wilson (6), **Grimsdell** (5), Mercer (1), Seed (2), Osborne (1), Chambers (4), Williams (1)

FACT FILE

Max Woosnam may have been a 1922 one-cap international wonder, but he also won the men's tennis doubles at the 1920 Olympics and had similar success at Wimbledon.

1923

Home International Championship

DATE	VENUE	OPPONENTS	SCORE	GOALSCORERS	ATTENDANCE	TEAM
Mar 5	Ninian Park, Cardiff	WALES	D 2-2	Chambers, Watson	15,000	Taylor (2), Longworth (3), Titmuss (2), Magee (1), Wilson (7), **Grimsdell** (6), Carr (2), Seed (3), Watson (1), Chambers (5), Williams (2)

Friendly

DATE	VENUE	OPPONENTS	SCORE	GOALSCORERS	ATTENDANCE	TEAM
Mar 19	Highbury, London	BELGIUM	W 6-1	Hegan 2, Chambers, Mercer, Seed, Bullock	14,052	Taylor (3), Longworth (4), Wadsworth (2), Kean (1), **Wilson** (8), Bromilow (4), Mercer (2), Seed (4), Bullock (1), Chambers (6), Hegan (1)

Home International Championship

DATE	VENUE	OPPONENTS	SCORE	GOALSCORERS	ATTENDANCE	TEAM
Apr 14	Hampden Park, Glasgow	SCOTLAND	D 2-2	Kelly, Watson	71,000	Taylor (4), Longworth (5), Wadsworth (3), Kean (2), **Wilson** (9), Tresadern (1), Chedgzoy (6), Kelly (7), Watson (2), Chambers (7), Tunstall (1)

Friendlies

DATE	VENUE	OPPONENTS	SCORE	GOALSCORERS	ATTENDANCE	TEAM
May 10	Paris	FRANCE	W 4-1	Hegan 2, Buchan, Creek	30,000	Alderson (1), Cresswell (2), Jones H (1), Plum (1), Seddon (1), Barton (3), Osborne (2), **Buchan** (5), Creek (1), Hartley (1), Hegan (2)
May 21	Stockholm	SWEDEN	W 4-2	Walker 2, Moore J, Thornewell	14,500	Williamson (1), Ashurst (1), Harrow (2), **Patchitt** (1), Seddon (2), Tresadern (2), Thornewell (1), Moore J (1), Bedford (1), Walker (5), Urwin (1)
May 24	Stockholm	SWEDEN	W 3-1	Moore W 2, Miller	12,000	Williamson (2), Ashurst (2), Silcock (3), Magee (2), Seddon (3), **Patchitt** (2), Thornewell (2), Moore W (1), Walker (6), Miller (1), Urwin (2)

Home International Championship

DATE	VENUE	OPPONENTS	SCORE	GOALSCORERS	ATTENDANCE	TEAM
Oct 20	Windsor Park, Belfast	IRELAND	L 1-2	Bradford	23,000	Taylor (5), Bower (1), Wadsworth (4), Pantling (1), **Wilson** (10), Meehan (1), Hegan (3), Kelly (8), Bradford (1), Chambers (8), Tunstall (2)

Friendly

DATE	VENUE	OPPONENTS	SCORE	GOALSCORERS	ATTENDANCE	TEAM
Nov 1	Antwerp	BELGIUM	D 2-2	Brown W, Roberts W	40,000	Hufton (1), Cresswell (3), Bower (2), Moss (4), Seddon (4), Barton (4), Hegan (4), Brown W (1), Roberts W (1), **Doggart** (1), Urwin (3)

FACT FILE

Kenneth Edward Hegan, known as 'Jackie' and a serving Army officer with a lieutenant's rank, made the most appearances for England by an amateur in the period after World War I. His first of four caps was against Belgium in 1923. He played regularly for the Corinthians.

1924

Home International Championship

DATE	VENUE	OPPONENTS	SCORE	GOALSCORERS	ATTENDANCE	TEAM
Mar 3	Ewood Park, Blackburn	WALES	L 1-2	Roberts W	30,000	Sewell (1), Smart (2), Mort (1), Kean (3), **Wilson** (11), Barton (5), Chedgzoy (7), Jack (1), Roberts W (2), Stephenson (1), Tunstall (3)
Apr 12	Wembley, London	SCOTLAND	D 1-1	Walker	37,250	Taylor (6), Smart (3), Wadsworth (5), **Moss** (5), Spencer (1), Barton (6), Butler W (1), Jack (2), Buchan (6), Walker (7), Tunstall (4)

Friendly

DATE	VENUE	OPPONENTS	SCORE	GOALSCORERS	ATTENDANCE	TEAM
May 17	Paris	FRANCE	W 3-1	Gibbins 2, Storer	20,000	Taylor (7), Lucas (2), Mort (2), Ewer (1), **Wilson** (12), Blackburn (1), Thornewell (3), Earle (1), Gibbins (1), Storer (1), Tunstall (5)

Home International Championship

DATE	VENUE	OPPONENTS	SCORE	GOALSCORERS	ATTENDANCE	TEAM
Oct 22	Goodison Park, Liverpool	IRELAND	W 3-1	Kelly, Bedford, Walker	25,000	Mitchell (1), Cresswell (4), **Wadsworth** (6), Kean (4), Healless (1), Barton (7), Chedgzoy (8), Kelly (9), Bedford (2), Walker (8), Tunstall (6)

Friendly

DATE	VENUE	OPPONENTS	SCORE	GOALSCORERS	ATTENDANCE	TEAM
Dec 8	The Hawthorns, West Bromwich	BELGIUM	W 4-0	Bradford 2, Walker 2,	15,405	Hardy (1), Ashurst (3), **Bower** (3), Magee (3), Butler J (1), Ewer (2), Osborne (3), Roberts F (1), Bradford (2), Walker (9), Dorrell (1)

1925

Home International Championship

DATE	VENUE	OPPONENTS	SCORE	GOALSCORERS	ATTENDANCE	TEAM
Feb 28	Vetch Field, Swansea	WALES	W 2-1	Roberts F 2	8,000	Pym (1), Ashurst (4), **Bower** (4), Hill J (1), Spencer (2), Graham (1), Kelly (10), Roberts F (2), Cook (1), Walker (10), Dorrell (2)
Apr 4	Hampden Park, Glasgow	SCOTLAND	L 0-2		92,000	Pym (1), Ashurst (5), **Wadsworth** (7), Magee (4), Townrow (1), Graham (2), Kelly (11), Seed (5), Roberts F (3), Walker (11), Tunstall (7)

Friendly

DATE	VENUE	OPPONENTS	SCORE	GOALSCORERS	ATTENDANCE	TEAM
May 21	Paris	FRANCE	W 3-2	Gibbins, Dorrell, own goal	35,000	Fox (1), Parker (1), Felton (1), Magee (5), Bryant (1), Green (1), Thornewell (4), Roberts F (4), Gibbins (2), **Walker** (12), Dorrell (3)

Home International Championship

DATE	VENUE	OPPONENTS	SCORE	GOALSCORERS	ATTENDANCE	TEAM
Oct 24	Windsor Park, Belfast	IRELAND	D 0-0		35,000	Baker H (2), Smart (4), Hudspeth (1), Kean (5), Armitage (1), Bromilow (5), Austin (1), Puddefoot (1), **Ashton** (1), Walker (13), Dorrell (4)

1926

Home International Championship

DATE	VENUE	OPPONENTS	SCORE	GOALSCORERS	ATTENDANCE	TEAM
Mar 1	Selhurst Park, London	WALES	L 1-3	Walker	23,000	Pym (3), Cresswell (5), **Wadsworth** (8), Edwards (1), Townrow (2), Green (2), Urwin (4), Kelly (12), Bullock (2), Walker (14), Dimmock (2)
Apr 17	Old Trafford, Manchester	SCOTLAND	L 0-1		49,000	Taylor (8), Goodall (1), Mort (3), Edwards (2), Hill J (2), Green (3), York (2), Puddefoot (2), Harper (1), **Walker** (15), Ruffell (1)

Friendly

DATE	VENUE	OPPONENTS	SCORE	GOALSCORERS	ATTENDANCE	TEAM
May 24	Antwerp	BELGIUM	W 5-3	Osborne 3, Carter J, Johnson	33,000	Ashmore (1), **Lucas** (3), Hill R (1), Kean (6), Cowan (1), Green (4), Spence (1), Carter J (1), Osborne (4), Johnson (1), Dimmock (3)

Home International Championship

DATE	VENUE	OPPONENTS	SCORE	GOALSCORERS	ATTENDANCE	TEAM
Oct 20	Anfield, Liverpool	IRELAND	D 3-3	Brown G, Spence, Bullock	20,000	McInroy (1), Cresswell (6), **Wadsworth** (9), Edwards (3), Hill J (3), Green (5), Spence (2), Brown G (1), Bullock (3), Walker (16), Ruffell (2)

1927

Home International Championship

DATE	VENUE	OPPONENTS	SCORE	GOALSCORERS	ATTENDANCE	TEAM
Feb 12	Racecourse Ground, Wrexham	WALES	D 3-3	Dean 2, Walker	16,100	Brown J (1), **Bower** (5), Waterfield (1), Edwards (4), Seddon (5), Green (6), Pease (1), Brown G (2), Dean (1), Walker (17), Page (1)
Apr 2	Hampden Park, Glasgow	SCOTLAND	W 2-1	Dean 2	111,214	Brown J (2), Goodall (2), Jones H (1), Edwards (5), **Hill J** (4), Bishop (1), Hulme (1), Brown G (3), Dean (2), Rigby (1), Page (2)

Friendlies

DATE	VENUE	OPPONENTS	SCORE	GOALSCORERS	ATTENDANCE	TEAM
May 11	Brussels	BELGIUM	W 9-1	Dean 3, Brown G 2, Rigby 2, Page, Hulme	35,000	Brown J (3), Goodall (3), Jones H (2), Edwards (6), **Hill J** (5), Bishop (2), Hulme (2), Brown G (4), Dean (3), Rigby (2), Page (3)
May 21	Luxembourg	LUXEMBOURG	W 5-2	Dean 3, Kelly, Bishop	5,000	Brown J (4), Goodall (4), Jones H (3), Edwards (7), **Kean** (7), Bishop (3), Kelly (13), Brown G (5), Dean (4), Rigby (3), Page (4)
May 26	Paris	FRANCE	W 6-0	Dean 2, Brown G 2, Rigby, own goal	25,000	Brown J (5), Goodall (5), Jones H (4), Edwards (8), **Hill J** (6), Bishop (4), Hulme (3), Brown G (6), Dean (5), Rigby (4), Page (5)

Home International Championship

DATE	VENUE	OPPONENTS	SCORE	GOALSCORERS	ATTENDANCE	TEAM
Oct 22	Windsor Park, Belfast	IRELAND	L 0-2		30,000	Hufton (2), Cooper (1), Jones H (5), Nuttall (1), **Hill J** (7), Storer (2), Hulme (4), Earle (2), Dean (6), Ball (1), Page (6)
Nov 28	Turf Moor, Burnley	WALES	L 1-2	own goal	32,089	Tremelling (1), Goodall (6), Osborne (1), Baker (1), **Hill J** (8), Nuttall (2), Hulme (5), Brown G (7), Dean (7), Rigby (5), Page (7)

1928

Home International Championship

DATE	VENUE	OPPONENTS	SCORE	GOALSCORERS	ATTENDANCE	TEAM
Mar 31	Wembley, London	SCOTLAND	L 1-5	Kelly	80,868	Hufton (3), **Goodall** (7), Jones H (6), Edwards (9), Wilson (1), Healless (2), Hulme (6), Kelly (14), Dean (8), Bradford (3), Smith WH (3)

Friendlies

DATE	VENUE	OPPONENTS	SCORE	GOALSCORERS	ATTENDANCE	TEAM
May 17	Paris	FRANCE	W 5-1	Stephenson 2, Dean 2, Jack	40,000	Olney (1), **Goodall** (8), Blenkinsop (1), Edwards (10), Matthews (1), Green (7), Bruton (1), Jack (3), Dean (9), Stephenson (1), Barry (1)
May 19	Antwerp	BELGIUM	W 3-1	Dean 2, Matthews	25,000	Olney (2), **Goodall** (9), Blenkinsop (2), Edwards (11), Matthews (2), Green (8), Bruton (2), Jack (4), Dean (10), Stephenson (2), Barry (2)

Home International Championship

DATE	VENUE	OPPONENTS	SCORE	GOALSCORERS	ATTENDANCE	TEAM
Oct 22	Goodison Park, Liverpool	IRELAND	W 2-1	Hulme, Dean	34,000	Hacking (1), Cooper (2), Blenkinsop (3), **Edwards** (12), Barrett (1), Campbell (1), Hulme (7), Hine (1), Dean (11), Bradford (4), Ruffell (3)
Nov 17	Vetch Field, Swansea	WALES	W 3-2	Hulme 2, Hine	22,000	Hacking (2), Cooper (3), Blenkinsop (4), **Edwards** (13), Hart (1), Campbell (2), Hulme (8), Hine (2), Dean (12), Bradford (5), Ruffell (4)

FACT FILE

Jim Barrett had the shortest international career of any player starting a match for England. He was carried off injured in the eighth minute of his debut against Ireland in 1928 and was never subsequently selected.

1929

Home International Championship

DATE	VENUE	OPPONENTS	SCORE	GOALSCORERS	ATTENDANCE	TEAM
Apr 13	Hampden Park, Glasgow	SCOTLAND	L 0-1		110,512	Hacking (3), Cooper (4), Blenkinsop (5), **Edwards** (14), Seddon (6), Nuttall (3), Bruton (3), Brown G (8), Dean (13), Wainscoat (1), Ruffell (5)

Friendlies

DATE	VENUE	OPPONENTS	SCORE	GOALSCORERS	ATTENDANCE	TEAM
May 9	Paris	FRANCE	W 4-1	Kail 2, Camsell 2	35,000	Hufton (4), Blenkinsop (6), Cooper (5), Kean (8), **Hill J** (9), Peacock (1), Adcock (1), Kail (1), Camsell (1), Bradford (6), Barry (3)
May 11	Brussels	BELGIUM	W 5-1	Camsell 4, Carter J	35,000	Hufton (5), Cooper (6), Blenkinsop (7), Oliver (1), **Hill J** (10), Peacock (2), Adcock (2), Kail (2), Camsell (2), Carter J (2), Barry (4)
May 15	Madrid	SPAIN	L 3-4	Carter J 2, Bradford	50,000	Hufton (6), Cooper (7), Blenkinsop (8), Kean (9), **Hill J** (11), Peacock (3), Adcock (3), Kail (3), Bradford (7), Carter J (3), Barry (5)

Home International Championship

DATE	VENUE	OPPONENTS	SCORE	GOALSCORERS	ATTENDANCE	TEAM
Oct 19	Windsor Park, Belfast	IRELAND	W 3-0	Camsell 2, Hine (pen)	40,000	Brown J (6), Cresswell (7), Blenkinsop (9), **Edwards** (15), Hart (2), Barrett (1), Adcock (4), Hine (3), Camsell (3), Bradford (8), Brook (1)
Nov 20	Stamford Bridge, London	WALES	W 6-0	Adcock, Camsell 3, Johnson 2	32,945	Hibbs (1), Smart (5), Blenkinsop (10), **Edwards** (16), Hart (3), Marsden (1), Adcock (5), Hine (4), Camsell (4), Johnson (2), Ruffell (6)

FACT FILE

In 1929 Edgar Kail became the last non-league amateur to win a full cap for England. He played for Dulwich Hamlet and was an experienced amateur international. Bernard Joy, in 1936, was the last amateur to win a full cap.

1930

Home International Championship

DATE	VENUE	OPPONENTS	SCORE	GOALSCORERS	ATTENDANCE	TEAM
Apr 5	Wembley, London	SCOTLAND	W 5-2	Jack, Watson 2, Rimmer 2	87,375	Hibbs (2), Goodall (10), Blenkinsop (11), Strange (1), Webster (1), Marsden (2), Crooks (1), **Jack** (5), Watson (3), Bradford (9), Rimmer (1)

Friendlies

DATE	VENUE	OPPONENTS	SCORE	GOALSCORERS	ATTENDANCE	TEAM
May 10	Berlin	GERMANY	D 3-3	Bradford 2, Jack	60,000	Hibbs (3), Goodall (11), Blenkinsop (12), Strange (2), Webster (2), Marsden (3), Crooks (2), **Jack** (6), Watson (4), Bradford (10), Rimmer (2)
May 14	Vienna	AUSTRIA	D 0-0		61,000	Hibbs (4), Goodall (12), Blenkinsop (13), Strange (3), Webster (3), Cowan (2), Crooks (3), **Jack** (7), Watson (5), Bradford (11), Rimmer (3)

Home International Championship

DATE	VENUE	OPPONENTS	SCORE	GOALSCORERS	ATTENDANCE	TEAM
Oct 20	Bramall Lane, Sheffield	IRELAND	W 5-1	Burgess 2, Crooks, Hampson, Houghton	35,000	Hibbs (5), **Goodall** (13), Blenkinsop (14), Strange (4), Leach (1), Campbell (3), Crooks (4), Hodgson (1), Hampson (1), Burgess (1), Houghton (1)
Nov 22	Racecourse Ground, Wrexham	WALES	W 4-0	Hodgson, Bradford, Hampson 2	11,282	Hibbs (6), **Goodall** (14), Blenkinsop (15), Strange (5), Leach (2), Campbell (4), Crooks (5), Hodgson (2), Hampson (2), Bradford (12), Houghton (2)

1931

Home International Championship

DATE	VENUE	OPPONENTS	SCORE	GOALSCORERS	ATTENDANCE	TEAM
Mar 28	Hampden Park, Glasgow	SCOTLAND	L 0-2		129,810	Hibbs (7), **Goodall** (15), Blenkinsop (16), Strange (6), Roberts H (1), Campbell (5), Crooks (6), Hodgson (3), Dean (14), Burgess (2), Crawford (1),

Friendlies

DATE	VENUE	OPPONENTS	SCORE	GOALSCORERS	ATTENDANCE	TEAM
May 14	Paris	FRANCE	L 2-5	Crooks, Waring	35,000	Turner (1), Cooper (8), Blenkinsop (17), **Strange** (7), Graham (1), Tate (1), Crooks (7), Stephenson (3), Waring (1), Burgess (3), Houghton (3)
May 16	Brussels	BELGIUM	W 4-1	Burgess 2, Houghton (pen), Roberts (Henry)	30,000	Turner (2), Goodall (16), Blenkinsop (18), **Strange** (8), Cowan (3), Tate (2), Crooks (8), Roberts (Henry) (1), Waring (2), Burgess (4), Houghton (4)

Home International Championship

DATE	VENUE	OPPONENTS	SCORE	GOALSCORERS	ATTENDANCE	TEAM
Oct 17	Windsor Park, Belfast	IRELAND	W 6-2	Waring 2, Smith JW, Hine, Houghton 2	40,000	Hibbs (8), **Goodall** (17), Blenkinsop (19), Strange (9), Graham (2), Campbell (6), Crooks (9), Smith JW (1), Waring (3), Hine (5), Houghton (5)
Nov 18	Anfield, Liverpool	WALES	W 3-1	Smith JW, Crooks, Hine	30,000	Hibbs (9), Cooper (9), Blenkinsop (20), **Strange** (10), Gee (1), Campbell (7), Crooks (10), Smith JW (2), Waring (4), Hine (6), Bastin (1)

Friendly

DATE	VENUE	OPPONENTS	SCORE	GOALSCORERS	ATTENDANCE	TEAM
Dec 9	Highbury, London	SPAIN	W 7-1	Smith JW 2, Johnson 2, Crooks 2, Dean	55,000	Hibbs (10), Cooper (10), **Blenkinsop** (21), Strange (11), Gee (2), Campbell (8), Crooks (11), Smith JW (3), Dean (15), Johnson (3), Rimmer (4)

Spanish goalkeeper Ricardo Zamora punches the ball clear of the England forwards at Highbury in December 1931. England won the match 7-1.

1932

Home International Championship

DATE	VENUE	OPPONENTS	SCORE	GOALSCORERS	ATTENDANCE	TEAM
Apr 9	Wembley, London	SCOTLAND	W 3-0	Waring, Crooks, Barclay	92,180	Pearson (1), Shaw (1), **Blenkinsop** (22), Strange (12), O'Dowd (1), Weaver (1), Crooks (12), Barclay (1), Waring (5), Johnson (4), Houghton (6)
Oct 17	Bloomfield Road, Blackpool	IRELAND	W 1-0	Barclay	23,000	Hibbs (11), Goodall (18), **Blenkinsop** (23), Strange (13), O'Dowd (2), Weaver (2), Crooks (13), Barclay (2), Dean (16), Johnson (5), Cunliffe (1)
Nov 16	Racecourse Ground, Wrexham	WALES	D 0-0		25,250	Hibbs (12), Goodall (19), Blenkinsop (24), Stoker (1), Young (1), Tate (3), Crooks (14), **Jack** (8), Brown G (9), Sandford (1), Cunliffe (2)

Friendly

DATE	VENUE	OPPONENTS	SCORE	GOALSCORERS	ATTENDANCE	TEAM
Dec 7	Stamford, Bridge, London	AUSTRIA	W 4-3	Hampson 2, Houghton, Crooks	42,000	Hibbs (13), Goodall (20), Blenkinsop (25), Strange (14), Hart (4), Keen (1), Crooks (15), Jack (9), Hampson (3), **Walker** (18), Houghton (7)

1933

Home International Championship

DATE	VENUE	OPPONENTS	SCORE	GOALSCORERS	ATTENDANCE	TEAM
Apr 1	Hampden Park, Glasgow	SCOTLAND	L 1-2	Hunt	134,710	Hibbs (14), Cooper (11), **Blenkinsop** (26), Strange (15), Hart (5), Weaver (3), Hulme (9), Starling (1), Hunt (1), Pickering (1), Arnold (1)

Friendlies

DATE	VENUE	OPPONENTS	SCORE	GOALSCORERS	ATTENDANCE	TEAM
May 13	Rome	ITALY	D 1-1	Bastin	50,000	Hibbs (15), **Goodall** (21), Hapgood (1), Strange (16), White (1), Copping (1), Geldard (1), Richardson J (1), Hunt (2), Furness (1), Bastin (2)
May 20	Berne	SWITZERLAND	W 4-0	Bastin 2, Richardson J 2	20,000	Hibbs (16), **Goodall** (22), Hapgood (2), Strange (17), O'Dowd (3), Copping (2), Geldard (2), Richardson J (2), Hunt (3), Bastin (3), Brook (2)

Home International Championship

DATE	VENUE	OPPONENTS	SCORE	GOALSCORERS	ATTENDANCE	TEAM
Oct 14	Windsor Park, Belfast	IRELAND	W 3-0	Brook, Grosvenor, Bowers	40,000	Hibbs (17), **Goodall** (23), Hapgood (3), Strange (18), Allen (1), Copping (3), Crooks (16), Grosvenor (1), Bowers (1), Bastin (4), Brook (3)
Nov 15	St James' Park, Newcastle	WALES	L 1-2	Brook	15,000	Hibbs (18), **Goodall** (24), Hapgood (4), Strange (19), Allen (2), Copping (4), Crooks (17), Grosvenor (2), Bowers (2), Bastin (5), Brook (4)

Friendly

DATE	VENUE	OPPONENTS	SCORE	GOALSCORERS	ATTENDANCE	TEAM
Dec 6	White Hart Lane, London	FRANCE	W 4-1	Camsell 2, Brook, Grosvenor	17,097	Hibbs (19), **Goodall** (25), Fairhurst (1), Strange (20), Rowe (1), Copping (5), Crooks (18), Grosvenor (3), Camsell (5), Hall (1), Brook (5)

1934

Home International Championship

DATE	VENUE	OPPONENTS	SCORE	GOALSCORERS	ATTENDANCE	TEAM
Apr 14	Wembley, London	SCOTLAND	W 3-0	Brook, Bastin, Bowers	92,693	Moss (1), **Cooper** (12), Hapgood (5), Stoker (2), Hart (6), Copping (6), Crooks (19), Carter H (1), Bowers (3), Bastin (6), Brook (6)

Friendlies

DATE	VENUE	OPPONENTS	SCORE	GOALSCORERS	ATTENDANCE	TEAM
May 10	Budapest	HUNGARY	L 1-2	Tilson	35,000	Moss (2), **Cooper** (13), Hapgood (6), Stoker (3), Hart (7), Burrows (1), Crooks (20), Carter H (2), Tilson (1), Bastin (7), Brook (7)
May 16	Prague	CZECHOSLOVAKIA	L 1-2	Tilson	35,000	Moss (3), **Cooper** (14), Hapgood (7), Gardner (1), Hart (8), Burrows (2), Crooks (21), Beresford (1), Tilson (2), Bastin (8), Brook (8)

Home International Championship

DATE	VENUE	OPPONENTS	SCORE	GOALSCORERS	ATTENDANCE	TEAM
Sept 29	Ninian Park, Cardiff	WALES	W 4-0	Tilson 2, Brook, Matthews	51,000	Hibbs (20), **Cooper** (15), Hapgood (8), Britton (1), Barker (1), Bray (1), Matthews (1), Bowden (1), Tilson (3), Westwood (1), Brook (9)

Friendly

DATE	VENUE	OPPONENTS	SCORE	GOALSCORERS	ATTENDANCE	TEAM
Nov 14	Highbury, London	ITALY	W 3-2	Brook 2, Drake	56,044	Moss (4), Male (1), **Hapgood** (9), Britton (2), Barker (2), Copping (7), Matthews (2), Bowden (2), Drake (1), Bastin (9), Brook (10)

FACT FILE

Arsenal supplied a record seven players for the match with Italy at Highbury in 1934: Frank Moss, George Male, Eddie Hapgood, Wilf Copping, Ray Bowden, Ted Drake and Cliff Bastin. But Male was only a late replacement for the injured Tom Cooper and Drake was second choice after first Fred Tilson and then George Hunt had to withdraw. Arsenal's Tom Whittaker was trainer. The club also provided six players against both Wales and Austria in 1936.

Eric Brook missed a penalty against Italy in 1934, depriving himself of a hat-trick against the World Cup holders.

1935

Home International Championship

DATE	VENUE	OPPONENTS	SCORE	GOALSCORERS	ATTENDANCE	TEAM
Feb 6	Goodison Park, Liverpool	IRELAND	W 2-1	Bastin 2	32,000	Hibbs (21), Male (2), **Hapgood** (10), Britton (3), Barker (3), Copping (8), Crooks (22), Bestall (1), Drake (2), Bastin (10), Brook (11)
Apr 6	Hampden Park, Glasgow	SCOTLAND	L 0-2		129,613	Hibbs (22), Male (3), **Hapgood** (11), Britton (4), Barker (4), Alsford (1), Geldard (3), Bastin (11), Gurney (1), Westwood (2), Brook (12)

Friendly

May 18	Amsterdam	HOLLAND	W 1-0	Worrall	33,000	Hibbs (23), Male (4), **Hapgood** (12), Gardner (2), Barker (5), Burrows (3), Worrall (1), Eastham (1), Richardson W (1), Westwood (3), Boyes (1)

Jubilee Fund match

Aug 21	Hampden Park, Glasgow	SCOTLAND	L 2-4	Westwood, Gurney	56,316	Hibbs, Male, **Hapgood**, Britton, Millership, Bray, (Smith S), Morton, Carter, Gurney, Westwood, Boyes

Home International Championship

Oct 19	Windsor Park, Belfast	IRELAND	W 3-1	Tilson 2, Brook	28,000	Sagar (1), Male (5), **Hapgood** (13), Smith S (1), Barker (6), Bray (2), Birkett (1), Bowden (3), Tilson (4), Westwood (4), Brook (13)

Friendly

Dec 4	White Hart Lane, London	GERMANY	W 3-0	Camsell 2, Bastin	54,164	Hibbs (24), Male (6), **Hapgood** (14), Crayston (1), Barker (7), Bray (3), Matthews (3), Carter H (3), Camsell (6), Westwood (5), Bastin (12)

1936

Home International Championship

DATE	VENUE	OPPONENTS	SCORE	GOALSCORERS	ATTENDANCE	TEAM
Feb 5	Molineux, Wolverhampton	WALES	L 1-2	Bowden	22,613	Hibbs (25), Male (7), **Hapgood** (15), Crayston (2), Barker (8), Bray (4), Crooks (23), Bowden (4), Drake (3), Bastin (13), Brook (14)
Apr 4	Wembley, London	SCOTLAND	D 1-1	Camsell	93,267	Sagar (2), Male (8), **Hapgood** (16), Crayston (3), Barker (9), Bray (5), Crooks (24), Barclay (3), Camsell (7), Bastin (14), Brook (15)

Friendlies

May 6	Vienna	AUSTRIA	L 1-2	Camsell	60,000	Sagar (3), Male (9), **Hapgood** (17), Crayston (4), Barker (10), Copping (9), Spence (1), Bowden (5), Camsell (8), Bastin (15), Hobbis (1)
May 9	Brussels	BELGIUM	L 2-3	Camsell, Hobbis	40,000	Sagar (4), Male (10), **Hapgood** (18), Crayston (5), Joy (1), Copping (10), Spence (2), Barkas (1), Camsell (9), Cunliffe (1), Hobbis (2)

Home International Championship

Oct 17	Ninian Park, Cardiff	WALES	L 1-2	Bastin	50,000	Holdcroft (1), Sproston (1), Catlin (1), Smalley (1), **Barker** (11), Keen (2), Crooks (25), Scott (1), Steele (1), Westwood (6), Bastin (16)
Nov 18	Victoria Ground, Stoke	IRELAND	W 3-1	Carter H, Bastin, Worrall	47,882	Holdcroft (2), **Male** (11), Catlin (2), Britton (5), Gee (3), Keen (3), Worrall (2), Carter H (4), Steele (2), Bastin (17), Johnson (1)

Friendly

Dec 2	Highbury, London	HUNGARY	W 6-2	Drake 3, Brook, Britton, Carter H	36,000	Tweedy (1), **Male** (12), Catlin (3), Britton (6), Young (2), Keen (4), Crooks (26), Bowden (6), Drake (4), Carter H (5), Brook (16)

Bert Sproston earned his first cap in 1936 as a Leeds United player. He kept his place in the side despite his transfer to Tottenham in 1938.

1937

Home International Championship

DATE	VENUE	OPPONENTS	SCORE	GOALSCORERS	ATTENDANCE	TEAM
Apr 17	Hampden Park, Glasgow	SCOTLAND	L 1-3	Steele	149,547	Woodley (1), **Male** (13), Barkas (2), Britton (7), Young (3), Bray (6), Matthews (4), Carter H (6), Steele (3), Starling (2), Johnson (2)

Friendlies

DATE	VENUE	OPPONENTS	SCORE	GOALSCORERS	ATTENDANCE	TEAM
May 14	Oslo	NORWAY	W 6-0	Steele 2, Kirchen, Galley, Goulden, own goal	20,000	Woodley (2), **Male** (14), Catlin (4), Britton (8), Young (4), Copping (11), Kirchen (1), Galley (1), Steele (4), Goulden (1), Johnson (3)
May 17	Stockholm	SWEDEN	W 4-0	Steele 3, Johnson	34,119	Woodley (3), **Male** (15), Catlin (5), Britton (9), Young (5), Copping (12), Kirchen (2), Galley (2), Steele (5), Goulden (2), Johnson (4)
May 20	Helsinki	FINLAND	W 8-0	Payne 2, Steele 2, Kirchen, Willingham, Johnson, Robinson	9,533	Woodley (4), **Male** (16), Hapgood (19), Willingham (1), Betmead (1), Copping (13), Kirchen (3), Robinson (1), Payne (1), Steele (6), Johnson (5)

Home International Championship

DATE	VENUE	OPPONENTS	SCORE	GOALSCORERS	ATTENDANCE	TEAM
Oct 23	Windsor Park, Belfast	IRELAND	W 5-1	Mills 3, Hall, Brook	36,000	Woodley (5), Sproston (2), **Barkas** (3), Crayston (6), Cullis (1), Copping (14), Geldard (4), Hall (2), Mills (1), Goulden (3), Brook (17)
Nov 17	Ayresome Park, Middlesbrough	WALES	W 2-1	Matthews, Hall	30,608	Woodley (6), Sproston (3), **Barkas** (4), Crayston (7), Cullis (2), Copping (15), Matthews (5), Hall (3), Mills (2), Goulden (4), Brook (18)

Friendly

DATE	VENUE	OPPONENTS	SCORE	GOALSCORERS	ATTENDANCE	TEAM
Dec 1	White Hart Lane, London	CZECHOSLOVAKIA	W 5-4	Crayston, Morton, Matthews 3	45,879	Woodley (7), Sproston (4), **Barkas** (5), Crayston (8), Cullis (3), Copping (16), Matthews (6), Hall (4), Mills (3), Goulden (5), Morton (1)

FACT FILE

In 1937 the 149,547 crowd at Hampden Park for the Scotland v England international was the highest for a Home International Championship match in the competition's history.

1938

Home International Championship

DATE	VENUE	OPPONENTS	SCORE	GOALSCORERS	ATTENDANCE	TEAM
Apr 9	Wembley, London	SCOTLAND	L 0-1		93,267	Woodley (8), Sproston (5), **Hapgood** (20), Willingham (2), Cullis (4), Copping (17), Matthews (7), Hall (5), Fenton (1), Stephenson (1), Bastin (18)

Friendlies

DATE	VENUE	OPPONENTS	SCORE	GOALSCORERS	ATTENDANCE	TEAM
May 14	Berlin	GERMANY	W 6-3	Robinson 2, Bastin, Broome, Matthews, Goulden	120,000	Woodley (9), Sproston (6), **Hapgood** (21), Willingham (3), Young (6), Welsh (1), Matthews (8), Robinson (2), Broome (1), Goulden (6), Bastin (19)
May 21	Zurich	SWITZERLAND	L 1-2	Bastin (pen)	25,000	Woodley (10), Sproston (7), **Hapgood** (22), Willingham (4), Young (7), Welsh (2), Matthews (9), Robinson (3), Broome (2), Goulden (7), Bastin (20)
May 26	Paris	FRANCE	W 4-2	Drake 2, Broome, Bastin (pen)	46,920	Woodley (11), Sproston (8), **Hapgood** (23), Willingham (5), Young (8), Cullis (5), Broome (3), Matthews (10), Drake (5), Goulden (8), Bastin (21)

Home International Championship

DATE	VENUE	OPPONENTS	SCORE	GOALSCORERS	ATTENDANCE	TEAM
Oct 22	Ninian Park, Cardiff	WALES	L 2-4	Lawton (pen), Matthews	55,000	Woodley (12), Sproston (9), **Hapgood** (24), Willingham (6), Young (9), Copping (18), Matthews (11), Robinson (4), Lawton (1), Goulden (9), Boyes (2)

Friendlies

DATE	VENUE	OPPONENTS	SCORE	GOALSCORERS	ATTENDANCE	TEAM
Oct 26	Highbury, London	REST OF EUROPE	W 3-0	Hall, Lawton, Goulden	40,185	Woodley (13), Sproston (10), **Hapgood** (25), Willingham (7), Cullis (6), Copping (19), Matthews (12), Hall (6), Lawton (2), Goulden (10), Boyes (3)
Nov 9	St James' Park, Newcastle	NORWAY	W 4-0	Smith JR 2, Dix, Lawton	39,887	Woodley (14), Sproston (11), **Hapgood** (26), Willingham (8), Cullis (7), Wright D (1), Matthews (13), Broome (4), Lawton (3), Dix (1), Smith JR (1)

Home International Championship

DATE	VENUE	OPPONENTS	SCORE	GOALSCORERS	ATTENDANCE	TEAM
Nov 16	Old Trafford, Manchester	IRELAND	W 7-0	Hall 5, Lawton, Matthews	40,386	Woodley (15), Morris (1), **Hapgood** (27), Willingham (9), Cullis (8), Mercer (1), Matthews (14), Hall (7), Lawton (4), Stephenson (2), Smith JR (2)

FACT FILE

Willie Hall's hat-trick for England against Northern Ireland in 1938 came in 3.5 minutes: 34th, 36th and 38th.

The crowd at Hampden Park for the Scotland v England match in 1937 was the highest in the history of the Home International Championship.

1939

Home International Championship

DATE	VENUE	OPPONENTS	SCORE	GOALSCORERS	ATTENDANCE	TEAM
Apr 15	Hampden Park, Glasgow	SCOTLAND	W 2-1	Beasley, Lawton	149,269	Woodley (16), Morris (2), **Hapgood** (28), Willingham (10), Cullis (9), Mercer (2), Matthews (15), Hall (8), Lawton (5), Goulden (11), Beasley (1)

Friendlies

DATE	VENUE	OPPONENTS	SCORE	GOALSCORERS	ATTENDANCE	TEAM
May 13	Milan	ITALY	D 2-2	Lawton, Hall	70,000	Woodley (17), Male (17), **Hapgood** (29), Willingham (11), Cullis (10), Mercer (3), Matthews (16), Hall (9), Lawton (6), Goulden (12), Broome (5)
May 18	Belgrade	YUGOSLAVIA	L 1-2	Broome	40,000	Woodley (18), Male (18), **Hapgood** (30), Willingham (12), Cullis (11), Mercer (4), Matthews (17), Hall (10), Lawton (7), Goulden (13), Broome (6)
May 24	Bucharest	ROMANIA	W 2-0	Goulden, Welsh	5,000	Woodley (19), Male (19), Morris (3), Mercer (5), **Cullis** (12), Copping (20), Broome (7), Goulden (14), Lawton (8), Welsh (3), Smith L (1)

Wartime Internationals

DATE	VENUE	OPPONENTS	SCORE	GOALSCORERS	ATTENDANCE	TEAM
Nov 11	Ninian Park, Cardiff	WALES	D 1-1	Goulden	28,000	Woodley (1), Bacuzzi (1), (Lewis (1), **Hapgood** (1), Crayston (1), Oakes (1), Fenton (1), Smith L (1), Hall (1), Compton L (1), Goulden (1), Smith R (1)
Nov 18	Racecourse Ground, Wrexham	WALES	W 3-2	Martin, Balmer, own goal	17,000	Swift (1), Sproston (1), Crook (1), Willingham (1), **Cullis** (1), Mercer (1), Matthews (1), Martin (1), Lawton (1), Balmer (1), Brook (1)
Dec 2	St James' Park, Newcastle	SCOTLAND	W 2-1	Carter, Lawton	15,000	Swinburne (1), Richardson (1), Greenhalgh (1), **Goslin** (1), Harper (1), Mercer (2), Matthews (2), Carter (1), Lawton (2), Clifton (1), Pearson (1)

FACT FILE

Tommy Pearson, a Scot, had to be commandeered into the England team for the 1939 match with Scotland at Newcastle because Eric Brook had been injured in a car crash on the way to the ground. Injuries received in this accident caused Brook's retirement.

1940

Wartime Internationals

DATE	VENUE	OPPONENTS	SCORE	GOALSCORERS	ATTENDANCE	TEAM
Apr 13	Wembley, London	WALES	L 0-1		40,000	Bartram (1), Bacuzzi (2), **Hapgood** (2), Willingham (2), Cullis (2), Copping (1), Matthews (3), Hall (2), Westcott (1), Goulden (2), Compton D (1)
May 11	Hampden Park, Glasgow	SCOTLAND	D 1-1	Welsh	75,000	Woodley (2), Sproston (2), **Hapgood** (3), Willingham (3), Cullis (3), Mercer (4), Matthews (4), Martin (2), Broome (1), Welsh (1), Smith R (2)

Corporal Stanley Matthews played regularly for the RAF as well as for England during the war years.

1941

Wartime Internationals

DATE	VENUE	OPPONENTS	SCORE	GOALSCORERS	ATTENDANCE	TEAM
Feb 8	St James' Park, Newcastle	SCOTLAND	L 2-3	Birkett, Lawton	25,000	Bartram (2), Bacuzzi (3), Mountford (1), Willingham (4), **Cullis** (4), Mercer (4), Birkett (1), Mannion (1), Lawton (3), Goulden (3), Hanson (1)
Apr 16	City Ground, Nottingham	WALES	W 4-1	Welsh 4	13,016	Mapson (1), Bacuzzi (4), Hardwick (1), Britton (1), **Cullis** (5), Buckingham (1), Fisher (1), Edelston (1), Welsh (2), Hagan (1), Smith R (3)
May 3	Hampden Park, Glasgow	SCOTLAND	W 3-1	Welsh 2, Goulden	78,000	Swift (2), Bacuzzi (5), **Hapgood** (4), Goslin (2), Cullis (6), Mercer (5), Matthews (5), Mannion (2), Welsh (3), Goulden (4), Compton D (2)
Jun 7	Ninian Park, Cardiff	WALES	W 3-2	Hagan 2, Welsh	20,000	Bartram (3), Bacuzzi (6), **Hapgood** (5), Britton (2), Cullis (7), Buckingham (2), Kirchen (1), Hagan (2), Welsh (4), Goulden (5), Finch (1)
Oct 4	Wembley, London	SCOTLAND	W 2-0	Hagan, Welsh	65,000	Marks (1), Bacuzzi (7), **Hapgood** (6), Goslin (3), Cullis (8), Mercer (6), Matthews (6), Mannion (3), Welsh (5), Hagan (3), Compton D (3)
Oct 25	St Andrew's, Birmingham	WALES	W 2-1	Hagan, Edelston	25,000	Marks (2), Bacuzzi (8), **Hapgood** (7), Goslin (4), Cullis (9), Mercer (7), Matthews (7), Edelston (2), Welsh (6), Hagan (4), Compton D (4)

1942

Wartime Internationals

DATE	VENUE	OPPONENTS	SCORE	GOALSCORERS	ATTENDANCE	TEAM
Jan 17	Wembley, London	SCOTLAND	W 3-0	Hagan, Lawton 2	64,000	Marks (3), Bacuzzi (9), **Hapgood** (8), Willingham (5), Cullis (10), Welsh (7), Matthews (8), Mannion (4), Lawton (4), Hagan (5), Compton D (5)
Apr 18	Hampden Park, Glasgow	SCOTLAND	L 4-5	Lawton 3, Hagan	91,000	Marks (4), Bacuzzi (10), **Hapgood** (9), Willingham (6), Mason (1), Mercer (8), Matthews (9), Edelston (3), Lawton (5), Hagan (6), Kirchen (2)
May 9	Ninian Park, Cardiff	WALES	L 0-1		30,000	Marks (5), Scott (1), **Hapgood** (10), Britton (3), Mason (2), Soo (1), Kirchen (3), Hall (3), Lawton (6), Edelston (4), Smith L (2)
Oct 10	Wembley, London	SCOTLAND	D 0-0		75,000	Marks (6), Bacuzzi (11), **Hapgood** (11), Britton (4), Cullis (11), Mercer (9), Matthews (10), Edelston (5), Lawton (7), Hagan (7), Compton D (6)
Oct 24	Molineux, Wolverhampton	WALES	L 1-2	Lawton	25,097	Marks (7), Hardwick (2), **Hapgood** (12), Britton (5), Cullis (12), Mercer (10), Matthews (11), Rooke (1), Lawton (8), Gibbons (1), Mullen (1)

Action from a snowbound Wembley in 1942 as England met Scotland. England won 3-0 with two goals from Tommy Lawton and one from Jimmy Hagan.

1943

Wartime Internationals

DATE	VENUE	OPPONENTS	SCORE	GOALSCORERS	ATTENDANCE	TEAM
Feb 27	Wembley, London	WALES	W 5-3	Westcott 3, Carter 2	75,000	Marks (8), Bacuzzi (12), **Hapgood** (13), Britton (6), Cullis (13), Mercer (11), Matthews (12), Carter (2), Westcott (2), Hagan (8), Compton D (7)
Apr 17	Hampden Park, Glasgow	SCOTLAND	W 4-0	Carter 2, Westcott, Compton D	105,000	Swift (3), Hardwick (3), Compton L (2), Britton (7), **Cullis** (14), Mercer (12), Matthews (13), Carter (3), Westcott (3), Hagan (9), Compton D (8)
May 8	Ninian Park, Cardiff	WALES	D 1-1	Westcott	25,000	Swift (4), Hardwick (4), Compton L (3), Britton (8), **Cullis** (15), Mercer (13), Matthews (14), Carter (4), Westcott (4), Hagan (10), Compton D (9)
Sep 25	Wembley, London	WALES	W 8-3	Welsh 2, Carter 2, Hagan 2, Compton D 2	80,000	Roxburgh (1), Scott (3), Hardwick (5), Britton (9), **Cullis** (16), Soo (2), Matthews (15), Carter (5), Welsh (8), Hagan (11), Compton D (10)
Oct 16	Maine Road, Manchester	SCOTLAND	W 8-0	Lawton 4, Hagan 2, Carter, Matthews	60,000	Swift (5), Scott (3), Hardwick (6), Britton (10), **Cullis** (17), Mercer (14), Matthews (16), Carter (6), Lawton (9), Hagan (12), Compton D (11)

FACT FILE

After England's 8-0 win over Scotland at Maine Road, Manchester, in 1943, Wreford Brown, then a life vice-president of the Football Association said: 'This England team which has won such a magnificent victory showed perhaps the greatest combination and team work in the whole history of international football. I myself have never seen anything like it before.' The secret lay in the fact that most of the England team were playing with and against each other regularly in service and representative matches as well as club games; a situation unheard of in peacetime.

Stan Mortensen made his international debut for Wales in wartime against his own country. In 1943 at Wembley he was reserve for England, sitting on the bench in RAF uniform, but when Wales lost their wing-half Ivor Powell to injury, it was agreed that Mortensen should take his place in the second half, as the Welsh team had no 12th man.

When Eddie Hapgood was chosen to play against Wales in 1943 at Wembley it was his 43rd appearance, including the wartime matches for which no official caps were awarded. Having overtaken Crompton's total in the summer he was presented with a cheque for £100 as a testimonial for his achievement. This was the first time the FA had given cash in this manner.

1944

Wartime Internationals

DATE	VENUE	OPPONENTS	SCORE	GOALSCORERS	ATTENDANCE	TEAM
Feb 19	Wembley	SCOTLAND	W 6-2	Hagan 2, Carter, Lawton, Mercer, own goal	80,000	Ditchburn (1), Scott (4), Hardwick (7), Britton (11), **Cullis** (18), Mercer (15), Matthews (17), Carter (7), Lawton (10), Hagan (13), Smith L (3)
Apr 22	Hampden Park, Glasgow	SCOTLAND	W 3-2	Lawton 2, Carter	133,000	Swift (6), Compton L (4), Taylor (1), Soo (3), **Cullis** (19), Mercer (16), Matthews (18), Carter (8), Lawton (11), Hagan (14), Smith L (4),
May 6	Ninian Park, Cardiff	WALES	W 2-0	Lawton, Smith L	50,000	Ditchburn (2), Scott (5), Compton L (5), Britton (12), **Cullis** (20), Mercer (17), Elliott (1), Carter (9), Lawton (12), Rowley (1), Smith L (5)
Sep 16	Anfield, Liverpool	WALES	D 2-2	Carter, Lawton	38,483	Swift (7), Scott (6), Hardwick (8), **Mercer** (18), Flewin (1), Welsh (9), Matthews (19), Carter (10), Lawton (13), Mortensen (1), Mullen (2)
Oct 14	Wembley, London	SCOTLAND	W 6-2	Lawton 3, Carter, Goulden, Smith L	90,000	Swift (8), Scott (7), Hardwick (9), Soo (4), Joy (1), **Mercer** (19), Matthews (20), Carter (11), Lawton (14), Goulden (6), Smith L (6)

1945

Wartime Internationals

DATE	VENUE	OPPONENTS	SCORE	GOALSCORERS	ATTENDANCE	TEAM
Feb 3	Villa Park, Birmingham	SCOTLAND	W 3-2	Mortensen 2, Brown	65,780	Swift (9), Scott (8), Hardwick (10), Soo (5), Franklin (1), **Mercer** (20), Matthews (21), Brown (1), Lawton (15), Mortensen (2), Smith L (7)
Apr 14	Hampden Park, Glasgow	SCOTLAND	W 6-1	Lawton 2, Brown, Carter, Matthews, Smith L	133,000	Swift (10), Scott (9), Hardwick (11), Soo (6), Franklin (2), **Mercer** (21), Matthews (22), Carter (12), Lawton (16), Brown (2), Smith L (8)
May 5	Ninian Park, Cardiff	WALES	W 3-2	Carter 3	25,000	Williams (1), Scott (10), Hardwick (12), Smith G (1), Franklin (3), **Mercer** (22), Matthews (23), Carter (13), Lawton (17), Brown (3), Smith L (9)

Victory Internationals

DATE	VENUE	OPPONENTS	SCORE	GOALSCORERS	ATTENDANCE	TEAM
May 26	Wembley, London	FRANCE	D 2-2	Carter, Lawton	65,000	Williams (2), Scott (11), Hardwick (13), Soo (7), Franklin (4), Mercer (23), Matthews (24), Carter (14), **Lawton** (18), Brown (4), Smith L (10)
Sep 15	Windsor Park, Belfast	N. IRELAND	W 1-0	Mortensen	45,061	Swift (11), Scott (12), Kinsell (1), Soo (8), Franklin (5), **Mercer** (24), Matthews (25), Carter (15), Lawton (19), Mortensen (3), Smith L (11)
Oct 20	The Hawthorns, West Bromwich	WALES	L 0-1		54,611	Williams (3), Scott (13), Kinsell (2), Soo (9), Franklin (6), **Mercer** (25), Matthews (26), Fenton M (1), Stubbins (1), Barrass (1), Watson (1)

1946

Victory Internationals

DATE	VENUE	OPPONENTS	SCORE	GOALSCORERS	ATTENDANCE	TEAM
Jan 19	Wembley, London	BELGIUM	W 2-0	Brown, Pye	85,000	Swift (12), Scott (14), Hardwick (14), Wright (1), Franklin (7), **Mercer** (26), Matthews (27), Pye (1), Lawton (20), Brown (5), Mullen (3)
Apr 13	Hampden Park, Glasgow	SCOTLAND	L 0-1		139,468	Swift (13), Scott (15), Hardwick (15), Wright (2), Franklin (8), **Mercer** (27), Elliott (2), Shackleton (1), Lawton (21), Hagan (15), Compton D (12)

Bolton Disaster Fund match

DATE	VENUE	OPPONENTS	SCORE	GOALSCORERS	ATTENDANCE	TEAM
Apr 24	Maine Road, Manchester	SCOTLAND	D 2-2	Welsh 2	70,000	Swift, Walton, **Hardwick**, Wright, Leuty, Mitchell, Matthews, Welsh, Lewis, Fielding, Mannion

Victory Internationals

DATE	VENUE	OPPONENTS	SCORE	GOALSCORERS	ATTENDANCE	TEAM
May 11	Stamford Bridge, London	SWITZERLAND	W 4-1	Carter 2, Brown, Lawton	75,000	Swift (14), Scott (16), Hardwick (16), Wright (3), Franklin (9), Johnson (1), Matthews (28), Carter (16), **Lawton** (22), Brown (6), Smith L (12)
May 19	Paris	FRANCE	L 1-2	Hagan	58,481	Williams (4), Bacuzzi (13), Hardwick (17), Wright (4), Franklin (10), Johnson (2), Matthews (29), Carter (17), **Lawton** (23), Hagan (16), Smith L (13)

Home International Championship

DATE	VENUE	OPPONENTS	SCORE	GOALSCORERS	ATTENDANCE	TEAM
Sep 28	Windsor Park, Belfast	N. IRELAND	W 7-2	Carter H, Mannion 3, Finney, Lawton, Langton	57,111	Swift (1), Scott (1), **Hardwick** (1), Wright W (1), Franklin (1), Cockburn (1), Finney (1), Carter H (7), Lawton (9), Mannion (1), Langton (1)

Friendly

DATE	VENUE	OPPONENTS	SCORE	GOALSCORERS	ATTENDANCE	TEAM
Sep 30	Dalymount Park, Dublin	R. of IRELAND	W 1-0	Finney	32,000	Swift (2), Scott (2), **Hardwick** (2), Wright W (2), Franklin (2), Cockburn (2), Finney (2), Carter H (8), Lawton (10), Mannion (2), Langton (2)

Home International Championship

DATE	VENUE	OPPONENTS	SCORE	GOALSCORERS	ATTENDANCE	TEAM
Nov 13	Maine Road, Manchester	WALES	W 3-0	Mannion 2, Lawton	59,121	Swift (3), Scott (3), **Hardwick** (3), Wright W (3), Franklin (3), Cockburn (3), Finney (3), Carter H (9), Lawton (11), Mannion (3), Langton (3)

Friendly

DATE	VENUE	OPPONENTS	SCORE	GOALSCORERS	ATTENDANCE	TEAM
Nov 27	Leeds Road, Huddersfield	HOLLAND	W 8-2	Lawton 4, Carter H 2, Mannion, Finney	32,435	Swift (4), Scott (4), **Hardwick** (4), Wright W (4), Franklin (4), Johnston (1), Finney (4), Carter H (10), Lawton (12), Mannion (4), Langton (4)

FACT FILE

Playing for England against Scotland in 1946, Denis Compton took a pass from Jimmy Hagan, ran down the wing and crossed the ball, falling as he did on the corner flag, which broke at its base. A spectator emerged from the crowd, snatched the post and vanished.

1947

Home International Championship

DATE	VENUE	OPPONENTS	SCORE	GOALSCORERS	ATTENDANCE	TEAM
Apr 12	Wembley, London	SCOTLAND	D 1-1	Carter H	98,200	Swift (5), Scott (5), **Hardwick** (5), Wright W (5), Franklin (5), Johnston (2), Matthews (18), Carter H (11), Lawton (13), Mannion (5), Mullen (1)

Friendlies

DATE	VENUE	OPPONENTS	SCORE	GOALSCORERS	ATTENDANCE	TEAM
May 3	Highbury, London	FRANCE	W 3-0	Finney, Mannion, Carter H	54,389	Swift (6), Scott (6), **Hardwick** (6), Wright W (6), Franklin (6), Lowe (1), Finney (5), Carter H (12), Lawton (14), Mannion (6), Langton (5)
May 18	Zurich	SWITZERLAND	L 0-1		34,000	Swift (7), Scott (7), **Hardwick** (7), Wright W (7), Franklin (7), Lowe (2), Matthews (19), Carter H (13), Lawton (15), Mannion (7), Langton (6)
May 25	Lisbon	PORTUGAL	W 10-0	Lawton 4, Mortensen 4, Finney, Matthews	65,000	Swift (8), Scott (8), **Hardwick** (8), Wright W (8), Franklin (8), Lowe (3), Matthews (20), Mortensen (1), Lawton (16), Mannion (8), Finney (6)
Sep 21	Brussels	BELGIUM	W 5-2	Lawton 2, Mortensen Finney 2	54,326	Swift (9), Scott (9), **Hardwick** (9), Ward (1), Franklin (9), Wright W (9), Matthews (21), Mortensen (2), Lawton (17), Mannion (9), Finney (7)

Home International Championship

DATE	VENUE	OPPONENTS	SCORE	GOALSCORERS	ATTENDANCE	TEAM
Oct 18	Ninian Park, Cardiff	WALES	W 3-0	Finney, Mortensen, Lawton	55,000	Swift (10), Scott (10), **Hardwick** (10), Taylor P (1), Franklin (10), Wright W (10), Matthews (22), Mortensen (3), Lawton (18), Mannion (10), Finney (8)
Nov 5	Goodison Park, Liverpool	N. IRELAND	D 2-2	Mannion, Lawton	67,980	Swift (11), Scott (11), **Hardwick** (11), Taylor P (2), Franklin (11), Wright W (11), Matthews (23), Mortensen (4), Lawton (19), Mannion (11), Finney (9)

Friendly

DATE	VENUE	OPPONENTS	SCORE	GOALSCORERS	ATTENDANCE	TEAM
Nov 19	Highbury, London	SWEDEN	W 4-2	Mortensen 3, Lawton (pen)	44,282	Swift (12), Scott (12), **Hardwick** (12), Taylor P (3), Franklin (12), Wright W (12), Finney (10), Mortensen (5), Lawton (20), Mannion (12), Langton (7)

FACT FILE

At Goodison Park in 1947, the 2-2 draw with Northern Ireland saw three of the four goals scored in the last seven minutes. Northern Ireland equalised in the last minute.

1948

Home International Championship

DATE	VENUE	OPPONENTS	SCORE	GOALSCORERS	ATTENDANCE	TEAM
Apr 10	Hampden Park, Glasgow	SCOTLAND	W 2-0	Finney, Mortensen	135,376	Swift (13), Scott (13), **Hardwick** (13), Wright W (13), Franklin (13), Cockburn (4), Matthews (24), Mortensen (6), Lawton (21), Pearson (1), Finney (11)

Friendlies

DATE	VENUE	OPPONENTS	SCORE	GOALSCORERS	ATTENDANCE	TEAM
May 16	Turin	ITALY	W 4-0	Mortensen, Lawton, Finney 2	58,000	**Swift** (14), Scott (14), Howe (1), Wright W (14), Franklin (14), Cockburn (5), Matthews (25), Mortensen (7), Lawton (22), Mannion (13), Finney (12)
Sep 26	Copenhagen	DENMARK	D 0-0		41,000	**Swift** (15), Scott (15), Aston (1), Wright W (15), Franklin (15), Cockburn (6), Matthews (26), Hagan (1), Lawton (23), Shackleton (1), Langton (8)

Home International Championship

DATE	VENUE	OPPONENTS	SCORE	GOALSCORERS	ATTENDANCE	TEAM
Oct 9	Windsor Park, Belfast	N. IRELAND	W 6-2	Matthews, Mortensen 3, Milburn, Pearson	53,629	Swift (16), Scott (16), Howe (2), **Wright W** (16), Franklin (16), Cockburn (7), Matthews (27), Mortensen (8), Milburn (1), Pearson (2), Finney (13)
Nov 10	Villa Park, Birmingham	WALES	W 1-0	Finney	67,770	Swift (17), Scott (17), Aston (2), Ward (2), Franklin (17), **Wright W** (17), Matthews (28), Mortensen (9), Milburn (2), Shackleton (2), Finney (14)

Friendly

DATE	VENUE	OPPONENTS	SCORE	GOALSCORERS	ATTENDANCE	TEAM
Dec 2	Highbury, London	SWITZERLAND	W 6-0	Haines 2, Hancocks 2, Rowley, Milburn	48,000	Ditchburn (1), Ramsey (1), Aston (3), **Wright W** (18), Franklin (18), Cockburn (8), Matthews (29), Rowley (1), Milburn (3), Haines (1), Hancocks (1)

1949

Home International Championship

DATE	VENUE	OPPONENTS	SCORE	GOALSCORERS	ATTENDANCE	TEAM
Apr 9	Wembley, London	SCOTLAND	L 1-3	Milburn	98,188	Swift (18), Aston (4), Howe (3), **Wright W** (19), Franklin (19), Cockburn (9), Matthews (30), Mortensen (10), Milburn (4), Pearson (3), Finney (15)

Friendlies

DATE	VENUE	OPPONENTS	SCORE	GOALSCORERS	ATTENDANCE	TEAM
May 13	Stockholm	SWEDEN	L 1-3	Finney	37,500	Ditchburn (2), Shimwell (1), Aston (5), **Wright W** (20), Franklin (20), Cockburn (10), Finney (16), Mortensen (11), Bentley (1), Rowley J (2), Langton (9)
May 18	Oslo	NORWAY	W 4-1	Mullen, Finney, Morris, own goal	36,000	Swift (19), Ellerington (1), Aston (6), **Wright W** (21), Franklin (21), Dickinson (1), Finney (17), Morris (1), Mortensen (12), Mannion (14), Mullen (2)
May 22	Paris	FRANCE	W 3-1	Morris 2, Wright W	61,308	Williams (1), Ellerington (2), Aston (7), **Wright W** (22), Franklin (22), Dickinson (2), Finney (18), Morris (2), Rowley J (3), Mannion (15), Mullen (3)
Sep 21	Goodison Park, Liverpool	R. of IRELAND	L 0-2		51,487	Williams (2), Mozley (1), Aston (8), **Wright W** (23), Franklin (23), Dickinson (3), Harris P (1), Morris (3), Pye (1), Mannion (16), Finney (19)

Home International Championship/World Cup Qualifiers

DATE	VENUE	OPPONENTS	SCORE	GOALSCORERS	ATTENDANCE	TEAM
Oct 15	Ninian Park, Cardiff	WALES	W 4-1	Mortensen, Milburn 3	61,079	Williams (3), Mozley (2), Aston (9), **Wright W** (24), Franklin (24), Dickinson (4), Finney (20), Mortensen (13), Milburn (5), Shackleton (3), Hancocks (2)
Nov 16	Maine Road, Manchester	N. IRELAND	W 9-2	Rowley J 4, Froggatt J, Pearson 2, Mortensen 2	69,762	Streten (1), Mozley (3), Aston (10), Watson (1), Franklin (25), **Wright W** (25), Finney (21), Mortensen (14), Rowley J (4), Pearson (4), Froggatt J (1)

Friendly

DATE	VENUE	OPPONENTS	SCORE	GOALSCORERS	ATTENDANCE	TEAM
Nov 30	White Hart Lane, London	ITALY	W 2-0	Rowley J, Wright W	71,797	Williams (4), Ramsey (2), Aston (11), Watson (2), Franklin (26), **Wright W** (26), Finney (22), Mortensen (15), Rowley J (5), Pearson (5), Froggatt J (2)

FACT FILE

Against Wales in 1949, Len Shackleton's 50-yard dribble led to a goal by Jackie Milburn.

England's 9-2 win over Northern Ireland in the 1949 World Cup qualifier was their biggest win for 50 years.

1950

Home International Championship/World Cup Qualifiers

DATE	VENUE	OPPONENTS	SCORE	GOALSCORERS	ATTENDANCE	TEAM
Apr 15	Hampden Park, Glasgow	SCOTLAND	W 1-0	Bentley	133,300	Williams (5), Ramsey (3), Aston (12), **Wright W** (27), Franklin (27), Dickinson (5), Finney (23), Mannion (17), Mortensen (16), Bentley (2), Langton (10)

Friendlies

DATE	VENUE	OPPONENTS	SCORE	GOALSCORERS	ATTENDANCE	TEAM
May 14	Lisbon	PORTUGAL	W 5-3	Finney 4 (2 pens), Mortensen	65,000	Williams (6), Ramsey (4), Aston (13), **Wright W** (28), Jones WH (1), Dickinson (6), Milburn (6), Mortensen (17), Bentley (3), Mannion (18), Finney (24)
May 18	Brussels	BELGIUM	W 4-1	Mullen, Mortensen, Mannion, Bentley	55,854	Williams (7), Ramsey (5), Aston (14), **Wright W** (29), Jones WH (2), Dickinson (7), Milburn (7), (Mullen) (4), Mortensen (18), Bentley (4), Mannion (19), Finney (25)

FACT FILE

Though Leslie Compton is recognised as the oldest England debutant at 38 years 64 days in 1950, he had made wartime appearances for his country prior to his 'official' debut.

In 1950 Jimmy Mullen became England's first substitute in an international for which caps were awarded. He replaced Jackie Milburn against Belgium and then became the first sub to score a goal. In the Jubilee match with Scotland in 1935, Sep Smith had replaced the injured Jackie Bray at half-time.

Members of the England squad do stretching exercises during a pre-World Cup training session at Dulwich (left to right) Bill Eckersley, Wilf Mannion, Roy Bentley, Billy Wright, Eddie Baily and Tom Finney.

THE WORLD CUP FINALS 1950 (BRAZIL)

Group Stage – Pool 2

DATE	VENUE	OPPONENTS	SCORE	GOALSCORERS	ATTENDANCE	TEAM
Jun 25	Rio	CHILE	W 2-0	Mortensen, Mannion	29,703	Williams (8), Ramsey (6), Aston (15), **Wright W** (30), Hughes L (1), Dickinson (8), Finney (26), Mannion (20), Bentley (5), Mortensen (19), Mullen (5)
Jun 29	Belo Horizonte	USA	L 0-1		10,151	Williams (9), Ramsey (7), Aston (16), **Wright W** (31), Hughes L (2), Dickinson (9), Finney (27), Mannion (21), Bentley (6), Mortensen (20), Mullen (6)
July 2	Rio	SPAIN	L 0-1		74,462	Williams (10), Ramsey (8), Eckersley (1), **Wright W** (32), Hughes L (3), Dickinson (10), Matthews (31), Mortensen (21), Milburn (8), Baily E (1), Finney (28)

POOL 2

	P	W	D	L	F	A	Pts
SPAIN	3	3	0	0	6	1	6
ENGLAND	3	1	0	2	2	2	2
CHILE	3	1	0	2	5	6	2
USA	3	1	0	2	4	8	2

England captain Billy Wright (left) and Ed McIlvenny, captain of the USA, exchange souvenirs before the start of their World Cup group match in Belo Horizonte, Brazil. Little did they know how the result of the match would shock the football world.

1950 (continued)

Home International Championship

Oct 7	Windsor Park, Belfast	N. IRELAND	W 4-1	Baily E 2, Lee J, Wright W	50,000	Williams (11), Ramsey (9), Aston (17), **Wright W** (33), Chilton (1), Dickinson (11), Matthews (32), Mannion (22),
Nov 15	Roker Park, Sunderland	WALES	W 4-2	Baily E 2, Mannion, Milburn	59,137	Williams (12), **Ramsey** (10), Smith L (1), Watson (3), Compton L (1), Dickinson (12), Finney (29), Mannion (23), Milburn (9), Baily E (3), Medley (1)

Friendly

Nov 22	Highbury, London	YUGOSLAVIA	D 2-2	Lofthouse 2	61,454	Williams (13), **Ramsey** (11), Eckersley (2), Watson (4), Compton L (2), Dickinson (13), Hancocks (3), Mannion (24), Lofthouse (1), Baily E (4), Medley (2)

1951

Home International Championship

DATE	VENUE	OPPONENTS	SCORE	GOALSCORERS	ATTENDANCE	TEAM
Apr 14	Wembley, London	SCOTLAND	L 2-3	Hassall, Finney	98,000	Williams (14), Ramsey (12), Eckersley (3), Johnston (3), Froggatt J (3), **Wright W** (34), Matthews (33), Mannion (25), Mortensen (22), Hassall (1), Finney (30)

Friendlies

May 9	Wembley, London	ARGENTINA	W 2-1	Mortensen, Milburn	60,000	Williams (15), Ramsey (13), Eckersley (4), **Wright W** (35), Taylor J (1), Cockburn (11), Finney (31), Mortensen (23), Milburn (10), Hassall (2), Metcalfe (1)
May 19	Goodison Park, Liverpool	PORTUGAL	W 5-2	Nicholson, Milburn 2, Finney, Hassall	52,686	Williams (16), **Ramsey** (14), Eckersley (5), Nicholson (1), Taylor J (2), Cockburn (12), Finney (32), Pearson (6), Milburn (11), Hassall (3), Metcalfe (2)
Oct 3	Highbury, London	FRANCE	D 2-2	Medley, own goal	57,603	Williams (17), Ramsey (15), Willis (1), **Wright W** (36), Chilton (2), Cockburn (13), Finney (33), Mannion (26), Milburn (12), Hassall (4), Medley (3)

Home International Championship

Oct 20	Ninian Park, Cardiff	WALES	D 1-1	Baily E	60,000	Williams (18), Ramsey (16), Smith L (2), **Wright W** (37), Barrass (1), Dickinson (14), Finney (34), Thompson T (1), Lofthouse (2), Baily E (5), Medley (4)
Nov 14	Villa Park, Birmingham	N. IRELAND	W 2-0	Lofthouse 2	57,889	Merrick (1), Ramsey (17), Smith L (3), **Wright W** (38), Barrass (2), Dickinson (15), Finney (35), Sewell (1), Lofthouse (3), Phillips (1), Medley (5)

Friendly

Nov 28	Wembley, London	AUSTRIA	D 2-2	Ramsey (pen), Lofthouse	100,000	Merrick (2), Ramsey (18), Eckersley (6), **Wright W** (39), Froggatt J (4), Dickinson (16), Milton (1), Broadis (1), Lofthouse (4), Baily E (6), Medley (6)

FACT FILE

Billy Nicholson scored against Portugal in 1951 after just 19 seconds with an 18-yard shot in what proved to be his one and only full international appearance.

Plans before the 1951 game with Austria to use Billy Wright as a defensive inside left to curb the foraging activities of Ernst Ocwirk, the Austrian's attacking centre half, were scuppered by injuries which affected final team selection.

1952

Home International Championship

DATE	VENUE	OPPONENTS	SCORE	GOALSCORERS	ATTENDANCE	TEAM
Apr 5	Hampden Park, Glasgow	SCOTLAND	W 2-1	Pearson 2	133,991	Merrick (3), Ramsey (19), Garrett (1), **Wright W** (40), Froggatt J (5), Dickinson (17), Finney (36), Broadis (2), Lofthouse (5), Pearson (7), Rowley J (6)

Friendlies

DATE	VENUE	OPPONENTS	SCORE	GOALSCORERS	ATTENDANCE	TEAM
May 18	Florence	ITALY	D 1-1	Broadis	93,000	Merrick (4), Ramsey (20), Garrett (2), **Wright W** (41), Froggatt J (6), Dickinson (18), Finney (37), Broadis (3), Lofthouse (6), Pearson (8), Elliott (1)
May 25	Vienna	AUSTRIA	W 3-2	Lofthouse 2, Sewell	65,000	Merrick (5), Ramsey (21), Eckersley (7), **Wright W** (42), Froggatt J (7), Dickinson (19), Finney (38), Sewell (2), Lofthouse (7), Baily E (7), Elliott (2)
May 28	Zurich	SWITZERLAND	W 3-0	Sewell, Lofthouse 2	33,000	Merrick (6), Ramsey (22), Eckersley (8), **Wright W** (43), Froggatt J (8), Dickinson (20), Allen R (1), Sewell (3), Lofthouse (8), Baily E (8), Finney (39)

Home International Championship

DATE	VENUE	OPPONENTS	SCORE	GOALSCORERS	ATTENDANCE	TEAM
Oct 4	Windsor Park, Belfast	N. IRELAND	D 2-2	Lofthouse, Elliott	58,000	Merrick (7), Ramsey (23), Eckersley (9), **Wright W** (44), Froggatt J (9), Dickinson (21), Finney (40), Sewell (4), Lofthouse (9), Baily E (9), Elliott (3)
Nov 12	Wembley, London	WALES	W 5-2	Finney, Lofthouse 2, Froggatt J, Bentley	94,094	Merrick (8), Ramsey (24), Smith L (4), **Wright W** (45), Froggatt J (10), Dickinson (22), Finney (41), Froggatt R (1), Lofthouse (10), Bentley (7), Elliott (4)

Friendly

DATE	VENUE	OPPONENTS	SCORE	GOALSCORERS	ATTENDANCE	TEAM
Nov 26	Wembley, London	BELGIUM	W 5-0	Elliott 2, Lofthouse 2, Froggatt R	68,333	Merrick (9), Ramsey (25), Smith L (5), **Wright W** (46), Froggatt J (11), Dickinson (23), Finney (42), Bentley (8), Lofthouse (11), Froggatt R (2), Elliott (5)

FACT FILE

Billy Wright set a world record of 70 consecutive appearances starting with the match with France in 1951 and ending against the USA in 1959. He never refused to sign autographs, though it might have been slightly easier for him as he was ambidextrous and it was said he often signed two books at a time.

Portuguese keeper Ernesto punches clear from England forward Stan Pearson during their match against England at Goodison Park in May 1951. Jackie Milburn waits and watches, hoping to benefit for any mistake.

1953

Home International Championship

DATE	VENUE	OPPONENTS	SCORE	GOALSCORERS	ATTENDANCE	TEAM
Apr 18	Wembley, London	SCOTLAND	D 2-2	Broadis 2	97,000	Merrick (10), Ramsey (26), Smith L (6), **Wright W** (47), Barrass (3), Dickinson (24), Finney (43), Broadis (4), Lofthouse (12), Froggatt R (3), Froggatt J (12)

Friendlies

DATE	VENUE	OPPONENTS	SCORE	GOALSCORERS	ATTENDANCE	TEAM
May 17	Buenos Aires	ARGENTINA	D 0-0	(abandoned after 23 mins; waterlogged pitch)	80,000	Merrick (11), Ramsey (27), Eckersley (10), **Wright W** (48), Johnston (4), Dickinson (25), Finney (44), Broadis (5), Lofthouse (13), Taylor T (1), Berry (1)
May 24	Santiago	CHILE	W 2-1	Taylor T, Lofthouse	56,398	Merrick (12), Ramsey (28), Eckersley (11), **Wright W** (49), Johnston (5), Dickinson (26), Finney (45), Broadis (6), Lofthouse (14), Taylor T (2), Berry (2)
May 31	Montevideo	URUGUAY	L 1-2	Taylor T	66,072	Merrick (13), Ramsey (29), Eckersley (12), **Wright W** (50), Johnston (6), Dickinson (27), Finney (46), Broadis (7), Lofthouse (15), Taylor T (3), Berry (3)
Jun 8	New York	USA	W 6-3	Broadis, Finney 2, Lofthouse 2, Froggatt R	7,271	Ditchburn (3), Ramsey (30), Eckersley (13), **Wright W** (51), Johnston (7), Dickinson (28), Finney (47), Broadis (8), Lofthouse (16), Froggatt R (4), Froggatt J (13)

Home International Championship/World Cup Qualifier

DATE	VENUE	OPPONENTS	SCORE	GOALSCORERS	ATTENDANCE	TEAM
Oct 10	Ninian Park, Cardiff	WALES	W 4-1	Wilshaw 2, Lofthouse 2	61,000	Merrick (14), Garrett (3), Eckersley (14), **Wright W** (52), Johnston (8), Dickinson (29), Finney (48), Quixall (1), Lofthouse (17), Wilshaw (1), Mullen (7)

Friendly

DATE	VENUE	OPPONENTS	SCORE	GOALSCORERS	ATTENDANCE	TEAM
Oct 21	Wembley, London	REST OF EUROPE	D 4-4	Mullen 2, Mortensen, Ramsey (pen)	96,000	Merrick (15), Ramsey (31), Eckersley (15), **Wright W** (53), Ufton (1), Dickinson (30), Matthews (34), Mortensen (24), Lofthouse (18), Quixall (2), Mullen (8)

Home International Championship/World Cup Qualifier

DATE	VENUE	OPPONENTS	SCORE	GOALSCORERS	ATTENDANCE	TEAM
Nov 11	Goodison Park, Liverpool	N. IRELAND	W 3-1	Hassall 2, Lofthouse	70,000	Merrick (16), Rickaby (1), Eckersley (16), **Wright W** (54), Johnston (9), Dickinson (31), Matthews (35), Quixall (3), Lofthouse (19), Hassall (5), Mullen (9)

Friendly

DATE	VENUE	OPPONENTS	SCORE	GOALSCORERS	ATTENDANCE	TEAM
Nov 25	Wembley, London	HUNGARY	L 3-6	Sewell, Mortensen, Ramsey (pen)	100,000	Merrick (17), Ramsey (32), Eckersley (17), **Wright W** (55), Johnston (10), Dickinson (32), Matthews (36), Taylor E (1), Mortensen (25), Sewell (5), Robb (1),

FACT FILE

Unusually in England's 4-1 win over Wales in 1953, all five goals came from headers.

Only a last-minute penalty goal by Alf Ramsey salvaged a 4-4 draw for England against the Rest of Europe in the FA's 75th anniversary match in 1953.

On 29 August 1953, the four British national associations decided that each player who participated in the Home International Championship would receive one cap for each series rather than one for each actual appearance. Thus for example Billy Wright who turned out in 18 such championship matches after this date, received only six more caps, thereby reducing his overall total of 105 caps to 93!

Jimmy Mullen turns away having scored England's third goal in the friendly against a Rest of Europe XI at Wembley in October 1953. The final result was a thrilling 4-4 draw.

1954

Home International Championship/World Cup Qualifier

DATE	VENUE	OPPONENTS	SCORE	GOALSCORERS	ATTENDANCE	TEAM
Apr 3	Hampden Park, Glasgow	SCOTLAND	W 4-2	Broadis, Nicholls, Allen, Mullen	134,544	Merrick (18), Staniforth (1), Byrne R (1), **Wright W** (56), Clarke H (1), Dickinson (33), Finney (49), Broadis (9), Allen R (2), Nicholls (1), Mullen (10),

Friendlies

DATE	VENUE	OPPONENTS	SCORE	GOALSCORERS	ATTENDANCE	TEAM
May 16	Belgrade	YUGOSLAVIA	L 0-1		60,000	Merrick (19), Staniforth (2), Byrne R (2), **Wright W** (57), Owen (1), Dickinson (34), Finney (50), Broadis (10), Allen R (3), Nicholls (2), Mullen (11)
May 23	Budapest	HUNGARY	L 1-7	Broadis	92,000	Merrick (20), Staniforth (3), Byrne R (3), **Wright W** (58), Owen (2), Dickinson (35), Harris P (2), Sewell (6), Jezzard (1), Broadis (11), Finney (51)

FACT FILE

In 1953-54 Hungary achieved the feat of being the only continental team to score as many as six and seven goals against a full England side, winning 6-3 at Wembley and 7-1 in Budapest. Four of their six goals came from outside the penalty area and in the return match Hungarian fans chanted 'ra-ra-hajra', their version of 'hip-hip-hooray'. Before the Wembley game, the Hungarian team trained at Lake Bulaton, using a machine which simulated fog conditions, as a precaution against adverse weather.

THE WORLD CUP FINALS 1954 (SWITZERLAND)

Group Stage – Pool 4

DATE	VENUE	OPPONENTS	SCORE	GOALSCORERS	ATTENDANCE	TEAM
Jun 17	Basle	BELGIUM	D 4-4	Broadis 2, Lofthouse 2	14,000	Merrick (21), Staniforth (4), Byrne R (4), **Wright W** (59), Owen (3), Dickinson (36), Matthews (37), Broadis (12), Lofthouse (20), Taylor T (4), Finney (52)
Jun 20	Berne	SWITZERLAND	W 2-0	Wilshaw, Mullen	30,000	Merrick (22), Staniforth (5), Byrne R (5), McGarry (1), **Wright W** (60), Dickinson (37), Finney (53), Broadis (13), Taylor T (5), Wilshaw (2), Mullen (12)

Quarter-final

DATE	VENUE	OPPONENTS	SCORE	GOALSCORERS	ATTENDANCE	TEAM
Jun 26	Basle	URUGUAY	L 2-4	Lofthouse, Finney	35,000	Merrick (23), Staniforth (6), Byrne R (6), McGarry (2), **Wright W** (61), Dickinson (38), Matthews (38), Broadis (14), Lofthouse (21), Wilshaw (3), Finney (54)

Pool 4

	P	W	D	L	F	A	Pts
ENGLAND	2	1	1	0	6	4	3
ITALY	2	1	0	1	5	3	2
SWITZERLAND	2	1	0	1	2	3	2
BELGIUM	2	0	1	1	5	8	1

Tom Finney (second left) watches as Nat Lofthouse directs a header towards the Belgian goal during their 1954 World Cup opener. Tommy Taylor also rises in anticipation. The match ended 4-4.

1954 (continued)

Home International Championship

DATE	VENUE	OPPONENTS	SCORE	GOALSCORERS	ATTENDANCE	TEAM
Oct 2	Windsor Park, Belfast	N. IRELAND	W 2-0	Haynes, Revie	59,000	Wood (1), Foulkes (1), Byrne R (7), Wheeler (1), **Wright W** (62), Barlow (1), Matthews (39), Revie (1), Lofthouse (22), Haynes (1), Pilkington (1)
Nov 10	Wembley, London	WALES	W 3-2	Bentley 3	89,789	Wood (2), Staniforth (7), Byrne R (8), Phillips (2), **Wright W** (63), Slater (1), Matthews (40), Bentley (9), Allen R (4), Shackleton (4), Blunstone (1)

Friendly

DATE	VENUE	OPPONENTS	SCORE	GOALSCORERS	ATTENDANCE	TEAM
Dec 1	Wembley, London	W. GERMANY	W 3-1	Bentley, Allen R, Shackleton	100,000	Williams (19), Staniforth (8), Byrne R (9), Phillips (3), **Wright W** (64), Slater (2), Matthews (41), Bentley (10), Allen R (5), Shackleton (5), Finney (55)

1955

Home International Championship

DATE	VENUE	OPPONENTS	SCORE	GOALSCORERS	ATTENDANCE	TEAM
Apr 2	Wembley, London	SCOTLAND	W 7-2	Wilshaw 4, Lofthouse 2, Revie	96,847	Williams (20), Meadows (1), Byrne R (10), Armstrong (1), **Wright W** (65), Edwards (1), Matthews (42), Revie (2), Lofthouse (23), Wilshaw (4), Blunstone (2)

Friendlies

DATE	VENUE	OPPONENTS	SCORE	GOALSCORERS	ATTENDANCE	TEAM
May 15	Paris	FRANCE	L 0-1		54,696	Williams (21), Sillett P (1), Byrne R (11), Flowers (1), **Wright W** (66), Edwards (2), Matthews (43), Revie (3), Lofthouse (24), Wilshaw (5), Blunstone (3)
May 18	Madrid	SPAIN	D 1-1	Bentley	125,000	Williams (22), Sillett P (2), Byrne R (12), Dickinson (39), **Wright W** (67), Edwards (3), Matthews (44), Bentley (11), Lofthouse (25), Quixall (4), Wilshaw (6)
May 22	Oporto	PORTUGAL	L 1-3	Bentley	52,000	Williams (23), Sillett P (3), Byrne R (13), Dickinson (40), **Wright W** (68), Edwards (4), Matthews (45), Bentley (12), Lofthouse (26), (Quixall 5), Wilshaw (7), Blunstone (4)
Oct 2	Copenhagen	DENMARK	W 5-1	Revie 2 (1 pen), Lofthouse 2, Bradford	53,000	Baynham (1), Hall (1), Byrne R (14), McGarry (3), **Wright W** (69), Dickinson (41), Milburn (13), Revie (4), Lofthouse (27), Bradford (1), Finney (56)

Home International Championship

DATE	VENUE	OPPONENTS	SCORE	GOALSCORERS	ATTENDANCE	TEAM
Oct 22	Ninian Park, Cardiff	WALES	L 1-2	own goal	60,000	Williams (24), Hall (2), Byrne R (15), McGarry (4), **Wright W** (70), Dickinson (42), Matthews (46), Revie (5), Lofthouse (28), Wilshaw (8), Finney (57)
Nov 2	Wembley, London	N. IRELAND	W 3-0	Wilshaw 2, Finney	60,000	Baynham (2), Hall (3), Byrne R (16), Clayton (1), **Wright W** (71), Dickinson (43), Finney (58), Haynes (2), Jezzard (2), Wilshaw (9), Perry (1)

Friendly

DATE	VENUE	OPPONENTS	SCORE	GOALSCORERS	ATTENDANCE	TEAM
Nov 30	Wembley, London	SPAIN	W 4-1	Atyeo, Perry 2, Finney	95,550	Baynham (3), Hall (4), Byrne R (17), Clayton (2), **Wright W** (72), Dickinson (44), Finney (59), Atyeo (1), Lofthouse (29), Haynes (3), Perry (2)

FACT FILE

When England beat Scotland 7-2 in 1955, Denis Wilshaw became the first player to score as many as four goals in one match for England against the Scots.

1956

Home International Championship

DATE	VENUE	OPPONENTS	SCORE	GOALSCORERS	ATTENDANCE	TEAM
Apr 14	Hampden Park, Glasgow	SCOTLAND	D 1-1	Haynes	132,817	Matthews R (1), Hall (5), Byrne R (18), Dickinson (45), **Wright W** (73), Edwards (5), Finney (60), Taylor T (6), Lofthouse (30), Haynes (4), Perry (3)

Friendlies

DATE	VENUE	OPPONENTS	SCORE	GOALSCORERS	ATTENDANCE	TEAM
May 9	Wembley, London	BRAZIL	W 4-2	Taylor T 2, Grainger 2	97,000	Matthews R (2), Hall (6), Byrne R (19), Clayton (3), **Wright W** (74), Edwards (6), Matthews S (47), Ateyo (2), Taylor T (7), Haynes (5), Grainger (1)
May 16	Stockholm	SWEDEN	D 0-0		35,000	Matthews R (3), Hall (7), Byrne R (20), Clayton (4), **Wright W** (75), Edwards (7), Berry (4), Atyeo (3), Taylor T (8), Haynes (6), Grainger (2)
May 20	Helsinki	FINLAND	W 5-1	Wilshaw, Haynes, Astall, Lofthouse 2	20,177	Wood (3), Hall (8), Byrne R (21), Clayton (5), **Wright W** (76), Edwards (8), Astall (1), Haynes (7), Taylor T (9), (Lofthouse 31), Wilshaw (10), Grainger (3)
May 26	Berlin	W. GERMANY	W 3-1	Edwards, Grainger, Haynes	90,000	Matthews R (4), Hall (9), Byrne R (22), Clayton (6), **Wright W** (77), Edwards (9), Astall (2), Haynes (8), Taylor T (10), Wilshaw (11), Grainger (4)

Home International Championship

DATE	VENUE	OPPONENTS	SCORE	GOALSCORERS	ATTENDANCE	TEAM
Oct 6	Windsor Park, Belfast	N. IRELAND	D 1-1	Matthews S	58,420	Matthews R (5), Hall (10), Byrne R (23), Clayton (7), **Wright W** (78), Edwards (10), Matthews S (48), Revie (6), Taylor T (11), Wilshaw (12), Grainger (5)
Nov 14	Wembley, London	WALES	W 3-1	Haynes, Brooks, Finney	93,796	Ditchburn (4), Hall (11), Byrne R (24), Clayton (8), **Wright W** (79), Dickinson (46), Matthews S (49), Brooks (1), Finney (61), Haynes (9), Grainger (6)

Friendly

DATE	VENUE	OPPONENTS	SCORE	GOALSCORERS	ATTENDANCE	TEAM
Nov 28	Wembley, London	YUGOSLAVIA	W 3-0	Brooks, Taylor T 2	75,000	Ditchburn (5), Hall (12), Byrne R (25), Clayton (9), **Wright W** (80), Dickinson (47), Matthews S (50), Brooks (2), Finney (62), Haynes (10), (Taylor T 12), Blunstone (5)

World Cup Qualifier

DATE	VENUE	OPPONENTS	SCORE	GOALSCORERS	ATTENDANCE	TEAM
Dec 5	Molineux, Wolverhampton	DENMARK	W 5-2	Taylor T 3, Edwards 2	54,083	Ditchburn (6), Hall (13), Byrne R (26), Clayton (10), **Wright W** (81), Dickinson (48), Matthews S (51), Brooks (3), Taylor T (13), Edwards (11), Finney (63)

Tommy Taylor scores England's first goal in a 4-2 win against Brazil at Wembley in May 1956. In the end, Taylor scored twice amd Colin Grainger added two more on his debut.

1957

Home International Championship

DATE	VENUE	OPPONENTS	SCORE	GOALSCORERS	ATTENDANCE	TEAM
Apr 6	Wembley, London	SCOTLAND	W 2-1	Kevan, Edwards	97,520	Hodgkinson (1), Hall (14), Byrne R (27), Clayton (11), **Wright W** (82), Edwards (12), Matthews S (52), Thompson T (2), Finney (64), Kevan (1), Grainger (7)

World Cup Qualifiers

DATE	VENUE	OPPONENTS	SCORE	GOALSCORERS	ATTENDANCE	TEAM
May 8	Wembley, London	R. of IRELAND	W 5-1	Taylor T 3, Atyeo 2,	52,000	Hodgkinson (2), Hall (15), Byrne R (28), Clayton (12), **Wright W** (83), Edwards (13), Matthews S (53), Atyeo (4), Taylor T (14), Haynes (11), Finney (65)
May 15	Copenhagen	DENMARK	W 4-1	Haynes, Taylor T 2, Atyeo	35,000	Hodgkinson (3), Hall (16), Byrne R (29), Clayton (13), **Wright W** (84), Edwards (14), Matthews S (54), Atyeo (5), Taylor T (15), Haynes (12), Finney (66)
May 19	Dalymount Park, Dublin	R. of IRELAND	D 1-1	Atyeo	47,000	Hodgkinson (4), Hall (17), Byrne R (30), Clayton (14), **Wright W** (85), Edwards (15), Finney (67), Atyeo (6), Taylor T (16), Haynes (13), Pegg (1)

Home International Championship

DATE	VENUE	OPPONENTS	SCORE	GOALSCORERS	ATTENDANCE	TEAM
Oct 19	Ninian Park, Cardiff	WALES	W 4-0	Haynes 2, Finney, own goal	58,000	Hopkinson (1), Howe D (1), Byrne R (31), Clayton (15), **Wright W** (86), Edwards (16), Douglas (1), Kevan (2), Taylor T (17), Haynes (14), Finney (68)
Nov 6	Wembley, London	N. IRELAND	L 2-3	A'Court, Edwards	40,000	Hopkinson (2), Howe D (2), Byrne R (32), Clayton (16), **Wright W** (87), Edwards (17), Douglas (2), Kevan (3), Taylor T (18), Haynes (15), A'Court (1)

Friendly

DATE	VENUE	OPPONENTS	SCORE	GOALSCORERS	ATTENDANCE	TEAM
Nov 27	Wembley, London	FRANCE	W 4-0	Taylor T 2, Robson R 2	64,349	Hopkinson (3), Howe D (3), Byrne R (33), Clayton (17), **Wright W** (88), Edwards (18), Douglas (3), Robson R (1), Taylor T (19), Haynes (16), Finney (69)

FACT FILE

In 1957, Northern Ireland's 3-2 win at Wembley was the first such Irish success against England since 1927 and ended the home country's run of 16 unbeaten matches.

Stanley Matthews' career as an international lasted 22 years 228 days, until 1957, and he was also the oldest goalscorer at 41 years 248 days.

Derek Kevan (left) and Alan Hodgkinson run around White Hart Lane during a training session ahead of the home international against Scotland in 1957.

Johnny Haynes, seen here showing the Fulham youngsters how to do it during training, scored a hat-trick for England against the USSR at Wembley in 1958.

1958

Home International Championship

DATE	VENUE	OPPONENTS	SCORE	GOALSCORERS	ATTENDANCE	TEAM
Apr 19	Hampden Park, Glasgow	SCOTLAND	W 4-0	Douglas, Kevan 2, Charlton R	127,874	Hopkinson (4), Howe D (4), Langley (1), Clayton (18), **Wright W** (89), Slater (3), Douglas (4), Charlton R (1), Kevan (4), Haynes (17), Finney (70)

Friendlies

DATE	VENUE	OPPONENTS	SCORE	GOALSCORERS	ATTENDANCE	TEAM
May 7	Wembley, London	PORTUGAL	W 2-1	Charlton R 2	72,000	Hopkinson (5), Howe D (5), Langley (2), Clayton (19), **Wright W** (90), Slater (4), Douglas (5), Charlton R (2), Kevan (5), Haynes (18), Finney (71)
May 11	Belgrade	YUGOSLAVIA	L 0-5		55,000	Hopkinson (6), Howe D (6), Langley (3), Clayton (20), **Wright W** (91), Slater (5), Douglas (6), Charlton R (3), Kevan (6), Haynes (19), Finney (72)
May 18	Moscow	USSR	D 1-1	Kevan	102,000	McDonald (1), Howe D (7), Banks T (1), Clamp (1), **Wright W** (92), Slater (6), Douglas (7), Robson R (2), Kevan (7), Haynes (20), Finney (73)

FACT FILE

The three goals scored by Johnny Haynes against the USSR at Wembley in 1958 rank as the first hat-trick for England against an eastern European team.

From May to October 1958 England played seven matches without a win, drawing five times and losing twice.

THE WORLD CUP FINALS 1958 (SWEDEN)

Group Stage – Pool 2

DATE	VENUE	OPPONENTS	SCORE	GOALSCORERS	ATTENDANCE	TEAM
Jun 8	Gothenburg	USSR	D 2-2	Kevan, Finney (pen)	49,348	McDonald (2), Howe D (8), Banks T (2), Clamp (2), **Wright W** (93), Slater (7), Douglas (8), Robson R (3), Kevan (8), Haynes (21), Finney (74)
Jun 11	Gothenburg	BRAZIL	D 0-0		40,895	McDonald (3), Howe D (9), Banks T (3), Clamp (3), **Wright W** (94), Slater (8), Douglas (9), Robson R (4), Kevan (9), Haynes (22), A'Court (2)
Jun 15	Boras	AUSTRIA	D 2-2	Haynes, Kevan	16,800	McDonald (4), Howe D (10), Banks T (4), Clamp (4), **Wright W** (95), Slater (9), Douglas (10), Robson R (5), Kevan (10), Haynes (23), A'Court (3)

Play-off

DATE	VENUE	OPPONENTS	SCORE	GOALSCORERS	ATTENDANCE	TEAM
Jun 17	Gothenburg	USSR	L 0-1		23,182	McDonald (5), Howe D (11), Banks T (5), Clayton (21), **Wright W** (96), Slater (10), Brabrook (1), Broadbent (1), Kevan (11), Haynes (24), A'Court (4)

Pool 2

	P	W	D	L	F	A	Pts
Brazil	3	2	1	0	5	0	5
England	3	0	3	0	4	4	3
Soviet Union	3	1	1	1	4	4	3
Austria	3	0	1	2	2	7	1

Russian keeper Lev Yashin punches clear from an England attack during their opening match in Gothenburg. The match ended in a 2-2 draw. The two met again in a Play-off and the USSR went through 1-0.

265

1958 (continued)

Home International Championship

DATE	VENUE	OPPONENTS	SCORE	GOALSCORERS	ATTENDANCE	TEAM
Oct 4	Windsor Park, Belfast	N. IRELAND	D 3-3	Charlton R 2, Finney	58,000	McDonald (6), Howe D (12), Banks T (6), Clayton (22), Wright W (97), McGuinness (1), Brabrook (2), Broadbent (2), Charlton R (4), Haynes (25), Finney (75)

Friendly

DATE	VENUE	OPPONENTS	SCORE	GOALSCORERS	ATTENDANCE	TEAM
Oct 22	Wembley, London	USSR	W 5-0	Haynes 3, Charlton R (pen), Lofthouse	100,000	McDonald (7), Howe D (13), Shaw G (1), Clayton (23), Wright W (98), Slater (11), Douglas (11), Charlton R (5), Lofthouse (32), Haynes (26), Finney (76)

Home International Championship

DATE	VENUE	OPPONENTS	SCORE	GOALSCORERS	ATTENDANCE	TEAM
Nov 26	Villa Park, Birmingham	WALES	D 2-2	Broadbent 2	41,581	McDonald (8), Howe D (14), Shaw G (2), Clayton (24), Wright W (99), Flowers (2), Clapton (1), Broadbent (3), Lofthouse (33), Charlton R (6), A'Court (5)

Tom Finney (left), Maurice Setters and Bobby Charlton (right) give Billy Wright a lift during an England training session at Roehampton in London in 1958.

1959

Home International Championship

DATE	VENUE	OPPONENTS	SCORE	GOALSCORERS	ATTENDANCE	TEAM
Apr 11	Wembley, London	SCOTLAND	W 1-0	Charlton R	98,329	Hopkinson (7), Howe D (15), Shaw G (3), Clayton (25), **Wright W** (100), Flowers (3), Douglas (12), Broadbent (4), Charlton R (7), Haynes (27), Holden (1)

Friendlies

DATE	VENUE	OPPONENTS	SCORE	GOALSCORERS	ATTENDANCE	TEAM
May 6	Wembley, London	ITALY	D 2-2	Charlton R, Bradley	92,000	Hopkinson (8), Howe D (16), Shaw G (4), Clayton (26), **Wright W** (101), Flowers (4), Bradley (1), Broadbent (5), Charlton R (8), Haynes (28), Holden (2)
May 13	Rio	BRAZIL	L 0-2		160,000	Hopkinson (9), Howe D (17), Armfield (1), Clayton (27), **Wright W** (102), Flowers (5), Deeley (1), Broadbent (6), Charlton R (9), Haynes (29), Holden (3)
May 17	Lima	PERU	L 1-4	Greaves	50,306	Hopkinson (10), Howe D (18), Armfield (2), Clayton (28), **Wright W** (103), Flowers (6), Deeley (2), Greaves (1), Charlton R (10), Haynes (30), Holden (4)
May 24	Mexico City	MEXICO	L 1-2	Kevan	83,000	Hopkinson (11), Howe D (19), Armfield (3), Clayton (29), **Wright W** (104), McGuinness (2), (Flowers 7), Holden (5), (Bradley 2), Greaves (2), Kevan (12), Haynes (31), Charlton R (11)
May 28	Los Angeles	USA	W 8-1	Charlton R 3 (1 pen), Flowers 2, Bradley, Kevan, Haynes	14,000	Hopkinson (12), Howe D (20), Armfield (4), Clayton (30), **Wright W** (105), Flowers (8), Bradley (3), Greaves (3), Kevan (13), Haynes (32), Charlton R (12)

Home International Championship

DATE	VENUE	OPPONENTS	SCORE	GOALSCORERS	ATTENDANCE	TEAM
Oct 17	Ninian Park, Cardiff	WALES	D 1-1	Greaves	62,000	Hopkinson (13), Howe D (21), Allen A (1), **Clayton** (31), Smith T (1), Flowers (9), Connelly (1), Greaves (4), Clough (1), Charlton R (13), Holliday (1)

Friendly

DATE	VENUE	OPPONENTS	SCORE	GOALSCORERS	ATTENDANCE	TEAM
Oct 28	Wembley, London	SWEDEN	L 2-3	Connelly, Charlton R	80,000	Hopkinson (14), Howe D (22), Allen A (2), **Clayton** (32), Smith T (2), Flowers (10), Connelly (2), Greaves (5), Clough (2), Charlton R (14), Holliday (2)

Home International Championship

DATE	VENUE	OPPONENTS	SCORE	GOALSCORERS	ATTENDANCE	TEAM
Nov 18	Wembley, London	N. IRELAND	W 2-1	Baker, Parry	60,000	Springett R (1), Howe D (23), Allen A (3), **Clayton** (33), Brown (1), Flowers (11), Connelly (3), Haynes (33), Baker (1), Parry (1), Holliday (3)

FACT FILE

In May, 1959 in the friendly in Los Angeles, both Ron Flowers' goals against the USA were hit from 30 yards.

Captain Billy Wright is chaired off the pitch by the England players on the occasion of his 100th cap, against Scotland at Wembley in April 1959. England won the match 1-0.

1960

Home International Championship

DATE	VENUE	OPPONENTS	SCORE	GOALSCORERS	ATTENDANCE	TEAM
Apr 9	Hampden Park, Glasgow	SCOTLAND	D 1-1	Charlton R (pen)	129,193	Springett R (2), Armfield (5), Wilson (1), **Clayton** (34), Slater (12), Flowers (12), Connelly (4), Broadbent (7), Baker (2), Parry (2), Charlton R (15)

Friendlies

DATE	VENUE	OPPONENTS	SCORE	GOALSCORERS	ATTENDANCE	TEAM
May 11	Wembley, London	YUGOSLAVIA	D 3-3	Douglas, Greaves, Haynes	60,000	Springett R (3), Armfield (6), Wilson (2), **Clayton** (35), Swan (1), Flowers (13), Douglas (13), Haynes (34), Baker (3), Greaves (6), Charlton R (16)
May 15	Madrid	SPAIN	L 0-3		77,000	Springett R (4), Armfield (7), Wilson (3), Robson R (6), Swan (2), Flowers (14), Brabrook (3), **Haynes** (35), Baker (4), Greaves (7), Charlton R (17)
May 22	Budapest	HUNGARY	L 0-2		90,000	Springett R (5), Armfield (8), Wilson (4), Robson R (7), Swan (3), Flowers (15), Douglas (14), **Haynes** (36), Baker (5), Viollet (1), Charlton R (18)

Home International Championship

DATE	VENUE	OPPONENTS	SCORE	GOALSCORERS	ATTENDANCE	TEAM
Oct 8	Windsor Park, Belfast	N. IRELAND	W 5-2	Smith R, Greaves 2, Charlton R, Douglas	60,000	Springett R (6), Armfield (9), McNeil (1), Robson R (8), Swan (4), Flowers (16), Douglas (15), Greaves (8), Smith R (1), **Haynes** (37), Charlton R (19)

World Cup Qualifier

DATE	VENUE	OPPONENTS	SCORE	GOALSCORERS	ATTENDANCE	TEAM
Oct 19	Luxembourg	LUXEMBOURG	W 9-0	Greaves 3, Charlton R 3, Smith R 2, Haynes	5,500	Springett R (7), Armfield (10), McNeil (2), Robson R (9), Swan (5), Flowers (17), Douglas (16), Greaves (9), Smith R (2), **Haynes** (38), Charlton R (20)

Friendly

DATE	VENUE	OPPONENTS	SCORE	GOALSCORERS	ATTENDANCE	TEAM
Oct 26	Wembley, London	SPAIN	W 4-2	Greaves, Douglas, Smith R (2),	80,000	Springett R (8), Armfield (11), McNeil (3), Robson R (10), Swan (6), Flowers (18), Douglas (17), Greaves (10), Smith R (3), **Haynes** (39), Charlton R (21)

Home International Championship

DATE	VENUE	OPPONENTS	SCORE	GOALSCORERS	ATTENDANCE	TEAM
Nov 23	Wembley, London	WALES	W 5-1	Greaves 2, Charlton R, Smith R, Haynes	65,000	Hodgkinson (5), Armfield (12), McNeil (4), Robson R (11), Swan (7), Flowers (19), Douglas (18), Greaves (11), Smith R (4), **Haynes** (40), Charlton R (22)

FACT FILE

During the 1-1 draw with Scotland in 1960, Bobby Charlton scored one penalty and missed another – for which he actually had two attempts in fact.

Jimmy Greaves scored seven goals in the 1960-61 Home International Championship, the best by an England player in the competition from an overall total of 13 that season.

Ron Springett of Sheffield Wednesday was the number one choice goalkeeper for several years during the early 1960s

1961

Home International Championship

DATE	VENUE	OPPONENTS	SCORE	GOALSCORERS	ATTENDANCE	TEAM
Apr 15	Wembley, London	SCOTLAND	W 9-3	Robson R, Greaves 3, Douglas, Smith R 2, Haynes 2	97,350	Springett R (9), Armfield (13), McNeil (5), Robson R (12), Swan (8), Flowers (20), Douglas (19), Greaves (12), Smith R (5), **Haynes** (41), Charlton R (23)

Friendly

DATE	VENUE	OPPONENTS	SCORE	GOALSCORERS	ATTENDANCE	TEAM
May 10	Wembley, London	MEXICO	W 8-0	Hitchens, Charlton R 3, Robson R, Douglas 2, Flowers (pen)	77,000	Springett R (10), Armfield (14), McNeil (6), Robson R (13), Swan (9), Flowers (21), Douglas (20), Kevan (14), Hitchens (1), **Haynes** (42), Charlton R (24)

World Cup Qualifier

DATE	VENUE	OPPONENTS	SCORE	GOALSCORERS	ATTENDANCE	TEAM
May 21	Lisbon	PORTUGAL	D 1-1	Flowers	65,000	Springett R (11), Armfield (15), McNeil (7), Robson R (14), Swan (10), Flowers (22), Douglas (21), Greaves (13), Smith R (6), **Haynes** (43), Charlton R (25)

Friendlies

DATE	VENUE	OPPONENTS	SCORE	GOALSCORERS	ATTENDANCE	TEAM
May 24	Rome	ITALY	W 3-2	Hitchens 2, Greaves	90,000	Springett R (12), Armfield (16), McNeil (8), Robson R (15), Swan (11), Flowers (23), Douglas (22), Greaves (14), Hitchens (2), **Haynes** (44), Charlton R (26)
May 27	Vienna	AUSTRIA	L 1-3	Greaves	90,000	Springett R (13), Armfield (17), Angus (1), Miller (1), Swan (12), Flowers (24), Douglas (23), Greaves (15), Hitchens (3), **Haynes** (45), Charlton R (27)

World Cup Qualifier

DATE	VENUE	OPPONENTS	SCORE	GOALSCORERS	ATTENDANCE	TEAM
Sep 28	Highbury, London	LUXEMBOURG	W 4-1	Pointer, Viollet, Charlton R (2),	33,409	Springett R (14), **Armfield** (18), McNeil (9), Robson R (16), Swan (13), Flowers (25), Douglas (24), Fantham (1), Pointer (1), Viollet (2), Charlton R (28)

Home International Championship

DATE	VENUE	OPPONENTS	SCORE	GOALSCORERS	ATTENDANCE	TEAM
Oct 14	Ninian Park, Cardiff	WALES	D 1-1	Douglas	61,566	Springett R (15), Armfield (19), Wilson (5), Robson R (17), Swan (14), Flowers (26), Connelly (5), Douglas (25), Pointer (2), **Haynes** (46), Charlton R (29)

World Cup Qualifier

DATE	VENUE	OPPONENTS	SCORE	GOALSCORERS	ATTENDANCE	TEAM
Oct 25	Wembley, London	PORTUGAL	W 2-0	Connelly, Pointer	100,000	Springett R (16), Armfield (20), Wilson (6), Robson R (18), Swan (15), Flowers (27), Connelly (6), Douglas (26), Pointer (3), **Haynes** (47), Charlton R (30)

Home International Championship

DATE	VENUE	OPPONENTS	SCORE	GOALSCORERS	ATTENDANCE	TEAM
Nov 22	Wembley, London	N. IRELAND	D 1-1	Charlton R	30,000	Springett R (17), Armfield (21), Wilson (7), Robson R (19), Swan (16), Flowers (28), Douglas (27), Byrne J (1), Crawford (1), **Haynes** (48), Charlton R (31)

Jimmy Greaves scores one of his hat-trick of goals against Scotland in April 1961. Scotland's keeper, Frank Haffey, conceded six other goals in a 9-3 defeat that day.

1962

Friendly

DATE	VENUE	OPPONENTS	SCORE	GOALSCORERS	ATTENDANCE	TEAM
Apr 4	Wembley, London	AUSTRIA	W 3-1	Crawford, Flowers (pen), Hunt	50,000	Springett R (18), Armfield (22), Wilson (8), Anderson (1), Swan (17), Flowers (29), Connelly (7), Hunt (1), Crawford (2), **Haynes** (49), Charlton R (32)

Home International Championship

Apr 14	Hampden Park, Glasgow	SCOTLAND	L 0-2		132,441	Springett R (19), Armfield (23), Wilson (9), Anderson (2), Swan (18), Flowers (30), Douglas (28), Greaves (16), Smith R (7), **Haynes** (50), Charlton R (33)

Friendlies

May 9	Wembley, London	SWITZERLAND	W 3-1	Flowers, Hitchens, Connelly	35,000	Springett R (20), Armfield (24), Wilson (10), Robson R (20), Swan (19), Flowers (31), Connelly (8), Greaves (17), Hitchens (4), **Haynes** (51), Charlton R (34)
May 20	Lima	PERU	W 4-0	Flowers (pen), Greaves 3	32,565	Springett R (21), Armfield (25), Wilson (11), Moore (1), Norman (1), Flowers (32), Douglas (29), Greaves (18), Hitchens (5), **Haynes** (52), Charlton R (35)

FACT FILE

In 1962, when Scotland beat England 2-0, it was their first win at Hampden Park against their opponents for 25 years, and it was the first time England had failed to win a match in the Home International Championship for 35 years.

Manager Walter Winterbottom (left) welcomes new caps Stan Anderson (centre) and Roger Hunt to a training session at White City in April 1962. Both made their debuts in the match against Austria which England won 3-1.

THE WORLD CUP FINALS 1962 (CHILE)

Group Stage – Group 4

DATE	VENUE	OPPONENTS	SCORE	GOALSCORERS	ATTENDANCE	TEAM
May 31	Rancagua	HUNGARY	L 1-2	Flowers (pen)	7,938	Springett R (22), Armfield (26), Wilson (12), Moore (2), Norman (2), Flowers (33), Douglas (30), Greaves (19), Hitchens (6), **Haynes** (53), Charlton R (36)
Jun 2	Rancagua	ARGENTINA	W 3-1	Flowers (pen), Charlton R, Greaves	9,794	Springett R (23), Armfield (27), Wilson (13), Moore (3), Norman (3), Flowers (34), Douglas (31), Greaves (20), Peacock (1), **Haynes** (54), Charlton R (37)
Jun 7	Rancagua	BULGARIA	D 0-0		5,700	Springett R (24), Armfield (28), Wilson (14), Moore (4), Norman (4), Flowers (35), Douglas (32), Greaves (21), Peacock (2), **Haynes** (55), Charlton R (38)

Quarter-final

DATE	VENUE	OPPONENTS	SCORE	GOALSCORERS	ATTENDANCE	TEAM
Jun 10	Vina del Mar	BRAZIL	L 1-3	Hitchens	17,736	Springett R (25), Armfield (29), Wilson (15), Moore (5), Norman (5), Flowers (36), Douglas (33), Greaves (22), Hitchens (7), **Haynes** (56), Charlton R (39)

Group 4

	P	W	D	L	F	A	Pts
HUNGARY	3	2	1	0	8	2	5
ENGLAND	3	1	1	1	4	3	3
ARGENTINA	3	1	1	1	2	3	3
BULGARIA	3	0	1	2	1	7	1

Johnny Haynes (right) is all sweetness and light as he shakes hands with Argentina's captain before their World Cup match in Rancagua in Chile in June 1962. England won 3-1 that day with a penalty from Ron Flowers and other goals from Bobby Charlton and Jimmy Greaves.

271

1962 (continued)

European Nations Cup Qualifier

DATE	VENUE	OPPONENTS	SCORE	GOALSCORERS	ATTENDANCE	TEAM
Oct 3	Hillsborough, Sheffield	FRANCE	D 1-1	Flowers (pen)	35,380	Springett R (26), **Armfield** (30), Wilson (16), Moore (6), Norman (6), Flowers (37), Hellawell (1), Crowe (1), Charnley (1), Greaves (23), Hinton A (1)

Home International Championship

DATE	VENUE	OPPONENTS	SCORE	GOALSCORERS	ATTENDANCE	TEAM
Oct 20	Windsor Park, Belfast	N. IRELAND	W 3-1	Greaves, O'Grady 2	55,000	Springett R (27), **Armfield** (31), Wilson (17), Moore (7), Labone (1), Flowers (38), Hellawell (2), Hill F (1), Peacock (3), Greaves (24), O'Grady (1)
Nov 21	Wembley, London	WALES	W 4-0	Connelly, Peacock 2, Greaves	27,500	Springett R (28), **Armfield** (32), Shaw G (5), Moore (8), Labone (2), Flowers (39), Connelly (9), Hill F (2), Peacock (4), Greaves (25), Tambling (1)

1963

European Nations Cup Qualifier

DATE	VENUE	OPPONENTS	SCORE	GOALSCORERS	ATTENDANCE	TEAM
Feb 27	Paris	FRANCE	L 2-5	Smith R, Tambling	23,986	Springett R (29), **Armfield** (33), Henry (1), Moore (9), Labone (3), Flowers (40), Connelly (10), Tambling (2), Smith R (8), Greaves (26), Charlton R (40)

Home International Championship

DATE	VENUE	OPPONENTS	SCORE	GOALSCORERS	ATTENDANCE	TEAM
Apr 6	Wembley, London	SCOTLAND	L 1-2	Douglas	98,606	Banks (1), **Armfield** (34), Byrne G (1), Moore (10), Norman (7), Flowers (41), Douglas (34), Greaves (27), Smith R (9), Melia (1), Charlton R (41)

Friendlies

DATE	VENUE	OPPONENTS	SCORE	GOALSCORERS	ATTENDANCE	TEAM
May 8	Wembley, London	BRAZIL	D 1-1	Douglas	92,000	Banks (2), **Armfield** (35), Wilson (18), Milne (1), Norman (8), Moore (11), Douglas (35), Greaves (28), Smith R (10), Eastham (1), Charlton R (42)
May 29	Bratislava	CZECHOSLOVAKIA	W 4-2	Greaves 2, Smith R, Charlton R	50,000	Banks (3), Shellito (1), Wilson (19), Milne (2), Norman (9), **Moore** (12), Paine (1), Greaves (29), Smith R (11), Eastham (2), Charlton R (43)
Jun 2	Leipzig	E. GERMANY	W 2-1	Hunt, Charlton R	90,000	Banks (4), **Armfield** (36), Wilson (20), Milne (3), Norman (10), Moore (13), Paine (2), Hunt (2), Smith R (12), Eastham (3), Charlton R (44)
Jun 5	Basle	SWITZERLAND	W 8-1	Charlton R 3, Byrne J 2, Douglas, Kay, Melia	49,800	Springett R (30), **Armfield** (37), Wilson (21), Kay (1), Moore (14), Flowers (42), Douglas (36), Greaves (30), Byrne J (2), Melia (2), Charlton R (45)

Home International Championship

DATE	VENUE	OPPONENTS	SCORE	GOALSCORERS	ATTENDANCE	TEAM
Oct 12	Ninian Park, Cardiff	WALES	W 4-0	Smith R 2, Greaves, Charlton R	48,350	Banks (5), **Armfield** (38), Wilson (22), Milne (4), Norman (11), Moore (15), Paine (3), Greaves (31), Smith R (13), Eastham (4), Charlton R (46)

Friendly

DATE	VENUE	OPPONENTS	SCORE	GOALSCORERS	ATTENDANCE	TEAM
Oct 23	Wembley, London	REST OF WORLD	W 2-1	Paine, Greaves	100,000	Banks (6), **Armfield** (39), Wilson (23), Milne (5), Norman (12), Moore (16), Paine (4), Greaves (32), Smith R (14), Eastham (5), Charlton R (47)

Home International Championship

DATE	VENUE	OPPONENTS	SCORE	GOALSCORERS	ATTENDANCE	TEAM
Nov 20	Wembley, London	N. IRELAND	W 8-3	Greaves 4, Paine 3, Smith R	55,000	Banks (7), **Armfield** (40), Thomson R (1), Milne (6), Norman (13), Moore (17), Paine (5), Greaves (33), Smith R (15), Eastham (6), Charlton R (48)

FACT FILE

The 8-3 win over Northern Ireland at Wembley in 1963 was the first evening international under floodlights. That same season England played the Rest of the World as part of the FA's centenary and visited Brazil for that country's 50th anniversary. Their 10-0 win over the USA equalled the score against Portugal in 1947.

Billy Wright and Bobby Moore shared a record for England, having each captained their country on 80 occasions. Moore was 22 years, 47 days old when he led the team for the first time in 1963.

1964

Home International Championship

DATE	VENUE	OPPONENTS	SCORE	GOALSCORERS	ATTENDANCE	TEAM
Apr 11	Hampden Park, Glasgow	SCOTLAND	L 0-1		133,245	Banks (8), **Armfield** (41), Wilson (24), Milne (7), Norman (14), Moore (18), Paine (6), Hunt (3), Byrne J (3), Eastham (7), Charlton R (49)

Friendlies

DATE	VENUE	OPPONENTS	SCORE	GOALSCORERS	ATTENDANCE	TEAM
May 6	Wembley, London	URUGUAY	W 2-1	Byrne J 2	55,000	Banks (9), Cohen (1), Wilson (25), Milne (8), Norman (15), **Moore** (19), Paine (7), Greaves (34), Byrne J (4), Eastham (8), Charlton R (50)
May 17	Lisbon	PORTUGAL	W 4-3	Byrne J 3, Charlton R	40,000	Banks (10), Cohen (2), Wilson (26), Milne (9), Norman (16), **Moore** (20), Thompson P (1), Greaves (35), Byrne J (5), Eastham (9), Charlton R (51)
May 24	Dalymount Park, Dublin	R. of IRELAND	W 3-1	Eastham, Byrne J, Greaves	45,000	Waiters (1), Cohen (3), Wilson (27), Milne (10), Flowers (43), **Moore** (21), Thompson P (2), Greaves (36), Byrne J (6), Eastham (10), Charlton R (52)
May 27	New York	USA	W 10-0	Hunt 4, Pickering 3, Paine 2, Charlton R	5,000	Banks (11), Cohen (4), Thomson R (2), Bailey M (1), Norman (17), **Flowers** (44), Paine (8), Hunt (4), Pickering (1), Eastham (11), (Charlton R 53), Thompson P (3)

Brazilian Jubilee Tournament

DATE	VENUE	OPPONENTS	SCORE	GOALSCORERS	ATTENDANCE	TEAM
May 30	Rio	BRAZIL	L 1-5	Greaves	77,000	Waiters (2), Cohen (5), Wilson (28), Milne (11), Norman (18), **Moore** (22), Thompson P (4), Greaves (37), Byrne J (7), Eastham (12), Charlton R (54)
Jun 4	Sao Paulo	PORTUGAL	D 1-1	Hunt	25,000	Banks (12), Thomson R (3), Wilson (29), Flowers (45), Norman (19), **Moore** (23), Paine (9), Greaves (38), Byrne J (8), Hunt (5), Thompson P (5)
Jun 6	Rio	ARGENTINA	L 0-1		15,000	Banks (13), Thomson R (4), Wilson (30), Milne (12), Norman (20), **Moore** (24), Thompson P (6), Greaves (39), Byrne J (9), Eastham (13), Charlton R (55)

Home International Championship

DATE	VENUE	OPPONENTS	SCORE	GOALSCORERS	ATTENDANCE	TEAM
Oct 3	Windsor Park, Belfast	N. IRELAND	W 4-3	Pickering, Greaves 3	58,000	Banks (14), Cohen (6), Thomson R (5), Milne (13), Norman (21), **Moore** (25), Paine (10), Greaves (40), Pickering (2), Charlton R (56), Thompson P (7)

Friendly

DATE	VENUE	OPPONENTS	SCORE	GOALSCORERS	ATTENDANCE	TEAM
Oct 21	Wembley, London	BELGIUM	D 2-2	Pickering, Hinton	55,000	Waiters (3), Cohen (7), Thomson R (6), Milne (14), Norman (22), **Moore** (26), Thompson P (8), Greaves (41), Pickering (3), Venables (1), Hinton A (2)

Home International Championship

DATE	VENUE	OPPONENTS	SCORE	GOALSCORERS	ATTENDANCE	TEAM
Nov 18	Wembley, London	WALES	W 2-1	Wignall 2	40,000	Waiters (4), Cohen (8), Thomson R (7), Bailey M (2), **Flowers** (46), Young (1), Thompson P (9), Hunt (6), Wignall (1), Byrne J (10), Hinton A (3)

Friendly

DATE	VENUE	OPPONENTS	SCORE	GOALSCORERS	ATTENDANCE	TEAM
Dec 9	Amsterdam	HOLLAND	D 1-1	Greaves	60,000	Waiters (5), Cohen (9), Thomson R (8), Mullery (1), Norman (23), **Flowers** (47), Thompson P (10), Greaves (42), Wignall (2), Venables (2), Charlton R (57)

FACT FILE

In 1964 Jimmy Greaves' hat-trick in 12 minutes against Northern Ireland took his goals to 35, thus overtaking Bobby Charlton's total.

In 1965 England won 2-0 in Spain, their first win there. A 4-3-3 system was used for the first time. The following year in the 1-0 win over West Germany, Nobby Stiles wearing the No.9 shirt was the scorer in what was Geoff Hurst's international debut.

When Jack and Bobby Charlton first played together in the same full international team in 1965, they became the first pair of brothers to appear as such since Nottingham Forest's Frank and Fred Forman in 1899.

When Norman Hunter came on to replace Joe Baker against Spain in 1965, he became the first England player to win his first cap as a substitute.

In Jack Charlton's 35 international appearances at centre-back from 1965, he was on the losing side only against Austria and Scotland, while in 23 of the matches not a goal was conceded.

1965

Home International Championship

DATE	VENUE	OPPONENTS	SCORE	GOALSCORERS	ATTENDANCE	TEAM
Apr 10	Wembley, London	SCOTLAND	D 2-2	Charlton R, Greaves	98,199	Banks (15), Cohen (10), Wilson (31), Stiles (1), Charlton J (1), **Moore** (27), Thompson P (11), Greaves (43), Bridges (1), Byrne J (11), Charlton R (58)

Friendlies

DATE	VENUE	OPPONENTS	SCORE	GOALSCORERS	ATTENDANCE	TEAM
May 5	Wembley, London	HUNGARY	W 1-0	Greaves	70,000	Banks (16), Cohen (11), Wilson (32), Stiles (2), Charlton J (2), **Moore** (28), Paine (11), Greaves (44), Bridges (2), Eastham (14), Connelly (11)
May 9	Belgrade	YUGOSLAVIA	D 1-1	Bridges	70,000	Banks (17), Cohen (12), Wilson (33), Stiles (3), Charlton J (3), **Moore** (29), Paine (12), Greaves (45), Bridges (3), Ball (1), Connelly (12)
May 12	Nuremberg	W. GERMANY	W 1-0	Paine	70,000	Banks (18), Cohen (13), Wilson (34), Flowers (48), Charlton J (4), **Moore** (30), Paine (13), Ball (2), Jones M (1), Eastham (15), Temple (1)
May 16	Gothenburg	SWEDEN	W 2-1	Ball, Connelly	18,975	Banks (19), Cohen (14), Wilson (35), Stiles (4), Charlton J (5), **Moore** (31), Paine (14), Ball (3), Jones M (2), Eastham (16), Connelly (13)

Home International Championship

DATE	VENUE	OPPONENTS	SCORE	GOALSCORERS	ATTENDANCE	TEAM
Oct 2	Ninian Park, Cardiff	WALES	D 0-0		30,000	Springett (31), Cohen (15), Wilson (36), Stiles (5), Charlton J (6), **Moore** (32), Paine (15), Greaves (46), Peacock (5), Charlton R (59), Connelly (14)

Friendly

DATE	VENUE	OPPONENTS	SCORE	GOALSCORERS	ATTENDANCE	TEAM
Oct 20	Wembley, London	AUSTRIA	L 2-3	Charlton R, Connelly	65,000	Springett R (32), Cohen (16), Wilson (37), Stiles (6), Charlton J (7), **Moore** (33), Paine (16), Greaves (47), Bridges (4), Charlton R (60), Connelly (15)

Home International Championship

DATE	VENUE	OPPONENTS	SCORE	GOALSCORERS	ATTENDANCE	TEAM
Nov 10	Wembley, London	N. IRELAND	W 2-1	Baker, Peacock	70,000	Banks (20), Cohen (17), Wilson (38), Stiles (7), Charlton J (8), **Moore** (34), Thompson P (12), Baker (6), Peacock (6), Charlton R (61), Connelly (16)

Friendly

DATE	VENUE	OPPONENTS	SCORE	GOALSCORERS	ATTENDANCE	TEAM
Dec 8	Madrid	SPAIN	W 2-0	Baker, Hunt	30,000	Banks (21), Cohen (18), Wilson (39), Stiles (8), Charlton J (9), **Moore** (35), Ball (4), Hunt (7), Baker (7), (Hunter 1), Eastham (17), Charlton R (62)

England manager Alf Ramsey (centre) talks things through with assistant Harold Shepherdson (left) and Bobby Moore at a training session at Stamford Bridge in 1965.

Pickles the dog is photographed in Norwood close to where he found the World Cup trophy that had been stolen from a stamp exhibition in Westminster in March 1966.

1966

Friendlies

DATE	VENUE	OPPONENTS	SCORE	GOALSCORERS	ATTENDANCE	TEAM
Jan 5	Goodison Park, Liverpool	POLAND	D 1-1	Moore	47,839	Banks (22), Cohen (19), Wilson (40), Stiles (9), Charlton J (10), **Moore** (36), Ball (5), Hunt (8), Baker (8), Eastham (18), Harris G (1)
Feb 23	Wembley, London	W. GERMANY	W 1-0	Stiles	75,000	Banks (23), Cohen (20), Newton K (1), (Wilson 41), **Moore** (37), Charlton J (11), Hunter (2), Ball (6), Hunt (9), Stiles (10), Hurst (1), Charlton R (63)

Home International Championship

DATE	VENUE	OPPONENTS	SCORE	GOALSCORERS	ATTENDANCE	TEAM
Apr 2	Hampden Park, Glasgow	SCOTLAND	W 4-3	Hurst, Hunt 2, Charlton R	123,052	Banks (24), Cohen (21), Newton K (2), Stiles (11), Charlton J (12), **Moore** (38), Ball (7), Hunt (10), Charlton R (64), Hurst (2), Connelly (17)

Friendlies

DATE	VENUE	OPPONENTS	SCORE	GOALSCORERS	ATTENDANCE	TEAM
May 4	Wembley, London	YUGOSLAVIA	W 2-0	Greaves, Charlton R	55,000	Banks (25), **Armfield** (42), Wilson (42), Peters (1), Charlton J (13), Hunter (3), Paine (17), Greaves (48), Charlton R (65), Hurst (3), Tambling (3)
Jun 26	Helsinki	FINLAND	W 3-0	Peters, Hunt, Charlton J	12,899	Banks (26), **Armfield** (43), Wilson (43), Peters (2), Charlton J (14), Hunter (4), Callaghan (1), Hunt (11), Charlton R (66), Hurst (4), Ball (8)
Jun 29	Oslo	NORWAY	W 6-1	Greaves 4, Connelly, Moore	29,534	Springett R (33), Cohen (22), Byrne G (2), Stiles (12), Flowers (49), **Moore** (39), Paine (18), Greaves (49), Charlton R (67), Hunt (12), Connelly (18)
July 3	Copenhagen	DENMARK	W 2-0	Charlton J, Eastham	32,000	Bonetti (1), Cohen (23), Wilson (44), Stiles (13), Charlton J (15), **Moore** (40), Ball (9), Greaves (50), Hurst (5), Eastham (19), Connelly (19)
July 5	Chorzow	POLAND	W 1-0	Hunt	93,000	Banks (27), Cohen (24), Wilson (45), Stiles (14), Charlton J (16), **Moore** (41), Ball (10), Greaves (51), Charlton R (68), Hunt (13), Peters (3)

FACT FILE

In 1966 Jimmy Greaves' four goals against Norway was the sixth occasion he had scored three or more goals for his country in one match. The others were: Luxembourg 1960, Scotland 1961, Peru 1962, Northern Ireland 1963 (four goals) and again in 1964.

THE WORLD CUP FINALS 1966 (ENGLAND)

Group Stage – Group 1

England qualified as hosts

DATE	VENUE	OPPONENTS	SCORE	GOALSCORERS	ATTENDANCE	TEAM
Jul 11	Wembley, London	URUGUAY	D 0-0		87,148	Banks (28), Cohen (25), Wilson (46), Stiles (15), Charlton J (17), **Moore** (42), Ball (11), Greaves (52), Charlton R (69), Hunt (14), Connelly (20)
Jul 16	Wembley, London	MEXICO	W 2-0	Charlton R, Hunt	92,570	Banks (29), Cohen (26), Wilson (47), Stiles (16), Charlton J (18), **Moore** (43), Paine (19), Greaves (53), Charlton R (70), Hunt (15), Peters (4)
Jul 20	Wembley, London	FRANCE	W 2-0	Hunt 2	98,270	Banks (30), Cohen (27), Wilson (48), Stiles (17), Charlton J (19), **Moore** (44), Callaghan (2), Greaves (54), Charlton R (71), Hunt (16), Peters (5)

GROUP 1

	P	W	D	L	F	A	Prs
ENGLAND	3	2	1	0	4	0	5
URUGUAY	3	1	2	0	2	1	4
MEXICO	3	0	2	1	1	3	2
FRANCE	3	0	1	2	2	5	1

Ray Wilson makes sure this French attack comes to nothing in their group game on 20 July. Ian Callaghan looks relieved.

FACT FILE

The opening match of the 1966 World Cup finals between England and Uruguay was almost called off by referee Istvan Zsolt of Hungary when he discovered that seven England players had left their identity cards at the team hotel. A police dispatch rider had to be sent to retrieve them.

From the World Cup quarter-final in 1966 onwards, manager Alf Ramsey fielded the same 11 players in six consecutive matches, an England record.

To commemorate England's World Cup triumph in 1966, Peter Eastaway named his son Peter Derek Banks Cohen Wilson Stiles Charlton Moore Ball Hurst Hunt Peters Ramsey Eastaway.

England's successful World Cup team of 1966 each received a £1,000 bonus and £60 appearance money (less tax). Manager Alf Ramsey was given a £6,000 bonus by the FA.

Martin Peters (No. 16) wheels away to celebrate as he puts England 2-1 up in the World Cup final.

Quarter-final

DATE	VENUE	OPPONENTS	SCORE	GOALSCORERS	ATTENDANCE	TEAM
Jul 23	Wembley, London	ARGENTINA	W 1-0	Hurst	90,584	Banks (31), Cohen (28), Wilson (49), Stiles (18), Charlton J (20), **Moore** (45), Ball (12), Hurst (6), Charlton R (72), Hunt (17), Peters (6)

Semi-final

Jul 26	Wembley, London	PORTGUAL	W 2-1	Charlton R. 2	94,493	Banks (32), Cohen (29), Wilson (50), Stiles (19), Charlton J (21), **Moore** (46), Ball (13), Hurst (7), Charlton R (73), Hunt (18), Peters (7)

Final

Jul 30	Wembley, London	W. GERMANY	W 4-2	Hurst 3, Peters	96,924	Banks (33), Cohen (30), Wilson (51), Stiles (20), Charlton J (22), **Moore** (47), Ball (14), Hurst (8), Charlton R (74), Hunt (19), Peters (8)

Above: *Her Majesty the Queen presents England captain Bobby Moore with the Jules Rimet trophy after their World Cup triumph.*

Left: *Jack Charlton watches as Ray Wilson puts the World Cup on his head during their lap of honour.*

1966 (continued)

Home International Championship/European Nations Cup Qualifier

DATE	VENUE	OPPONENTS	SCORE	GOALSCORERS	ATTENDANCE	TEAM
Oct 22	Windsor Park, Belfast	N. IRELAND	W 2-0	Hunt, Peters	48,600	Banks (34), Cohen (31), Wilson (52), Stiles (21), Charlton J (23), **Moore** (48), Ball (15), Hurst (9), Charlton R (75), Hunt (20), Peters (9)

Friendly

DATE	VENUE	OPPONENTS	SCORE	GOALSCORERS	ATTENDANCE	TEAM
Nov 2	Wembley, London	CZECHOSLOVAKIA	D 0-0		75,000	Banks (35), Cohen (32), Wilson (53), Stiles (22), Charlton J (24), **Moore** (49), Ball (16), Hurst (10), Charlton R (76), Hunt (21), Peters (10)

Home International Championship/European Nations Cup Qualifier

DATE	VENUE	OPPONENTS	SCORE	GOALSCORERS	ATTENDANCE	TEAM
Nov 16	Wembley, London	WALES	W 5-1	Hurst 2, Charlton R, Charlton J, own goal	75,380	Banks (36), Cohen (33), Wilson (54), Stiles (23), Charlton J (25), **Moore** (50), Ball (17), Hurst (11), Charlton R (77), Hunt (22), Peters (11)

1967

Home International Championship/European Nations Cup Qualifiers

DATE	VENUE	OPPONENTS	SCORE	GOALSCORERS	ATTENDANCE	TEAM
Apr 15	Wembley, London	SCOTLAND	L 2-3	Charlton J, Hurst	99,063	Banks (37), Cohen (34), Wilson (55), Stiles (24), Charlton J (26), **Moore** (51), Ball (18), Greaves (55), Charlton R (78), Hurst (12), Peters (12)

Friendlies

DATE	VENUE	OPPONENTS	SCORE	GOALSCORERS	ATTENDANCE	TEAM
May 24	Wembley, London	SPAIN	W 2-0	Greaves, Hunt	97,500	Bonetti (2), Cohen (35), Newton K (3), Mullery (2), Labone (4), **Moore** (52), Ball (19), Greaves (56), Hurst (13), Hunt (23), Hollins (1)
May 27	Vienna	AUSTRIA	W 1-0	Ball	50,000	Bonetti (3), Newton K (4), Wilson (56), Mullery (3), Labone (5), **Moore** (53), Ball (20), Greaves (57), Hurst (14), Hunt (24), Hunter (5)

Home International Championship/European Nations Cup Qualifiers

DATE	VENUE	OPPONENTS	SCORE	GOALSCORERS	ATTENDANCE	TEAM
Oct 21	Ninian Park, Cardiff	WALES	W 3-0	Peters, Charlton R, Ball (pen)	44,960	Banks (38), Cohen (36), Newton K (5), Mullery (4), Charlton J (27), **Moore** (54), Ball (21), Hunt (25), Charlton R (79), Hurst (15), Peters (13)
Nov 22	Wembley, London	N. IRELAND	W 2-0	Hurst, Charlton R	85,000	Banks (39), Cohen (37), Wilson (57), Mullery (5), Sadler (1), **Moore** (55), Thompson P (13), Hunt (26), Charlton R (80), Hurst (16), Peters (14)

Friendly

DATE	VENUE	OPPONENTS	SCORE	GOALSCORERS	ATTENDANCE	TEAM
Dec 6	Wembley, London	USSR	D 2-2	Ball, Peters	93,000	Banks (40), Knowles (1), Wilson (58), Mullery (6), Sadler (2), **Moore** (56), Ball (22), Hunt (27), Charlton R (81), Hurst (17), Peters (15)

Geoff Hurst hooks the ball into the net to give England the lead against Northern Ireland at Wembley in November 1967.

1968

Home International Championship/European Nations Cup Qualifier

DATE	VENUE	OPPONENTS	SCORE	GOALSCORERS	ATTENDANCE	TEAM
Feb 24	Hampden Park, Glasgow	SCOTLAND	D 1-1	Peters	134,000	Banks (41), Newton K (6), Wilson (59), Mullery (7), Labone (6), **Moore** (57), Ball (23), Hurst (18), Summerbee (1), Charlton R (82), Peters (16)

European Nations Cup Quarter-final

DATE	VENUE	OPPONENTS	SCORE	GOALSCORERS	ATTENDANCE	TEAM
Apr 3	Wembley, London	SPAIN	W 1-0	Charlton R	100,000	Banks (42), Knowles (2), Wilson (60), Mullery (8), Charlton J (28), **Moore** (58), Ball (24), Hunt (28), Summerbee (2), Charlton R (83), Peters (17)
May 8	Madrid	SPAIN	W 2-1	Peters, Hunter	120,000	Bonetti (4), Newton K (7), Wilson (61), Mullery (9), Labone (7), **Moore** (59), Ball (25), Peters (18), Charlton R (84), Hunt (29), Hunter (6)

Friendlies

DATE	VENUE	OPPONENTS	SCORE	GOALSCORERS	ATTENDANCE	TEAM
May 22	Wembley, London	SWEDEN	W 3-1	Peters, Charlton R, Hunt	72,500	Stepney (1), Newton K (8), Knowles (3), Mullery (10), Labone (8), **Moore** (60), Bell (1), Peters (19), Charlton R (85), (Hurst 19), Hunt (30), Hunter (7)
Jun 1	Hanover	W. GERMANY	L 0-1		79,124	Banks (43), Newton K (9), Knowles (4), Hunter (8), Labone (9), **Moore** (61), Ball (26), Bell (2), Summerbee (3), Hurst (20), Thompson P (14)

European Nations Cup Semi-final

DATE	VENUE	OPPONENTS	SCORE	GOALSCORERS	ATTENDANCE	TEAM
Jun 5	Florence	YUGOSLAVIA	L 0-1		60,000	Banks (44), Newton K (10), Wilson (62), Mullery (11), Labone (10), **Moore** (62), Ball (27), Peters (20), Charlton R (86), Hunt (31), Hunter (9)

European Nations Cup Third Place Match

DATE	VENUE	OPPONENTS	SCORE	GOALSCORERS	ATTENDANCE	TEAM
Jun 8	Rome	USSR	W 2-0	Charlton R, Hurst	80,000	Banks (45), Wright T (1), Wilson (63), Stiles (25), Labone (11), **Moore** (63), Hunter (10), Hunt (32), Charlton R (87), Hurst (21), Peters (21)

Friendlies

DATE	VENUE	OPPONENTS	SCORE	GOALSCORERS	ATTENDANCE	TEAM
Nov 6	Bucharest	ROMANIA	D 0-0		80,000	Banks (46), Wright T (2), (McNab 1), Newton K (11), Mullery (12), Labone (12), Moore (64), Ball (28), Hunt (33), Charlton R (88), Hurst (22), Peters (22)
Dec 11	Wembley, London	BULGARIA	D 1-1	Hurst	80,000	West (1), Newton K (12), (Reaney 1), McNab (2), Mullery (13), Labone (13), **Moore** (65), Lee F (1), Bell (3), Charlton R (89), Hurst (23), Peters (23)

FACT FILE

Alan Mullery was the first England player to be sent off in a full international. It was against Yugoslavia in the 1968 European Nations Cup semi-final.

Sir Alf Ramsey chats to some new faces (left to right) Allan Clarke, Cyril Knowles, Len Badger and Howard Kendall as the Under-23 squad met at the England training ground at Roehampton in December 1968.

1969

Friendlies

DATE	VENUE	OPPONENTS	SCORE	GOALSCORERS	ATTENDANCE	TEAM
Jan 15	Wembley, London	ROMANIA	D 1-1	Charlton J	80,000	Banks (47), Wright T (3), McNab (3), Stiles (26), Charlton J (29), Hunter (11), Radford (1), Hunt (34), **Charlton R** (90), Hurst (24), Ball (29)
Mar 12	Wembley, London	FRANCE	W 5-0	Hurst 3 (2 pens), O'Grady, Lee F	85,000	Banks (48), Newton K (13), Cooper (1), Mullery (14), Charlton J (30), **Moore** (66), Lee F (2), Bell (4), Hurst (25), Peters (24), O'Grady (2)

Home International Championship

DATE	VENUE	OPPONENTS	SCORE	GOALSCORERS	ATTENDANCE	TEAM
May 3	Windsor Park, Belfast	N. IRELAND	W 3-1	Peters, Lee F, Hurst (pen)	23,000	Banks (49), Newton K (14), McNab (4), Mullery (15), Labone (14), **Moore** (67), Ball (30), Lee F (3), Charlton R (91), Hurst (26), Peters (25)
May 7	Wembley, London	WALES	W 2-1	Charlton R, Lee F	70,000	West (2), Newton K (15), Cooper (2), **Moore** (68), Charlton J (31), Hunter (12), Lee F (4), Bell (5), Astle (1), Charlton R (92), Ball (31)
May 10	Wembley, London	SCOTLAND	W 4-1	Peters 2, Hurst 2 (1 pen)	89,902	Banks (50), Newton K (16), Cooper (3), Mullery (16), Labone (15), **Moore** (69), Lee F (5), Ball (32), Charlton R (93), Hurst (27), Peters (26)

Friendlies

DATE	VENUE	OPPONENTS	SCORE	GOALSCORERS	ATTENDANCE	TEAM
Jun 1	Mexico City	MEXICO	D 0-0		105,000	West (3), Newton K (17), (Wright T 4), Cooper (4), Mullery (17), Labone (16), **Moore** (70), Lee F (6), Ball (33), Charlton R (94), Hurst (28), Peters (27)
Jun 8	Montevideo	URUGUAY	W 2-1	Lee F, Hurst	54,161	Banks (51), Wright T (5), Newton K (18), Mullery (18), Labone (17), **Moore** (71), Lee F (7), Bell (6), Hurst (29), Ball (34), Peters (28)
Jun 12	Rio	BRAZIL	L 1-2	Bell	135,000	Banks (52), Wright T (6), Newton K (19), Mullery (19), Labone (18), **Moore** (72), Ball (35), Bell (7), Charlton R (95), Hurst (30), Peters (29)
Nov 5	Amsterdam	HOLLAND	W 1-0	Bell	33,000	Bonetti (5), Wright T (7), Hughes (1), Mullery (20), Charlton J (32), **Moore** (73), Lee F (8), (Thompson P 15), Bell (8), Charlton R (96), Hurst (31), Peters (30)
Dec 10	Wembley, London	PORTUGAL	W 1-0	Charlton J	100,000	Bonetti (6), Reaney (2), Hughes (2), Mullery (21), Charlton J (33), **Moore** (74), Lee F (9), Bell (9), (Peters 31), Astle (2), Charlton R (97), Ball (36)

FACT FILE

In 1970 Bobby Charlton was presented with a silver salver by FA chairman Dr Andrew Stephen before the match with Northern Ireland to commemorate his 100th appearance, in which he captained the team.

Alan Mullery of Spurs put in some marvellous midfield performances for England during the late 60s and early 70s.

1970

Friendlies

DATE	VENUE	OPPONENTS	SCORE	GOALSCORERS	ATTENDANCE	TEAM
Jan 14	Wembley	HOLLAND	D 0-0		75,000	Banks (53), Newton K (20), Cooper (5), Peters (32), Charlton J (34), Hunter (13), Lee F (10), (Mullery 22), Bell (10), Jones M (3), (Hurst 32), **Charlton R** (98), Moore I (1)
Feb 25	Brussels	BELGIUM	W 3-1	Ball 2, Hurst	20,594	Banks (54), Wright T (8), Cooper (6), **Moore** (75), Labone (19), Hughes (3), Lee F (11), Ball (37), Osgood (1), Hurst (33), Peters (33)

Home International Championship

DATE	VENUE	OPPONENTS	SCORE	GOALSCORERS	ATTENDANCE	TEAM
Apr 18	Ninian Park, Cardiff	WALES	D 1-1	Lee F	50,000	Banks (55), Wright T (9), Hughes (4), Mullery (23), Labone (20), **Moore** (76), Lee F (12), Ball (38), Charlton R (99), Hurst (34), Peters (34)
Apr 21	Wembley	N. IRELAND	W 3-1	Peters, Hurst, Charlton R	100,000	Banks (56), Newton K (21), (Bell 11), Hughes (5), Mullery (24), Moore (77), Stiles (27), Coates (1), Kidd (1), **Charlton R** (100), Hurst (35), Peters (35)
Apr 25	Hampden Park, Glasgow	SCOTLAND	D 0-0		137,438	Banks (57), Newton K (22), Hughes (6), Stiles (28), Labone (21), **Moore** (78), Thompson P (16), (Mullery 25), Ball (39), Astle (3), Hurst (36), Peters (36)

Friendlies

DATE	VENUE	OPPONENTS	SCORE	GOALSCORERS	ATTENDANCE	TEAM
May 20	Bogota	COLOMBIA	W 4-0	Peters 2, Charlton R, Ball	36,000	Banks (58), Newton K (23), Cooper (7), Mullery (26), Labone (22), **Moore** (79), Lee F (13), Ball (40), Charlton R (101), Hurst (37), Peters (37)
May 24	Quito	ECUADOR	W 2-0	Lee F, Kidd	36,000	Banks (59), Newton K (24), Cooper (8), Mullery (27), Labone (23), **Moore** (80), Lee F (14), (Kidd 2), Ball (41), Charlton R (102), (Sadler 3), Hurst (38), Peters (38)

West Ham and England colleagues Geoff Hurst and Bobby Moore chat among the Ford Cortinas in the training ground car park in late 1969.

THE WORLD CUP FINALS 1970 (MEXICO)

Group Stage – Group 3

DATE	VENUE	OPPONENTS	SCORE	GOALSCORERS	ATTENDANCE	TEAM
Jun 2	Guadalajara	ROMANIA	W 1-0	Hurst	50,000	Banks (60), Newton K (25), (Wright T 10), Cooper (9), Mullery (28), Labone (24), **Moore** (81), Lee F (15), (Osgood 2), Ball (42), Charlton R (103), Hurst (39), Peters (39)
Jun 7	Guadalajara	BRAZIL	L 0-1		70,950	Banks (61), Wright T (11), Cooper (10), Mullery (29), Labone (25), **Moore** (82), Lee F (16), (Astle 4), Ball (43), Charlton R (104), (Bell 12), Hurst (40), Peters (40)
Jun 11	Guadalajara	CZECHOSLOVAKIA	W 1-0	Clarke A (pen)	49,000	Banks (62), Newton K (30), Charlton J (35), **Moore** (83), Bell (13), Charlton R (105), (Ball 44), Astle (5), (Osgood 3), Clarke A (1), Peters (41)

Quarter-final

Jun 14	Leon	W. GERMANY	L 2-3	Mullery, Peters	32,000	Bonetti (7), Newton K (27), Cooper (12), Mullery (31), Labone (26), **Moore** (84), Lee F (17), Ball (45), Charlton R (106), (Bell 14), Hurst (41), Peters (42), (Hunter 14)

Group 3

	P	W	D	L	F	A	Pts
BRAZIL	3	3	0	0	8	3	6
ENGLAND	3	2	0	1	2	1	4
ROMANIA	3	1	0	2	4	5	2
CZECHOSLOVAKIA	3	0	0	3	2	7	0

FACT FILE

When Allan Clarke made his debut for England against Czechoslovakia in the 1970 World Cup he scored the only goal of the match from a penalty. It was his wife's birthday, his wedding aniversary and the anniversary of his transfer from Fulham to Leicester City.

Gordon Banks hits the ground after making one of the most famous saves in the history of football from Pele in the group match between Brazil and England in Guadalajara.

1970 (continued)

Friendly

DATE	VENUE	OPPONENTS	SCORE	GOALSCORERS	ATTENDANCE	TEAM
Nov 25	Wembley, London	E. GERMANY	W 3-1	Lee F, Peters, Clarke A	93,000	Shilton (1), Hughes (7), Cooper (13), Mullery (32), Sadler (4), **Moore** (85), Lee F (18), Ball (46), Hurst (42), Clarke A (2), Peters (43)

1971

European Championship Qualifiers

DATE	VENUE	OPPONENTS	SCORE	GOALSCORERS	ATTENDANCE	TEAM
Feb 3	Valletta	MALTA	W 1-0	Peters	29,751	Banks (63), Reaney (3), Hughes (8), **Mullery** (33), McFarland (1), Hunter (15), Ball (47), Chivers (1), Royle (1), Harvey (1), Peters (44)
Apr 21	Wembley, London	GREECE	W 3-0	Chivers, Hurst, Lee F	55,123	Banks (64), Storey (1), Hughes (9), Mullery (34), McFarland (2), **Moore** (86), Lee F (19), Ball (48), (Coates 2), Chivers (2), Hurst (43), Peters (45)
May 12	Wembley, London	MALTA	W 5-0	Chivers 2, Lee F, Clarke A (pen), Lawler	41,534	Banks (65), Lawler (1), Cooper (14), **Moore** (87), McFarland (3), Hughes (10), Lee F (20), Coates (3), Chivers (3), Clarke A (3), Peters (46), (Ball 49)

Home International Championship

DATE	VENUE	OPPONENTS	SCORE	GOALSCORERS	ATTENDANCE	TEAM
May 15	Windsor Park, Belfast	N. IRELAND	W 1-0	Clarke A	33,000	Banks (66), Madeley (1), Cooper (15), Storey (2), McFarland (4), **Moore** (88), Lee F (21), Ball (50), Chivers (4), Clarke A (4), Peters (47)
May 19	Wembley, London	WALES	D 0-0		70,000	Shilton (2), Lawler (2), Cooper (16), Smith (1), Lloyd (1), Hughes (11), Lee F (22), Coates (4), (Clarke A 5), Hurst (44), Brown A (1), **Peters** (48)
May 22	Wembley, London	SCOTLAND	W 3-1	Peters, Chivers 2	91,469	Banks (67), Lawler (3), Cooper (17), Storey (3), McFarland (5), **Moore** (89), Lee F (23), (Clarke A 6), Ball (51), Chivers (5), Hurst (45), Peters (49)

European Championship Qualifiers

DATE	VENUE	OPPONENTS	SCORE	GOALSCORERS	ATTENDANCE	TEAM
Oct 13	Basle	SWITZERLAND	W 3-2	Hurst, Chivers, own goal	47,877	Banks (68), Lawler (4), Cooper (18), Mullery (35), McFarland (6), **Moore** (90), Lee F (24), Madeley (2), Chivers (6), Hurst (46), (Radford 2), Peters (50)
Nov 10	Wembley, London	SWITZERLAND	D 1-1	Summerbee	90,423	Shilton (3), Madeley (3), Cooper (19), Storey (4), Lloyd (2), **Moore** (91), Summerbee (4), (Chivers 7), Ball (52), Hurst (47), Lee F (25), (Marsh 1), Hughes (12)
Dec 1	Piraeus	GREECE	W 2-0	Hurst, Chivers	34,014	Banks (69), Madeley (4), Hughes (13), Bell (15), McFarland (7), **Moore** (92), Lee F (26), Ball (53), Chivers (8), Hurst (48), Peters (51)

Martin Peters scores in England's 3-1 victory over Scotland at Wembley in May 1971.

FACT FILE

Malta's 1971 visit to Wembley produced some unusual statistics. England had no goal-kicks, Malta no corners. Gordon Banks touched the ball just four times from back passes.

1972

European Championship Qualifiers

DATE	VENUE	OPPONENTS	SCORE	GOALSCORERS	ATTENDANCE	TEAM
Apr 29	Wembley, London	W. GERMANY	L 1-3	Lee F	100,000	Banks (70), Madeley (5), Hughes (14), Bell (16), **Moore** (93), Hunter (16), Lee F (27), Ball (54), Chivers (9), Hurst (49), (Marsh 2), Peters (52)
May 13	Berlin	W. GERMANY	D 0-0		76,200	Banks (71), Madeley (6), Hughes (15), Storey (5), McFarland (8), **Moore** (94), Ball (55), Bell (17), Chivers (10), Marsh (3), (Summerbee 5), Hunter (17), (Peters 53)

Home International Championship

DATE	VENUE	OPPONENTS	SCORE	GOALSCORERS	ATTENDANCE	TEAM
May 20	Ninian Park, Cardiff	WALES	W 3-0	Hughes, Bell, Marsh	34,000	Banks (72), Madeley (7), Hughes (16), Storey (6), McFarland (9), **Moore** (95), Summerbee (6), Bell (18), Macdonald (1), Marsh (4), Hunter (18)
May 23	Wembley, London	N. IRELAND	L 0-1		64,000	Shilton (4), Todd (1), Hughes (17), Storey (7), Lloyd (3), Hunter (19), Summerbee (7), **Bell** (19), Macdonald (2), (Chivers 11), Marsh (5), Currie (1), (Peters 54)
May 27	Hampden Park, Glasgow	SCOTLAND	W 1-0	Ball	119,325	Banks (73), Madeley (8), Hughes (18), Storey (8), McFarland (10), **Moore** (96), Ball (56), Bell (20), Chivers (12), Marsh (6), (Macdonald 3), Hunter (20)

Friendly

DATE	VENUE	OPPONENTS	SCORE	GOALSCORERS	ATTENDANCE	TEAM
Oct 11	Wembley, London	YUGOSLAVIA	D 1-1	Royle	50,000	Shilton (5), Mills (1), Lampard (1), Storey (9), Blockley (1), **Moore** (97), Ball (57), Channon (1), Royle (2), Bell (21), Marsh (7)

World Cup Qualifier

DATE	VENUE	OPPONENTS	SCORE	GOALSCORERS	ATTENDANCE	TEAM
Nov 15	Ninian Park, Cardiff	WALES	W 1-0	Bell	36,384	Clemence (1), Storey (10), Hughes (19), Hunter (21), McFarland (11), **Moore** (98), Keegan (1), Marsh (8), Chivers (13), Bell (22), Ball (58)

Günter Netzer slots a penalty past Gordon Banks to give West Germany a 2-1 lead in the European Championship qualifier at Wembley in April 1972. West Germany scored again to win 3-1.

1973

World Cup Qualifier

DATE	VENUE	OPPONENTS	SCORE	GOALSCORERS	ATTENDANCE	TEAM
Jan 24	Wembley, London	WALES	D 1-1	Hunter	62,273	Clemence (2), Storey (11), Hughes (20), Hunter (22), McFarland (12), **Moore** (99), Keegan (2), Bell (23), Chivers (14), Marsh (9), Ball (59)

Friendly

Feb 14	Hampden Park, Glasgow	SCOTLAND	W 5-0	Clarke A 2, Channon, Chivers, own goal	48,470	Shilton (6), Storey (12), Hughes (21), Bell (24), Madeley (9), **Moore** (100), Ball (60), Channon (2), Chivers (15), Clarke A (7), Peters (55)

Home International Championship

May 12	Goodison Park, Liverpool	N. IRELAND	W 2-1	Chivers 2	29,865	Shilton (7), Storey (13), Nish (1), Bell (25), McFarland (13), **Moore** (101), Ball (61), Channon (3), Chivers (16), Richards (1), Peters (56)
May 15	Wembley, London	WALES	W 3-0	Chivers, Channon, Peters	38,000	Shilton (8), Storey (14), Hughes (22), Bell (26), McFarland (14), **Moore** (102), Ball (62), Channon (4), Chivers (17), Clarke A (8), Peters (57)
May 19	Wembley, London	SCOTLAND	W 1-0	Peters	95,950	Shilton (9), Storey (15), Hughes (23), Bell (27), McFarland (15), **Moore** (103), Ball (63), Channon (5), Chivers (18), Clarke A (9), Peters (58)

Friendly

May 27	Prague	CZECHOSLOVAKIA	D 1-1	Clarke A	25,000	Shilton (10), Madeley (10), Storey (16), Bell (28), McFarland (16), **Moore** (104), Ball (64), Channon (6), Chivers (19), Clarke A (10), Peters (59)

World Cup Qualifier

Jun 6	Chorzow	POLAND	L 0-2		73,714	Shilton (11), Madeley (11), Hughes (24), Storey (17), McFarland (17), **Moore** (105), Ball (65), Bell (29), Chivers (20), Clarke A (11), Peters (60)

Friendlies

Jun 10	Moscow	USSR	W 2-1	Chivers, own goal	85,000	Shilton (12), Madeley (12), Hughes (25), Storey (18), McFarland (18), **Moore** (106), Currie (2), Channon (7), (Summerbee 8), Chivers (21), Clarke A (12), (Macdonald 4), Peters (61), (Hunter 23)
Jun 14	Turin	ITALY	L 0-2		60,000	Shilton (13), Madeley (13), Hughes (26), Storey (19), McFarland (19), **Moore** (107), Currie (3), Channon (8), Chivers (22), Clarke A (13), Peters (62)
Sep 26	Wembley, London	AUSTRIA	W 7-0	Channon 2, Clarke A 2, Chivers, Currie, Bell	48,000	Shilton (14), Madeley (14), Hughes (27), Bell (30), McFarland (20), Hunter (24), Currie (4), Channon (9), Chivers (23), Clarke A (14), **Peters** (63)

World Cup Qualifier

Oct 17	Wembley, London	POLAND	D 1-1	Clarke A (pen)	100,000	Shilton (15), Madeley (15), Hughes (28), Bell (31), McFarland (21), Hunter (25), Currie (5), Channon (10), Chivers (24), (Hector 1), Clarke A (15), **Peters** (64)

Friendly

Nov 14	Wembley, London	ITALY	L 0-1		88,000	Shilton (16), Madeley (16), Hughes (29), Bell (32), McFarland (22), **Moore** (108), Currie (6), Channon (11), Osgood (4), Clarke A (16), (Hector 2), Peters (65)

Roy McFarland tries to retrieve the ball from a disconsolate Norman Hunter whose mistake has just given Poland the lead in their World Cup qualifier in October 1973. The match ended all square at 1-1 and that point was enough for Poland to qualify at England's expense.

1974

Friendly

DATE	VENUE	OPPONENTS	SCORE	GOALSCORERS	ATTENDANCE	TEAM
Apr 3	Lisbon	PORTUGAL	D 0-0		20,000	Parkes (1), Nish (2), Pejic (1), Dobson (1), Watson (1), Todd (2), Bowles (1), Channon (12), Macdonald (5), (Ball 66), Brooking (1), **Peters** (66)

Home International Championship

May 11	Ninian Park, Cardiff	WALES	W 2-0	Bowles, Keegan	25,734	Shilton (17), Nish (3), Pejic (2), **Hughes** (30), McFarland (23), Todd (3), Keegan (3), Bell (33), Channon (13), Weller (1), Bowles (2)
May 15	Wembley, London	N. IRELAND	W 1-0	Weller	45,500	Shilton (18), Nish (4), Pejic (3), **Hughes** (31), McFarland (24), (Hunter 26), Todd (4), Keegan (4), Weller (2), Channon (14), Bell (34), Bowles (3), (Worthington 1),
May 18	Hampden Park, Glasgow	SCOTLAND	L 0-2		94,487	Shilton (19), Nish (5), Pejic (4), **Hughes** (32), Hunter (27), (Watson 2), Todd (5), Channon (15), Bell (35), Worthington (2), (Macdonald 6), Weller (3), Peters (67)

Friendlies

May 22	Wembley, London	ARGENTINA	D 2-2	Channon, Worthington	68,000	Shilton (20), **Hughes** (33), Lindsay (1), Todd (6), Watson (3), Bell (36), Keegan (5), Channon (16), Worthington (3), Weller (4), Brooking (2)
May 29	Leipzig	E. GERMANY	D 1-1	Channon	95,000	Clemence (3), **Hughes** (34), Lindsay (2), Todd (7), Watson (4), Dobson (2), Keegan (6), Channon (17), Worthington (4), Bell (37), Brooking (3)
Jun 1	Sofia	BULGARIA	W 1-0	Worthington	60,000	Clemence (4), **Hughes** (35), Lindsay (3), Todd (8), Watson (5), Dobson (3), Keegan (7), Channon (18), Worthington (5), Bell (38), Brooking (4)
Jun 5	Belgrade	YUGOSLAVIA	D 2-2	Channon, Keegan	90,000	Clemence (5), **Hughes** (36), Lindsay (4), Todd (9), Watson (6), Dobson (4), Keegan (8), Channon (19), Worthington (6), (Macdonald 7), Bell (39), Brooking (5)

European Championship Qualifiers

| Oct 30 | Wembley, London | CZECHOSLOVAKIA | W 3-0 | Channon, Bell 2 | 83,858 | Clemence (6), Madeley (17), **Hughes** (37), Dobson (5), (Brooking 6), Watson (7), Hunter (28), Bell (40), Francis G (1), Worthington (7), (Thomas 1), Channon (20), Keegan (9) |
| Nov 20 | Wembley, London | PORTUGAL | D 0-0 | | 84,461 | Clemence (7), Madeley (18), Cooper (20), (Todd 10), **Hughes** (38), Watson (8), Brooking (7), Bell (41), Francis G (2), Channon (21), Clarke A (17), (Worthington 8), Thomas (2) |

Maverick, genius, Leicester City's Frank Worthington was given his first cap by manager Sir Alf Ramsey against Northern Ireland in May 1974.

1975

Friendly

DATE	VENUE	OPPONENTS	SCORE	GOALSCORERS	ATTENDANCE	TEAM
Mar 12	Wembley, London	W. GERMANY	W 2-0	Bell, Macdonald	100,000	Clemence (8), Whitworth (1), Gillard (1), Bell (42), Watson (9), Todd (11), **Ball** (67), Macdonald (8), Channon (22), Hudson (1), Keegan (10)

European Championship Qualifiers

DATE	VENUE	OPPONENTS	SCORE	GOALSCORERS	ATTENDANCE	TEAM
Apr 16	Wembley, London	CYPRUS	W 5-0	Macdonald 5	68,245	Shilton (21), Madeley (19), Beattie (1), Todd (12), Watson (10), Bell (43), **Ball** (68), Macdonald (9), Channon (23), (Thomas 3), Hudson (2), Keegan (11)
May 11	Limassol	CYPRUS	W 1-0	Keegan	16,200	Clemence (9), Whitworth (2), Beattie (2), (Hughes 39), Todd (13), Watson (11), Bell (44), Thomas (4), (Tueart 1), Macdonald (10), Channon (24), **Ball** (69), Keegan (12)

Home International Championship

DATE	VENUE	OPPONENTS	SCORE	GOALSCORERS	ATTENDANCE	TEAM
May 17	Windsor Park, Belfast	N. IRELAND	D 0-0		36,500	Clemence (10), Whitworth (3), Hughes (40), Todd (14), Watson (12), Bell (45), **Ball** (70), Viljoen (1), Macdonald (11), (Channon 25), Keegan (13), Tueart (2)
May 21	Wembley, London	WALES	D 2-2	Johnson 2	53,000	Clemence (11), Whitworth (4), Gillard (2), Francis G (3), Watson (13), Todd (15), **Ball** (71), Channon (26), (Little 1), Johnson (1), Viljoen (2), Thomas (5)
May 24	Wembley, London	SCOTLAND	W 5-1	Francis G 2, Beattie, Bell, Johnson	98,241	Clemence (12), Whitworth (5), Beattie (3), Bell (46), Watson (14), Todd (16), **Ball** (72), Channon (27), Johnson (2), Francis G (4), Keegan (14), (Thomas 6)

Friendly

DATE	VENUE	OPPONENTS	SCORE	GOALSCORERS	ATTENDANCE	TEAM
Sep 3	Basle	SWITZERLAND	W 2-1	Keegan, Channon	30,000	Clemence (13), Whitworth (6), Beattie (4), Bell (47), Watson (15), Todd (17), Currie (7), Channon (28), Johnson (3), (Macdonald 12), **Francis G** (5), Keegan (15)

European Championship Qualifiers

DATE	VENUE	OPPONENTS	SCORE	GOALSCORERS	ATTENDANCE	TEAM
Oct 30	Bratislava	CZECHOSLOVAKIA	L 1-2	Channon	50,651	Clemence (14), Madeley (20), Gillard (3), **Francis G** (6), McFarland (25), (Watson 16), Todd (18), Keegan (16), Channon (29), (Thomas 7), Macdonald (13), Clarke A (18), Bell (48)
Nov 19	Lisbon	PORTUGAL	D 1-1	Channon	60,000	Clemence (15), Whitworth (7), Beattie (5), **Francis G** (7), Watson (17), Todd (19), Keegan (17), Channon (30), Macdonald (14), (Thomas 8), Brooking (8), Madeley (21), (Clarke A 19)

FACT FILE

Malcolm MacDonald became the first England player to score five for his country at Wembley with all the goals in the victory over Cyprus in 1975.

England's 2-0 win over Germany in 1975 was the 100th international match at Wembley.

Southampton's Mick Channon had established himself as a lively presence up front for England during the mid 1970s.

287

1976

Friendly

DATE	VENUE	OPPONENTS	SCORE	GOALSCORERS	ATTENDANCE	TEAM
Mar 24	Racecourse Ground, Wrexham	WALES	W 2-1	Kennedy, Taylor	20,927	Clemence (16), Cherry (1), (Clement 1), Mills (2), Neal (1), Thompson (1), Doyle (1), **Keegan** (18), Channon (31), (Taylor 1), Boyer (1), Brooking (9), Kennedy (1)

Home International Championship

May 8	Ninian Park, Cardiff	WALES	W 1-0	Taylor	24,592	Clemence (17), Clement (2), Mills (3), Towers (1), Greenhoff (1), Thompson (2), Keegan (19), **Francis G** (8), Pearson (1), Kennedy (2), Taylor (2)
May 11	Wembley, London	N. IRELAND	W 4-0	Francis G, Channon 2 (1 pen), Pearson	48,000	Clemence (18), Todd (20), Mills (4), Thompson (3), Greenhoff (2), Kennedy (3), Keegan (20), (Royle 3), **Francis G** (9), Pearson (2), Channon (32), Taylor (3), (Towers 2)
May 15	Hampden Park, Glasgow	SCOTLAND	L 1-2	Channon	85,165	Clemence (19), Todd (21), Mills (5), Thompson (4), McFarland (26), (Doyle 2), Kennedy (4), Keegan (21), **Francis G** (10), Pearson (3), (Cherry 2), Channon (33), Taylor (4)

US Bicentennial Tournament

May 23	Los Angeles	BRAZIL	L 0-1		32,900	Clemence (20), Todd (22), Mills (6), Thompson (5), Doyle (3), Cherry (3), Keegan (22), Brooking (10), Pearson (4), **Francis G** (11), Channon (34)
May 28	New York	ITALY	W 3-2	Channon 2, Thompson	40,650	Rimmer (1), (Corrigan 1), Clement (3), Neal (2), (Mills 7), Thompson (6), Doyle (4), Towers (3), Wilkins (1), **Channon** (35), Royle (4), Brooking (11), Hill (1)

England captain Gerry Francis poses with Team America's Bobby Moore and Pele during the US Bicentennial Tournament in May 1976.

World Cup Qualifier

Jun 13	Helsinki	FINLAND	W 4-1	Keegan 2, Channon, Pearson	24,336	Clemence (21), Todd (23), Mills (8), Thompson (7), Madeley (22), Cherry (4), Keegan (23), Channon (36), Pearson (5), Brooking (12), **Francis G** (12)

Friendly

Sep 8	Wembley, London	R. of IRELAND	D 1-1	Pearson	51,000	Clemence (22), Todd (24), Madeley (23), Greenhoff (3), McFarland (27), Cherry (5), **Keegan** (24), Wilkins (2), Pearson (6), Brooking (13), George (1), (Hill 2)

World Cup Qualifiers

Oct 13	Wembley, London	FINLAND	W 2-1	Tueart, Royle	92,000	Clemence (23), Todd (25), Beattie (6), Thompson (8), Greenhoff (4), Wilkins (3), **Keegan** (25), Channon (37), Royle (5), Brooking (14), (Mills 9), Tueart (3), (Hill 3)
Nov 17	Rome	ITALY	L 0-2		70,718	Clemence (24), Clement (4), (Beattie 7), Mills (10), Greenhoff (5), McFarland (28), Hughes (41), **Keegan** (26), Cherry (6), Channon (38), Bowles (4), Brooking (15)

FACT FILE

On 14 May 1976 Peter Shilton – with 21 caps for England – pulled out of the squad and asked not to be selected in the future. On 26 August he asked to be reconsidered and went on to play 125 times.

1977

Friendly

DATE	VENUE	OPPONENTS	SCORE	GOALSCORERS	ATTENDANCE	TEAM
Feb 9	Wembley, London	HOLLAND	L 0-2		90,260	Clemence (25), Clement (5), Beattie (8), Doyle (5), Watson (18), Madeley (24), (Pearson 7), **Keegan** (27), Greenhoff (6), (Todd 26), Francis T (1), Bowles (5), Brooking (16)

World Cup Qualifier

DATE	VENUE	OPPONENTS	SCORE	GOALSCORERS	ATTENDANCE	TEAM
Mar 30	Wembley, London	LUXEMBOURG	W 5-0	Keegan, Francis T, Kennedy, Channon 2 (1 pen)	81,718	Clemence (26), Gidman (1), Cherry (7), Kennedy (5), Watson (19), Hughes (42), **Keegan** (28), Channon (39), Royle (6), (Mariner 1), Francis T (2), Hill (4)

Home International Championship

DATE	VENUE	OPPONENTS	SCORE	GOALSCORERS	ATTENDANCE	TEAM
May 28	Windsor Park Belfast	N. IRELAND	W 2-1	Channon, Tueart	35,000	Shilton (22), Cherry (8), Mills (11), Greenhoff (7), Watson (20), Todd (27), Wilkins (4), (Talbot 1), **Channon** (40), Mariner (2), Brooking (17), Tueart (4)
May 31	Wembley, London	WALES	L 0-1		48,000	Shilton (23), Neal (3), Mills (12), Greenhoff (8), Watson (21), Hughes (43), **Keegan** (29), Channon (41), Pearson (8), Brooking (18), (Tueart 5), Kennedy (6)
Jun 4	Wembley, London	SCOTLAND	L 1-2	Channon (pen)	98,103	Clemence (27), Neal (4), Mills (13), Greenhoff (9), (Cherry 9), Watson (22), **Hughes** (44), Francis T (3), Channon (42), Pearson (9), Talbot (2), Kennedy (7), (Tueart 6)

Friendlies

DATE	VENUE	OPPONENTS	SCORE	GOALSCORERS	ATTENDANCE	TEAM
Jun 8	Rio	BRAZIL	D 0-0		77,000	Clemence (28), Neal (5), Cherry (10), Greenhoff (10), Watson (23), Hughes (45), **Keegan** (30), Francis T (4), Pearson (10), (Channon 43), Wilkins (5), (Kennedy 8), Talbot (3)
Jun 12	Buenos Aires	ARGENTINA	D 1-1	Pearson	60,000	Clemence (29), Neal (6), Cherry (11), Greenhoff (11), (Kennedy 9), Watson (24), Hughes (46), **Keegan** (31), Channon (44), Pearson (11), Wilkins (6), Talbot (4)
Jun 15	Montevideo	URUGUAY	D 0-0		25,000	Clemence (30), Neal (7), Cherry (12), Greenhoff (12), Watson (25), Hughes (47), **Keegan** (32), Channon (45), Pearson (12), Wilkins (7), Talbot (5)
Sep 7	Wembley, London	SWITZERLAND	D 0-0		42,000	Clemence (31), Neal (8), Cherry (13), McDermott (1), Watson (26), **Hughes** (48), Keegan (33), Channon (46), Francis T (5), Kennedy (10), Callaghan (3), (Wilkins 8)

World Cup Qualifiers

DATE	VENUE	OPPONENTS	SCORE	GOALSCORERS	ATTENDANCE	TEAM
Oct 12	Luxembourg	LUXEMBOURG	W 2-0	Kennedy, Mariner	10,621	Clemence (32), Cherry (14), **Hughes** (49), McDermott (2), (Whymark 1), Watson (27), (Beattie 9), Kennedy (11), Wilkins (9), Francis T (6), Mariner (3), Hill (6), Callaghan (4)
Nov 16	Wembley, London	ITALY	W 2-0	Keegan, Brooking	92,000	Clemence (33), Neal (9), Cherry (15), Wilkins (10), Watson (28), **Hughes** (50), Keegan (34), (Francis T 7), Coppell (1), Latchford (1), (Pearson 13), Brooking (19), Barnes (1)

FACT FILE

Against Switzerland in 1977, Liverpool had six players in the England team while a seventh was their former player Kevin Keegan, then playing for Hamburg.

Scottish fans celebrated their 2-1 victory over England at Wembley in June 1977 by pulling up the pitch and pulling down both sets of goalposts.

1978

Friendlies

DATE	VENUE	OPPONENTS	SCORE	GOALSCORERS	ATTENDANCE	TEAM
Feb 22	Munich	W. GERMANY	L 1-2	Pearson	77,850	Clemence (34), Neal (10), Mills (14), Wilkins (11), Watson (29), **Hughes** (51), Keegan (35), (Francis T 8), Coppell (2), Pearson (14), Brooking (20), Barnes (2)
Apr 19	Wembley, London	BRAZIL	D 1-1	Keegan	92,500	Corrigan (2), Mills (15), Cherry (16), Greenhoff (13), Watson (30), Currie (8), **Keegan** (36), Coppell (3), Latchford (2), Francis T (9), Barnes (3)

Home International Championship

DATE	VENUE	OPPONENTS	SCORE	GOALSCORERS	ATTENDANCE	TEAM
May 13	Ninian Park, Cardiff	WALES	W 3-1	Latchford, Currie, Barnes	17,698	Shilton (24), **Mills** (16), Cherry (17), (Currie 9), Greenhoff (14), Watson (31), Wilkins (12), Coppell (4), Francis T (10), Latchford (3), (Mariner 4), Brooking (21), Barnes (4)
May 16	Wembley, London	N. IRELAND	W 1-0	Neal	55,000	Clemence (35), Neal (11), Mills (17), Wilkins (13), Watson (32), **Hughes** (52), Currie (10), Coppell (5), Pearson (15), Woodcock (1), Greenhoff (15)
May 20	Hampden Park, Glasgow	SCOTLAND	W 1-0	Coppell	88,319	Clemence (36), Neal (12), Mills (18), Currie (11), Watson (33), **Hughes** (53), (Greenhoff 16), Wilkins (14), Coppell (6), Mariner (5), (Brooking 22), Francis T (11), Barnes (5)

Friendly

DATE	VENUE	OPPONENTS	SCORE	GOALSCORERS	ATTENDANCE	TEAM
May 24	Wembley, London	HUNGARY	W 4-1	Barnes, Neal (pen), Francis T, Currie	75,000	Shilton (25), Neal (13), Mills (19), Wilkins (15), Watson (34), (Greenhoff 17), **Hughes** (54), Keegan (37), Coppell (7), Francis T (12), Brooking (23), (Currie 12), Barnes (6)

European Championship Qualifiers

DATE	VENUE	OPPONENTS	SCORE	GOALSCORERS	ATTENDANCE	TEAM
Sep 20	Copenhagen	DENMARK	W 4-3	Keegan 2, Neal, Latchford	47,600	Clemence (37), Neal (14), Mills (20), Wilkins (16), Watson (35), **Hughes** (55), Keegan (38), Coppell (8), Latchford (4), Brooking (24), Barnes (7)
Oct 25	Lansdowne Road, Dublin	R. of IRELAND	D 1-1	Latchford	55,000	Clemence (38), Neal (15), Mills (21), Wilkins (17), Watson (36), (Thompson 9), **Hughes** (56), Keegan (39), Coppell (9), Latchford (5), Brooking (25), Barnes (8), (Woodcock 2)

Friendly

DATE	VENUE	OPPONENTS	SCORE	GOALSCORERS	ATTENDANCE	TEAM
Nov 29	Wembley, London	CZECHOSLOVAKIA	W 1-0	Coppell	92,000	Shilton (26), Anderson (1), Cherry (18), Thompson (10), Watson (37), Wilkins (18), **Keegan** (40), Coppell (10), Woodcock (3), (Latchford 6), Currie (13), Barnes (9)

FACT FILE

The first black player to play for England in a full international was Viv Anderson against Czechoslovakia in 1978. In 1982 Luther Blissett hit a hat-trick in the 9-0 win against Luxembourg to become the first black player to score for England. In the same game Mark Chamberlain was the second. It was also the first time as many as seven different players had scored in a full England international fixture. In 1993 Paul Ince became the first black player to captain England when he led the team against Brazil.

Managers Danny Blanchflower (left) and Ron Greenwood walk out together before the match between England and Northern Ireland at Wembley in May 1978. England won the match 1-0.

1979

European Championship Qualifier

DATE	VENUE	OPPONENTS	SCORE	GOALSCORERS	ATTENDANCE	TEAM
Feb 7	Wembley, London	N. IRELAND	W 4-0	Keegan, Latchford 2, Watson	92,000	Clemence (39), Neal (16), Mills (22), Currie (14), Watson (38), **Hughes** (57), Keegan (41), Coppell (11), Latchford (7), Brooking (26), Barnes (10)

Home International Championship

DATE	VENUE	OPPONENTS	SCORE	GOALSCORERS	ATTENDANCE	TEAM
May 19	Windsor Park, Belfast	N. IRELAND	W 2-0	Watson, Coppell	35,000	Clemence (40), Neal (17), **Mills** (23), Thompson (11), Watson (39), Currie (15), Coppell (12), Wilkins (19), Latchford (8), McDermott (3), Barnes (11)
May 23	Wembley, London	WALES	D 0-0		70,220	Corrigan (3), Cherry (19), Sansom (1), Currie (16), Watson (40), **Hughes** (58), Keegan (42), (Coppell 13), Wilkins (20), (Brooking 27), Latchford (9), McDermott (4), Cunningham (1)
May 26	Wembley, London	SCOTLAND	W 3-1	Barnes, Coppell, Keegan	100,000	Clemence (41), Neal (18), Mills (24), Thompson (12), Watson (41), Wilkins (21), **Keegan** (43), Coppell (14), Latchford (10), Brooking (28), Barnes (12)

Kevin Keegan celebrates his goal against Scotland at Wembley in May 1979.

European Championship Qualifier

DATE	VENUE	OPPONENTS	SCORE	GOALSCORERS	ATTENDANCE	TEAM
Jun 6	Sofia	BULGARIA	W 3-0	Keegan, Watson, Barnes	47,500	Clemence (42), Neal (19), Mills (25), Thompson (13), Watson (42), Wilkins (22), **Keegan** (44), Coppell (15), Latchford (11), (Francis T 13), Brooking (29), Barnes (13), (Woodcock 4)

Friendlies

DATE	VENUE	OPPONENTS	SCORE	GOALSCORERS	ATTENDANCE	TEAM
Jun 10	Stockholm	SWEDEN	D 0-0		35,691	Shilton (27), Anderson (2), Cherry (20), McDermott (5), (Wilkins 23), Watson (43), (Thompson 14), **Hughes** (59), Keegan (45), Francis T (14), (Brooking 30), Woodcock (5), Currie (17), Cunningham (2)
Jun 13	Vienna	AUSTRIA	L 3-4	Keegan, Coppell, Wilkins	60,000	Shilton (28), (Clemence 43), Neal (20), Mills (26), Thompson (15), Watson (44), Wilkins (24), **Keegan** (46), Coppell (16), Latchford (12), (Francis T 15), Brooking (31), Barnes (14), (Cunningham 3)

European Championship Qualifiers

DATE	VENUE	OPPONENTS	SCORE	GOALSCORERS	ATTENDANCE	TEAM
Sep 12	Wembley, London	DENMARK	W 1-0	Keegan	85,000	Clemence (44), Neal (21), Mills (27), Thompson (16), Watson (45), Wilkins (25), McDermott (6), Coppell (17), **Keegan** (47), Brooking (32), Barnes (15)
Oct 17	Windsor Park, Belfast	N. IRELAND	W 5-1	Francis T 2, Woodcock 2, own goal	25,000	Shilton (29), Neal (22), Mills (28), Thompson (17), Watson (46), Wilkins (26), **Keegan** (48), Coppell (18), Francis T (16), Brooking (33), (McDermott 7), Woodcock (6)
Nov 22	Wembley, London	BULGARIA	W 2-0	Watson, Hoddle	71,491	Clemence (45), Anderson (3), Sansom (2), **Thompson** (18), Watson (47), Wilkins (27), Reeves (1), Hoddle (1), Francis T (17), Kennedy (12), Woodcock (7)

FACT FILE

England's 1-0 victory over the USSR in Tbilisi in 1986 inflicted the first home defeat on the Soviets after 18 matches and the first goal conceded on local territory since 1979.

1980

European Championship Qualifiers

DATE	VENUE	OPPONENTS	SCORE	GOALSCORERS	ATTENDANCE	TEAM
Feb 6	Wembley, London	R. of IRELAND	W 2-0	Keegan 2	90,299	Clemence (46), Cherry (21), Sansom (3), Thompson (19), Watson (48), Robson (1), **Keegan** (49), McDermott (8), Johnson (4), (Coppell 19), Woodcock (8), Cunningham (4)

Friendlies

Mar 26	Barcelona	SPAIN	W 2-0	Woodcock, Francis T	50,000	Shilton (30), Neal (23), (Hughes 60) Mills (29), Thompson (20), Watson (49), Wilkins (28), **Keegan** (50), Coppell (20), Francis T (18), (Cunningham 5), Kennedy (13), Woodcock (9)
May 13	Wembley, London	ARGENTINA	W 3-1	Johnson 2, Keegan	92,000	Clemence (47), Neal (24), (Cherry 22), Sansom (4), Thompson (21), Watson (50), Wilkins (29), **Keegan** (51), Coppell (21), Johnson (5), (Birtles 1), Kennedy (14), (Brooking 34), Woodcock (10)

Home International Championship

May 17	Racecourse Ground, Wrexham	WALES	L 1-4	Mariner	24,386	Clemence (48), Neal (25), (Sansom 5), Cherry (23), **Thompson** (22), Lloyd (4), (Wilkins 30), Kennedy (15), Coppell (22), Hoddle (2), Mariner (6), Brooking (35), Barnes (16)
May 20	Wembley, London	N. IRELAND	D 1-1	Johnson	33,676	Corrigan (4), Cherry (24), Sansom (6), Wilkins (31), Watson (51), **Hughes** (61), Reeves (2), (Mariner 7), McDermott (9), Johnson (6), Brooking (36), Devonshire (1)
May 24	Hampden Park, Glasgow	SCOTLAND	W 2-0	Brooking, Coppell	85,000	Clemence (49), Cherry (25), Sansom (7), **Thompson** (23), Watson (52), Wilkins (32), Coppell (23), McDermott (10), Johnson (7), Brooking (37), Mariner (8), (Hughes 62)

Friendly

May 31	Sydney	AUSTRALIA	W 2-1	Hoddle, Mariner	30,000	Corrigan (5), **Cherry** (26), Lampard (2), Talbot (6), Osman (1), Butcher (1), Robson (2), (Greenhoff 18), Sunderland (1), (Ward 1), Mariner (9), Hoddle (3), Armstrong (1), (Devonshire 2)

FACT FILE

England's first all-seated international at Wembley was against Yugoslavia in 1989. The crowd was only 34,796 as the terracing behind each goal was closed for conversion. The first full attendance was in 1990 against Brazil with a capacity 80,000 paying £1.2 million.

Ray Clemence leaps high to take the ball from Scotland's Alec McLeish during England's 2-0 win at Hampden in May 1980.

EUROPEAN CHAMPIONSHIP FINALS 1980

Group Stage – Group 2

DATE	VENUE	OPPONENTS	SCORE	GOALSCORERS	ATTENDANCE	TEAM
Jun 12	Turin	BELGIUM	D 1-1	Wilkins	15,186	Clemence (50), Neal (26), Sansom (8), Thompson (24), Watson (53), Wilkins (33), **Keegan** (52), Coppell (24), (McDermott 11), Johnson (8), (Kennedy 16), Brooking (38), Woodcock (11)
Jun 15	Turin	ITALY	L 0-1		59,649	Shilton (31), Neal (27), Sansom (9), Thompson (25), Watson (54), Wilkins (34), **Keegan** (53), Coppell (25), Birtles (2), (Mariner 10), Kennedy (17), Woodcock (12)
Jun 18	Naples	SPAIN	W 2-1	Brooking, Woodcock	14,440	Clemence (51), Anderson (4), (Cherry 27), Mills (30), Thompson (26), Watson (55), Wilkins (35), **Keegan** (54), McDermott (12), Woodcock (13), Brooking (39), Hoddle (4), (Mariner 11)

Group 2

	P	W	D	L	F	A	Pts
BELGIUM	3	1	2	0	3	2	4
ITALY	3	1	2	0	1	0	4
ENGLAND	3	1	1	1	3	3	3
SPAIN	3	0	1	2	2	4	1

Ray Wilkins lifts the ball over the Belgian keeper to score in England's 1-1 draw in the opening group game of the 1980 European Championships.

1980 (continued)

World Cup Qualifiers

DATE	VENUE	OPPONENTS	SCORE	GOALSCORERS	ATTENDANCE	TEAM
Sep 10	Wembley, London	NORWAY	W 4-0	McDermott 2 (1 pen), Woodcock, Mariner	48,200	Shilton (32), Anderson (5), Sansom (10), **Thompson** (27), Watson (56), Robson (3), Gates (1), McDermott (13), Mariner (12), Woodcock (14), Rix (1)
Oct 15	Bucharest	ROMANIA	L 1-2	Woodcock	75,000	Clemence (52), Neal (28), Sansom (11), **Thompson** (28), Watson (57), Robson (4), Gates (2), (Coppell 26), McDermott (14), Birtles (3), (Cunningham 6), Woodcock (15), Rix (2)
Nov 19	Wembley, London	SWITZERLAND	W 2-1	Mariner, own goal	70,000	Shilton (33), Neal (29), Sansom (12), Robson (5), Watson (58), **Mills** (31), Coppell (27), McDermott (15), Mariner (13), Brooking (40), (Rix 3), Woodcock (16)

1981

Friendly

DATE	VENUE	OPPONENTS	SCORE	GOALSCORERS	ATTENDANCE	TEAM
Mar 25	Wembley, London	SPAIN	L 1-2	Hoddle	71,840	Clemence (53), Neal (30), Sansom (13), Robson (6), Osman (2), Butcher (2), **Keegan** (55), Francis T (19), (Barnes 17), Mariner (14), Brooking (41), (Wilkins 36), Hoddle (5)

World Cup Qualifier

Apr 29	Wembley, London	ROMANIA	D 0-0		62,500	Shilton (34), Anderson (6), Sansom (14), Robson (7), **Watson** (59), Osman (3), Coppell (28), Wilkins (37), Francis T (20), Brooking (42), (McDermott 16), Woodcock (17)

Friendly

May 12	Wembley, London	BRAZIL	L 0-1		75,000	**Clemence** (54), Neal (31), Sansom (15), Robson (8), Martin (1), Wilkins (38), Coppell (29), McDermott (17), Withe (1), Rix (4), Barnes (18)

Home International Championship

May 20	Wembley, London	WALES	D 0-0		34,280	Corrigan (6), Anderson (7), Sansom (16), Robson (9), **Watson** (60), Wilkins (39), Coppell (30), Hoddle (6), Withe (2), (Woodcock 18), Rix (5), Barnes (19)
May 23	Wembley, London	SCOTLAND	L 0-1		90,000	Corrigan (7), Anderson (8), Sansom (17), Wilkins (40), **Watson** (61), (Martin 2), Robson (10), Coppell (31), Hoddle (7), Withe (3), Woodcock (19), (Francis T 21), Rix (6)

World Cup Qualifiers

DATE	VENUE	OPPONENTS	SCORE	GOALSCORERS	ATTENDANCE	TEAM
May 30	Basle	SWITZERLAND	L 1-2	McDermott	40,000	Clemence (55), Mills (32), Sansom (18), Wilkins (41), Watson (62), (Barnes 20), Osman (4), **Keegan** (56), Coppell (32), Mariner (15), Francis T (22), (McDermott 18), Robson (11)
Jun 6	Budapest	HUNGARY	W 3-1	Brooking 2, Keegan (pen)	68,000	Clemence (56), Neal (32), Mills (33), Thompson (29), Watson (63), Robson (12), **Keegan** (57), Coppell (33), Mariner (16), Brooking (43), (Wilkins 42), McDermott (19)
Sep 9	Oslo	NORWAY	L 1-2	Robson	28,500	Clemence (57), Neal (33), Mills (34), Thompson (30), Osman (5), Robson (13), **Keegan** (58), Francis T (23), Mariner (17), (Withe 4), Hoddle (8), (Barnes 21), McDermott (20)
Nov 18	Wembley, London	HUNGARY	W 1-0	Mariner	92,000	Shilton (35), Neal (34), Mills (35), Thompson (31), Martin (3), Robson (14), **Keegan** (59), Coppell (34), (Morley 1), Mariner (18), Brooking (44), McDermott (21)

1982

Home International Championship

DATE	VENUE	OPPONENTS	SCORE	GOALSCORERS	ATTENDANCE	TEAM
Feb 23	Wembley, London	N. IRELAND	W 4-0	Robson, Keegan, Hoddle, Wilkins	54,900	Clemence (58), Anderson (9), Sansom (19), Wilkins (43), Watson (64), Foster (1), **Keegan** (60), Robson (15), Francis T (24), (Regis 1), Hoddle (9), Morley (2), (Woodcock 20)
Apr 27	Ninian Park, Cardiff	WALES	W 1-0	Francis T	25,000	Corrigan (8), Neal (35), Sansom (20), **Thompson** (32), Butcher (3), Wilkins (44), Robson (16), Francis T (25), (Regis 2), Withe (5), Hoddle (10), (McDermott 22), Morley (3)

Friendly

DATE	VENUE	OPPONENTS	SCORE	GOALSCORERS	ATTENDANCE	TEAM
May 25	Wembley, London	HOLLAND	W 2-0	Mariner, Woodcock	69,000	**Shilton** (36), Neal (36), Sansom (21), Thompson (33), Foster (2), Wilkins (45), Robson (17), McDermott (23), Mariner (19), (Barnes 22), Woodcock (21), Devonshire (3), (Rix 7)

Home International Championship

DATE	VENUE	OPPONENTS	SCORE	GOALSCORERS	ATTENDANCE	TEAM
May 29	Hampden Park, Glasgow	SCOTLAND	W 1-0	Mariner	80,529	Shilton (37), Mills (36), Sansom (22), Thompson (34), Butcher (4), Wilkins (46), **Keegan** (61), (McDermott 24), Coppell (35), Mariner (20), (Francis T 26), Brooking (45), Robson (18)

Friendlies

DATE	VENUE	OPPONENTS	SCORE	GOALSCORERS	ATTENDANCE	TEAM
Jun 2	Reykjavik	ICELAND	D 1-1	Goddard	11,110	Corrigan (9), Anderson (10), **Neal** (37), McDermott (25), Watson (65), Osman (6), Morley (4), Hoddle (11), Withe (6), Regis (3), (Goddard 1), Devonshire (4), (Perryman 1)
Jun 3	Helsinki	FINLAND	W 4-1	Robson 2, Mariner 2	21,521	Clemence (59), Mills (37), Sansom (23), Thompson (35), Martin (4), Wilkins (47), **Keegan** (62), Coppell (36), (Francis T 27), Mariner (21), Brooking (46), (Woodcock 22), Robson (19), (Rix 8)

FACT FILE

Against Luxembourg in 1982 the nine goals scored by England was, at the time, the highest score in a European Championship match.

Receipts for the 100th international between Scotland and England at Hampden Park in 1982 were £500,000, compared with £103 from the initial encounter in 1872, when the profit was £33.

England mascot Ken Bailey signals victory during the draw for the 1982 World Cup in Spain in January of that year.

THE WORLD CUP FINALS 1982 (SPAIN)

Group Stage – Group 4

DATE	VENUE	OPPONENTS	SCORE	GOALSCORERS	ATTENDANCE	TEAM
Jun 16	Bilbao	FRANCE	W 3-1	Robson 2, Mariner	44,172	Shilton (38), **Mills** (38), Sansom (24), (Neal 38), Thompson (36), Butcher (5), Wilkins (48), Coppell (37), Francis T (28), Mariner (22), Rix (9), Robson (20)
Jun 20	Bilbao	CZECHOSLOVAKIA	W 2-0	Francis T, own goal	42,000	Shilton (39), **Mills** (39), Sansom (25), Thompson (37), Butcher (6), Wilkins (49), Coppell (38), Francis T (29), Mariner (23), Rix (10), Robson (21), (Hoddle 12)
Jun 25	Bilbao	KUWAIT	W 1-0	Francis T	39,700	Shilton (40), Neal (39), **Mills** (40), Thompson (38), Foster (3), Wilkins (50), Coppell (39), Francis T (30), Mariner (24), Rix (11), Hoddle (13)

Second Round – Group B

DATE	VENUE	OPPONENTS	SCORE	GOALSCORERS	ATTENDANCE	TEAM
Jun 29	Madrid	W. GERMANY	D 0-0		90,089	Shilton (41), **Mills** (41), Sansom (26), Thompson (39), Butcher (7), Wilkins (51), Coppell (40), Francis T (31), (Woodcock 23), Mariner (25), Rix (12), Robson (22)
July 5	Madrid	SPAIN	D 0-0		60,000	Shilton (42), **Mills** (42), Sansom (27), Thompson (40), Butcher (8), Wilkins (52), Robson (23), Francis T (32), Mariner (26), Woodcock (24), (Keegan 63), Rix (13), (Brooking 47)

Group 4

	P	W	D	L	F	A	Pts
ENGLAND	3	3	0	0	6	1	6
FRANCE	3	1	1	1	6	5	3
CZECHOSLOVAKIA	3	0	2	1	2	4	2
KUWAIT	3	0	1	2	2	6	1

Group B

	P	W	D	L	F	A	Pts
WEST GERMANY	2	1	1	0	2	1	3
ENGLAND	2	0	2	0	0	0	2
SPAIN	2	0	1	1	1	2	1

The England team line up before their World Cup second round match with Spain in Madrid in July 1982. The result was a frustrating 0-0 draw that saw England drop out of the competition.

1982 (continued)

European Championship Qualifier

DATE	VENUE	OPPONENTS	SCORE	GOALSCORERS	ATTENDANCE	TEAM
Sep 22	Copenhagen	DENMARK	D 2-2	Francis T 2	44,300	Shilton (43), Neal (40), Sansom (28), **Wilkins** (53), Osman (7), Butcher (9), Morley (5), (Hill 1), Robson (24), Mariner (27), Francis T (33), Rix (14)

Friendly

| Oct 13 | Wembley, London | W. GERMANY | L 1-2 | Woodcock | 68,000 | Shilton (44), Mabbutt (1), Sansom (29), Thompson (41), Butcher (10), **Wilkins** (54), Hill (2), Regis (4), (Blissett 1), Mariner (28), (Woodcock 25), Armstrong (2), (Rix 15), Devonshire (5) |

European Championship Qualifiers

| Nov 17 | Salonika | GREECE | W 3-0 | Woodcock 2, Lee | 45,000 | Shilton (45), Neal (41), Sansom (30), Thompson (42), Martin (5), Mabbutt (2), **Robson** (25), Lee (1), Mariner (29), Woodcock (26), Morley (6) |
| Dec 15 | Wembley, London | LUXEMBOURG | W 9-0 | Blissett 3, Woodcock, Coppell, Hoddle, Chamberlain, Neal, own goal | 35,000 | Clemence (60), Neal (42), Sansom (31), Martin (6), Butcher (11), Mabbutt (3), (Hoddle 14), **Robson** (26), Lee (2), Blissett (2), Coppell (41), (Chamberlain 1), Woodcock (27) |

1983

Home International Championship

DATE	VENUE	OPPONENTS	SCORE	GOALSCORERS	ATTENDANCE	TEAM
Feb 23	Wembley, London	WALES	W 2-1	Butcher, Neal (pen)	24,000	**Shilton** (46), Neal (43), Statham (1), Mabbutt (4), Martin (7), Butcher (12), Lee (3), Blissett (3), Mariner (30), Cowans (1), Devonshire (6)

European Championship Qualifiers

| Mar 30 | Wembley, London | GREECE | D 0-0 | | 48,500 | **Shilton** (47), Neal (44), Sansom (32), Mabbutt (5), Martin (8), Butcher (13), Coppell (42), Lee (4), Francis T (34), Woodcock (28), (Blissett 4), Devonshire (7), (Rix 16) |
| Apr 27 | Wembley, London | HUNGARY | W 2-0 | Francis T, Withe | 55,000 | **Shilton** (48), Neal (45), Sansom (33), Mabbutt (6), Martin (9), Butcher (14), Lee (5), Francis T (35), Withe (7), Blissett (5), Cowans (2) |

Home International Championship

| May 28 | Windsor Park, Belfast | N. IRELAND | D 0-0 | | 22,000 | **Shilton** (49), Neal (46), Sansom (34), Mabbutt (7), Roberts (1), Butcher (15), Hoddle (15), Francis T (36), Withe (8), Blissett (6), (Barnes J 1), Cowans (3) |
| Jun 1 | Wembley, London | SCOTLAND | W 2-0 | Robson, Cowans | 84,000 | Shilton (50), Neal (47), Sansom (35), Lee (6), Roberts (2), Butcher (16), **Robson** (27), (Mabbutt 8), Francis T (37), Withe (9), (Blissett 7), Hoddle (16), Cowans (4) |

Friendlies

Jun 12	Sydney	AUSTRALIA	D 0-0		28,000	**Shilton** (51), Thomas (1), Statham (2), (Barnes J 2), Williams (1), Osman (8), Butcher (17), Barham (1), Gregory (1), Blissett (8), (Walsh 1), Francis T (38), Cowans (5)
Jun 15	Brisbane	AUSTRALIA	W 1-0	Walsh	10,000	**Shilton** (52), Neal (48), Statham (3), (Williams 2), Barham (2), Osman (9), Butcher (18), Gregory (2), Francis T (39), Walsh (2), Cowans (6), Barnes J (3)
Jun 19	Melbourne	AUSTRALIA	D 1-1	Francis T	20,000	**Shilton** (53), (Spink 1), Neal (49), (Thomas 2), Pickering (1), Lee (7), Osman (10), Butcher (19), Gregory (3), Francis T (40), Walsh (3), (Blissett 9), Cowans (7), Barnes J (4)

European Championship Qualifiers

Sep 21	Wembley, London	DENMARK	L 0-1		82,500	Shilton (54), Neal (50), Sansom (36), Lee (8), (Chamberlain 2), Osman (11), Butcher (20), **Wilkins** (55), Gregory (4), Mariner (31), Francis T (41), Barnes J (5), (Blissett 10)
Oct 12	Budapest	HUNGARY	W 3-0	Hoddle, Lee, Mariner	25,000	Shilton (55), Gregory (5), Sansom (37), Mabbutt (9), Martin (10), Butcher (21), **Robson** (28), Lee (9), Mariner (32), Hoddle (17), Blissett (11), (Withe 10)
Nov 16	Luxembourg	LUXEMBOURG	W 4-0	Robson 2, Mariner, Butcher	12,000	Clemence (61), Duxbury (1), Sansom (38), Lee (10), Martin (11), Butcher (22), **Robson** (29), Hoddle (18), Mariner (33), Woodcock (29), (Barnes J 6), Devonshire (8)

1984

Friendly

DATE	VENUE	OPPONENTS	SCORE	GOALSCORERS	ATTENDANCE	TEAM
Feb 29	Paris	FRANCE	L 0-2		45,554	Shilton (56), Duxbury (2), Sansom (39), Lee (11), (Barnes J 7), Roberts (3), Butcher (23), **Robson** (30), Stein (1), (Woodcock 30), Walsh (4), Hoddle (19), Williams (3)

Home International Championship

Apr 4	Wembley, London	N. IRELAND	W 1-0	Woodcock	24,000	Shilton (57), Anderson (11), Kennedy A (1), Lee (12), Roberts (4), Butcher (24), **Robson** (31), Wilkins (56), Woodcock (31), Francis T (42), Rix (17)
May 2	Racecourse Ground, Wrexham	WALES	L 0-1		14,250	Shilton (58), Duxbury (3), Kennedy A (2), Lee (13), Martin (12), (Fenwick 1), Wright (1), **Wilkins** (57), Gregory (6), Walsh (5), Woodcock (32), Armstrong (3), (Blissett 12)
May 26	Hampden Park, Glasgow	SCOTLAND	D 1-1	Woodcock	73,064	Shilton (59), Duxbury (4), Sansom (40), Wilkins (58), Roberts (5), Fenwick (2), Chamberlain (3), (Hunt 1), **Robson** (32), Woodcock (33), (Lineker 1), Blissett (13), Barnes J (8)

Friendlies

Jun 2	Wembley, London	USSR	L 0-2		38,125	Shilton (60), Duxbury (5), Sansom (41), Wilkins (59), Roberts (6), Fenwick (3), Chamberlain (4), **Robson** (33), Francis T (43), (Hateley 1), Blissett (14), Barnes J (9), (Hunt 2)
Jun 10	Rio	BRAZIL	W 2-0	Barnes J, Hateley	56,126	Shilton (61), Duxbury (6), Sansom (42), Wilkins (60), Watson (1), Fenwick (4), **Robson** (34), Chamberlain (5), Hateley (2), Woodcock (34), (Allen 1), Barnes J (10)
Jun 13	Montevideo	URUGUAY	L 0-2		34,500	Shilton (62), Duxbury (7), Sansom (43), Wilkins (61), Watson (2), Fenwick (5), **Robson** (35), Chamberlain (6), Hateley (3), Allen (2), (Woodcock 35), Barnes J (11)
Jun 17	Santiago	CHILE	D 0-0		9,876	Shilton (63), Duxbury (8), Sansom (44), Wilkins (62), Watson (3), Fenwick (6), **Robson** (36), Chamberlain (7), (Lee 14), Hateley (4), Allen (3), Barnes J (12)
Sep 12	Wembley, London	E. GERMANY	W 1-0	Robson	23,951	Shilton (64), Duxbury (9), Sansom (45), Williams (4), Wright (2), Butcher (25), **Robson** (37), Wilkins (63), Mariner (34), (Hateley 5), Woodcock (36), (Francis T 44), Barnes J (13)

World Cup Qualifiers

Oct 17	Wembley, London	FINLAND	W 5-0	Hateley 2, Woodcock, Robson, Sansom	47,234	Shilton (65), Duxbury (10), (Stevens G 1), Sansom (46), Williams (5), Wright (3), Butcher (26), **Robson** (38), (Chamberlain 8), Wilkins (64), Hateley (6), Woodcock (37), Barnes J (14)
Nov 14	Istanbul	TURKEY	W 8-0	Robson 3, Woodcock 2, Barnes J 2, Anderson	40,000	Shilton (66), Anderson (12), Sansom (47), Williams (6), (Stevens G 2), Wright (4), Butcher (27), **Robson** (39), Wilkins (65), Withe (11), (Francis T 45), Woodcock (38), Barnes J (15)

Stoke City's Mark Chamberlain is outmuscled by a Russian defender during their friendly in June 1984. England lost 2-0.

1985

World Cup Qualifier

DATE	VENUE	OPPONENTS	SCORE	GOALSCORERS	ATTENDANCE	TEAM
Feb 27	Windsor Park, Belfast	N. IRELAND	W 1-0	Hateley	28,500	Shilton (67), Anderson (13), Sansom (48), **Wilkins** (66), Martin (13), Butcher (28), Steven (1), Stevens G (3), Hateley (7), Woodcock (39), (Francis T 46), Barnes J (16)

Friendly

DATE	VENUE	OPPONENTS	SCORE	GOALSCORERS	ATTENDANCE	TEAM
Mar 26	Wembley, London	R. of IRELAND	W 2-1	Steven, Lineker	34,793	Bailey (1), Anderson (14), Sansom (49), Steven (2), Wright (5), Butcher (29), **Robson** (40), (Hoddle 20), Wilkins (67), Hateley (8), (Davenport 1), Lineker (2), Waddle (1)

World Cup Qualifiers

DATE	VENUE	OPPONENTS	SCORE	GOALSCORERS	ATTENDANCE	TEAM
May 1	Bucharest	ROMANIA	D 0-0		70,000	Shilton (68), Anderson (15), Sansom (50), Steven (3), Wright (6), Butcher (30), **Robson** (41), Wilkins (68), Mariner (35), (Lineker 3), Francis T (47), Barnes J (17), (Waddle 2)
May 22	Helsinki	FINLAND	D 1-1	Hateley	30,311	Shilton (69), Anderson (16), Sansom (51), Steven (4), (Waddle 3), Butcher (31), Fenwick (7), **Robson** (42), Wilkins (69), Hateley (9), Francis T (48), Barnes J (18)

Rous Cup

DATE	VENUE	OPPONENTS	SCORE	GOALSCORERS	ATTENDANCE	TEAM
May 25	Hampden Park, Glasgow	SCOTLAND	L 0-1		66,489	Shilton (70), Anderson (17), Sansom (52), Hoddle (21), (Lineker 4), Butcher (32), Fenwick (8), **Robson** (43), Wilkins (70), Hateley (10), Francis T (49), Barnes J (19), (Waddle 4)

Mexico City Tournament

DATE	VENUE	OPPONENTS	SCORE	GOALSCORERS	ATTENDANCE	TEAM
Jun 6	Mexico City	ITALY	L 1-2	Hateley	8,000	Shilton (71), Stevens M (1), Sansom (53), Steven (5), (Hoddle 22), Wright (7), Butcher (33), **Robson** (44), Wilkins (71), Hateley (11), Francis T (50), (Lineker 5), Waddle (5), (Barnes J 20)
Jun 9	Mexico City	MEXICO	L 0-1		15,000	Bailey (2), Anderson (18), Sansom (54), Hoddle (23), (Dixon 1), Watson (4), Fenwick (9), **Robson** (45), Wilkins (72), (Reid 1), Hateley (12), Francis T (51), Barnes J (21), (Waddle 6)
Jun 12	Mexico City	W. GERMANY	W 3-0	Robson, Dixon 2	10,000	Shilton (72), Stevens M (2), Sansom (55), Hoddle (24), Wright (8), Butcher (34), **Robson** (46), (Bracewell 1), Reid (2), Dixon (2), Lineker (6), (Barnes J 22), Waddle (7)

Friendly

DATE	VENUE	OPPONENTS	SCORE	GOALSCORERS	ATTENDANCE	TEAM
Jun 16	Los Angeles	USA	W 5-0	Lineker 2, Dixon 2, Steven	10,145	Woods (1), Anderson (19), Sansom (56), (Watson 5), Hoddle (25), (Reid 3), Butcher (35), Fenwick (10), **Robson** (47), (Steven 6), Bracewell (2), Dixon (3), Lineker (7), Waddle (8), (Barnes J 23)

World Cup Qualifiers

DATE	VENUE	OPPONENTS	SCORE	GOALSCORERS	ATTENDANCE	TEAM
Sep 11	Wembley, London	ROMANIA	D 1-1	Hoddle	59,500	Shilton (73), Stevens M (3), Sansom (57), Hoddle (26), Wright (9), Fenwick (11), **Robson** (48), Reid (4), Hateley (13), Lineker (8), (Woodcock 40), Waddle (9), (Barnes J 24)
Oct 16	Wembley, London	TURKEY	W 5-0	Waddle, Lineker 3, Robson	52,500	Shilton (74), Stevens M (4), Sansom (58), Hoddle (27), Wright (10), Fenwick (12), **Robson** (49), (Steven 7), Wilkins (73), Hateley (14), (Woodcock 41), Lineker (9), Waddle (10)
Nov 13	Wembley, London	N. IRELAND	D 0-0		70,500	Shilton (75), Stevens M (5), Sansom (59), **Wilkins** (74), Wright (11), Fenwick (13), Hoddle (28), Bracewell (3), Dixon (4), Lineker (10), Waddle (11)

FACT FILE

Peter Shilton made his 74th appearance against Turkey in 1985 to become England's most capped goalkeeper. He won his 100th cap against Holland in 1988.

1986

Friendlies

DATE	VENUE	OPPONENTS	SCORE	GOALSCORERS	ATTENDANCE	TEAM
Jan 29	Cairo	EGYPT	W 4-0	Steven, Wallace, Cowans, own goal	20,000	Shilton (76), (Woods 2), Stevens M (6), Sansom (60), Cowans (8), Wright (12), Fenwick (14), Steven (8), (Hill 3), **Wilkins** (75), Hateley (15), Lineker (11), (Beardsley 1), Wallace (1)
Feb 26	Tel Aviv	ISRAEL	W 2-1	Robson 2 (1 pen)	15,000	Shilton (77), (Woods 3), Stevens M (7), Sansom (61), Wilkins (76), Martin (14), Butcher (36), **Robson** (50), Hoddle (29), Dixon (5), (Woodcock 42) Beardsley (2), Waddle (12), (Barnes J 25)
Mar 26	Tbilisi	USSR	W 1-0	Waddle	62,500	Shilton (78), Anderson (20), Sansom (62), **Wilkins** (77), Wright (13), Butcher (37), Hoddle (30), Cowans (9), (Hodge 1), Beardsley (3), Lineker (12), Waddle (13), (Steven 9)

Rous Cup

DATE	VENUE	OPPONENTS	SCORE	GOALSCORERS	ATTENDANCE	TEAM
Apr 23	Wembley, London	SCOTLAND	W 2-1	Butcher, Hoddle	68,357	Shilton (79), Stevens M (8), Sansom (63), Hoddle (31), Watson (6), Butcher (38), **Wilkins** (78), (Reid 5), Hodge (2), (Stevens G 4), Hateley (16), Francis T (52), Waddle (14)

Friendlies

DATE	VENUE	OPPONENTS	SCORE	GOALSCORERS	ATTENDANCE	TEAM
May 17	Los Angeles	MEXICO	W 3-0	Hateley 2, Beardsley	45,000	Shilton (80), Anderson (21), Sansom (64), Hoddle (32), Butcher (39), Fenwick (15), **Robson** (51), (Stevens G 5), Wilkins (79), (Steven 10), Hateley (17), (Dixon 6), Beardsley (4), Waddle (15), (Barnes J 26)
May 24	Vancouver	CANADA	W 1-0	Hateley	8,150	Shilton (81), (Woods 4), Stevens M (9), Sansom (65), Hoddle (33), Martin (15), Butcher (40), **Wilkins** (80), (Reid 6), Hodge (3), Hateley (18), Lineker (13), (Beardsley 5), Waddle (16), (Barnes J 27)

FACT FILE

Mark Hateley's diving headed goal against Mexico in Los Angeles in 1986 was too quick for the television cameramen, who missed it completely.

After scoring a hat-trick for England against Poland in the 1986 World Cup, Gary Lineker's sequence of scoring in the next ten matches was: 2 1 2 0 4 0 0 1 1 3, for a total of 17 goals.

D for disgrace day – on 6 June 1986 Ray Wilkins became the first England player to be sent off in the World Cup finals, when he was dismissed against Morocco in Monterrey.

Tottenham's Gary Stevens (right) came on as a substitute for England against Scotland in 1986 with Everton's Gary Stevens (left) already on the pitch. The fans were soon heard chanting, 'There's only two Gary Stevens, Two Gary Stevens'.

THE WORLD CUP FINALS 1986 (MEXICO)

Group Stage – Group F

DATE	VENUE	OPPONENTS	SCORE	GOALSCORERS	ATTENDANCE	TEAM
Jun 3	Monterrey	PORTUGAL	L 0-1		19,998	Shilton (82), Stevens M (10), Sansom (66), Hoddle (34), Butcher (41), Fenwick (16), **Robson** (52), (Hodge 4), Wilkins (81), Hateley (19), Lineker (14), Waddle (17), (Beardsley 6)
Jun 6	Monterrey	MOROCCO	D 0-0		20,200	Shilton (83), Stevens M (11), Sansom (67), Hoddle (35), Butcher (42), Fenwick (17), **Robson** (53), (Hodge 5), Wilkins (82), Hateley (20), (Stevens G 6), Lineker (15), Waddle (18)
Jun 11	Mexico City	POLAND	W 3-0	Lineker 3	22,700	**Shilton** (84), Stevens M (12), Sansom (68), Hoddle (36), Martin (16), Butcher (43), Hodge (6), Reid (7), Beardsley (7), (Waddle 19), Lineker (16), (Dixon 7), Steven (11)

Second Round

Jun 18	Mexico City	PARAGUAY	W 3-0	Lineker 2, Beardsley	98,728	**Shilton** (85), Stevens M (13), Sansom (69), Hoddle (37), Martin (16), Butcher (44), Hodge (7), Reid (8), (Stevens G 7), Beardsley (8), (Hateley 21), Lineker (17), Steven (12)

Quarter-final

Jun 22	Mexico City	ARGENTINA	L 1-2	Lineker	114,580	**Shilton** (86), Stevens M (14), Sansom (70), Hoddle (38), Butcher (45), Fenwick (19), Hodge (8), Reid (9), (Waddle 20), Beardsley (9), Lineker (18), Steven (13), (Barnes J 28)

Group F

	P	W	D	L	F	A	Pts
MOROCCO	3	1	2	0	3	1	4
ENGLAND	3	1	1	1	3	1	3
POLAND	3	1	1	1	1	3	3
PORTUGAL	3	1	0	2	2	4	2

Diego Maradona gets between Peter Reid (left) and Steve Hodge en route to scoring his second goal in Argentina's 2-1 victory in Mexico City in June 1986.

1986 (continued)

Friendly

DATE	VENUE	OPPONENTS	SCORE	GOALSCORERS	ATTENDANCE	TEAM
Sep 10	Stockholm	SWEDEN	L 0-1		15,646	**Shilton** (87), Anderson (22), Sansom (71), Steven (14), (Cottee 1), Martin (17), Butcher (46), Hodge (9), Wilkins (83), Dixon (8), Hoddle (39), Barnes J (29), (Waddle 21)

European Championship Qualifiers

DATE	VENUE	OPPONENTS	SCORE	GOALSCORERS	ATTENDANCE	TEAM
Oct 15	Wembley, London	N. IRELAND	W 3-0	Lineker 2, Waddle	35,300	Shilton (88), Anderson (23), Sansom (72), Hoddle (40), Watson (7), Butcher (47), **Robson** (54), Hodge (10), Beardsley (10), (Cottee 2), Lineker (19), Waddle (22)
Nov 12	Wembley, London	YUGOSLAVIA	W 2-0	Mabbutt, Anderson	60,000	Woods (5), Anderson (24), Sansom (73), Mabbutt (10), Wright (14), **Butcher** (48), Hoddle (41), Hodge (11), (Wilkins 84), Beardsley (11), Lineker (20), Waddle (23), (Steven 15)

1987

Friendly

DATE	VENUE	OPPONENTS	SCORE	GOALSCORERS	ATTENDANCE	TEAM
Feb 18	Madrid	SPAIN	W 4-2	Lineker 4	35,000	Shilton (89), (Woods 6), Anderson (25), Sansom (74), Hoddle (42), Butcher (49), Adams (1), **Robson** (55), Hodge (12), Beardsley (12), Lineker (21), Waddle (24), (Steven 16)

European Championship Qualifiers

DATE	VENUE	OPPONENTS	SCORE	GOALSCORERS	ATTENDANCE	TEAM
Apr 1	Windsor Park, Belfast	N. IRELAND	W 2-0	Robson, Waddle	20,578	Shilton (90), (Woods 7), Anderson (26), Sansom (75), Mabbutt (11), Wright (15), Butcher (50), **Robson** (56), Hodge (13), Beardsley (13), Lineker (22), Waddle (25)
Apr 29	Izmir	TURKEY	D 0-0		25,000	Woods (8), Anderson (27), Sansom (76), Hoddle (43), Adams (2), Mabbutt (12), **Robson** (57), Hodge (14), (Barnes J 30), Allen (4), (Hateley 22) Lineker (23), Waddle (26)

Rous Cup

DATE	VENUE	OPPONENTS	SCORE	GOALSCORERS	ATTENDANCE	TEAM
May 19	Wembley, London	BRAZIL	D 1-1	Lineker	92,000	Shilton (91), Stevens M (15), Pearce (1), Reid (10), Butcher (51), Adams (3), **Robson** (58), Barnes J (31), Beardsley (14), Lineker (24), (Hateley 23) Waddle (27)
May 23	Hampden Park, Glasgow	SCOTLAND	D 0-0		64,713	Woods (9), Stevens M (16), Pearce (2), Hoddle (44), Wright (16), Butcher (52), **Robson** (59), Hodge (15), Hateley (24), Beardsley (15), Waddle (28)

Friendly

DATE	VENUE	OPPONENTS	SCORE	GOALSCORERS	ATTENDANCE	TEAM
Sep 9	Dusseldorf	W. GERMANY	L 1-3	Lineker	50,000	**Shilton** (92), Anderson (28), Sansom (77), (Pearce 3), Hoddle (45), (Webb 1), Adams (4), Mabbutt (13), Reid (11), Barnes J (32), Beardsley (16), Lineker (25), Waddle (29), (Hateley 25)

European Championship Qualifiers

DATE	VENUE	OPPONENTS	SCORE	GOALSCORERS	ATTENDANCE	TEAM
Oct 14	Wembley, London	TURKEY	W 8-0	Lineker 3, Barnes J 2, Robson, Beardsley, Webb	45,528	Shilton (93), Stevens M (17), Sansom (78), Steven (17), (Hoddle 46), Butcher (53), Adams (5), **Robson** (60), Webb (2), Beardsley (17), (Regis 5), Lineker (26), Barnes J (33)
Nov 11	Belgrade	YUGOSLAVIA	W 4-1	Beardsley, Barnes J, Robson, Adams	70,000	Shilton (94), Stevens M (18), Sansom (79), Steven (18), Butcher (54), Adams (6), **Robson** (61), (Reid 12), Webb (3), (Hoddle 47), Beardsley (18), Lineker (27), Barnes J (34)

FACT FILE

Stuart Pearce was the 999th player to play for England when selected against Brazil in 1987. Neil Webb, as substitute for Glenn Hoddle against West Germany, became the 1000th.

1988

Friendlies

DATE	VENUE	OPPONENTS	SCORE	GOALSCORERS	ATTENDANCE	TEAM
Feb 17	Tel Aviv	ISRAEL	D 0-0		6,000	Woods (10), Stevens M (19), Pearce (4), Webb (4), Watson (8), Wright (17), (Fenwick 20), Allen (5), (Harford 1), McMahon (1), **Beardsley** (19), Barnes J (35), Waddle (30)
Mar 23	Wembley, London	HOLLAND	D 2-2	Lineker, Adams	74,590	Shilton (95), Stevens M (20), Sansom (80), Steven (19), Watson (9), (Wright 18), Adams (7), **Robson** (62), Webb (5), (Hoddle 48), Beardsley (20), (Hateley 26), Lineker (28), Barnes J (36)
Apr 27	Budapest	HUNGARY	D 0-0		35,000	Woods (11), Anderson (29), Pearce (5), (Stevens M 21), Steven (20), Adams (8), Pallister (1), **Robson** (63), McMahon (2), Beardsley (21), (Hateley 27), Lineker (29), (Cottee 3), Waddle (31), (Hoddle 49)

Rous Cup

DATE	VENUE	OPPONENTS	SCORE	GOALSCORERS	ATTENDANCE	TEAM
May 21	Wembley, London	SCOTLAND	W 1-0	Beardsley	70,480	Shilton (96), Stevens M (22), Sansom (81), Webb (6), Watson (10), Adams (9), Steven (21), (Waddle 32), Beardsley (22), Lineker (30), Barnes J (37)
May 24	Wembley, London	COLOMBIA	D 1-1	Lineker	25,756	Shilton (97), Anderson (30), Sansom (82), McMahon (3), Wright (19), Adams (10), **Robson** (65), Waddle (33), (Hoddle 50), Beardsley (23), Lineker (31), Barnes J (38), (Hateley 28)

Friendly

DATE	VENUE	OPPONENTS	SCORE	GOALSCORERS	ATTENDANCE	TEAM
May 28	Lausanne	SWITZERLAND	W 1-0	Lineker	10,000	Shilton (98), (Woods 12), Stevens M (23), Sansom (83), Steven (22), (Waddle 34), Wright (20), Adams (11), (Watson 11), **Robson** (66), (Reid 13), Webb (7), Beardsley (24), Lineker (32), Barnes J (39)

Dave Watson outjumps Scotland's Ally McCoist during the Rous Cup match at Wembley in May 1988.

EUROPEAN CHAMPIONSHIP FINALS 1988

Group Stage – Group 2

DATE	VENUE	OPPONENTS	SCORE	GOALSCORERS	ATTENDANCE	TEAM
Jun 12	Stuttgart	R. of IRELAND	L 0-1		53,000	Shilton (99), Stevens M (24), Sansom (84), Webb (8), (Hoddle 51), Wright (21), Adams (12), **Robson** (67), Waddle (35), Beardsley (25), (Hateley 29), Lineker (33), Barnes J (40)
Jun 15	Dusseldorf	HOLLAND	L 1-3	Robson	65,000	Shilton (100), Stevens M (25), Sansom (85), Steven (23), (Waddle 36), Wright (22), Adams (13), **Robson** (68), Hoddle (52), Beardsley (26), (Hateley 30), Lineker (34), Barnes J (41)
Jun 18	Frankfurt	USSR	L 1-3	Adams	53,000	Woods (13), Stevens M (26), Sansom (86), Hoddle (53), Watson (12), Adams (14), **Robson** (69), McMahon (4), (Webb 9), Lineker (35), (Hateley 31), Steven (24), Barnes J (42)

Group 2

	P	W	D	L	F	A	Pts
Soviet Union	3	2	1	0	5	2	5
Netherlands	3	2	0	1	4	2	4
Rep. of Ireland	3	1	1	1	2	2	3
England	3	0	0	3	2	7	0

John Barnes outmanoeuvres the Republic of Ireland's Ray Houghton during their European Championship match in Stuttgart. England lost 1-0.

1988 (continued)

Friendly

Sep 14   Wembley,   DENMARK   W 1-0   Webb   25,837   Shilton (101), (Woods 14), Stevens M (27), Pearce (6),
         London   Rocastle (1), Butcher (55), Adams (15), (Walker 1),
                                                                 Robson (70), Webb (10), Harford (2), (Cottee 4),
                                                                 Beardsley (27), (Gascoigne 1), Hodge (16)

World Cup Qualifier

Oct 19   Wembley,   SWEDEN   D 0-0   65,628   Shilton (102), Stevens M (28), Pearce (7), Webb (11),
         London   Butcher (56), Adams (16), (Walker 2), **Robson** (71),
                                                                 Waddle (37), Beardsley (28), Lineker (36), Barnes J (43),
                                                                 (Cottee 5)

Friendly

Nov 16   Riyadh   SAUDI ARABIA D 1-1   Adams   8,000   Seaman (1), Sterland (1), Pearce (8), Thomas M (1),
                                                                 (Gascoigne 2), Adams (17), Pallister (2), **Robson** (72),
                                                                 Rocastle (2), Beardsley (29), (Smith A 1), Lineker (37),
                                                                 Waddle (38), (Marwood 1)

FACT FILE

In 1988 Brian Marwood played nine minutes of his international debut as substitute against Saudi Arabia; there were just 17 minutes for Peter Davenport; and 18 over two games for Kevin Hector also as substitute in 1973. Davenport with almost his first touch of the ball, set up a goal for Gary Lineker against the Republic of Ireland in 1985.

1989

Friendly

DATE	VENUE	OPPONENTS	SCORE	GOALSCORERS	ATTENDANCE	TEAM
Feb 8	Athens	GREECE	W 2-1	Barnes J, Robson	6,000	Shilton (103), Stevens M (29), Pearce (9), Rocastle (3), Butcher (57), Walker (3), **Robson** (73), Webb (12), Smith A (2), (Beardsley 30), Lineker (38), Barnes J (44)

World Cup Qualifiers

| Mar 8 | Tirana | ALBANIA | W 2-0 | Barnes J, Robson | 25,000 | Shilton (104), Stevens M (30), Pearce (10), Rocastle (4), Butcher (58), Walker (4), **Robson** (74), Webb (13), Barnes J (45), Lineker (39), (Smith A 3), Waddle (39), (Beardsley 31) |
| Apr 26 | Wembley, London | ALBANIA | W 5-0 | Lineker, Beardsley 2, Waddle, Gascoigne | 60,602 | Shilton (105), Stevens M (31), (Parker 1), Pearce (11), Webb (14), Butcher (59), Walker (5), **Robson** (75), Rocastle (5), (Gascoigne 3), Beardsley (32), Lineker (40), Waddle (40) |

Rous Cup

| May 23 | Wembley, London | CHILE | D 0-0 | | 15,628 | Shilton (106), Parker (2), Pearce (12), Webb (15), Butcher (60), Walker (6), **Robson** (76), Gascoigne (4), Clough (1), Fashanu (1), (Cottee 6), Waddle (41) |
| May 27 | Hampden Park, Glasgow | SCOTLAND | W 2-0 | Waddle, Bull | 63,282 | Shilton (107), Stevens M (32), Pearce (13), Steven (25), Butcher (61), Walker (7), **Robson** (77), Webb (16), Fashanu (2), (Bull 1), Cottee (7), (Gascoigne 5), Waddle (42) |

World Cup Qualifier

| Jun 3 | Wembley, London | POLAND | W 3-0 | Lineker, Barnes J, Webb | 69,203 | Shilton (108), Stevens M (33), Pearce (14), Webb (17), Butcher (62), Walker (8), **Robson** (78), Waddle (43), (Rocastle 6), Beardsley (33), (Smith A 4), Lineker (41), Barnes J (46) |

Friendly

| Jun 7 | Copenhagen | DENMARK | D 1-1 | Lineker | 18,400 | Shilton (109), (Seaman 2), Parker (3), Pearce (15), Webb (18), (McMahon 5), Butcher (63), Walker (9), **Robson** (79), Rocastle (7), Beardsley (34), (Bull 2), Lineker (42), Barnes J (47), (Waddle 44) |

1989 (continued)

World Cup Qualifiers

Sep 6	Stockholm	SWEDEN	D 0-0		38,588	Shilton (110), Stevens M (34), Pearce (16), McMahon (6), **Butcher** (64), Walker (10), Waddle (45), Webb (19), (Gascoigne 6), Beardsley (35), Lineker (43), Barnes J (48), (Rocastle 8)
Oct 11	Katowice	POLAND	D 0-0		32,423	Shilton (111), Stevens M (35), Pearce (17), McMahon (7), Butcher (65), Walker (11), **Robson** (80), Rocastle (9), Beardsley (36), Lineker (44), Waddle (46)

Friendlies

Nov 15	Wembley, London	ITALY	D 0-0		67,500	Shilton (112), (Beasant 1), Stevens M (36), Pearce (18), (Winterburn 1), McMahon (8), (Hodge 17), Butcher (66), Walker (12), **Robson** (81), (Phelan 1), Waddle (47), Beardsley (37), (Platt 1), Lineker (45), Barnes J (49)
Dec 13	Wembley, London	YUGOSLAVIA	W 2-1	Robson 2	34,796	Shilton (113), (Beasant 2), Parker (4), Pearce (19), (Dorigo 1), Thomas M (2), (Platt 2), Butcher (67), Walker (13), **Robson** (82), (McMahon 9), Rocastle (10), (Hodge 18), Bull (3), Lineker (46), Waddle (48)

FACT FILE

When Nigel Clough was capped by England against Chile in 1989 he emulated the achievement of George Eastham junior by following in his own father's footsteps. Brian Clough had been capped in 1959-60, George Eastham senior once in pre-war days. Frank Lampard jnr, first capped in 1999, also equalled father Frank snr, who had played for England in 1973.

In 1989 England's 2-1 win over Yugoslavia registered their 100th Wembley win, and captain Bryan Robson's goal in 38 seconds was the fastest there by the national team. Robson's 27 seconds goal in the 1982 World Cup finals against Spain was the quickest for his country overall.

Bryan Robson scores against Yugoslavia in December 1989 to secure England's 100th win at Wembley.

Gary Lineker (on ground) fires England's winner against Brazil at Wembley in March 1990.

1990

Friendlies

DATE	VENUE	OPPONENTS	SCORE	GOALSCORERS	ATTENDANCE	TEAM
Mar 28	Wembley, London	BRAZIL	W 1-0	Lineker	80,000	Shilton (114), (Woods 15), Stevens M (37), Pearce (20), McMahon (10), **Butcher** (68), Walker (14), Platt (3), Waddle (49), Beardsley (38), (Gascoigne 7), Lineker (47), Barnes J (50)
Apr 25	Wembley, London	CZECHOSLOVAKIA	W 4-2	Bull 2, Pearce, Gascoigne	21,342	Shilton (115), (Seaman 3), Dixon (1), Pearce (21), (Dorigo 2), Steven (26), Butcher (69), Walker (15), (Wright 23), **Robson** (83), (McMahon 11), Gascoigne (8), Bull (4), Lineker (48), Hodge (19)
May 15	Wembley, London	DENMARK	W 1-0	Lineker	27,643	Shilton 116, (Woods 16), Stevens M (38), Pearce (22), (Dorigo 3), McMahon (12), (Platt 4), **Butcher** (70), Walker (16), Hodge (20), Gascoigne (9), Waddle (50), (Rocastle 11), Lineker (49), (Bull 5). Barnes J (51)
May 22	Wembley, London	URUGUAY	L 1-2	Barnes J	38,751	Shilton (117), Parker (5), Pearce (23), Hodge (21), (Beardsley 39), Butcher (71), Walker (17), **Robson** (84), Gascoigne (10), Waddle (51), Lineker (50), (Bull 6), Barnes J (52)
Jun 2	Tunis	TUNISIA	D 1-1	Bull	25,000	Shilton (118), Stevens M (39), Pearce (24), Hodge (22), (Beardsley 40), Butcher (72), (Wright 24), Walker (18), **Robson** (85), Gascoigne (11), Waddle (52), (Platt 5), Lineker (51), (Bull 7), Barnes J (53)

THE WORLD CUP FINALS 1990 (ITALY)

Group Stage – Group F

DATE	VENUE	OPPONENTS	SCORE	GOALSCORERS	ATTENDANCE	TEAM
Jun 11	Cagliari	R. of IRELAND	D 1-1	Lineker	35,238	Shilton (119), Stevens M (40), Pearce (25), Gascoigne (12), Butcher (73), Walker (19), **Robson** (86), Beardsley (41), (McMahon 13), Waddle (53), Lineker (52), (Bull 8), Barnes J (54)
Jun 16	Cagliari	HOLLAND	D 0-0		35,267	Shilton (120), Parker (6), Pearce (26), Wright (25), Butcher (74), Walker (20), **Robson** (87), (Platt 6), Gascoigne (13), Waddle (54), (Bull 9), Lineker (53), Barnes J (55)
Jun 21	Cagliari	EGYPT	W 1-0	Wright	34,959	**Shilton** (121), Parker (7), Pearce (27), McMahon (14), Wright (26), Walker (21), Waddle (55), (Platt 7), Gascoigne (14), Bull (10), (Beardsley 42), Lineker (54), Barnes J (56)

Second Round

DATE	VENUE	OPPONENTS	SCORE	GOALSCORERS	ATTENDANCE	TEAM
Jun 26	Bologna	BELGIUM	W 1-0	Platt	34,520	Shilton (122), Parker (8), Pearce (28), Wright (27), **Butcher** (75), Walker (22), McMahon (15), (Platt 8), Gascoigne (15), Waddle (56), Lineker (55), Barnes J (57), (Bull 11)

Quarter-final

DATE	VENUE	OPPONENTS	SCORE	GOALSCORERS	ATTENDANCE	TEAM
July 1	Naples	CAMEROON	W 3-2	Platt, Lineker 2 (2 pens)	55,205	Shilton (123), Parker (9), Pearce (29), Wright (28), **Butcher** (76), (Steven 27), Walker (23), Platt (9), Gascoigne (16), Waddle (57), Lineker (56), Barnes J (58), (Beardsley 43)

Semi-final

DATE	VENUE	OPPONENTS	SCORE	GOALSCORERS	ATTENDANCE	TEAM
July 4	Turin	W. GERMANY	D 1-1	Lineker England lost 4-3 on penalties	62,628	Shilton (124), Parker (10), Pearce (30), Wright (29), **Butcher** (77), (Steven 28), Walker (24), Platt (10), Gascoigne (17), Beardsley (44), Lineker (57), Waddle (58)

Third Place Play-off

DATE	VENUE	OPPONENTS	SCORE	GOALSCORERS	ATTENDANCE	TEAM
July 7	Bari	ITALY	L 1-2	Platt	51,426	**Shilton** (125), Stevens M (41), Dorigo (4), Parker (11), Wright (30), Walker (25), Platt (11), McMahon (16), (Webb 20), Beardsley (45), Lineker (58), Steven (29), (Waddle 59)

Group F

	P	W	D	L	F	A	Pts
ENGLAND	3	1	2	0	2	1	4
NETHERLANDS	3	0	3	0	2	2	3
REP. OF IRELAND	3	0	3	0	2	2	3
EGYPT	3	0	2	1	1	2	2

Although chiefly remembered for his penalty miss against West Germany, Chris Waddle put in some superb performances for England during Italia 90.

FACT FILE

In June 1990 Peter Shilton set a then world record for a goalkeeper by making his 120th appearance against Holland in Cagliari. The previous year he had overtaken Bobby Moore as England's most capped player.

1990 (continued)

Friendly

DATE	VENUE	OPPONENTS	SCORE	GOALSCORERS	ATTENDANCE	TEAM
Sep 12	Wembley, London	HUNGARY	W 1-0	Lineker	51,459	Woods (17), Dixon (2), Pearce (31), (Dorigo 5), Parker (12), Wright (31), Walker (26), Platt (12), Gascoigne (18), Bull (12), (Waddle 60), **Lineker** (59), Barnes J (59)

European Championship Qualifiers

DATE	VENUE	OPPONENTS	SCORE	GOALSCORERS	ATTENDANCE	TEAM
Oct 17	Wembley, London	POLAND	W 2-0	Lineker (pen), Beardsley	77,040	Woods (18), Dixon (3), Pearce (32), Parker (13), Wright (32), Walker (27), Platt (13), Gascoigne (19), Bull (13), (Waddle 61), **Lineker** (60), (Beardsley 46), Barnes J (60)
Nov 14	Lansdowne Road, Dublin	R. of IRELAND	D 1-1	Platt	46,000	Woods (19), Dixon (4), Pearce (33), Adams (18), Wright (33), Walker (28), Platt (14), McMahon (17), Beardsley (47), **Lineker** (61), Cowans (10)

1991

Friendly

DATE	VENUE	OPPONENTS	SCORE	GOALSCORERS	ATTENDANCE	TEAM
Feb 6	Wembley, London	CAMEROON	W 2-0	Lineker 2 (1 pen)	61,075	Seaman (4), Dixon (5), Pearce (34), Steven (30), Wright (34), Walker (29), **Robson** (88), (Pallister 3), Gascoigne (20), (Hodge 23), Wright I (1), Lineker (62), Barnes J (61)

European Championship Qualifiers

DATE	VENUE	OPPONENTS	SCORE	GOALSCORERS	ATTENDANCE	TEAM
Mar 27	Wembley, London	R. of IRELAND	D 1-1	Dixon	77,753	Seaman (5), Dixon (6), Pearce (35), Adams (19), (Sharpe 1), Wright (35), Walker (30), **Robson** (89), Platt (15), Beardsley (48), Lineker (63), (Wright I 2), Barnes J (62)
May 1	Izmir	TURKEY	W 1-0	Wise	25,000	Seaman (6), Dixon (7), Pearce (36), Wise (1), Pallister (4), Walker (31), Platt (16), Thomas (1), (Hodge 24), Smith (5), **Lineker** (64), Barnes J (63)

England Challenge Cup

DATE	VENUE	OPPONENTS	SCORE	GOALSCORERS	ATTENDANCE	TEAM
May 21	Wembley, London	USSR	W 3-1	Smith, Platt 2 (1 pen)	23,789	Woods (20), Stevens M (42), Dorigo (6), Wise (2), (Batty 1), **Wright** (36), (Beardsley 49), Parker (14), Platt (17), Thomas (2), Smith (6), Wright I (3), Barnes J (64)
May 25	Wembley, London	ARGENTINA	D 2-2	Lineker, Platt	44,497	Seaman (7), Dixon (8), Pearce (37), Batty (2), Wright (37), Walker (32), Platt (18), Thomas (3), Smith (7), **Lineker** (65), Barnes J (65), (Clough 2)

Friendlies

DATE	VENUE	OPPONENTS	SCORE	GOALSCORERS	ATTENDANCE	TEAM
Jun 1	Sydney	AUSTRALIA	W 1-0	own goal	35,472	Woods (21), Parker (15), Pearce (38), Batty (3), Wright (38), Walker (33), Platt (19), Thomas (4), Clough (3), **Lineker** (66), (Wise 3), Hirst (1), (Salako 1)
Jun 3	Auckland	NEW ZEALAND	W 1-0	Lineker	17,520	Woods (22), Parker (16), Pearce (39), Batty (4), (Deane 1), Barrett (1), Walker (34), Platt (20), Thomas (5), Walters (1), (Salako 2), **Lineker** (67), Wise (4)
Jun 8	Wellington	NEW ZEALAND	W 2-0	Pearce, Hirst	12,000	Woods (23), Charles (1), **Pearce** (40), Wise (5), Wright (39), Walker (35), Platt (21), Thomas (6), Deane (2), (Hirst 2), Wright I (4), Salako (3)
Jun 12	Kuala Lumpur	MALAYSIA	W 4-2	Lineker 4	45,000	Woods (24), Charles (2), Pearce (41), Batty (5), Wright (40), Walker (36), Platt (22), Thomas (7), Clough (4), **Lineker** (68), Salako (4)
Sep 11	Wembley, London	GERMANY	L 0-1		59,493	Woods (25), Dixon (9), Dorigo (7), Batty (6), Parker (17), Pallister (5), Platt (23), Steven (31), (Merson 1), Smith (8), **Lineker** (69), Salako (5), (Stewart 1)

European Championship Qualifiers

DATE	VENUE	OPPONENTS	SCORE	GOALSCORERS	ATTENDANCE	TEAM
Oct 16	Wembley, London	TURKEY	W 1-0	Smith	50,896	Woods (26), Dixon (10), Pearce (42), Batty (7), Mabbutt (14), Walker (37), Robson (90), Platt (24), Smith (9), **Lineker** (70), Waddle (62)
Nov 13	Poznan	POLAND	D 1-1	Lineker	15,000	Woods (27), Dixon (11), Pearce (43), Gray (1), (Smith 10), Mabbutt (15), Walker (38), Platt (25), Thomas (8), Rocastle (12), **Lineker** (71), Sinton (1), (Daley 1)

FACT FILE

Gary Lineker's fastest goal for England was scored against Malaysia in 1991, 42 seconds from the kick-off.

The king is dead, long live the king. Gary Lineker (left) and Alan Shearer, the two goalscorers against France in February 1992. It was Alan Shearer's first goal for England and very nearly Lineker's last as his England career was coming to an end.

1992

Friendlies

DATE	VENUE	OPPONENTS	SCORE	GOALSCORERS	ATTENDANCE	TEAM
Feb 19	Wembley, London	FRANCE	W 2-0	Shearer, Lineker	58,723	Woods (28), Jones (1), **Pearce** (44), Keown (1), Wright (41), Walker (39), Webb (21), Thomas (9), Clough (5), Shearer (1), Hirst (3), (Lineker 72)
Mar 25	Prague	CZECHOSLOVAKIA	D 2-2	Merson, Keown	6,000	Seaman (8), Keown (2), **Pearce** (45), Rocastle (13), (Dixon 12), Mabbutt (16), (Lineker 73), Walker (40), Platt (26), Merson (2), Clough (6), (Stewart 2), Hateley (32), Barnes J (66), (Dorigo 8)
Apr 29	Moscow	CIS	D 2-2	Lineker, Steven	25,000	Woods (29), (Martyn 1), Stevens M (43), Sinton (2), (Curle 1), Steven (32), (Stewart 3), Keown (3), Walker (41), Platt (27), Palmer (1), Shearer (2), (Clough 7), **Lineker** (74), Daley (2)
May 12	Budapest	HUNGARY	W 1-0	Webb	25,000	Martyn (2), (Seaman 9), Stevens M (44), Dorigo (9), Curle (2), (Sinton 3), Keown (4), Walker (42), Webb (22), (Batty 8), Palmer (2), Merson (3), (Smith 11), **Lineker** (75), Daley (3), (Wright I 5)
May 17	Wembley, London	BRAZIL	D 1-1	Platt	53,428	Woods (30), Stevens M (45), Dorigo (10), (Pearce 46), Steven (33), (Rocastle 14), Keown (5), Walker (43), Daley (4), (Merson 4), Palmer (3), Platt (28), **Lineker** (76), Sinton (4), (Webb 23)
Jun 3	Helsinki	FINLAND	W 2-1	Platt 2	16,101	Woods (31), Stevens M (46), (Palmer 4), Pearce (47), Keown (6), Wright (42), Walker (44), Platt (29), Steven (34), (Daley 5), Webb (24), **Lineker** (77), Barnes J (67), (Merson 5)

EUROPEAN CHAMPIONSHIP FINALS 1992

Group Stage – Pool 2

DATE	VENUE	OPPONENTS	SCORE	GOALSCORERS	ATTENDANCE	TEAM
Jun 11	Malmo	DENMARK	D 0-0		26,385	Woods (32), Keown (7), Pearce (48), Steven (35), Curle (3), (Daley 6), Walker (45), Platt (30), Palmer (5), Smith (12), **Lineker** (78), Merson (6), (Webb 25)
Jun 14	Malmo	FRANCE	D 0-0		26,535	Woods (33), Keown (8), Pearce (49), Batty (9), Palmer (6), Walker (46), Platt (31), Steven (36), Shearer (3), **Lineker** (79), Sinton (5)
Jun 17	Stockholm	SWEDEN	L 1-2	Platt	30,126	Woods (34), Keown (9), Pearce (50), Batty (10), Palmer (7), Walker (47), Daley (7), Webb (26), Platt (32), **Lineker** (80), (Smith 13), Sinton (6), (Merson 7)

POOL 2

	P	W	D	L	F	A	Pts
SWEDEN	3	2	1	0	4	2	5
DENMARK	3	1	1	1	2	2	3
FRANCE	3	0	2	1	2	3	2
ENGLAND	3	0	2	1	1	2	2

Keith Curle (right) ghosts past Denmark's Brian Laudrup in England's opening match of the European Championships in Sweden.

1992 (continued)

Friendly

DATE	VENUE	OPPONENTS	SCORE	GOALSCORERS	ATTENDANCE	TEAM
Sep 9	Santander	SPAIN	L 0-1		22,000	Woods (35), Dixon (13), (Bardsley 1), (Palmer 8), **Pearce** (51), Ince (1), Wright (43), Walker (48), White (1), (Merson 8), Platt (33), Clough (8), Shearer (4), Sinton (7), (Deane 3)

World Cup Qualifiers

DATE	VENUE	OPPONENTS	SCORE	GOALSCORERS	ATTENDANCE	TEAM
Oct 14	Wembley, London	NORWAY	D 1-1	Platt	51,441	Woods (36), Dixon (14), (Palmer 9), **Pearce** (52), Batty (11), Adams (20), Walker (49), Platt (34), Gascoigne (21), Shearer (5), Wright I (6), (Merson 9), Ince (2)
Nov 18	Wembley, London	TURKEY	W 4-0	Gascoigne 2, Shearer, Pearce	42,984	Woods (37), Dixon (15), **Pearce** (53), Palmer (10), Adams (21), Walker (50), Platt (35), Gascoigne (22), Shearer (6), Wright I (7), Ince (3)

1993

World Cup Qualifiers

DATE	VENUE	OPPONENTS	SCORE	GOALSCORERS	ATTENDANCE	TEAM
Feb 17	Wembley, London	SAN MARINO	W 6-0	Platt 4, Palmer, Ferdinand	51,154	Woods (38), Dixon (16), Dorigo (11), Palmer (11), Adams (22), Walker (51), **Platt** (36), Gascoigne (23), Ferdinand (1), Batty (12), Barnes J (68)
Mar 31	Izmir	TURKEY	W 2-0	Platt, Gascoigne	60,000	Woods (39), Dixon (17), (Clough 9), Sinton (8), Palmer (12), Adams (23), Walker (52), **Platt** (37), Gascoigne (24), Wright I (8), (Sharpe 2), Ince (4), Barnes J (69)
Apr 28	Wembley, London	HOLLAND	D 2-2	Barnes J, Platt	73,163	Woods (40), Dixon (18), Keown (10), Palmer (13), Adams (24), Walker (53), **Platt** (38), Gascoigne (25), (Merson 10), Ferdinand (2), Ince (5), Barnes J (70)
May 29	Katowice	POLAND	D 1-1	Wright I	60,000	Woods (41), Bardsley (2), Dorigo (12), Palmer (14), (Wright I 9), Adams (25), Walker (54), **Platt** (39), Gascoigne (26), (Clough 10), Sheringham (1), Ince (6), Barnes J (71)
Jun 2	Oslo	NORWAY	L 0-2		22,250	Woods (42), Dixon (19), Sharpe (3), Pallister (6), Adams (26), Walker (55), (Clough 11), **Platt** (40), Palmer (15), Ferdinand (3), Sheringham (2), (Wright I 10), Gascoigne (27)

US Cup

DATE	VENUE	OPPONENTS	SCORE	GOALSCORERS	ATTENDANCE	TEAM
Jun 9	Boston	USA	L 0-2		37,652	Woods (43), Dixon (20), Dorigo (13), Batty (13), Pallister (7), Palmer (16), (Walker 56), **Ince** (7), Clough (12), Ferdinand (4), (Wright I 11), Barnes J (72), Sharpe (4)
Jun 13	Washington	BRAZIL	D 1-1	Platt	54,118	Flowers (1), Barrett (2), Dorigo (14), Batty (14), (Platt 41), Pallister (8), Walker (57), **Ince** (8), (Palmer 17), Clough (13), (Merson 11), Wright I (12), Sinton (9), Sharpe (5)
Jun 19	Detroit	GERMANY	L 1-2	Platt	62,126	Martyn (3), Barrett (3), Sinton (10), Sharpe (6), (Winterburn 2), Pallister (9), (Keown 11), Walker (58), **Platt** (42), Ince (9), Clough (14), (Wright I 13), Merson (12), Barnes J (73)

World Cup Qualifiers

DATE	VENUE	OPPONENTS	SCORE	GOALSCORERS	ATTENDANCE	TEAM
Sep 8	Wembley, London	POLAND	W 3-0	Ferdinand, Gascoigne, Pearce,	71,220	Seaman (10), Jones (2), **Pearce** (54), Ince (10), Adams (27), Pallister (10), Platt (43), Gascoigne (28), Ferdinand (5), Wright I (14), Sharpe (7)
Oct 13	Rotterdam	HOLLAND	L 0-2		48,000	Seaman (11), Parker (18), Dorigo (15), Palmer (18), (Sinton 11), Adams (28), Pallister (11), **Platt** (44), Ince (11), Shearer (7), Merson (13), (Wright I 15), Sharpe (8)
Nov 17	Bologna	SAN MARINO	W 7-1	Ince 2, Wright I 4, Ferdinand	2,378	Seaman (12), Dixon (21), **Pearce** (55), Ince (12), Pallister (12), Walker (59), Ripley (1), Platt (45), Ferdinand (6), Wright I (16), Sinton (12)

FACT FILE

The England v Germany match at the Pontiac Silverdome in Detroit in 1993 was the first international to be played indoors on natural grass.

1994

Friendlies

DATE	VENUE	OPPONENTS	SCORE	GOALSCORERS	ATTENDANCE	TEAM
Mar 9	Wembley, London	DENMARK	W 1-0	Platt	71,970	Seaman (13), Parker (19), Le Saux (1), Ince (13), (Batty 15), Adams (29), Pallister (13), Anderton (1), Gascoigne (29), (Le Tissier 1), Shearer (8), Beardsley (50), **Platt** (46)
May 17	Wembley, London	GREECE	W 5-0	Anderton, Beardsley, Platt 2 (1 pen), Shearer	23,659	Flowers (2), Jones (3), (Pearce 56), Le Saux (2), Richardson (1), Bould (1), Adams (30), Anderton (2), (Le Tissier 2), Merson (14), Shearer (9), Beardsley (51), (Wright I 17), **Platt** (47)
May 22	Wembley, London	NORWAY	D 0-0		64,327	Seaman (14), Jones (4), Le Saux (3), Ince (14), (Wright I 18), Bould (2), Adams (31), Anderton (3), (Le Tissier 3), **Platt** (48), Shearer (10), Beardsley (52), Wise (6)
Sep 7	Wembley, London	USA	W 2-0	Shearer 2	38,629	Seaman (15), Jones (5), Le Saux (4), Venison (1), Adams (32), Pallister (14), Anderton (4), **Platt** (49), Shearer (11), (Wright I 19), Sheringham (3), (Ferdinand 7), Barnes J (74)
Oct 12	Wembley, London	ROMANIA	D 1-1	Lee	48,754	Seaman (16), Jones (6), (Pearce 57), Le Saux (5), Ince (15), **Adams** (33), Pallister (15), Le Tissier (4), Lee (1), (Wise 7), Shearer (12), Wright I (20), (Sheringham 4), Barnes J (75)
Nov 16	Wembley, London	NIGERIA	W 1-0	Platt	37,196	Flowers (3), Jones (7), Le Saux (6), Wise (8), Howey (1), Ruddock (1), **Platt** (50), Lee (2), (McManaman 1), Shearer (13), (Sheringham 5), Beardsley (53), (Le Tissier 5), Barnes J (76)

FACT FILE

The current England caps on blue velvet are made by Toye Kenning and Spencer. While one cap is still awarded for each friendly, only one is given for such competitions as the World Cup and European Championship.

Alan Shearer lashes home the first of his two goals against the USA at Wembley in September 1994.

1995

Friendly

DATE	VENUE	OPPONENTS	SCORE	GOALSCORERS	ATTENDANCE	TEAM
Feb 15	Lansdowne Road Dublin	R. of IRELAND	L 0-1	(Abandoned after 27 minutes due to crowd trouble)	46,000	Seaman (17), Barton (1), Le Saux (7), Ince (16), Adams (34), Pallister (16), Anderton (5), **Platt** (51), Shearer (14), Beardsley (54), Le Tissier (6)
Mar 29	Wembley, London	URUGUAY	D 0-0		34,849	Flowers (4), Jones (8), Le Saux (8), (McManaman 2), Venison (2), Adams (35), Pallister (17), Anderton (6), **Platt** (52), Beardsley (55), (Barmby 1), Sheringham (6), (Cole 1), Barnes J (77)

Umbro International Trophy

DATE	VENUE	OPPONENTS	SCORE	GOALSCORERS	ATTENDANCE	TEAM
Jun 3	Wembley, London	JAPAN	W 2-1	Anderton, Platt (pen)	21,142	Flowers (5), Neville G (1), Pearce (58), Batty (16), (Gascoigne 30), Scales (1), Unsworth (1), Anderton (7), Beardsley (56), (McManaman 3), Shearer (15), Collymore (1), (Sheringham 7), **Platt** (53)
Jun 8	Elland Road, Leeds	SWEDEN	D 3-3	Sheringham, Platt, Anderton	32,008	Flowers (6), Barton (2), Le Saux (9), **Platt** (54), Cooper (1), Pallister (18), (Scales 2), Anderton (8), Beardsley (57), (Barmby 2), Shearer (16), Sheringham (8), Barnes J (78), (Gascoigne 31)
Jun 11	Wembley, London	BRAZIL	L 1-3	Le Saux	67,318	Flowers (7), Neville G (2), Pearce (59), Batty (17), (Gascoigne 32), Cooper (2), Scales (3), (Barton 3), Anderton (9), **Platt** (55), Shearer (17), Sheringham (9), (Collymore 2), Le Saux (10)

Friendlies

DATE	VENUE	OPPONENTS	SCORE	GOALSCORERS	ATTENDANCE	TEAM
Sep 6	Wembley, London	COLOMBIA	D 0-0		20,038	Seaman (18), Neville G (3), Le Saux (11), Redknapp (1), (Lee 3), **Adams** (36), Howey (2), McManaman (4), Barmby (3), Shearer (18), (Sheringham 10), Gascoigne (33), (Barnes J 79), Wise (9)
Oct 11	Oslo	NORWAY	D 0-0		21,006	Seaman (19), Neville G (4), Pearce (60), Redknapp (2), **Adams** (37), Pallister (19), Lee (4), Barmby (4), (Sheringham 11), Shearer (19), McManaman (5), Wise (10), (Stone 1)
Nov 15	Wembley, London	SWITZERLAND	W 3-1	Pearce, Sheringham, Stone	29,874	Seaman (20), Neville G (5), Pearce (61), Redknapp (3), (Stone 2), **Adams** (38), Pallister (20), Lee (5), Gascoigne (34), Shearer (20), Sheringham (12), McManaman (6)
Dec 12	Wembley, London	PORTUGAL	D 1-1	Stone	28,592	Seaman (21), Neville G (6), Pearce (62), (Le Saux 12), Stone (3), **Adams** (39), Howey (3), Barmby (5), (McManaman 7), Gascoigne (35), Shearer (21), Ferdinand (8), (Beardsley 58), Wise (11), (Southgate 1)

FACT FILE

Andy Cole and Nick Barmby, the first graduates from the FA National School to be fully capped by England, were playing substitutes against Uruguay in 1995.

1996

Friendlies

DATE	VENUE	OPPONENTS	SCORE	GOALSCORERS	ATTENDANCE	TEAM
Mar 27	Wembley, London	BULGARIA	W 1-0	Ferdinand	29,708	Seaman (22), Neville G (7), **Pearce** (63), Stone (4), Southgate (2), Howey (4), McManaman (8), Gascoigne (36), (Lee 6), Ferdinand (9), (Platt 56), Sheringham (13), (Fowler 1), Ince (17)
Apr 24	Wembley, London	CROATIA	D 0-0		33,650	Seaman (23), Neville G (8), Pearce (64), Stone (5), Wright (44), Ince (18), McManaman (9), Gascoigne (37), Fowler (2), Sheringham (14), **Platt** (57)
May 18	Wembley, London	HUNGARY	W 3-0	Anderton 2, Platt	34,184	Seaman (24), (Walker 1), Neville G (9), Pearce (65), **Platt** (58), (Wise 12), Wright (45), (Southgate 3), Ince (19), (Campbell 1), Anderton (10), Lee (7), Ferdinand (10), (Shearer 22), Sheringham (15), Wilcox (1)
May 23	Beijing	CHINA	W 3-0	Barmby 2, Gascoigne	65,000	Flowers (8), (Walker 2), Neville G (10), Neville P (1), Redknapp (4), **Adams** (40), (Ehiogu 1), Southgate (4), Anderton (11), Barmby (6), (Beardsley 59), Shearer (23), (Fowler 3), Gascoigne (38), McManaman (10), (Stone 6)

EUROPEAN CHAMPIONSHIP FINALS 1996

Group Stage – Group A

DATE	VENUE	OPPONENTS	SCORE	GOALSCORERS	ATTENDANCE	TEAM
Jun 8	Wembley, London	SWITZERLAND	D 1-1	Shearer	76,567	Seaman (25), Neville G (11), Pearce (66), Ince (20), **Adams** (41), Southgate (5), Anderton (12), Gascoigne (39), (Platt 59), Shearer (24), Sheringham (16), (Barmby 7), McManaman (11), (Stone 7)
Jun 15	Wembley, London	SCOTLAND	W 2-0	Shearer, Gascoigne	76,864	Seaman (26), Neville G (12), Pearce (67), (Redknapp 5), (Campbell 2), Ince (21), (Stone 8), **Adams** (42), Southgate (6), Anderton (13), Gascoigne (40), Shearer (25), Sheringham (17), McManaman (12)
Jun 18	Wembley, London	HOLLAND	W 4-1	Shearer 2 (1 pen), Sheringham 2	76,798	Seaman (27), Neville G (13), Pearce (68), Ince (22), (Platt 60), **Adams** (43), Southgate (7), Anderton (14), Gascoigne (41), Shearer (26), (Barmby 8), Sheringham (18), (Fowler 4), McManaman (13)

Quarter-final

DATE	VENUE	OPPONENTS	SCORE	GOALSCORERS	ATTENDANCE	TEAM
Jun 22	Wembley, London	SPAIN	D 0-0	(England won 4-2 on penalties)	75,440	Seaman (28), Neville G (14), Pearce (69), Platt (61), **Adams** (44), Southgate (8), Anderton (15), (Fowler 5), Gascoigne (42), Shearer (27), Sheringham (19), (Stone 9), McManaman (14), (Barmby 9)

Semi-final

DATE	VENUE	OPPONENTS	SCORE	GOALSCORERS	ATTENDANCE	TEAM
Jun 26	Wembley, London	GERMANY	D 1-1	Shearer (England lost 6-5 on penalties)	75,862	Seaman (29), Ince (23), Pearce (70), Platt (62), **Adams** (45), Southgate (9), Anderton (16), Gascoigne (43), Shearer (28), Sheringham (20), McManaman (15)

Group A

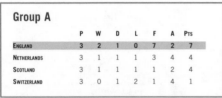

	P	W	D	L	F	A	Pts
ENGLAND	3	2	1	0	7	2	7
NETHERLANDS	3	1	1	1	3	4	4
SCOTLAND	3	1	1	1	1	2	4
SWITZERLAND	3	0	1	2	1	4	1

In one of England's finest victories of recent years, Teddy Sheringham scores England's fourth goal against Holland during their group match at Euro 96.

1996 (continued)

World Cup Qualifiers

DATE	VENUE	OPPONENTS	SCORE	GOALSCORERS	ATTENDANCE	TEAM
Sep 1	Chisinau	MOLDOVA	W 3-0	Gascoigne, Shearer, Barmby	15,000	Seaman (30), Neville G (15), Pearce (71), Ince (24), Pallister (21), Southgate (10), Beckham (1), Gascoigne (44), (Batty 18), **Shearer** (29), Barmby (10), (Le Tissier 7), Hinchcliffe (1)
Oct 9	Wembley, London	POLAND	W 2-1	Shearer 2	74,663	Seaman (31), Neville G (16), Pearce (72), Ince (25), Southgate (11), (Pallister 22), Hinchcliffe (2), Beckham (2), Gascoigne (45), **Shearer** (30), Ferdinand (11), McManaman (16)
Nov 9	Tbilisi	GEORGIA	W 2-0	Ferdinand, Sheringham	48,000	Seaman (32), Campbell (3), Hinchcliffe (3), Ince (26), **Adams** (46), Southgate (12), Beckham (3), Gascoigne (46), Ferdinand (12), (Wright I 21), Sheringham (21), Batty (19)

1997

World Cup Qualifier

DATE	VENUE	OPPONENTS	SCORE	GOALSCORERS	ATTENDANCE	TEAM
Feb 12	Wembley, London	ITALY	L 0-1		75,055	Walker (3), Neville G (17), Pearce (73), Ince (27), Campbell (4), Le Saux (13), Beckham (4), Batty (20), (Wright I 22), **Shearer** (31), Le Tissier (8), (Ferdinand 13), McManaman (17), (Merson 15)

Friendly

DATE	VENUE	OPPONENTS	SCORE	GOALSCORERS	ATTENDANCE	TEAM
Mar 29	Wembley, London	MEXICO	W 2-0	Fowler, Sheringham	48,076	James (1), Keown (12), Pearce (74), Batty (21), (Redknapp 6), Southgate (13), Le Saux (14), Lee (8), **Ince** (28), Fowler (6), Sheringham (22), (Wright I 23), McManaman (18), (Butt 1)

World Cup Qualifier

DATE	VENUE	OPPONENTS	SCORE	GOALSCORERS	ATTENDANCE	TEAM
Apr 30	Wembley, London	GEORGIA	W 2-0	Shearer, Sheringham	71,206	Seaman (33), Neville G (18), Campbell (5), Batty (22), Adams (47), (Southgate 14), Le Saux (15), Beckham (5), Ince (29), (Redknapp 7), **Shearer** (32), Sheringham (23), Lee (9)

Friendly

DATE	VENUE	OPPONENTS	SCORE	GOALSCORERS	ATTENDANCE	TEAM
May 24	Old Trafford	SOUTH AFRICA	W 2-1	Wright I, Lee	52,676	Martyn (4), Neville P (2), **Pearce** (75), Keown (13), Southgate (15), Le Saux (16), (Beckham 6), Redknapp (8), (Batty 23), Gascoigne (47), (Campbell 6), Wright I (24), Sheringham (24), (Scholes 1), Lee (10), (Butt 2)

World Cup Qualifier

DATE	VENUE	OPPONENTS	SCORE	GOALSCORERS	ATTENDANCE	TEAM
May 31	Katowice	POLAND	W 2-0	Shearer, Sheringham	35,000	Seaman (34), Neville G (19), Campbell (7), Ince (30), Southgate (16), Le Saux (17), Beckham (7), (Neville P 3), Gascoigne (48), (Batty 24), **Shearer** (33), Sheringham (25), Lee (11)

Tournoi de France

DATE	VENUE	OPPONENTS	SCORE	GOALSCORERS	ATTENDANCE	TEAM
Jun 4	Nantes	ITALY	W 2-0	Wright I, Scholes	25,000	Flowers (9), Neville P (4), Pearce (76), Keown (14), Southgate (17), Le Saux (18), (Neville G 20), Beckham (8), **Ince** (31), Wright I (25), (Cole 2), Sheringham (26), (Gascoigne 49), Scholes (2)
Jun 7	Montpellier	FRANCE	W 1-0	Shearer	25,000	Seaman (35), Neville G (21), Campbell (8), Neville P (5), Southgate (18), Le Saux (19), Beckham (9), (Lee 12), Gascoigne (50), **Shearer** (34), Wright I (26), (Sheringham 27), Batty (25), (Ince 32)
Jun 10	Paris	BRAZIL	L 0-1		50,000	Seaman (36), Keown (15), (Neville G 22), Campbell (9), Ince (33), Southgate (19), Le Saux (20), Neville P (6), Gascoigne (51), **Shearer** (35), Sheringham (28), (Wright I 27), Scholes (3), (Lee 13)

World Cup Qualifiers

DATE	VENUE	OPPONENTS	SCORE	GOALSCORERS	ATTENDANCE	TEAM
Sep 10	Wembley, London	MOLDOVA	W 4-0	Scholes, Wright I 2, Gascoigne	74,102	**Seaman** (37), Neville G (23), Neville P (7), Batty (26), Southgate (20), Campbell (10), Beckham (10), (Ripley 2), (Butt 3), Gascoigne (52), Ferdinand (14), (Collymore 3), Wright I (28), Scholes (4)
Oct 11	Rome	ITALY	D 0-0		81,200	Seaman (38), Beckham (11), Le Saux (21), Southgate (21), **Adams** (48), Campbell (11), Gascoigne (53), (Butt 4), Batty (27), Wright I (29), Sheringham (29), Ince (34)

Friendly

DATE	VENUE	OPPONENTS	SCORE	GOALSCORERS	ATTENDANCE	TEAM
Nov 15	Wembley, London	CAMEROON	W 2-0	Fowler, Scholes	46,176	Martyn (5), Beckham (12), Hinchcliffe (4), Neville P (8), Southgate (22), (Ferdinand R 1), Campbell (12), McManaman (19), Gascoigne (54), (Lee 14), Fowler (7), Scholes (5), (Sutton 1), **Ince** (35)

1998

Friendlies

DATE	VENUE	OPPONENTS	SCORE	GOALSCORERS	ATTENDANCE	TEAM
Feb 11	Wembley, London	CHILE	L 0-2		65,228	Martyn (6), Lee (15), Neville P (9), (Le Saux 22), Neville G (24), **Adams** (49), Campbell (13), Butt (5), Batty (28), (Ince 36), Dublin (1), Sheringham (30), (Shearer 36), Owen (1)
Mar 25	Berne	SWITZERLAND	D 1-1	Merson	17,100	Flowers (10), Lee (16), Hinchcliffe (5), Southgate (23), Keown (16), Ferdinand R (2), McManaman (20), Ince (37), **Shearer** (37), Merson (16), (Batty 29), Owen (2), (Sheringham 31)
Apr 22	Wembley, London	PORTUGAL	W 3-0	Shearer 2, Sheringham	63,463	Seaman (39), Beckham (13), (Merson 17), Le Saux (23), Neville G (25), (Neville P 10), Adams (50), Campbell (14), Batty (30), Ince (38), **Shearer** (38), Sheringham (32), (Owen 3), Scholes (6)
May 23	Wembley, London	SAUDI ARABIA	D 0-0		63,733	Seaman (40), Anderton (17), Hinchcliffe (6), (Neville P 11), Neville G (26), Adams (51), Southgate (24), Beckham (14), (Gascoigne 55), Batty (31), **Shearer** (39), (Ferdinand 15), Sheringham (33), (Wright I 30), Scholes (7)

King Hassan II Cup

DATE	VENUE	OPPONENTS	SCORE	GOALSCORERS	ATTENDANCE	TEAM
May 27	Casablanca	MOROCCO	W 1-0	Owen	80,000	Flowers (11), Anderton (18), Le Saux (24), Southgate (25), Keown (17), Campbell (15), McManaman (21), Gascoigne (56), Dublin (2), (Ferdinand 16), Wright I (31), (Owen 4), **Ince** (39)
May 29	Casablanca	BELGIUM	D 0-0	(England lost 4-3 on penalties)	25,000	Martyn (7), Neville G (27), (Owen 5), Neville P (12), (Ferdinand R 3), Gascoigne (57), (Beckham 15), Keown (18), **Campbell** (16), (Dublin 3), Lee (17), Butt (6), Ferdinand (17), Merson (18), Le Saux (25)

In a rare display of defensive solidity, England secured the necessary point to qualify for the World Cup finals in 1998 by drawing 0-0 against Italy in Rome. There was even no way past for Demetrio Albertini's free kick.

THE WORLD CUP FINALS 1998 (FRANCE)

Group Stage _ Group G

DATE	VENUE	OPPONENTS	SCORE	GOALSCORERS	ATTENDANCE	TEAM
Jun 15	Marseille	TUNISIA	W 2-0	Shearer, Scholes	54,587	Seaman (41), Anderton (19), Le Saux (26), Southgate (26), Adams (52), Campbell (17), Scholes (8), Batty (32), **Shearer** (40), Sheringham (34), (Owen 6), Ince (40)
Jun 22	Toulouse	ROMANIA	L 1-2	Owen	37,500	Seaman (42), Neville G (28), Le Saux (27), Batty (33), Adams (53), Campbell (18), Anderton (20), Ince (41), (Beckham 16), **Shearer** (41), Sheringham (35), (Owen 7), Scholes (9)
Jun 26	Lens	COLOMBIA	W 2-0	Anderton, Beckham	41,275	Seaman (43), Neville G (29), Le Saux (28), Beckham (17), Adams (54), Campbell (19), Anderton (21), (Lee 18), Ince (42), (Batty 34), **Shearer** (42), Scholes (10), (McManaman 22), Owen (8)

Second Round

DATE	VENUE	OPPONENTS	SCORE	GOALSCORERS	ATTENDANCE	TEAM
Jun 30	St Etienne	ARGENTINA	D 2-2	Shearer (pen), Owen (England lost 4-3 on penalties)	30,600	Seaman (44), Neville G (30), Le Saux (29), (Southgate 27), Beckham (18), Adams (55), Campbell (20), Anderton (22), (Batty 35), Ince (43), **Shearer** (43), Scholes (11), (Merson 19), Owen (9)

Group G

	P	W	D	L	F	A	Pts
ROMANIA	3	2	1	0	4	2	7
ENGLAND	3	2	0	1	5	2	6
COLOMBIA	3	1	0	2	1	3	3
TUNISIA	3	0	1	2	1	4	1

Sol Campbell leaps to score what every Englishman thought was a legitimate winner for 10-man England against Argentina in St Etienne. But the goal was ruled out for a foul by Alan Shearer on the Argentinian keeper.

1998

European Championship Qualifiers

DATE	VENUE	OPPONENTS	SCORE	GOALSCORERS	ATTENDANCE	TEAM
Sep 5	Stockholm	SWEDEN	L 1-2	Shearer	35,394	Seaman (45), Campbell (21), (Merson 20), Le Saux (30), Ince (44), Adams (56), Southgate (28), Anderton (23), (Lee 19), Redknapp (9), **Shearer** (44), Owen (10), Scholes (12), (Sheringham 36)
Oct 10	Wembley, London	BULGARIA	D 0-0		72,974	Seaman (46), Neville G (31), Hinchcliffe (7), (Le Saux 31), Lee (20), Campbell (22), Southgate (29), Anderton (24), (Batty 36), Redknapp (10), **Shearer** (45), Owen (11), Scholes (13), (Sheringham 37)
Oct 14	Luxembourg	LUXEMBOURG	W 3-0	Southgate, Shearer, Owen	8,000	Seaman (47), Ferdinand R (4), Neville P (13), Batty (37), Campbell (23), Southgate (30), Beckham (19), Anderton (25), (Lee 21), **Shearer** (46), Owen (12), Scholes (14), (Wright I 32)

Friendly

DATE	VENUE	OPPONENTS	SCORE	GOALSCORERS	ATTENDANCE	TEAM
Nov 18	Wembley, London	CZECH REPUBLIC	W 2-0	Anderton, Merson	38,535	Martyn (8), Ferdinand R (5), Le Saux (32), Butt (7), **Campbell** (24), Keown (19), Beckham (20), Anderton (26), Dublin (4), Wright I (33), (Fowler 8), Merson (21), (Hendrie 1)

1999

Friendly

DATE	VENUE	OPPONENTS	SCORE	GOALSCORERS	ATTENDANCE	TEAM
Feb 10	Wembley, London	FRANCE	L 0-2		74,111	Seaman (48), (Martyn 9), Dixon (22), (Ferdinand R 6), Le Saux (33), Ince (45), Keown (20), (Wilcox 2), Adams (57), Beckham (21), Redknapp (11), (Scholes 15), **Shearer** (47), Owen (13), (Cole 3), Anderton (27)

European Championship Qualifier

DATE	VENUE	OPPONENTS	SCORE	GOALSCORERS	ATTENDANCE	TEAM
Mar 27	Wembley, London	POLAND	W 3-1	Scholes 3	73,836	Seaman (49), Neville G (32), Le Saux (34), Sherwood (1), Campbell (25), Keown (21), Beckham (22), (Neville P 14), Scholes (16), (Redknapp 12), **Shearer** (48), Cole (4), McManaman (23), (Parlour 1)

Friendly

DATE	VENUE	OPPONENTS	SCORE	GOALSCORERS	ATTENDANCE	TEAM
Apr 28	Budapest	HUNGARY	D 1-1	Shearer	20,000	Seaman (50), Brown W (1), Gray (1), Neville P (15), Batty (38), Ferdinand R (7), (Carragher 1), Keown (22), Butt (8), Sherwood (2), **Shearer** (49), Phillips (1), (Heskey 1), McManaman (24), (Redknapp 13)

European Championship Qualifiers

DATE	VENUE	OPPONENTS	SCORE	GOALSCORERS	ATTENDANCE	TEAM
Jun 5	Wembley, London	SWEDEN	D 0-0		75,824	Seaman (51), Neville P (16), Le Saux (35), (Gray 2), Sherwood (3), Campbell (26), Keown (23), (Ferdinand R 8), Beckham (23), (Parlour 2), Batty (39), **Shearer** (50), Cole (5), Scholes (17)
Jun 9	Sofia	BULGARIA	D 1-1	Shearer	22,000	Seaman (52), Neville P (17), Gray (3), Southgate (31), Campbell (27), Woodgate (1), (Parlour 3), Redknapp (14), Batty (40), **Shearer** (51), Sheringham (38), Fowler (9), (Heskey 2)
Sep 4	Wembley, London	LUXEMBOURG	W 6-0	Shearer 3, McManaman 2, Owen	68,772	Martyn (10), Dyer (1), (Neville G 33), Pearce (77), Batty (41), Keown (24), Adams (58), (Neville P 18), Beckham (24), (Owen 14), Parlour (4), **Shearer** (52), Fowler (10), McManaman (25)
Sep 8	Warsaw	POLAND	D 0-0		17,000	Martyn (11), Neville G (34), (Neville P 19), Pearce (78), Batty (42), Keown (25), Adams (59), Beckham (25), Scholes (18), **Shearer** (53), Fowler (11), (Owen 15), McManaman (26), (Dyer 2)

Friendly

DATE	VENUE	OPPONENTS	SCORE	GOALSCORERS	ATTENDANCE	TEAM
Oct 10	Sunderland	BELGIUM	W 2-1	Shearer, Redknapp	40,897	Seaman (53), (Martyn 12), Dyer (3), (Neville P 20), Guppy (1), Southgate (32), Keown (26), Adams (60), Lampard (1), (Wise 13), Redknapp (15), **Shearer** (54), (Heskey 3), Phillips (2), (Owen 16), Ince (46)

European Championship Qualifiers

DATE	VENUE	OPPONENTS	SCORE	GOALSCORERS	ATTENDANCE	TEAM
Nov 13	Hampden Park, Glasgow	SCOTLAND	W 2-0	Scholes 2	50,132	Seaman (54), Campbell (28), Neville P (21), Ince (47), Keown (27), Adams (61), Beckham (26), Scholes (19), **Shearer** (55), Owen (17), (Cole 6), Redknapp (16)
Nov 17	Wembley, London	SCOTLAND	L 0-1		75,848	Seaman (55), Campbell (29), Neville P (22), Ince (48), Southgate (33), Adams (62), Beckham (27), Scholes (20), (Parlour 5), **Shearer** (56), Owen (18), (Heskey 4), Redknapp (17)

2000

Friendlies

DATE	VENUE	OPPONENTS	SCORE	GOALSCORERS	ATTENDANCE	TEAM
Feb 23	Wembley, London	ARGENTINA	D 0-0		74,008	Seaman (56), Dyer (4), (Neville P 23), Campbell (30), Wise (14), Keown (28), Ferdinand R 9), Southgate (24), Beckham (28), (Parlour 6), Scholes (21), **Shearer** (57), (Phillips 3), Heskey (5), (Cole 7), Wilcox (3)
May 27	Wembley, London	BRAZIL	D 1-1	Owen	73,956	Seaman (57), Neville G (35), Neville P (24), Ince (49), (Parlour 7), (Barmby 11), Keown (29), Campbell (31), Beckham (29), Scholes (22), **Shearer** (58), (Fowler 12), Owen (19), (Phillips 4), Wise (15)
May 31	Wembley, London	UKRAINE	W 2-0	Adams, Fowler	55,975	Martyn (13), Gerrard (1), (Dyer 5), Neville P (25), (Barry 1), Southgate (25), Campbell (32), Adams (63), Beckham (30), Scholes (23), (Barmby 12), **Shearer** (59), Fowler (13), (Heskey 6), McManaman (27)
Jun 3	Valletta	MALTA	W 2-1	Keown, Heskey	10,023	Wright R (1), Neville G (36), Neville P (26), Wise (16), (Ince 50), Keown (30), (Southgate 26), Campbell (33), Beckham (31), (Barry 2), Scholes (24), (McManaman 28), **Shearer** (60), (Heskey 7), Phillips (5), (Fowler 14), Barmby (13)

FACT FILE

In 1999 seven Arsenal players took part in the match between England and France. David Seaman, Lee Dixon, Tony Adams and Martin Keown were in the England side; Nicolas Anelka and Emmanuel Petit started for the French and Patrick Vieira came on as a substitute for Anelka.

The England team to face Brazil at Wembley in May 2000. The match ended in a 1-1 draw.

EUROPEAN CHAMPIONSHIP FINALS 2000

Group Stage – Group A

DATE	VENUE	OPPONENTS	SCORE	GOALSCORERS	ATTENDANCE	TEAM
Jun 12	Eindhoven	PORTUGAL	L 2-3	Scholes, McManaman	33,000	Seaman (58), Neville G (37), Neville P (27), Ince (51), Campbell (34), Adams (64), (Keown 31) Beckham (32), Scholes (25), **Shearer** (61), Owen (20), (Heskey 8), McManaman (29), (Wise 17)
Jun 17	Charleroi	GERMANY	W 1-0	Shearer	30,000	Seaman (59), Neville G (38), Neville P (28), Ince (52), Keown (32), Campbell (35), Beckham (33), Scholes (26), (Barmby 13), **Shearer** (62), Owen (21), (Gerrard 2), Wise (18)
Jun 20	Charleroi	ROMANIA	L 2-3	Shearer (pen), Owen	30,000	Martyn (14), Neville G (39), Neville P (29), Ince (53), Keown (33), Campbell (36), Beckham (34), Scholes (27), (Southgate 27), **Shearer** (63), Owen (22), (Heskey 9), Wise (19), (Barmby 14)

Group A

	P	W	D	L	F	A	Pᴛs
PORTUGAL	3	3	0	0	7	2	9
ROMANIA	3	1	1	1	4	4	4
ENGLAND	3	1	0	2	5	6	3
GERMANY	3	0	1	2	1	5	1

Alan Shearer in familiar pose celebrates an unfamiliar feeling, winning against Germany. His goal was enough to win the match, but England's performance at the European Championships in 2000 was hugely disappointing.

2000 (continued)

Friendly

DATE	VENUE	OPPONENTS	SCORE	GOALSCORERS	ATTENDANCE	TEAM
Sep 2	Paris	FRANCE	D 1-1	Owen	70,000	Seaman (60), Campbell (37), Barry (3), Wise (20), Keown (34), **Adams** (65), (Southgate 28), Beckham (35), Scholes (28), (Owen 23), Cole (8), Barmby (15), (McManaman 30), Anderton (28), (Dyer 6)

World Cup Qualifiers

DATE	VENUE	OPPONENTS	SCORE	GOALSCORERS	ATTENDANCE	TEAM
Oct 7	Wembley, London	GERMANY	L 0-1		76,377	Seaman (61), Neville G (40), (Dyer 7), Le Saux (36), (Barry 4), Southgate (29), Keown (35), **Adams** (66), Beckham (36), (Parlour 8), Scholes (29), Cole (9), Owen (24), Barmby (16)
Oct 11	Helsinki	FINLAND	D 0-0		36,210	Seaman (62), Neville P (30), Barry (5), (Brown W 2), Wise (21), **Keown** (36), Southgate (30), Parlour (9), Scholes (30), Cole (10), Sheringham (39), (McManaman 31), Heskey (10)

Friendly

DATE	VENUE	OPPONENTS	SCORE	GOALSCORERS	ATTENDANCE	TEAM
Nov 15	Turin	ITALY	L 0-1		22,000	James (2), Neville G (41), Barry (6), (Johnson 1), Butt (9), (Carragher 2), Ferdinand R (10), Southgate (31), **Beckham** (37), Parlour (10), (Anderton 29), Heskey (11), (Phillips 6), Barmby (17), Dyer (8), (Fowler 15)

2001

Friendly

DATE	VENUE	OPPONENTS	SCORE	GOALSCORERS	ATTENDANCE	TEAM
Feb 28	Villa Park, Birmingham	SPAIN	W 3-0	Barmby, Ehiogu, Heskey	42,129	James (3), (Martyn 15), Neville P (31), (Neville G 42), Powell (1), (Ball 1), Butt (10), (Lampard 2), Ferdinand R (11), (Ehiogu 2), Campbell (38), **Beckham** (38), (McCann 1), Scholes (31), (Heskey 12), Cole (11), Owen (25), Barmby (18)

World Cup Qualifiers

DATE	VENUE	OPPONENTS	SCORE	GOALSCORERS	ATTENDANCE	TEAM
Mar 24	Anfield, Liverpool	FINLAND	W 2-1	Beckham, Owen	44,262	Seaman (63), Neville G (43), Powell (2), Gerrard (3), Ferdinand R (12), Campbell (39), **Beckham** (39), Scholes (32), Cole (12), (Fowler 16), Owen (26), (Butt 11), McManaman (32), (Heskey 13)
Mar 28	Tirana	ALBANIA	W 3-0	Scholes, Cole, Owen	18,000	Seaman (64), Neville G (44), Cole A (1), Butt (12), Ferdinand R (13), Campbell (40), (Brown W 3), **Beckham** (40), Scholes (33), Cole (13), Owen (27), (Sheringham 40), McManaman (33), (Heskey 14)

Friendly

DATE	VENUE	OPPONENTS	SCORE	GOALSCORERS	ATTENDANCE	TEAM
May 25	Derby	MEXICO	W 4-0	Beckham, Scholes, Fowler, Sheringham	33,597	Martyn (16), (James 4), Neville P (32), Cole A (2), (Powell 3), Gerrard (4), (Butt 13), Ferdinand R (14), (Carragher 3), Keown (37), (Southgate 42), **Beckham** (41), (Cole J 1), Scholes (34), (Carrick 1), Fowler (17), (Sheringham 41), Owen (28), (Smith 1), Heskey (15), (Mills 1)

World Cup Qualifier

DATE	VENUE	OPPONENTS	SCORE	GOALSCORERS	ATTENDANCE	TEAM
Jun 6	Athens	GREECE	W 2-0	Beckham, Scholes,	46,000	Seaman (65), Neville P (33), Cole A (3), Gerrard (5), Ferdinand R (15), Keown (38), **Beckham** (42), Scholes (35), (Butt 14), Fowler (18), (Smith 2), Owen (29), Heskey (16), (McManaman 34)

Friendly

DATE	VENUE	OPPONENTS	SCORE	GOALSCORERS	ATTENDANCE	TEAM
Aug 15	White Hart Lane, London	HOLLAND	L 0-2		35,238	Martyn (17), (James 5), (Wright 2), Neville G (45), (Mills 2), Cole A (4), (Powell 4), Carragher (4), Keown (39), (Ehiogu 3), Brown (4), (Southgate 43), **Beckham** (43), (Lampard 3), Scholes (36), (Carrick 2), Cole (14), (Smith 3), Fowler (19), (Owen 30), Hargreaves (1), (Barmby 20)

World Cup Qualifiers

DATE	VENUE	OPPONENTS	SCORE	GOALSCORERS	ATTENDANCE	TEAM
Sep 1	Munich	GERMANY	W 5-1	Owen 3, Gerrard, Heskey	63,000	Seaman (66), Neville G (46), Cole A (5), Gerrard (6), (Hargreaves 2), Campbell (41), Ferdinand R (16), **Beckham** (44), Scholes (37), (Carragher 5), Heskey (17), Owen (31), Barmby (21), (McManaman 35)
Sep 5	St. James' Park, Newcastle	ALBANIA	W 2-0	Fowler, Owen	51,046	Seaman (67), Neville G (47), Cole A (6), Gerrard (7), (Carragher 6), Campbell (42), Ferdinand R (17), **Beckham** (45), Scholes (38), Heskey (18), (Fowler 20), Owen (32), Barmby (22), (McManaman 36)
Oct 6	Old Trafford, Manchester	GREECE	D 2-2	Sheringham, Beckham	66,009	Martyn (18), Neville G (48), Cole A (7), McManaman (37), Gerrard (8), Keown (40), Ferdinand R (18), **Beckham** (46), Scholes (39), Heskey (19), Fowler (21), (Sheringham 42), Barmby (23), (Cole 15)

Friendly

DATE	VENUE	OPPONENTS	SCORE	GOALSCORERS	ATTENDANCE	TEAM
Nov 10	Old Trafford, Manchester	SWEDEN	D 1-1	Beckham (pen)	64,413	Martyn (19), Neville G (49), (Mills 3), Carragher (7), (Neville P 34), Southgate (44), Ferdinand R (19), **Beckham** (47), Butt (15), Murphy (1), Heskey (20), (Sheringham 43), Phillips (7), (Fowler 22), Scholes (40), (Lampard 4), Sinclair (1), (Anderton 30)

Steven Gerrard scores a magnificent goal against Germany in Munich in September 2001, England's 5-1 victory signalling a surge of optimism amongst England fans in the run up to the World Cup in Korea and Japan.

2002

Friendlies

DATE	VENUE	OPPONENTS	SCORE	GOALSCORERS	ATTENDANCE	TEAM
Feb 13	Amsterdam	HOLLAND	D 1-1	Vassell	48,500	Martyn (20), (James 6), Neville G (50), (Neville P 35), Bridge (1), (Powell 5), Gerrard (9), (Lampard 5), Campbell (43), (Southgate 45), Ferdinand R (20), **Beckham** (48), Ricketts (1), (Phillips 8), Heskey (21), Vassell (1), (Cole J 2), Scholes (41), (Butt 16)
Mar 27	Elland Road, Leeds	ITALY	L 1-2	Fowler	36,635	Martyn (21), (James 7), Mills (4), (Neville P 36), Bridge (2), (Neville G 51), Butt (17), (Hargreaves 3), Campbell (44), (King 1), Southgate (46), (Ehiogu 4), **Beckham** (49), (Murphy 2), Lampard (6), (Cole J 3), Heskey (22), (Fowler 23), Owen (33), (Vassell 2), Sinclair (2), (Sheringham 44)
Apr 17	Anfield, Liverpool	PARAGUAY	W 4-0	Owen, Murphy, Vassell, own goal	42,713	Seaman (68), Neville G (52), (Lampard 7), Bridge (3), (Neville P 37), Butt (18), (Hargreaves 4), Keown (41), (Mills 5), Southgate (47), (Carragher 8), Gerrard (10), (Sinclair 3), Scholes (42), (Murphy 3), Vassell (3), (Sheringham 45), **Owen** (34), (Fowler 24), Dyer 9, (Cole J 4)
May 21	Seoguipo	SOUTH KOREA	D 1-1	Owen	39,876	Martyn (22), (James 8), Mills (6), (Brown 5), Cole A (8), (Bridge 4), Scholes (43), (Cole J 5), Campbell (45), (Keown 42), Ferdinand R (21), (Southgate 48), Murphy (4), (Sinclair 4), Vassell (4), Heskey (23), **Owen** (35), (Sheringham 46), Hargreaves (5)
May 26	Kobe	CAMEROON	D 2-2	Fowler, Vassell	42,000	Martyn (23), (James 9), Brown (6), Bridge (5), Scholes (44), (Mills 7), Campbell (46), (Keown 43), Ferdinand R (22), (Southgate 49), Cole J (6), Vassell (5), (Fowler 25), Heskey (24), (Sinclair 5), **Owen** (36), (Sheringham 47), Hargreaves (6)

FACT FILE

On 17 April 2002, at the age of 22 years 124 days, Michael Owen became the youngest England captain since Bobby Moore. Owen had been the youngest goalscorer at 18 years 164 days against Morocco in 1998.

THE WORLD CUP FINALS 2002 (JAPAN/KOREA)

Group Stage – Group F

DATE	VENUE	OPPONENTS	SCORE	GOALSCORERS	ATTENDANCE	TEAM
Jun 2	Saitama	SWEDEN	D 1-1	Campbell	52,271	Seaman (69), Mills (8), Cole A (9), Scholes (45), Campbell (47), Ferdinand R (23), **Beckham** (50), (Dyer 10), Vassell (6), (Cole J 7), Heskey (25), Owen (37), Hargreaves (7)
Jun 7	Sapporo	ARGENTINA	W 1-0	Beckham (pen)	35,927	Seaman (70), Mills (9), Cole A (10), Butt (19), Campbell (48), Ferdinand R (24), **Beckham** (51), Scholes (46), Heskey (26), (Sheringham 48), Owen (38), (Bridge 6), Hargreaves (8), (Sinclair 6)
Jun 12	Osaka	NIGERIA	D 0-0		44,864	Seaman (71), Mills (10), Cole A (11), (Bridge 7), Butt (20), Campbell (49), Ferdinand R (25), **Beckham** (52), Scholes (47), Heskey (27), (Sheringham 49), Owen (39), (Vassell 7), Sinclair (7)

Second Round

DATE	VENUE	OPPONENTS	SCORE	GOALSCORERS	ATTENDANCE	TEAM
Jun 15	Niigata	DENMARK	W 3-0	Owen, Ferdinand, Heskey	40,582	Seaman (72), Mills (11), Cole A (12), Butt (21), Campbell (50), Ferdinand R (26), **Beckham** (53), Scholes (48), (Dyer 11), Heskey (28), (Sheringham 50), Owen (40), (Fowler 26), Sinclair (8)

Quarter-final

DATE	VENUE	OPPONENTS	SCORE	GOALSCORERS	ATTENDANCE	TEAM
Jun 21	Shizuoka	BRAZIL	L 1-2	Owen	47,436	Seaman (73), Mills (12), Cole A (13), (Sheringham 51), Butt (22), Campbell (51), Ferdinand R (27), **Beckham** (54), Scholes (49), Heskey (29), Owen (41), (Vassell 8), Sinclair (9), (Dyer 12)

Group F

	P	W	D	L	F	A	Pts
SWEDEN	3	1	2	0	4	3	5
ENGLAND	3	1	2	0	2	1	5
ARGENTINA	3	1	1	1	2	2	4
NIGERIA	3	0	1	2	1	3	1

Sol Campbell drives his header into the Swedish net to give England the lead in their opening game of the tournament.

2002 (continued)

Friendly

DATE	VENUE	OPPONENTS	SCORE	GOALSCORERS	ATTENDANCE	TEAM
Sept 7	Villa Park, Birmingham	PORTUGAL	D 1-1	Smith	40,058	James (10), Mills (13), (Bridge 8), Cole A (14), (Hargreaves 9), Gerrard (11), (Dunn 1), Ferdinand (28), (Woodgate 2), Southgate (50), Bowyer (1), (Sinclair 10), Butt (23), (Murphy 5), Smith (4), **Owen** (42), (Cole J 8), Heskey (30)

European Championship Qualifiers

DATE	VENUE	OPPONENTS	SCORE	GOALSCORERS	ATTENDANCE	TEAM
Oct 12	Bratislava	SLOVAKIA	W 2-1	Beckham, Owen	30,000	Seaman (74), Neville G (53), Cole A (15), Gerrard (12), (Dyer 13), Woodgate (3), Southgate (51), **Beckham** (55), Scholes (50), Heskey (31), (Smith 5), Owen (43), (Hargreaves 10), Butt (24)
Oct 16	St Mary's, Southampton	MACEDONIA	D 2-2	Beckham, Gerrard	32,095	Seaman (75), Neville G (54), Cole A (16), Gerrard (13), (Butt 25), Woodgate (4), Campbell (52), **Beckham** (56), Scholes (51), Smith (6), Owen (44), Bridge (9), (Vassell 9)

2003

Friendly

DATE	VENUE	OPPONENTS	SCORE	GOALSCORERS	ATTENDANCE	TEAM
Feb 12	Upton Park, West Ham	AUSTRALIA	L 1-3	Jeffers	34,590	James (11), (Robinson 1), Neville G (55), (Mills 14), Cole A (17), (Konchesky 1), Lampard (8), (Hargreaves 11), Ferdinand (29), (Brown 7), Campbell (53), (King 2), **Beckham** (57), (Murphy 6), Scholes (52), (Jenas 1), Beattie (1), (Vassell 10), Owen (45), (Jeffers 1), Dyer (14), (Rooney 1)

European Championship Qualifiers

DATE	VENUE	OPPONENTS	SCORE	GOALSCORERS	ATTENDANCE	TEAM
Mar 29	Vaduz	LIECHTENSTEIN	W 2-0	Owen, Beckham	3,548	James (12), Neville G (56), Bridge (10), Gerrard (14), (Butt 26), Ferdinand (30), Southgate (52), **Beckham** (58), (Murphy 7), Scholes (53), Heskey (32), (Rooney 2), Owen (46), Dyer (15)
Apr 2	Stadium of Light, Sunderland	TURKEY	W 2-0	Vassell, Beckham (pen)	47,667	James (13), Neville G (57), Bridge (11), Gerrard (15), Ferdinand (31), Campbell (54), **Beckham** (59), Scholes (54), Rooney (3), (Dyer 16), Owen (47), (Vassell 11), Butt (27)

Friendlies

DATE	VENUE	OPPONENTS	SCORE	GOALSCORERS	ATTENDANCE	TEAM
May 22	Durban	SOUTH AFRICA	W 2-1	Southgate, Heskey	48,000	James (14), (Robinson 2), Mills (15), Neville P (38), Gerrard (16), (Barry 7), Ferdinand (32), (Upson 1), Southgate (53), **Beckham** (60), (Jenas 2), Scholes (55), (Cole J 9), Heskey (33), (Vassell 12), Owen (48), Sinclair (11), (Lampard 9)
Jun 3	Walkers Stadium, Leicester	SERBIA & MONTENEGRO	W 2-1	Gerrard, Cole J	30,900	James (15), Mills (16), (Carragher 9), Cole A (18), (Bridge 12), Gerrard (17), (Hargreaves 12), Upson (2), (Barry 8), Southgate (54), (Terry 1), Lampard (10), (Cole J 10), Scholes (56), (Jenas 3), Heskey (34) Vassell 13), **Owen** (49), (Rooney 4), Neville P (39), (Beattie 2)

European Championship Qualifier

DATE	VENUE	OPPONENTS	SCORE	GOALSCORERS	ATTENDANCE	TEAM
Jun 11	Riverside Stadium, Middlesbrough	SLOVAKIA	W 2-1	Owen 2 (1 pen)	35,000	James (16), Mills (17), (Hargreaves 13), Cole A (19), Gerrard (18), Upson (3), Southgate (55), Lampard (11), Scholes (57), Rooney (5), (Vassell 14), **Owen** (50), Neville P (40)

FACT FILE

Against Australia in 2003, Wayne Rooney became England's youngest debutant at 17 years 111 days.

Against Slovakia in 2003, Michael Owen became the youngest player to reach 50 caps at 23 years 179 days.

2003 (continued)

Friendly

DATE	VENUE	OPPONENTS	SCORE	GOALSCORERS	ATTENDANCE	TEAM
Aug 20	Ipswich	CROATIA	W 3-1	Beckham (pen) Owen, Lampard	28,700	James (17), (Robinson 3), Neville P (41), (Mills 18), Cole A (20), (Bridge 13), Butt (28), (Lampard 12), Terry (2), Ferdinand (33), (Upson 4), **Beckham** (61), (Sinclair 12), Scholes (58), (Cole J 11), Heskey (35), (Beattie 3), Owen (51), (Dyer 17), Gerrard (19), (Murphy 8)

European Championship Qualifiers

DATE	VENUE	OPPONENTS	SCORE	GOALSCORERS	ATTENDANCE	TEAM
Sept 6	Skopje	MACEDONIA	W 2-1	Rooney, Beckham (pen)	20,500	James (18), Neville G (58), Cole A (21), Butt (29), Terry (3), Campbell (55), **Beckham** (62), Lampard (13), (Heskey 36), Rooney (6), (Neville P 42), Owen (52), (Dyer 18), Hargreaves (14)
Sept 10	Old Trafford, Manchester	LIECHTENSTEIN	W 2-0	Owen, Rooney	64,931	James (19), Neville G (59), Bridge (14), Gerrard (20), (Neville P 43), Terry (4), Upson (5), **Beckham** (63), (Hargreaves 15), Rooney (7), (Cole J 12), Owen (53), Beattie (4), Lampard (14)
Oct 11	Istanbul	TURKEY	D 0-0		42,000	James (20), Neville G (60), Cole A (22), Butt (30), Terry (5), Campbell (56), **Beckham** (64), Gerrard (21), Heskey (37), (Vassell 15), Rooney (8), (Dyer 19), Scholes (59), (Lampard 15)

Friendly

DATE	VENUE	OPPONENTS	SCORE	GOALSCORERS	ATTENDANCE	TEAM
Nov 15	Old Trafford, Manchester	DENMARK	L 2-3	Rooney, Cole J	64,159	James (21), (Robinson 4), Neville G (61), Johnson 1), Cole A (23), (Bridge 15), Butt (31), (Neville P 44), Terry (6), Upson (6), **Beckham** (65), (Jenas 4), Lampard (16), Heskey (38), (Beattie 5), Rooney (9), (Parker 1), Cole J (13), (Murphy 9)

Michael Owen gives England the lead in the European Championship qualifier against Liechtenstein in September 2003.

2004

Friendlies

DATE	VENUE	OPPONENTS	SCORE	GOALSCORERS	ATTENDANCE	TEAM
Feb 18	Faro-Loule	PORTUGAL	D 1-1	King	27,000	James (22), Neville P (45), (Mills 19), Cole A (24), (Bridge 16), (Carragher 10), Butt (32), (Jenas 5), Southgate (56), King (3), **Beckham** (66), (Hargreaves 16), Rooney (10), (Heskey 39), Owen (54), (Smith 7), Scholes (60), (Dyer 20), Lampard (17), (Cole J 14)
Mar 31	Gothenburg	SWEDEN	L 0-1		40,464	James (23), Neville P (46), Carragher (11), Butt (33), (Parker 2), Terry (7), (Gardner 1), Woodgate (5), (Southgate 57), Hargreaves (17), (Jenas 6), **Gerrard** (22), (Cole J 15), Rooney (11), (Smith 8), Vassell (16), (Defoe 1), Thompson (1), (Heskey 40)
Jun 1	City of Manchester Stadium	JAPAN	D 1-1	Owen	38,581	James (24), Neville G (62), (Neville P 47), Cole A (25), Gerrard (23), (Hargreaves 18), Terry (8), (King 4), Campbell (57), **Beckham** (67), (Cole J 16), Lampard (18), (Butt 34), Rooney (12), (Heskey 41), Owen (55), (Vassell 17), Scholes (61), (Dyer 21)
Jun 5	City of Manchester Stadium	ICELAND	W 6-1	Lampard, Rooney 2 Vassell 2, Bridge	43,500	Robinson (5), (Walker 4), Neville G (63), (Neville P 48), Cole A (26), (Bridge 17), Gerrard 24 (Hargreaves 19), Carragher (12), (Defoe 2), Campbell (58), (King 5), **Beckham** (68), (Dyer 22), Lampard (19), (Butt 35), Rooney (13), (Vassell 18), Owen (56), (Heskey 42), Scholes (62), (Cole J 17)

EUROPEAN CHAMPIONSHIP FINALS 2004

Group Stage – Group B

DATE	VENUE	OPPONENTS	SCORE	GOALSCORERS	ATTENDANCE	TEAM
Jun 13	Estadio Da Luz, Lisbon	FRANCE	L 1-2	Lampard	62,487	James (25), Neville G (64), Cole A (27), Gerrard (25), Campbell (59), King (6), **Beckham** (69), Lampard (20), Rooney (14), (Heskey 43), Owen (57), Vassell 19), Scholes (63), (Hargreaves 20)
Jun 17	Coimbra	SWITZERLAND	W 3-0	Rooney 2, Gerrard	30,616	James (26), Neville G (65), Cole A (28), Gerrard (26), Terry (9), Campbell (60), **Beckham** (70), Lampard (21), Rooney (15), (Dyer 23), Owen (58), (Vassell 20), Scholes (64), (Hargreaves 21)
Jun 21	Estadio Da Luz, Lisbon	CROATIA	W 4-2	Scholes, Rooney 2, Lampard	63,000	James (27), Neville G (66), Cole A (29), Gerrard (27), Terry (10), Campbell (61), **Beckham** (71), Lampard (22), (Neville P 49), Rooney (16), (Vassell 21), Owen (59), Scholes (65), (King 7)

Group B

	P	W	D	L	F	A	Pts
FRANCE	3	2	1	0	7	4	7
ENGLAND	3	2	0	1	8	4	6
CROATIA	3	0	2	1	4	6	2
SWITZERLAND	3	0	1	2	1	6	1

Quarter-final

DATE	VENUE	OPPONENTS	SCORE	GOALSCORERS	ATTENDANCE	TEAM
Jun 24	Estadio Da Luz, Lisbon	PORTUGAL	D 2-2	Owen, Lampard England lost 6-5 on penalties	62,564	James (28), Neville G (67), Cole A (30), Gerrard (28), (Hargreaves 22), Terry (11), Campbell (62), **Beckham** (72), Lampard (23), Rooney (17), (Vassell 22), Owen (60), Scholes (66), (Neville P 50)

FACT FILE

Wayne Rooney, at 17 years 317 days became England's youngest ever goalscorer. In Euro 2004, he was the competition's youngest ever marksman at the age of 18 years 236 days for four days, until Johan Vonlanthen (Switzerland) set a new record when he scored against France.

Frank Lampard scores to make it 2-2 in extra time against Portugal and take the quarter-final to penalties.

England Appearances (as at July 2004)

Bury, L. (Cambridge University, Old Etonians) 2
Butcher, T. (Ipswich T, Rangers) 77
Butler, J.D. (Arsenal) 1
Butler, W. (Bolton W) 1
Butt, N. (Manchester U) 35
Byrne, G. (Liverpool) 2
Byrne, J.J. (C Palace), West Ham U 11
Byrne, R.W. (Manchester U) 33

Callaghan, I.R. (Liverpool) 4
Calvey, J. (Nottingham F) 1
Campbell, A.F. (Blackburn R, Huddersfield T) 8
Campbell, S. (Tottenham H, Arsenal) 62
Camsell, G.H. (Middlesbrough) 9
Capes, A.J. (Stoke C) 1
Carr, J. (Middlesbrough) 2
Carr, J. (Newcastle U) 2
Carr, W.H. (Owlerton, Sheffield) 1
Carragher, J.L. (Liverpool) 12
Carrick, M. (West Ham U) 2
Carter, H.S. (Sunderland, Derby Co) 13
Carter, J.H. (WBA) 3
Catlin, A.E. (Sheffield W) 5
Chadwick, A. (Southampton) 2
Chadwick, E. (Everton) 7
Chamberlain, M (Stoke C) 8
Chambers, H. (Liverpool) 8
Channon, M.R. (Southampton, Manchester C) 46
Charles, G.A. (Nottingham F) 2
Charlton, J. (Leeds U) 35
Charlton, R. (Manchester U) 106
Charnley, R.O. (Blackpool) 1
Charsley, C.C. (Small Heath) 1
Chedgzoy, S. (Everton) 8
Chenery, C.J. (C Palace) 3
Cherry, T.J. (Leeds U) 27
Chilton, A. (Manchester U) 2
Chippendale, H. (Blackburn R) 1
Chivers, M. (Tottenham H) 24
Christian, E. (Old Etonians) 1
Clamp, E. (Wolverhampton W) 4
Clapton, D.R. (Arsenal) 1
Clare, T. (Stoke C) 4
Clarke, A.J. (Leeds U) 19
Clarke, H.A. (Tottenham H) 1
Clay, T. (Tottenham H) 4
Clayton, R. (Blackburn R) 35
Clegg, J.C. (Sheffield W) 1
Clegg, W.E. (Sheffield W, Sheffield Albion) 2
Clemence, R.N. (Liverpool, Tottenham H) 61
Clement, D.T. (QPR) 5
Clough, B.H. (Middlesbrough) 2
Clough, N.H. (Nottingham F) 14
Coates, R. (Burnley, Tottenham H) 4
Cobbold, W.N. (Cambridge University, Old Carthusians) 9
Cock, J.G. (Huddersfield T, Chelsea) 2
Cockburn, H. (Manchester U) 13
Cohen, G.R. (Fulham) 37
Cole, A. (Manchester U) 15
Cole, A. (Arsenal) 30
Cole, J.J. (West Ham U, Chelsea) 17
Colclough, H. (C Palace) 1
Coleman, E.H. (Dulwich Hamlet) 1
Coleman, J. (Woolwich Arsenal) 1
Collymore, S.V. (Nottingham F, Aston Villa) 3

Common, A. (Sheffield U, Middlesbrough) 3
Compton, L.H. (Arsenal) 2
Conlin, J. (Bradford C) 1
Connelly, J.M. (Burnley, Manchester U) 20
Cook, T.E.R. (Brighton) 1
Cooper, C.T. (Nottingham F) 2
Cooper, N.C. (Cambridge University) 1
Cooper, T. (Derby Co) 15
Cooper, T. (Leeds U) 20
Coppell, S.J. (Manchester U) 42
Copping, W. (Leeds U, Arsenal, Leeds U) 20
Corbett, B.O. (Corinthians) 1
Corbett, R. (Old Malvernians) 1
Corbett, W.S. (Birmingham) 3
Corrigan, J.T. (Manchester C) 9
Cottee, A.R. (West Ham U, Everton) 7
Cotterill, G.H. (Cambridge University, Old Brightonians) 4
Cottle, J.R. (Bristol C) 1
Cowan, S. (Manchester C) 3
Cowans, G. (Aston Villa, Bari, Aston Villa) 10
Cowell, A. (Blackburn R) 1
Cox, J. (Liverpool) 3
Cox, J.D. (Derby Co) 1
Crabtree, J.W. (Burnley, Aston Villa) 14
Crawford, J.F. (Chelsea) 1
Crawford, R. (Ipswich T) 2
Crawshaw, T.H. (Sheffield W) 10
Crayston, W.J. (Arsenal) 8
Creek, F.N.S. (Corinthians) 1
Cresswell, W. (South Shields, Sunderland, Everton) 7
Crompton, R. (Blackburn R) 41
Crooks, S.D. (Derby Co) 26
Crowe, C. (Wolverhampton W) 1
Cuggy, F. (Sunderland) 2
Cullis, S. (Wolverhampton W) 12
Cunliffe, A. (Blackburn R) 2
Cunliffe, D. (Portsmouth) 1
Cunliffe, J.N. (Everton) 1
Cunningham, L. (WBA, Real Madrid) 6
Curle, K. (Manchester C) 3
Currey, E.S. (Oxford University) 2
Currie, A.W. (Sheffield U, Leeds U) 17
Cursham, A.W. (Notts Co) 6
Cursham, H.A. (Notts Co) 8

Daft, H.B. (Notts Co) 5
Daley, A.M. (Aston Villa) 7
Danks, T. (Nottingham F) 1
Davenport, P. (Nottingham F) 1
Davenport, J.K. (Bolton W) 2
Davis, G. (Derby Co) 2
Davis, H. (Sheffield W) 3
Davison, J.E. (Sheffield W) 1
Dawson, J. (Burnley) 2
Day, S.H. (Old Malvernians) 3
Dean, W.R. (Everton) 16
Deane, B.C. (Sheffield U) 3
Deeley, N.V. (Wolverhampton W) 2
Defoe, J.C. (Tottenham H) 2
Devey, J.H.G. (Aston Villa) 2
Devonshire, A. (West Ham U) 8
Dewhurst, F. (Preston NE) 9
Dewhurst, G.P. (Liverpool Ramblers) 1
Dickinson, J.W. (Portsmouth) 48
Dimmock, J.H. (Tottenham H 3
Ditchburn, E.G. (Tottenham H) 6

Dix, R.W. (Derby Co) 1
Dixon, J.A. (Notts Co) 1
Dixon, K.M. (Chelsea) 8
Dixon, L.M. (Arsenal) 22
Dobson, A.T.C. (Notts Co) 4
Dobson, C.F. (Notts Co) 1
Dobson, J.M. (Burnley, Everton) 5
Doggart, A.G. (Corinthians) 1
Dorigo, A.R. (Chelsea, Leeds U) 15
Dorrell, A.R. (Aston Villa) 4
Douglas, B. (Blackburn R) 36
Downs, R.W. (Everton) 1
Doyle, M. (Manchester C) 5
Drake, E.J. (Arsenal) 5
Dublin, D. (Coventry C, Aston Villa) 4
Ducat, A. (Woolwich Arsenal, Aston Villa) 6
Dunn, A.T.B. (Cambridge University, Old Etonians) 4
Dunn, D.J.I. (Blackburn R) 1
Duxbury, M. (Manchester U) 10
Dyer, K.C. (Newcastle U) 23

Earle, S.G.J. (Clapton, West Ham U) 2
Eastham, G. (Arsenal) 19
Eastham, G.R. (Bolton W) 1
Eckersley, W. (Blackburn R) 17
Edwards, D. (Manchester U) 18
Edwards, J.H. (Shropshire Wanderers) 1
Edwards, W. (Leeds U) 16
Ehiogu, U. (Aston Villa, Middlesbrough) 4
Ellerington, W. (Southampton) 2
Elliott, G.W. (Middlesbrough) 3
Elliott, W.H. (Burnley) 5
Evans, R.E. (Sheffield U) 4
Ewer, F.H. (Casuals) 2

Fairclough, P. (Old Foresters) 1
Fairhurst, D. (Newcastle U) 1
Fantham, J. (Sheffield W) 1
Fashanu, J. (Wimbledon) 2
Felton, W. (Sheffield W) 1
Fenton, M. (Middlesbrough) 1
Fenwick, T. (QPR, Tottenham H) 20
Ferdinand, L. (QPR, Newcastle U, Tottenham H) 17
Ferdinand, R.G. (West Ham U, Leeds U, Manchester U) 33
Field, E. (Clapham Rovers) 2
Finney, T. (Preston NE) 76
Fleming, H.J. (Swindon T) 11
Fletcher, A. (Wolverhampton W) 2
Flowers, R. (Wolverhampton W) 49
Flowers, T.D. (Southampton, Blackburn R) 11
Forman, Frank (Nottingham F) 9
Forman, F.R. (Nottingham F) 3
Forrest, J.H. (Blackburn R) 11
Fort, J. (Millwall) 1
Foster, R.E. (Oxford University, Corinthians) 5
Foster, S. (Brighton & HA) 3
Foulke, W.J. (Sheffield U) 1
Foulkes, W.A. (Manchester U) 1
Fowler, R.B. (Liverpool, Leeds U) 26
Fox, F.S. (Millwall) 1
Francis, G.C.J. (QPR) 12
Francis, T. (Birmingham C, Nottingham F, Manchester C, Sampdoria) 52

Kail, E.I.L. (Dulwich Hamlet) 3
Kay, A.H. (Everton) 1
Kean, F.W. (Sheffield W, Bolton W) 9
Keegan, J.K. (Liverpool, SV Hamburg, Southampton) 63
Keen, E.R.L. (Derby Co) 4
Kelly, R. (Burnley, Sunderland, Huddersfield T) 14
Kennedy, A. (Liverpool) 2
Kennedy, R. (Liverpool) 17
Kenyon-Slaney, W.S. (Wanderers) 1
Keown, M.R. (Everton, Arsenal) 43
Kevan, D.T. (WBA) 14
Kidd, B. (Manchester U) 2
King, L.B. (Tottenham H) 7
King, R.S. (Oxford University) 1
Kingsford, R.K. (Wanderers) 1
Kingsley, M. (Newcastle U) 1
Kinsey, G. (Wolverhampton W, Derby Co) 4
Kirchen, A.J. (Arsenal) 3
Kirton, W.J. (Aston Villa) 1
Knight, A.E. (Portsmouth) 1
Knowles, C. (Tottenham H) 4
Konchesky, P.M. (Charlton Ath) 1

Labone, B.L. (Everton) 26
Lampard, F.J. (West Ham U, Chelsea) 23
Lampard, F.R.G. (West Ham U) 2
Langley, E.J. (Fulham) 3
Langton, R. (Blackburn R, Preston NE, Bolton W) 11
Latchford, R.D. (Everton) 12
Latheron, E.G. (Blackburn R) 2
Lawler, C. (Liverpool) 4
Lawton, T. (Everton, Chelsea, Notts Co) 23
Leach, T. (Sheffield W) 2
Leake, A. (Aston Villa) 5
Lee, E.A. (Southampton) 1
Lee, F.H. (Manchester C) 27
Lee, J. (Derby Co) 1
Lee, R.M. (Newcastle U) 21
Lee, S. (Liverpool) 14
Leighton, J.E. (Nottingham F) 1
Le Saux, G.P. (Blackburn R, Chelsea) 36
Le Tissier, M.P. (Southampton) 8
Lilley, H.E. (Sheffield U) 1
Linacre, H.J. (Nottingham F) 2
Lindley, T. (Cambridge University, Nottingham F) 13
Lindsay, A. (Liverpool) 4
Lindsay, W. (Wanderers) 1
Lineker, G. (Leicester C, Everton, Barcelona, Tottenham H) 80
Lintott, E.H. (QPR, Bradford C) 7
Lipsham, H.B. (Sheffield U) 1
Little, B. (Aston Villa) 1
Lloyd, L.V. (Liverpool, Nottingham F) 4
Lockett, A. (Stoke C) 1
Lodge, L.V. (Cambridge University, Corinthians) 5
Lofthouse, J.M. (Blackburn R, Accrington, Blackburn R) 7
Lofthouse, N. (Bolton W) 33
Longworth, E. (Liverpool), 5
Lowder, A. (Wolverhampton W) 1
Lowe, E. (Aston Villa) 3
Lucas, T. (Liverpool) 3

Luntley, E. (Nottingham F) 2
Lyttelton, Hon. A. (Cambridge University) 1
Lyttelton, Hon. E. (Cambridge University) 1

McCall, J. (Preston NE) 5
McCann, G.P. (Sunderland) 1
McDermott, T. (Liverpool) 25
McDonald, C.A. (Burnley) 8
McFarland, R.L. (Derby Co) 28
McGarry, W.H. (Huddersfield T) 4
McGuinness, W. (Manchester U) 2
McInroy, A. (Sunderland) 1
McMahon, S. (Liverpool) 17
McManaman, S. (Liverpool, Real Madrid) 37
McNab, R. (Arsenal) 4
McNeal, R. (WBA) 2
McNeil, M. (Middlesbrough) 9
Mabbutt, G. (Tottenham H) 16
Macaulay, R.H. (Cambridge University) 1
Macdonald, M. (Newcastle U) 14
Macrae, S. (Notts Co) 5
Maddison, F.B. (Oxford University) 1
Madeley, P.E. (Leeds U) 24
Magee, T.P. (WBA) 5
Makepeace, H. (Everton) 4
Male, C.G. (Arsenal) 19
Mannion, W.J. (Middlesbrough) 26
Mariner, P. (Ipswich T, Arsenal) 35
Marsden, J.T. (Darwen) 1
Marsden, W. (Sheffield W) 3
Marsh, R. W. (QPR, Manchester C) 9
Marshall, T. (Darwen) 2
Martin, A. (West Ham U) 17
Martin, H. (Sunderland) 1
Martyn, A.N. (C Palace, Leeds U) 23
Marwood, B. (Arsenal) 1
Maskrey, H.M. (Derby Co) 1
Mason, C. (Wolverhampton W) 3
Matthews, R.D. (Coventry C) 5
Matthews, S. (Stoke C, Blackpool) 54
Matthews, V. (Sheffield U) 2
Maynard, W J. (1st Surrey Rifles) 2
Meadows, J. (Manchester C) 1
Medley, L.D. (Tottenham H) 6
Meehan, T. (Chelsea) 1
Melia, J. (Liverpool) 2
Mercer, D.W. (Sheffield U) 2
Mercer, J. (Everton) 5
Merrick, G.H. (Birmingham C) 23
Merson, P.C. (Arsenal, Middlesbrough, Aston Villa) 21
Metcalfe, V. (Huddersfield T) 2
Mew, J.W. (Manchester U) 1
Middleditch, B. (Corinthians) 1
Milburn, J.E.T. (Newcastle U) 13
Miller, B.G. (Burnley) 1
Miller, H.S. (Charlton Ath) 1
Mills, D.J. (Leeds U) 19
Mills, G.R. (Chelsea) 3
Mills, M.D. (Ipswich T) 42
Milne, G. (Liverpool) 14
Milton, C.A. (Arsenal) 1
Milward, A. (Everton) 4
Mitchell, C. (Upton Park) 5
Mitchell, J.F. (Manchester C) 1
Moffat, H. (Oldham Ath) 1
Molyneux, G. (Southampton) 4
Moon, W.R. (Old Westminsters) 7
Moore, H.T. (Notts Co) 2
Moore, J. (Derby Co) 1

Moore, R.F. (West Ham U) 108
Moore, W.G.B. (West Ham U) 1
Mordue, J. (Sunderland) 2
Morice, C.J. (Barnes) 1
Morley, A. (Aston Villa) 6
Morley, H. (Notts Co) 1
Morren, T. (Sheffield U) 1
Morris, F. (WBA) 2
Morris, J. (Derby Co) 3
Morris, W.W. (Wolverhampton W) 3
Morse, H. (Notts Co) 1
Mort, T. (Aston Villa) 3
Morten, A. (C Palace) 1
Mortensen, S.H. (Blackpool) 25
Morton, J.R. (West Ham U) 1
Mosforth, W. (Sheffield W, Sheffield Albion, Sheffield W) 9
Moss, F. (Arsenal) 4
Moss, F. (Aston Villa) 5
Mosscrop, E. (Burnley) 2
Mozley, B. (Derby Co) 3
Mullen, J. (Wolverhampton W) 12
Mullery, A.P. (Tottenham H) 35
Murphy, D.B. (Liverpool) 9

Neal, P.G. (Liverpool) 50
Needham, E. (Sheffield U) 16
Neville, G.A. (Manchester U) 67
Neville, P.J. (Manchester U) 50
Newton, K.R. (Blackburn R, Everton) 27
Nicholls, J. (WBA) 2
Nicholson, W.E. (Tottenham H) 1
Nish, D.J. (Derby Co) 5
Norman, M. (Tottenham H) 23
Nuttall, H. (Bolton W) 3

Oakley, W.J. (Oxford University, Corinthians) 16
O'Dowd, J.P. (Chelsea) 3
O'Grady, M. (Huddersfield T, Leeds U) 2
Ogilvie, R.A.M.M. (Clapham R) 1
Oliver, L. F. (Fulham) 1
Olney, B.A. (Aston Villa) 2
Osborne, F.R. (Fulham, Tottenham H) 4
Osborne, R. (Leicester C) 1
Osgood, P.L. (Chelsea) 4
Osman, R. (Ipswich T) 11
Ottaway, C.J. (Oxford University) 2
Owen, J.R.B. (Sheffield) 1
Owen, M.J. (Liverpool) 60
Owen, S.W. (Luton T) 3

Page, L.A. (Burnley) 7
Paine, T.L. (Southampton) 19
Pallister, G.A. (Middlesbrough, Manchester U) 22
Palmer, C.L. (Sheffield W) 18
Pantling, H.H. (Sheffield U) 1
Paravacini, P.J. de (Cambridge University) 3
Parker, P.A. (QPR, Manchester U) 19
Parker, S.M. (Charlton Ath, Chelsea) 2
Parker, T.R. (Southampton) 1
Parkes, P.B. (QPR) 1
Parkinson, J. (Liverpool) 2
Parlour, R. (Arsenal) 10
Parr, P.C. (Oxford University) 1
Parry, E.H. (Old Carthusians) 3
Parry, R.A. (Bolton W) 2
Patchitt, B.C.A. (Corinthians) 2

Stevens, G.A. (Tottenham H) 7
Stevens, M.G. (Everton, Rangers) 46
Stewart, J. (Sheffield W, Newcastle U) 3
Stewart, P.A. (Tottenham H) 3
Stiles, N.P. (Manchester U) 28
Stoker, J. (Birmingham) 3
Stone, S.B. (Nottingham F) 9
Storer, H. (Derby Co) 2
Storey, P.E. (Arsenal) 19
Storey-Moore, I. (Nottingham F) 1
Strange, A.H. (Sheffield W) 20
Stratford, A.H. (Wanderers) 1
Streten, B. (Luton T) 1
Sturgess, A. (Sheffield U) 2
Summerbee, M.G. (Manchester C) 8
Sunderland, A. (Arsenal) 1
Sutcliffe, J.W. (Bolton W, Millwall) 5
Sutton, C.R. (Blackburn R) 1
Swan, P. (Sheffield W) 19
Swepstone, H.A. (Pilgrims) 6
Swift, F.V. (Manchester C) 19

Tait, G. (Birmingham Excelsior) 1
Talbot, B. (Ipswich T, Arsenal) 6
Tambling, R.V. (Chelsea) 3
Tate, J. T. (Aston Villa) 3
Taylor, E. (Blackpool) 1
Taylor, E.H. (Huddersfield T) 8
Taylor, J.G. (Fulham) 2
Taylor, P.H. (Liverpool) 3
Taylor, P.J. (C Palace) 4
Taylor, T. (Manchester U) 19
Temple, D.W. (Everton) 1
Terry, J.G. (Chelsea) 11
Thickett, H. (Sheffield U) 2
Thomas, D. (Coventry C) 2
Thomas, D. (QPR) 8
Thomas, G.R. (C Palace) 9
Thomas, M.L. (Arsenal) 2
Thompson, A. (Celtic) 1
Thompson, P. (Liverpool) 16
Thompson, P.B. (Liverpool) 42
Thompson T. (Aston Villa, Preston NE) 2
Thomson, R.A. (Wolverhampton W) 8
Thornewell, G. (Derby Co) 4
Thornley, I. (Manchester C) 1
Tilson, S.F. (Manchester C) 4
Titmuss, F. (Southampton) 2
Todd, C. (Derby Co) 27
Toone, G. (Notts Co) 2
Topham, A.G. (Casuals) 1
Topham, R. (Wolverhampton W, Casuals) 2
Towers, M.A. (Sunderland) 3
Townley, W.J. (Blackburn R) 2
Townrow, J.E. (Clapton Orient) 2
Tremelling, D.R. (Birmingham) 1
Tresadern, J. (West Ham U) 2
Tueart, D. (Manchester C) 6
Tunstall, F.E. (Sheffield U) 7
Turnbull, R.J. (Bradford) 1
Turner, A. (Southampton) 2
Turner, H. (Huddersfield T) 2
Turner, J.A. (Bolton W, Stoke C, Derby Co) 3
Tweedy, G.J. (Grimsby T) 1

Ufton, D.G. (Charlton Ath) 1
Underwood A. (Stoke C) 2
Unsworth, D.G. (Everton) 1
Upson, M.J. (Birmingham C) 6

Urwin, T. (Middlesbrough, Newcastle U) 4
Utley, G. (Barnsley) 1

Vassell, D. (Aston Villa) 22
Vaughton, O.H. (Aston Villa) 5
Veitch, C.C.M. (Newcastle U) 6
Veitch, J.G. (Old Westminsters) 1
Venables, T.F. (Chelsea) 2
Venison, B. (Newcastle U) 2
Vidal, R.W.S. (Oxford University) 1
Viljoen, C. (Ipswich T) 2
Viollet, D.S. (Manchester U) 2
Von Donop (Royal Engineers) 2

Wace, H. (Wanderers) 3
Waddle, C.R. (Newcastle U, Tottenham H, Marseille) 62
Wadsworth, S.J. (Huddersfield T) 9
Wainscoat, W.R. (Leeds U) 1
Waiters, A.K. (Blackpool) 5
Walden, F.I. (Tottenham H) 2
Walker, D.S. (Nottingham F, Sampdoria, Sheffield W) 59
Walker, I.M. (Tottenham H, Leicester C) 4
Walker, W.H. (Aston Villa) 18
Wall, G. (Manchester U) 7
Wallace, C.W. (Aston Villa) 3
Wallace, D.L. (Southampton) 1
Walsh, P. (Luton T) 5
Walters, A.M. (Cambridge University, Old Carthusians) 9
Walters, K.M. (Rangers) 1
Walters, P.M. (Oxford University, Old Carthusians) 13
Walton, N. (Blackburn R) 1
Ward, J.T. (Blackburn Olympic) 1
Ward, P. (Brighton & HA) 1
Ward, T.V. (Derby Co) 2
Waring, T. (Aston Villa) 5
Warner, C. (Upton Park) 1
Warren, B. (Derby Co, Chelsea) 22
Waterfield, G.S. (Burnley) 1
Watson, D. (Norwich C, Everton) 12
Watson, D.V. (Sunderland, Manchester C, Werder Bremen, Southampton, Stoke C) 65
Watson, V.M. (West Ham U) 5
Watson, W. (Burnley) 3
Watson, W. (Sunderland) 4
Weaver, S. (Newcastle U) 3
Webb, G.W. (West Ham U) 2
Webb, N.J. (Nottingham F, Manchester U) 26
Webster, M. (Middlesbrough) 3
Wedlock, W.J. (Bristol C) 26
Weir, D. (Bolton W) 2
Welch, R. de C. (Wanderers, Harrow Chequers) 2
Weller, K. (Leicester C) 4
Welsh, D. (Charlton Ath) 3
West, G. (Everton) 3
Westwood, R.W. (Bolton W) 6
Whateley, O. (Aston Villa) 2
Wheeler, J.E. (Bolton W) 1
Wheldon, G.F. (Aston Villa) 4
White, D. (Manchester C) 1
White, T.A. (Everton) 1
Whitehead, J. (Accrington, Blackburn R) 2
Whitfeld, H. (Old Etonians) 1
Whitham, M. (Sheffield U) 1
Whitworth, S. (Leicester C) 7

Whymark, T.J. (Ipswich T) 1
Widdowson, S.W. (Nottingham F) 1
Wignall, F. (Nottingham F) 2
Wilcox, J.M. (Blackburn R, Leeds U) 3
Wilkes, A. (Aston Villa) 5
Wilkins, R.G. (Chelsea, Manchester U, AC Milan) 84
Wilkinson, B. (Sheffield U) 1
Wilkinson, L.R. (Oxford University) 1
Williams, B.F. (Wolverhampton W) 24
Williams, O. (Clapton Orient) 2
Williams, S. (Southampton) 6
Williams, W. (WBA) 6
Williamson, E.C. (Arsenal) 2
Williamson, R.G. (Middlesbrough) 7
Willingham, C.K. (Huddersfield T) 12
Willis, A. (Tottenham H) 1
Wilshaw, D.J. (Wolverhampton W) 12
Wilson, C.P. (Hendon) 2
Wilson, C.W. (Oxford University) 2
Wilson, G. (Sheffield W) 12
Wilson, G.P. (Corinthians) 2
Wilson, R. (Huddersfield T, Everton) 63
Wilson, T. (Huddersfield T) 1
Winckworth, W.N. (Old Westminsters) 2
Windridge, J.E. (Chelsea) 8
Wingfield-Stratford, C.V. (Royal Engineers) 1
Winterburn, N. (Arsenal) 2
Wise, D.F. (Chelsea) 21
Withe, P. (Aston Villa) 11
Wollaston, C.H.R. (Wanderers) 4
Wolstenholme, S. (Everton, Blackburn R) 3
Wood, H. (Wolverhampton W) 3
Wood, R.E. (Manchester U) 3
Woodcock, A.S. (Nottingham F, Cologne, Arsenal) 42
Woodgate, J.S. (Leeds U, Newcastle U) 5
Woodger, G. (Oldham Ath) 1
Woodhall, G. (WBA) 2
Woodley, V.R. (Chelsea) 19
Woods, C.C.E. (Norwich C, Rangers, Sheffield W) 43
Woodward, V.J. (Tottenham H, Chelsea) 23
Woosnam, M. (Manchester C) 1
Worrall, F. (Portsmouth) 2
Worthington, F.S. (Leicester C) 8
Wreford-Brown, C. (Oxford University, Old Carthusians) 4
Wright, E.G.D. (Cambridge University) 1
Wright, I.E. (C Palace, Arsenal, West Ham U) 33
Wright, J.D. (Newcastle U) 1
Wright, M. (Southampton, Derby Co, Liverpool) 45
Wright, R.I. (Ipswich T, Arsenal) 2
Wright, T.J. (Everton) 11
Wright, W.A. (Wolverhampton W) 105
Wylie, J.G. (Wanderers) 1

Yates, J. (Burnley) 1
York, R. E. (Aston Villa) 2
Young, A. (Huddersfield T) 9
Young, G.M. (Sheffield W) 1

R.E. Evans also played for Wales against England, N. Ireland, Scotland; J. Reynolds also played for Ireland against England, Wales, Scotland.

333

England Goalscorers (as at July 2004)

A'Court, A.	1	Brown, W.	1	Fleming, H.J.	9
Adams, T.A.	5	Buchan, C.M.	4	Flowers, R.	10
Adcock, H.	1	Bull, S.G.	4	Forman, Frank	1
Alcock, C.W.	1	Bullock, N.	2	Forman, Fred	3
Allen, A.	3	Burgess, H.	4	Foster, R.E.	3
Allen, R.	2	Butcher, T.	3	Fowler, R.B.	7
Amos, A.	1	Byrne, J.J.	8	Francis, G.C.J.	3
Anderson, V.	2			Francis, T.	12
Anderton, D.R.	7	Campbell, S.J.	1	Freeman, B.C.	3
Astall, G.	1	Camsell, G.H.	18	Froggatt, J.	2
Athersmith, W.C.	3	Carter, H.S.	7	Froggatt, R.	2
Atyeo, P.J.W.	5	Carter, J.H.	4		
		Chadwick, E.	3	Galley, T.	1
Bache, J.W.	4	Chamberlain, M.	1	Gascoigne, P.J.	10
Bailey, N.C.	2	Chambers, H.	5	Geary, F.	3
Baily, E.F.	5	Channon, M.R.	21	Gerrard, S.G.	4
Baker, J.H.	3	Charlton, J.	6	Gibbins, W.V.T.	3
Ball, A.J.	8	Charlton, R.	49	Gilliatt, W.E.	3
Bambridge, A.L.	1	Chenery, C.	1	Goddard, P.	1
Bambridge, E.C.	11	Chivers, M.	13	Goodall, J.	12
Barclay, R.	2	Clarke, A.J.	10	Goodyer, A.C.	1
Barmby, N.J.	4	Cobbold, W.N.	6	Gosling, R.C.	2
Barnes, J.	11	Cock, J.G.	2	Goulden, L.A.	4
Barnes, P.S.	4	Cole, A.	1	Grainger, C.	3
Barton, J.	1	Cole, J.J.	2	Greaves, J.	44
Bassett, W.I.	8	Common, A.	2	Grovesnor, A.T.	2
Bastin, C.S.	12	Connelly, J.M.	7	Gunn, W.	1
Beardsley, P.A.	9	Coppell, S.J.	7		
Beasley, A.	1	Cotterill, G.H.	2	Haines, J.T.W.	2
Beattie, T.K.	1	Cowans, G.	2	Hall, G.W.	9
Beckham, D.R.J.	13	Crawford, R.	1	Halse, H.J.	2
Becton, F.	2	Crawshaw, T.H.	1	Hampson, J.	5
Bedford, H.	1	Crayston, W.J.	1	Hampton, H.	2
Bell, C.	9	Creek, F.N.S.	1	Hancocks, J.	2
Bentley, R.T.F.	9	Crooks, S.D.	7	Hardman, H.P.	1
Bishop, S.M.	1	Currey, E.S.	2	Harris, S.S.	2
Blackburn, F.	1	Currie, A.W.	3	Hassall, H.W.	4
Blissett, L.	3	Cursham, A.W.	2	Hateley, M.	9
Bloomer, S.	28	Cursham, H.A.	5	Haynes, J.N.	18
Bond, R.	2			Hegan, K.E.	4
Bonsor, A.G.	1	Daft, H.B.	3	Henfrey, A.G.	2
Bowden, E.R.	1	Davenport, J.K.	2	Heskey, E.W.	5
Bowers, J.W.	2	Davis, G.	1	Hilsdon, G.R.	14
Bowles, S.	1	Davis, H.	1	Hine, E.W.	4
Bradford, G.R.W.	1	Day, S.H.	2	Hinton, A.T.	1
Bradford, J.	7	Dean, W.R.	18	Hirst, D.E.	1
Bradley, W.	2	Devey, J.H.G.	1	Hitchens, G.A.	5
Bradshaw, F.	3	Dewhurst, F.	11	Hobbis, H.H.F.	1
Brann, G.	1	Dix, W.R.	1	Hoddle, G.	8
Bridges, B.J.	1	Dixon, K.M.	4	Hodgetts, D.	1
Bridge, W.M.	1	Dixon, L.M.	1	Hodgson, G.	1
Bridgett, A.	3	Dorrell, A.R.	1	Holley, G.H.	8
Brindle, T.	1	Douglas, B.	11	Houghton, W.E.	5
Britton, C.S.	1	Drake, E.J.	6	Howell, R.	1
Broadbent, P.F.	2	Ducat, A.	1	Hughes, E.W.	1
Broadis, I.A.	8	Dunn, A.T.B.	2	Hulme, J.H.A.	4
Brodie, J.B.	1			Hunt, G.S.	1
Bromley-Davenport, W.	2	Eastham, G.	2	Hunt, R.	18
Brook, E.F.	10	Edwards, D.	5	Hunter, N.	2
Brooking, T.D.	5	Ehiogu, U.	1	Hurst, G.C.	24
Brooks, J.	2	Elliott, W.H.	3		
Broome, F.H.	3	Evans, R.E.	1	Ince, P.E.C.	2
Brown, A.	4				
Brown, A.S.	1	Ferdinand, L.	5	Jack, D.N.B.	3
Brown, G.	5	Ferdinand, R.G.	1	Jeffers, F.	1
Brown, J.	3	Finney, T.	30	Johnson, D.E.	6

Johnson, E.	2	Nicholls, J.	1	Southworth, J.	3
Johnson, J.A.	2	Nicholson, W.E.	1	Sparks, F.J.	3
Johnson, T.C.F.	5			Spence, J.W.	1
Johnson, W.H.	1	O'Grady, M.	3	Spiksley, F.	5
		Osborne, F.R.	3	Spilsbury, B.W.	5
Kail, E.I.L.	2	Owen, M.J.	26	Steele, F.C.	8
Kay, A.H.	1	Own goals	24	Stephenson, G.T.	2
Keegan, J.K.	21			Steven, T.M.	4
Kelly, R.	8	Page, L.A.	1	Stewart, J.	2
Kennedy, R.	3	Paine, T.L.	7	Stiles, N.P.	1
Kenyon-Slaney, W.S.	2	Palmer, C.L.	1	Storer, H.	1
Keown, M.R.	2	Parry, E.H.	1	Stone, S.B.	2
Kevan, D.T.	8	Parry, R.A.	1	Summerbee, M. G.	1
Kidd, B.	1	Pawson, F.W.	1		
King, L.B.	1	Payne, J.	2	Tambling, R.V.	1
Kingsford, R.K.	1	Peacock, A.	3	Taylor, P.J.	2
Kirchen, A.J.	2	Pearce, S.	5	Taylor, T.	16
Kirton, W.J.	1	Pearson, J.S.	5	Thompson, P.B.	1
		Pearson, S.C.	5	Thornewell, G.	1
Lampard, F.J.	5	Perry, W.	2	Tilson, S.F.	6
Langton, R.	1	Peters, M.	20	Townley, W.J.	2
Latchford, R.D.	5	Pickering, F.	5	Tueart, D.	2
Latherton, E.G.	1	Platt, D.	27		
Lawler, C.	1	Pointer, R.	2	Vassell, D.	6
Lawton, T.	22			Vaughton, O.H.	6
Lee, F.	10	Quantrill, A.	1	Veitch, J.G.	3
Lee, J.	1			Violett, D.S.	1
Lee, R.M.	2	Ramsay, A.E.	3		
Lee, S.	2	Revie, D.G.	4	Waddle, C.R.	6
Le Saux, G. P.	1	Redknapp, J.F.	1	Walker, W.H.	9
Lindley, T.	14	Reynolds, J.	3	Wall, G.	2
Lineker, G.	48	Richardson, J.R.	2	Wallace, D.	1
Lofthouse, J. M.	3	Rigby, A.	3	Walsh, P.	1
Lofthouse, N.	30	Rimmer, E. J.	2	Waring, T.	4
Hon. A. Lyttelton	1	Roberts, F.	2	Warren, B.	2
		Roberts, H.	1	Watson, D.V.	4
Mabbutt, G.	1	Roberts, W. T.	2	Watson, V.M.	4
Macdonald, M.	6	Robinson, J.	3	Webb, G.W.	1
Mannion, W.J.	11	Robson, B.	26	Webb, N.	4
Mariner, P.	13	Robson, R.	4	Wedlock, W.J.	2
Marsh, R.W.	1	Rooney, W.	9	Weller, K.	1
Matthews, S.	11	Rowley, J. F.	6	Welsh, D.	1
Matthews, V.	1	Royle, J.	2	Whateley, O.	2
McCall, J.	1	Rutherford, J.	3	Wheldon, G.F.	6
McDermott, T.	3			Whitfield, H.	1
McManaman, S.	3	Sagar, C.	1	Wignall, F.	2
Medley, L.D.	1	Sandilands, R.R.	3	Wilkes, A.	1
Melia, J.	1	Sansom, K.	1	Wilkins, R.G.	3
Mercer, D.W.	1	Schofield, J.	1	Willingham, C.K.	1
Merson, P.C.	3	Scholes, P.	14	Wilshaw, D.J.	10
Milburn, J.E.T.	10	Seed, J.M.	1	Wilson, G.P.	1
Miller, H.S.	1	Settle, J.	6	Winckworth, W.N.	1
Mills, G.R.	3	Sewell, J.	3	Windridge, J.E.	7
Milward, A.	3	Shackleton, L.F.	1	Wise, D.F.	1
Mitchell, C.	5	Sharp, J.	1	Withe, P.	1
Moore, J.	1	Shearer, A.	30	Wollaston, C.H.R.	1
Moore, R.F.	2	Shelton, A.	1	Wood, H.	1
Moore, W.G.B.	2	Shepherd, A.	2	Woodcock, T.	16
Morren, T.	1	Sheringham, E.P.	11	Woodhall, G.	1
Morris, F.	1	Simpson, J.	1	Woodward, V.J.	29
Morris, J.	3	Smith, A.	1	Worrall, F.	2
Mortensen, S.H.	23	Smith, A.M.	2	Worthington, F.S.	2
Morton, J. R.	1	Smith, G.O.	11	Wright, I.E.	9
Mosforth, W.	3	Smith, Joe	1	Wright, M.	1
Mullen, J.	6	Smith, J.R.	2	Wright, W.A.	3
Mullery, A.P.	1	Smith, J.W.	4	Wylie, J.G.	1
Murphy, D.B	1	Smith, R.	13		
		Smith, S.	1	Yates, J.	3
Neal, P.G.	5	Sorby, T.H.	1		
Needham, E.	3	Southgate, G.	2		

headline

Now you can buy any of these other bestselling sports titles from your bookshop or *direct from the publisher.*

FREE P&P AND UK DELIVERY
(Overseas and Ireland £3.50 per book)

Sky Sports Football Yearbook 2004–2005	Glenda Rollin and Jack Rollin	**£19.99**
Playfair Football Annual 2004–2005	Glenda Rollin and Jack Rollin	**£6.99**
1966 and All That	Geoff Hurst	**£6.99**
Psycho	Stuart Pearce	**£6.99**
King John	John Charles	**£7.99**
The Autobiography	Gareth Edwards	**£7.99**
Vinnie	Vinnie Jones	**£6.99**
My Autobiography	Tom Finney	**£7.99**
A Lot of Hard Yakka	Simon Hughes	**£7.99**
Left Foot Forward	Garry Nelson	**£6.99**
The Way It Was	Stanley Matthews	**£7.99**
The Autobiography	Niall Quinn	**£7.99**
Fathers, Sons and Football	Colin Shindler	**£6.99**
Cloughie	Brian Clough	**£7.99**
My Autobiography	Garry Sobers	**£6.99**
Lions and Falcons	Jonny Wilkinson	**£6.99**
Taking Fresh Guard	Tony Lewis	**£7.99**
Menace	Dennis Lillee	**£7.99**

TO ORDER SIMPLY CALL THIS NUMBER
01235 400 414

or visit our website
www.madaboutbooks.com

Prices and availability subject to change without notice.